Serpents of War

Serpents of War

An American Officer's Story of World War I Combat and Captivity

Harry Dravo Parkin

Edited by Steven Trout and Ian Isherwood

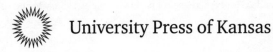

University Press of Kansas

Published by the University Press of Kansas (Lawrence, Kansas 66045), which was
organized by the Kansas Board of Regents and is operated and funded by Emporia
State University, Fort Hays State University, Kansas State University, Pittsburg State
University, the University of Kansas, and Wichita State University.

Library of Congress Cataloging-in-Publication Data
Names: Parkin, Harry Dravo, 1880–1946 author. | Trout, Steven, 1963–
   editor. | Isherwood, Ian Andrew, editor.
Title: Serpents of war : an American officer's story of World War I combat
   and captivity / Harry Dravo Parkin ; edited by Steven Trout and Ian Isherwood.
Other titles: American officer's story of World War I combat and captivity
Description: Lawrence, Kansas : University Press of Kansas, [2023] |
   Series: Modern war studies | Includes index.
Identifiers: LCCN 2022049952 (print) | LCCN 2022049953 (ebook)
   ISBN 9780700635054 (cloth) | ISBN 9780700635061 (ebook)
Subjects: LCSH: Argonne, Battle of the, France, 1918. | Parkin, Harry
   Dravo, 1880–1946. | United States. Army. Infantry Regiment,
   316th—Biography. | United States. Army. Division, 79th—Biography. |
   Argonne, Battle of the, France, 1918. | World War, 1914–1918—Personal
   narratives, American. | World War, 1914–1918--Campaigns—Western Front.
   | World War, 1914–1918—Prisoners and prisons, German.
Classification: LCC D570.3 79th .P37 2023 (print) | LCC D570.3 79th
   (ebook) | DDC 940.4/1273 [B]—dc23/eng/20230215
LC record available at https://lccn.loc.gov/2022049952.
LC ebook record available at https://lccn.loc.gov/2022049953.

British Library Cataloguing-in-Publication Data is available.

Printed in the United States of America

10 9 8 7 6 5 4 3 2 1

The paper used in this publication is acid free and meets the minimum requirements of
the American National Standard for Permanence of Paper for Printed Library Materials
Z39.48–1992.

Contents

Illustrations

Acknowledgments

The editors owe a debt of gratitude to many who have helped with this project over the three difficult years since its inception. First and foremost, we would like to thank Pete Parkin for his help and support of our editing and publishing his grandfather's war memoir. Pete not only provided us with insights into his grandfather's life, but he also shared his grandfather's photo album with us, providing the images of faces and places that we have included in this book.

This book would not be possible without the staff of Gettysburg College Special Collections. Alice Dangerfield Parkin donated the memoir to the college where it was preserved, catalogued, and digitized. Specifically, we are grateful to Carolyn Sautter, Catherine Perry, and Joy Zanghi. We owe a particularly large debt to college archivist Amy Lucadamo, who went above and beyond the call of duty to help us bring this book into print. Amy provided both sage historical advice and technical help; her work has been essential to the book's completion. If they give archivists medals for distinguished service, Amy has earned one for her work on *Serpents of War*. Officially, we acknowledge that this book is published courtesy of Special Collections and College Archives, Musselman Library, Gettysburg College, Gettysburg, Pennsylvania.

As we pursued this project, we benefited from the work of other scholars. We owe a debt of gratitude to William Walker, whose book *Betrayal at Little Gibraltar* propelled Harry Parkin to the forefront of the debate over the fight for Montfaucon. Walker provided us both with encouragement and research assistance. We also thank David Fort, Gettysburg College Class of 2000, who helped us with research at the National Archives at the height of the pandemic; Dr. Joseph Messina, Dean of the College of Arts and Sciences at the University of Alabama, who offered invaluable support; and Emma Allmann, a wonderful research assistant, who prepared the index. Of special note is the work of our two readers—Dr. Richard Faulkner and Dr. Michael Neiberg—whose careful reports helped to make this a much better book.

We are exceptionally grateful to our editor at the University Press of Kansas, Joyce Harrison. Joyce encouraged us from the first email we sent her and displayed considerable patience as the two of us struggled to deliver the manuscript on time. Off the clock, Joyce also worked as Parkin's transcriber, typing verbatim all five volumes of his memoir, a monumental task.

Personally, the editors would like to thank our families for putting up with stories about the western front, often told at random, and for nights and weekend time spent on the manuscript of a long-deceased American officer who left behind his record of the Great War.

Steven Trout
Ian Isherwood

Serpents of War

Introduction

Steven Trout and Ian Isherwood

In 1950, Alice Dangerfield Parkin, the widow of former American Expeditionary Forces (AEF) officer Major Harry Dravo Parkin, donated her husband's library of more than 350 volumes on World War I to Gettysburg College. She selected a fitting home for her gift: Parkin had commanded the 1st Battalion of the 316th Infantry Regiment, part of the 79th Division, as it fought in the Meuse-Argonne Offensive, and many of the men with whom he served hailed from the rolling hills of southeastern Pennsylvania, as well as from nearby Baltimore and Washington, DC.

Today housed in Gettysburg College's Musselman Library, the collection includes seemingly every significant title on the Great War published in English from 1914 through the late 1930s. One finds important volumes of history such as Basil Liddle Hart's *The Real War, 1914–1918* (1930), Thomas M. Johnson's *Without Censor* (1928), and Peyton C. March's *The Nation at War* (1932), as well as memoirs by high-level commanders like Erich Ludendorff, Alfred P. F. Tirpitz, Ian S. M. Hamilton, and, of course, John J. Pershing. Parkin sought out firsthand accounts by eyewitnesses of more modest rank as well. His library abounds in works of personal literature, including, to name just a few, Ellen N. LaMotte's *The Backwash of War* (1916), John W. Thomason's *Fix Bayonets!* (1926), T. E. Lawrence's *Revolt in the Desert* (1927), Edmund Blunden's *Undertones of War* (1928), John Lewis Barkley's *No Hard Feelings!* (1930), and Emilio Lussu's *Sardinian Brigade* (1939).[1]

Parkin read and probably reread every single volume. We know this because he penned a paragraph-length appraisal inside many of his books, as if preparing to write his own annotated bibliography of

1. Accession sheet, January 1950, Parkin Collection, Musselman Library, Gettysburg College.

sources on the Great War. On the flyleaf of Kermit Roosevelt's *War in the Garden of Eden* (1919), for example, he described Roosevelt's account of service with the British Army in Mesopotamia as "grade 'A' war literature." Kermit Roosevelt, Parkin went on to say, "is a more pleasing writer than was his distinguished father, who had not the style his son has." In contrast, Albert N. Depew's *Gunner Depew* (1918), the supposed adventures of a gun-turret officer who served with both the US Navy and the French Foreign Legion, received a failing grade. Parkin doubted the authenticity of this propagandistic account, which he dismissed as having "small value." More to his taste was Ferenc Imray's account of service in the Austro-Hungarian Army, *Through Blood and Ice* (1929), a "very unusual and interesting" book. The major's signature follows each of these assessments, along with a date. Thus, we not only know what Parkin read, as he absorbed a huge amount of World War I writing, we also know when he read it.

In addition to inscribing his volumes with often-perceptive critical overviews, the major marked up the text of his books as well, and his marginalia next to passages related to the 79th Division's infamous attack on Montfaucon—one of worst debacles of the Meuse-Argonne—shows that he had strong opinions about how America's deadliest battle might have been conducted differently. Parkin, who received legal training at Harvard, even penned an "affidavit" at the back of his copy of General James Harbord's *The American Army in France, 1917–1919*; in it, he alleged that soldiers who fought alongside the beleaguered 79th Division might have come to the division's assistance (and were, in fact, under orders to do so), had it not been for the ambitions of a particular AEF general. Eighty years later, Parkin's statement, long hidden away inside a volume buried deep in the Musselman's stacks, became a key piece of evidence in historian William Walker's book-length treatment of the 79th Division in World War I and its alleged betrayal on the battlefield.[2]

But this piece of damning testimony, delivered from beyond the grave, as it were, is hardly the most important item in Gettysburg College's Parkin collection. The centerpiece is a nearly 200,000-word

---

2. See William Walker, *Betrayal at Little Gibraltar: A German Fortress, a Treacherous American General, and the Battle to End World War I* (New York: Scribners, 2016), 4–11.

personal narrative, which someone recopied on a 1940s-era manual typewriter and then divided into five volumes, each bound, thesis-style, in black cloth with gold lettering. The text bears a title that was almost certainly added long after its original composition: *Memoirs of World War I, being an account of the experiences of an American Officer wounded and captured by the Germans* by Major Harry Dravo Parkin. Now retitled *Serpents of War,* a phrase Parkin used to describe hated German machine guns, and lightly edited to remove unnecessary repetition, this extraordinary account represents a major addition to the nonfictional literature of America and the Great War and stands alongside works such as Hervey Allen's *Toward the Flame* (1926), John Lewis Barkley's *Scarlet Fields* (1930), and William S. Triplet's *A Youth in the Meuse-Argonne* (2000).

Offering the perspective of a mid-level officer responsible for the lives and welfare of over a thousand men, this is a war narrative like no other. Parkin conveys the stress of command at a time when one innocent blunder could cost an officer his combat assignment, brings the inferno of the Meuse-Argonne Offensive to life in terrifying, gory detail, and recounts an experience undergone by very few American soldiers in 1918—that of being taken prisoner (while wounded no less) by the Imperial German Army. This is a book by a brave soldier, a recipient of the Distinguished Service Cross for his heroism on the battlefield, who was also a gifted writer. Though Parkin read a staggering number of published firsthand accounts (perhaps partly as preparation for his own book) and was exposed to World War I writing at its best, from Edmund Blunden to Erich Maria Remarque, he mercifully lacked literary pretentions. His narrative seldom strains for effect. Its prose is unassuming and workmanlike. Nevertheless, readers of *Serpents of War* will likely agree that Parkin possessed of a strong sense of setting, a knack for capturing the chaos and strange exhilaration of battle, and a sharp eye for the interpersonal, social dynamics of military life—the personality clashes and simmering feuds, as well as the moments of comradeship and accord.

At the same time, a deep sadness, born of survivor's guilt, haunts his account and leaves a lasting impression. So many lost comrades. So many young lives cut short. And for what exactly? It is almost shocking that this one-of-a-kind memoir, filled with closely observed details and moving reflections on wartime loss, has remained obscure for so long, attracting the attention of a World War I scholar every now and then, but otherwise forgotten.

Everything about Parkin's narrative suggests that he wrote it in the 1920s. There is no mention of the Great Depression, the rise of fascism in Europe, or the Second World War. Moreover, Parkin indicated that he composed his account primarily so that his son (Harry Dravo Parkin, Jr., born 1909) would someday be able to understand his father's experiences. One speculates that Parkin retitled his narrative near the end of his life (he died in 1946) or his widow may have done so; Alice Dangerfield Parkin may also have been responsible for having the volumes bound before presenting them to Gettysburg College. Each bears an elegant bookplate, a memorial to a proud soldier. Above a pen-and-ink drawing of the Distinguished Service Cross, the text reads "In memory of Harry Dravo Parkin, 1880–1946, Major, 316th Infantry, 79th Division, World War I."

Serpents of War opens with its author's arrival at Camp Meade, the massive cantonment outside Baltimore where the 79th Division received its stateside training (such as it was), and then offers a vivid rendering of his miserable transatlantic passage, followed by a harrowing eyewitness account of the 79th Division's attack on Montfaucon, as well as the woods and hills located north of that sinister prominence, an attack that left Parkin's battalion shattered—and humiliated. Just a handful of the dozens of officers under his command passed through the shelling and machinegun fire without injury. Afterwards, the survivors were greeted with reprimands handed down by Pershing's staff, which blamed the 79th Division for the American Army's failure to achieve its objectives in the first phase of the Meuse-Argonne battle.

Parkin then goes on to describe a military action all but forgotten today. After a period of "rest" amid trenches in the Troyon sector, the 79th Division was fed into the American offensive for a second time. Placed on the far right—or easternmost section—of the American line, on ground already well-churned by the terrible 1916 battle for Verdun, the Major's battalion once again went "over the top" on November 4, 1918, and attacked a German-held prominence called the Borne de Cornouiller (aka Hill 378 or "Corn Willy Hill"). Parkin led his troops to the summit, repelled a German counterattack, and in the process received multiple wounds in his legs, wounds that left him helpless when German stormtroopers finally recaptured the hill. In its closing chapters, *Serpents of War* becomes a unique captivity narrative, detailing the Major's experiences as he surrendered, received excellent care as a POW (even as the German Army showed clear signs of collapse), and, post-Armistice, made his way back to France.

Parkin's depiction of the Meuse-Argonne fighting is vivid and dramatic, and his depiction of passage into Germany offers a fascinating snapshot of an army—and a nation—tilting into political chaos. However, *Serpents of War* has historical value that goes beyond these two set pieces. Because he wrote his memoir primarily for his son, Parkin frequently pauses to explain features of military experience that would be unfamiliar to a non-veteran. For example, he outlines the command structure of an AEF battalion and explains the roles of the various individuals—chaplain, battalion gas officer, YMCA representative, etc.—attached to his command post. Parkin also dwells on small details often ignored in other accounts, including the ever-present difficulty of securing sleeping quarters for his men (barns and stables, if they were lucky) during their long marches to and from the front and the frustrations he encountered when trying to ensure that the troops received hot meals (an infrequent luxury, as it turned out). More than anything, he conveys the stresses and strains of leadership in situations for which no volunteer officer—even one as obviously captivated by military life as Parkin was—could possibly have been prepared.

This introduction will provide an outline of Parkin's education and business career prior to the Great War, as well as his qualities as a commander and his cultural outlook, followed by a historical discussion of the Meuse-Argonne Offensive. The final section offers a brief account of the Major's time in captivity and his life during the interwar decades, decades he spent revisiting—via reading and writing—wartime experience that left behind painful, unanswered questions.

A Pittsburgh Blueblood

On June 9, 1880, Harry Dravo Parkin was born—the second oldest of five children—into a prominent Pittsburgh family whose wealth flowed from the city's booming steel industry. Ironically, given his general contempt for officers in the Regular Army, who mostly come off badly in *Serpents of War*, he was something of a born soldier, and one wonders whether he ever considered applying to West Point. Military history fascinated the young Pittsburgher from the start. Indeed, while still a child, he began to collect artifacts from the American Civil War and the Napoleonic Wars, a hobby he would keep up throughout his life. In 2021, grandson Pete Parkin vividly recalled the fascinating assortment of breast plates, sabers, lances, and black-powder firearms that decorated his grandfather's den. No one knew quite what to do with the contents of this private war museum when Parkin died in 1946.[3]

The future major's love of all things martial led him to attend the Michigan Military Academy near Detroit. He would gladly have stayed at the so-called "West Point of the West" for his entire course of preparatory studies—the drill and "barracks life" were to his liking—but after his first year, the institution began to show signs of financial instability.[4] Parkin returned to Pittsburgh and completed his high-school education at Shady Side Academy, an illustrious private institution that drew its pupils from the city's upper crust. After that, he entered Harvard, as a young man of his social class and training simply did at that time. None other than Franklin D. Roosevelt, another creature of privilege, was one of his classmates. A member of the Sigma Alpha Epsilon fraternity, Parkin received his baccalaureate degree in 1904 and went on to study law. But his interest in the legal profession quickly waned. After just a few semesters, he dropped out of Harvard Law School and once again found himself back in Pittsburgh, where he went to work in the family business, a lucrative concern that supplied crucial industrial equipment to the Pennsylvania steel mills.[5]

In 1907, Parkin married Alice Marie Dangerfield, and two years later the couple had a son, Harry Dravo Parkin Jr. The family settled into a comfortable existence in Pittsburgh's exclusive Shadyside neighborhood, but Parkin's fascination with soldiering remained, simmering in the background of his otherwise contented life as a husband, father, and business executive. By 1915, the year of the *Lusitania* sinking and its

3. Interview with Pete Parkin, October 15, 2021.
4. Walker, *Betrayal at Little Gibraltar*, 76.
5. Walker, 76–77.

more than 120 American deaths, he knew that war in Europe would en-snare the United States eventually, whatever Woodrow Wilson might say, and he wanted to be ready. More than that, he wanted to fight. He was thirty-five now and realized that his one and only opportunity to become part of military history (as opposed to merely studying that history through artifact collecting and reading) was about to arrive. Along with thousands of other college-educated men, most of them devout Anglophiles or Francophiles all stirred by the fiery anti-neutral-ity rhetoric of Theodore Roosevelt, Parkin made his way to Plattsburg, New York, where General Leonard Wood had established a six-week training course designed to toughen-up future officers while they were still civilians. Amid the formidable physical training, Parkin acquired a rudimentary knowledge of military regulations, as well as the strange world of trenches and barbed wire awaiting him in France. After the American declaration of war in April 1917, he joined the Officer Train-ing Camp at Fort Niagara, where he obviously impressed his superiors: upon completion of the three-month course, Parkin received the rank of captain rather than lieutenant, a rare honor.[6] He was a ninety-day wonder, indeed.

The Company (about 250 soldiers) assigned to Parkin at Camp Meade consisted entirely of drafted men, members of the so-called Na-tional Army, as distinct from the Regular Army and the National Guard. The major made a virtue of conscription. Indeed, with a few notable ex-ceptions, the career soldiers who populate his narrative form a rogues' gallery of fossilized bureaucrats, bullying martinets, and alcoholics. Even professional NCOs come up short; for the most part, Parkin found them too sly, too adept at gaming the system, to ever trust them com-pletely. As for National Guardsmen, while he praised their courage in battle and noted the abundance of underage volunteers among their ranks (a sign of the robust patriotism endemic to militia), he was ap-palled by the informality that existed between officers in the Guard and enlisted men. To the major's horror, the latter sometimes even *elected* their commanders (or so he believed).[7] Convinced, like any soldier,

6. Walker, 77–78.

7. This practice was far from universal in National Guard units. Captain Harry S. Tru-man, for example, was assigned to Battery D of the 129th Field Artillery, not elected. At first, the Irish American National Guardsmen in this unit, a notoriously rowdy group,

that his branch of the service was superior to all others, Parkin held that the National Army represented the very best of America. A brand new fighting organization, constructed on a scale never before seen in American history, the National Army took in citizens of all walks of life and avoided (ideally, at least) the narrow doctrine and unnecessarily harsh discipline of the Regular Army, as well as the politics and cronyism common to the Guard.

What did the major's soldiers think of him? Though it's hard to know for certain, enough shared attitudes appear in the letters and memoirs of American enlisted men, regardless of unit or regional background, to support some speculation. For example, most doughboys in National Army divisions viewed their officers as creatures from an altogether alien realm for reasons that went beyond rank. This would certainly have been the case here. Parkin's men—mostly working class, many of them first-generation immigrants—could hardly have been unaware of the educational and social differences that profoundly separated them from their blueblood commander. And the major's manner, shaped by Pittsburgh high society and further refined at Harvard, probably did little to push those differences into the background.

His ethnic and class-based biases would have come across as well. In his memoir, Parkin consistently praises so-called hyphenated Americans under his command. But there's often condescension in his praise. The doughboys he leads are "fellows," sometimes *"little* fellows"— especially if they happen to be Jewish or Italian American. Given Parkin's background, it would be surprising if snobbishness and ethnic prejudice didn't color his perceptions to at least some degree—and even more surprising if his subordinates failed to notice.

The major's age also set him apart from his men, most of whom would have been in their mid-to-late twenties. This too would have shaped how he was viewed. Parkin was thirty-eight when he led his battalion in France. He was ten years older than Dwight D. Eisenhower, five years older than George S. Patton, four years older than Harry S. Truman, six months older than George C. Marshall, and just six months younger than Douglas McArthur. Few of the soldiers under

didn't know what to make of the spectacled farmer from Grandview, Missouri. They soon learned they were in good hands.

his command had any memories of the nineteenth century. In contrast, Parkin came of age in an era that predated the automobile and the airplane. Biographer David McCullough notes that Truman, born in 1884, remained, in many respects, a man of the late nineteenth century, always a little out of step with modernity.[8] Parkin may have shared the Missourian's outlook. Certainly, his antiquarianism, fascination with Napoleon, and fondness for military brass-bands and sing-alongs—just three of the often-eccentric personality features that emerge in his memoir—all seem incongruous with the hyper-modern Jazz Age ushered-in by the Great War.

So too does his enthusiasm for the YMCA, an organization many doughboys loathed. Along with the Salvation Army, the Jewish Welfare Board, and the Knights of Columbus, the "Y," for short, provided commissary services for the AEF, selling fruit, candy, and cigarettes primarily, along with pens and stationery so that troops could write home to their families. With the full support of the US Army, the Y also traded in moral uplift, steering soldiers on leave, for example, away from brothels and binge-drinking and toward more healthy recreations, such as theatricals and educational tours. This was, after all, the first war in American history in which the US military attempted to regulate the sex lives of its members; thus, the Y served as a crucial partner in Pershing's almost obsessive campaign against venereal disease.

By the time the 316th Infantry arrived in France in the late summer of 1918, the YMCA and its wholesome propaganda were ubiquitous. Hardly a town or village in the American sector failed to feature its own "Y hut," a portable shop or stand usually managed by a middle-aged volunteer, often a protestant clergyman, who would dispense moral guidance and pep talks along with the chocolate bars and tobacco. Parkin became a close friend of the YMCA representative in his own unit, Judge Donald M. Kimbrough, and he heartily approved of the organization's mission of promoting chastity and patriotic good cheer. Enlisted men took a different view—especially after they had seen combat. Many found the Y's moral messaging obnoxiously sanctimonious. Others accused the organization of money-grubbing and denounced its proselytizing volunteers as shirkers, a term front-line

8. David McCullough, *Truman* (New York: Simon & Schuster, 1992), 141–142.

soldiers eagerly applied to anyone who did not share in the dangers of battle.[9]

Though Parkin may have come across as elitist and old-fashioned at times, blind to the faults of supposed do-gooders pledged to keeping America's Christian crusaders on the straight and narrow, his troops likely appreciated his philosophy of military leadership. As seen in *Serpents of War*, the major understood that he was commanding citizen-soldiers, not hard-bitten regulars accustomed to unquestioningly following orders. Thus, while avoiding the kind of familiarity displayed by officers in the National Guard, he regularly held meeting with his troops (where he explained the rationale behind drill exercises and other military mysteries), maintained an open-door policy, and, when possible, softened the punishments that his soldiers received for acts of disobedience or insubordination.

An episode early in the narrative is illuminating in this regard. When an entire company of soldiers briefly goes AWOL, to protest a policy that the major also finds objectionable, Parkin is all for letting the matter drop. Only at the insistence of the regiment's Regular-Army commander, Colonel Oscar J. Charles, does he demote the NCOs involved. Here it should be noted that Charles, whom Parkin detested, serves throughout much of the memoir as a walking case study in how *not* to lead. Parkin's hectoring CO never explains anything, preferring to bark orders and constantly issue reprimands, behavior likely born of insecurity. Even worse, once the regiment enters combat, Charles's bullying gives way to paralyzing indecisiveness. How this unpopular officer manages to lose the respect of his men entirely and become a laughingstock is a story in *Serpents of War* too cruelly amusing to reveal here.

More than anything, Parkin's physical courage would have cemented his relationship with his troops—or at least those who remained on hand once 1st Battalion moved to the point of the spear. Straggling was a chronic problem in the AEF, and it included everything from four or five men helping a wounded comrade to the rear (when one would have sufficed) to soldiers conveniently becoming "separated from their

9. For more on the perception of the Y among Doughboys, see Joel Bius, "The Damn Y Man in WWI: Service, Perception, and Cigarettes," in Jeffrey Copeland and Yan Xu, eds., *The YMCA at War* (Lanham, MD: Lexington Books, 2018).

unit," i.e., hiding out somewhere safe during an advance and then re-appearing afterwards. During the Meuse-Argonne, Parkin saw little of this behavior among his troops—in part, as he explains, because his attention was constantly fixed on the soldiers who advanced alongside him. Few would have advanced at all without the major's inspirational example. While admitting to near-constant fear, Parkin maintains that he always risked just as much exposure to enemy fire as his enlisted men, to the point that he eventually lost any hope of avoiding injury or death. There is little reason to doubt him in this regard. The casualty rate among officers in his battalion—well over 75 percent during the unit's first passage through the Meuse-Argonne—demonstrates both the determination with which combat leaders in the AEF set out to prove their courage and the accuracy of the German snipers who targeted them specifically. Indeed, in places, Parkin's memoir becomes an anguished memorial volume as he details the deaths of various lieutenants, captains, and majors with whom he served. One senses that Parkin never quite forgave himself for not joining these brave comrades in death.

When the battalion was away from the front line, Parkin's connection with his troops took a different form: namely, shared grumbling about most things French. Given the major's reverence for Napoleon and interest in French military history, his frequent displays of cultural xenophobia are more than a little ironic. When describing his soldiers' horrified reaction to the tiny French trains into which they were squeezed (forty troops per railcar), he remarks, "The men were beginning to realize that France, as far as comforts and decencies of life are concerned, was a century behind their own country." Next comes the only underscored sentence in the entire memoir: *"And they never had cause to change their minds about this."* Like other American memoirists of World War I, Parkin was appalled by the austerity and backwardness of French rural life. He complains, for example, about the enormous manure piles heaped-up next to farmhouses and at one point even offends his French host so that he can escape proximity to this fragrant agricultural tradition. French villages, he notes, are devoid of cinemas or other modern diversions. Life there "would be terrible for the average American." Parkin also has much to say about the French attitude toward money, which he presents as a stereotypical blend of intractable parsimony and opportunistic price-gouging. The major actively combats the latter. When predatory street merchants, ready to fleece the well-paid Americans, show up in Percey-le-Grand, the Burgundian village where the 316th Infantry received its overseas training, he places armed guards next to their wagons and keeps them there until the prices drop by fifty percent.

In the time-honored tradition of educated Americans, Parkin was, of course, monolingual. Thus, his interactions with the French remained largely superficial until he became a POW. For most of the memoir, he behaves like a history-loving tourist, eagerly seeking out examples of Roman or medieval architecture and sites associated with the Napoleonic Wars. The French past often interests him more than the nation's drab and war-weary present. His one significant encounter with a French civilian, a meeting of aristocrats (French and American), occurs, appropriately enough, in a medieval castle located near Percey-le-Grand. The local count takes him on a tour of the fortifications and then, to the major's astonishment, gives the dazzled American a Legion of Honor medal that originally belonged to an ancestor in the *Grande Armée*. For Parkin, this encounter is pure magic, a collector's dream come true, and it marks a rare moment of intercultural connection between the Pittsburgher and a French citizen, albeit in a setting that reminds the major of *Ivanhoe*. (Readers of *Serpents of War* will be intrigued to learn that this very castle, known as the *Commanderie de la Romagne*, operates today as a bed and breakfast).

Ultimately, Parkin's detailed and chatty memoir opens a window on far more than the experience of battle circa 1918 or the nuts and bolts of battalion-level command. His narrative offers thoughtful reflections on the nature of leadership amid a brand new military organization, the National Army, which contained new kinds of conscripted citizen-soldiers. Judging from his account, Parkin probably fared better than most commanders when it came to leading such troops, though he was not without certain handicaps attributable to his age and upbringing. *Serpents of War* also captures the social-class dynamics of the US Army in the World War I era, when an Ivy-League degree all but guaranteed a commission (in much the same way that a public-school background made one a subaltern in the British Army), as well as the ethic prejudices that—despite apparent progress during wartime—would fuel anti-immigration legislation in the 1920s, along with other expressions of nativism, such as the Red Scare and the growth of the Ku Klux Klan. Parkin's view of the French is instructive as well. Ironically, despite his fascination with the First Empire and its military history, the major shared most of the attitudes of the typical doughboy: France, he concluded, was beautiful to look at, but hopeless to live in. As a number of social historians have demonstrated, participation in the Great Adventure only reinforced the values of a newly emergent American mass culture fortified by notions of American superiority and exceptionalism.[10] Filled with criticisms of French inefficiency and technological backwardness, Parkin's memoir reflects this dynamic on every page.

What *Serpents of War* has to say specifically as a work of battlefield testimony receives consideration below, along with the memoir's military-historical context. As we will see, Parkin's eyewitness account takes us straight into the dark heart of the Meuse-Argonne, capturing the full fury of this often murderously mismanaged offensive at a pivotal and, as it turned out, disastrous moment for the AEF.

Parkin and the Meuse-Argonne

The Meuse-Argonne, a terrible battle even by World War I standards, was America's version of the Somme, and it remains to this day the most lethal military engagement in American history, worse than any of the better-known bloodbaths from World War II, including Anzio, the D-Day Landings, the Battle of the Bulge, Iwo Jima, or Okinawa. At 26,000 killed, the number of US fatalities in this notorious forty-seven-day "Drive," as Parkin called it, equals roughly half the total for the *entire Vietnam War*. Even Ulysses S. Grant's infamous Overland Campaign through Virginia in 1864, an operation so casualty-ridden and unpopular that it nearly cost Abraham Lincoln the presidential election that year, produced less carnage than America's largest World War I battle.

One reason for the staggering number of losses in the fall of 1918 was the superabundance of American bodies on hand for the outnumbered but still capable Germans to destroy with their notoriously accurate

10. See especially Mark Meigs's excellent study, *Optimism at Armageddon: Voices of American Participants in the First World War* (Palgrave, 1997).

artillery and interlocking fields of machine gun fire. Determined to break through the belts of German defenses at the Meuse-Argonne, the toughest sector on the western front, with overwhelming brute force, Pershing crammed 750,000 American troops at a time into an area just twenty miles wide. The result was a proverbial shooting gallery for the Kaiser's forces and a supply nightmare for the Americans, who were forced to rely upon just three main roads leading into the battlefield. The American juggernaut became a victim of its own mass. Ever a critic of Pershing, the French Premier Georges Clemenceau famously motored to the Meuse-Argonne to see the AEF in action with his own eyes. He never reached the battle. Stuck for hours in a massive American traffic jam, which extended over miles of mud-churned road, he gave up and ordered his chauffeur to turn around.[11] With too many men, not enough experience, and zero interest in learning military lessons from their allies, the Americans had created a quagmire.

How the American Army got into this mess had everything to do with the bitter politics of coalition warfare. Badgered from the start by French and British commanders who demanded that American troops be fed into their own units (not entirely without reason since valuable time would be lost while the United States, ill-prepared for war, created its own autonomous fighting organization), Pershing finally achieved his goal of establishing an all-American army in the late summer of 1918. France's Ferdinand Foch, the supreme commander of all Allied forces (though not always recognized as such by either the British or the Americans), assigned to this new force the task of reducing the St. Mihiel Salient, a German-occupied bulge in the western front located southeast of Verdun, in preparation for an attack on the fortress city of Metz.

Then, on August 30, 1918, just days before the American operation was to begin, the Generalissimo met with Pershing to announce that he had changed his mind. Foch now wanted the Americans to abandon their plans for the salient and to join a French attack in the Meuse-Argonne sector. Even worse, he ordered Pershing to split his just-formed army into two halves, each of which would be subject to French

---

11. Geoffrey Wawro, *Sons of Freedom: The Forgotten American Soldiers Who Defeated Germany in World War I* (New York: Basic Books, 2018), 348–349.

command. A stunned Pershing refused, and the meeting turned, in the words of historian Geoffrey Wawro, "heated and ugly."[12] But Marshal Phillipe Petain intervened and proposed a compromise: the American Army would be left intact and allowed to proceed with its plans at St. Mihiel—but only if Pershing agreed to shift his forces to the Meuse-Argonne immediately afterwards. The AEF's commander accepted these terms, which committed the fledgling American Army to two gigantic operations back-to-back in two different sectors with seventy miles of bad roads between them.

The arrangement sealed the fate of Parkin and his men. Because Pershing needed his experienced divisions to lead the assault at St. Mihiel, novice divisions held in reserve (like the 79th) were the first ones to take up positions at the Meuse-Argonne. Thus, they would be the first to cross no-man's land in the coming battle. Putting so much trust in untested troops was a risky gamble, to put it mildly, but by the time the Meuse-Argonne Offensive opened on September 26, 1918—with an artillery barrage that consumed more projectiles than the entire American Civil War—the AEF's high command was brimming with confidence. Things had gone remarkably well at St. Mihiel (though aided, in no small measure, by a German withdrawal just prior to the American attack), and Pershing and his staff were now more certain than ever that gung-ho doughboys, uncorrupted by years of trench warfare and the defeatist mentality it supposedly fostered, would achieve the coveted breakthrough into "open warfare" that had so far eluded Allied and German war planners alike. Everything depended upon the element of surprise, as well as the swift capture of Montfaucon (the "Mount of Falcons"), a prominence at the center of the Meuse-Argonne sector, where the Germans had concealed an elaborate sighting instrument used to direct artillery fire across the entire American front. This crucial observatory would have to be taken in less than a day. Otherwise, the Germans would have time to reinforce their positions and thus force Pershing's operation into a familiar World War I–style stalemate. Which, as it turned out, is exactly what happened.

The task of seizing the Mount of Falcons fell to Parkin's 79th Division, a dubious choice given the unit's abbreviated period of overseas

12. Wawro, *Sons of Freedom*, 268.

training, which clocked in at barely a month and a half. Indeed, of all the green divisions assigned to the opening phase of the Meuse-Argonne Offensive, the 79th was probably the greenest. In addition to its dangerously incomplete instruction in modern warfare, the division had spent exactly zero days in a combat zone. But probably no group of soldiers in the AEF could have delivered the unrealistic results that Pershing expected. As historian Edward Lengel remarks, the timetable for the advance was built for "an army of supermen."[13] German positions that had resisted attacks earlier in the war, costing thousands of French lives, were to be taken by the Americans in just a few hours.

Parkin's firsthand account details all that inevitably went wrong. For one thing, Mountfaucon's defenses were far more formidable than suspected, and included, for example, two soon-to-be notorious death traps known as the Redoute du Golfe and the Oeuvre du Demon. Each of these networks of camouflaged machine gun nests was ingeniously positioned *in front* of the woods and ridges where the Germans knew their attackers would concentrate their artillery fire. And each utilized the concept of "defense in depth," which meant that once the Americans overran one seemingly isolated nest, they would immediately come under fire from others hidden in almost any direction.[14] This pair of killing fields was just the beginning. More traps, one after another, waited for the Americans in the open pastures and scattered woods north of Montfaucon, the area where the *real* belt of defenses, the *Kreimhelde Stellung*, began.

Tactical preparation was a problem as well. Parkin tells us that his troops were taught to move forward, at the start of an attack, in lines with "ten paces" of open ground between each soldier, a measure that supposedly minimized losses from artillery fire. But instructions on what to do next never had time to sink in, thanks to the 79th Division's hurried and incomplete training. Translations of French military manuals, used by the AEF in 1918, reflected hard-won lessons for advances across No Man's Land, including the importance of coordination between small groups of soldiers, who would alternate between

13. Edward Lengel, *To Conquer Hell: The Meuse-Argonne, 1918* (New York: Henry Holt, 2008), 61.
14. Walker, *Betrayal at Little Gibraltar*, 139–142.

rushing enemy positions and providing covering fire.[15] Unfortunately, many of the inadequately prepared doughboys in Parkin's unit never fully grasped such lessons—or forgot them completely the minute enemy bullets and shells starting flying. Another tactical failure involved the so-called rolling barrage, a precisely controlled storm of steel designed to land just ahead of attacking soldiers and to sweep forward with them as they penetrated enemy defenses. By 1918, the rolling barrage had become an essential ingredient in almost any successful assault. However, so ruinous were the roads leading across the battlefield at the Meuse-Argonne—roads the Germans had meticulously demolished and, for good measure, mined—that once the advance was underway it took days, even with engineers working around the clock, to move American guns into new positions. As a result, Parkin reports that his soldiers fought with little or no artillery support, a recipe for mass casualties.

And then there was the issue of coordination between different divisions and corps within the AEF, each of which was assigned a specific zone along the twenty-mile front. Per orders from GHQ, once they advanced far enough, units of the American 4th Division, located to the 79th Division right and facing easier terrain, were supposed to swing in behind Montfaucon, a so-called enveloping maneuver. It never happened. Instead, Parkin's division was left to fight its way to the summit on its own. Officially, a misunderstanding caused this deadly snafu. However, William Walker has offered a more sinister explanation, alleging that General Robert Lee Bullard, the head of III Corps, disregarded orders so that the Fourth Division, part of his command, could push as far into German territory as possible, thereby garnering maximum glory for the General, who was angling for a promotion.[16] The truth may never be known with absolute certainty (the costly attack on Montfaucon remains a controversial subject among historians), but Parkin, for one, held Bullard personally responsible for the 79th Division's ordeal, hence his incendiary affidavit.

Thanks to these various factors—underestimation of German defenses, poor training, tactical shortcomings, and lack of coordination

15. Our thanks to Richard S. Faulkner for this information on manuals and AEF tactics.

16. Walker, *Betrayal*, 357.

across Corps lines—it took two days for the 79th Division to battle its way to the top of Montfaucon, and, as feared, the delay gave the Germans time to move reserve divisions into place. Pershing's offensive stalled as a result, with the Americans hung up for three weeks on the *Kreimhelde Stellung*. Unfortunately for Parkin and his men, the 316th Infantry, which had operated in a support role during the initial attack, now shifted into the lead position, and its advance through the countryside north of Montfaucon turned into a crash-course in the advantages enjoyed by defenders on a World War I battlefield. German artillery fire pulverized the inexperienced Americans whenever they grouped together, became snagged on barbed wire, or were caught in the open. Hidden enemy machine guns—those "serpents of war"—laid down deadly crossfires. And snipers, camouflaged in the treetops, picked off unwary messengers and officers. Three days of this reduced Parkin's command of 1,200 troops by three-quarters and left him with just five officers.

What happened afterwards reflected yet another problem with Pershing's army: blame for tardy gains in battle typically landed on the soldiers involved—with, of course, little or no acknowledgement of miscalculations and faulty assumptions at the top. On October 1, 1918, the AEF's veteran 3rd Division relieved the shattered 79th, and Parkin, half-comatose by this point from four days of sleep deprivation and constant stress, led his men on a brutal twenty-mile march to the rear. Pride sustained the major as he staggered through the rain, mud, and near-freezing temperatures. His battalion had advanced further than any other unit in the division, and from what he could tell, the novice draftees of the 79th had performed well in their first battle.

But they hadn't. Or at least not according to the Pershing and his staff. The bitterest moment in *Serpents of War*—perhaps the bitterest moment in Harry Dravo Parkin's life—comes when the major and his fellow officers (the handful still alive by this point) receive a thorough "bawling out" from their brigade commander, who, doubtless under pressure from above, accuses them of "everything but cowardice" during the Meuse-Argonne fighting. Such morale-killing rebukes occurred frequently in the AEF, where the pressure to meet impossible goals sometimes created a toxic military culture, and Pershing helped set the negative tone from the top by instantly removing any officer who lacked appropriate "aggressiveness" (i.e., the willingness to throw American soldiers at enemy machineguns, regardless of cost).[17] Officers in the AEF lived in constant fear of being sent to Blois, the site of a dreaded reassignment center where disgraced combat commanders received orders to report to the Services of Supply, the ultimate humiliation. An anxious Major Parkin narrowly avoided this fate on more than one occasion.

By the time the 316th Infantry reentered the Meuse-Argonne battle, more than a month after its attack on Montfaucon, German forces had finally started to crack. Improvements in American tactics, combined with Foch's strategy of applying pressure along the entire western front (to say nothing of civil unrest and political turmoil in Germany), would soon push the Kaiser's army to the verge of collapse. Indeed, during the final days of the war, American troops could often barely keep up with their retreating adversaries. But Parkin's account demonstrates that not every area along the Meuse-Argonne front was relinquished so easily. There were still places where the enemy would fight to the last man. On November 4, just seven days before the Armistice, the 316th Infantry attacked Hill 378 (aka "Corn Willy Hill"), a position the Germans had no intention of giving up. The geography of the region explains their resolve. Located on the far-right side of the American front, Hill 378 formed part of the notorious Heights on the east bank of the Meuse River. From here, German artillery had tormented the AEF for weeks. Now Corn Willy was the last piece of high ground left in enemy hands, the only place remaining from which German observers could view the entire battlefield. It would not be given up easily.

Serpents of War offers an oddly fragmented and jumbled account of Parkin's final engagement. The text describes the lead-up to the 316th Infantry's assault on the hill, and then jumps abruptly to the moment when Parkin is taken prisoner at its summit. The trauma of the major's wounding may explain this uncharacteristic breakdown in the narrative. Or perhaps modesty. After all, the actions for which Parkin

17. The soldiers of the 35th Division, another unit that failed to meet its objectives during Phase One of the Meuse-Argonne, received similar reprimands after it was pulled from the battle and sent to a quiet sector in disgrace. See Robert Ferrell, *Collapse at the Meuse-Argonne: The Failure of the Missouri-Kansas Division* (Columbia: University of Missouri Press, 2004).

received the Distinguished Service Cross transpired during the period missing from his account. Or, again, survivor's guilt. Just a fraction of the soldiers who followed the major in his last attack were still standing by the end. Attached to a different battalion, Parkin's closest friend, William Sinkler Manning, died on Hill 378 as well, a loss that haunted the major for the rest of his life.

Such speculation is complicated by the fact that Parkin *did* include the attack in an earlier version of his memoir. In 1924, he received a request from Xenophon Price, the Secretary of the American Battle Monuments Commission (ABMC), to review for accuracy a set of official maps showing American positions near the end of the Meuse-Argonne Offensive. In his response (today housed in the National Archives), the major made one significant correction: the line marking American positions at the close of day on November 4, 1918, should, he explained, be adjusted to show that the 316th Infantry held the eastern half of Hill 378. To support this claim, Parkin enclosed a seven-page account of his experiences during the Corn Willy attack up the point when he was captured—precisely the information missing from *Serpents of War*. And he noted that these pages were "an extract from the war memoirs of H. D. Parkin."[18]

The existence of this curious excerpt (included in this edition as Appendix B) does not, of course, solve the mystery of why Parkin omitted such key information from the final version of his manuscript. Did he perhaps misplace his copy of the pages sent to the ABMC? Or did he decide to leave out the details of the attack for one or more of the hypothetical reasons offered above? We will never know. What is clear is that the fire fight on November 4 surpassed in violence and intensity anything Parkin had experienced earlier. Even the costly advance north from Montfaucon in September paled in comparison. On Hill 378, the major fought his last and most desperate battle.

Readers of *Serpents of War* may appreciate a quick summary of the November 4 attack and the actions for which Parkin received the

18. Harry Dravo Parkin, "Description of the Attack on Hill 378, the Borne de Cornouiller, France, November 4, 1918, by Companies B and C, First Battalion, 316th Infantry, 79th Division, AEF, Under the Command of Major H. D. Parkin." RG 127 Records of the American Battle Monuments Commission, Box 243, National Archives, College Park, MD.

nation's second-highest decoration for valor. According to the major's seven-page account, the operation against Corn Willy Hill seemed to go well at first. After a preliminary barrage, Parkin led two companies from 1st Battalion to the crest of the prominence, where they found the German trenches all but obliterated and filled with dead or dying enemy soldiers. But French troops to the Americans' left apparently failed to advance, leaving a dangerous opening on Parkin's flank. A German counterattack soon poured through this gap, only to be broken up by an action so remarkable (in a World War I context) that it requires some willing suspension of disbelief on the part of the reader. *If* we can trust Parkin's testimony (and there is no reason not to, apart from the sheer implausibility of what he describes), the major rose from his position in the captured German trenches and joined his troops as—a la the defense of Little Roundtop—they pushed their attackers down the hillside at bayonet point, a moment of wild hand-to-hand combat.

Parkin's description of what happened next, a return to the familiar conditions of industrialized warfare, is much easier to believe: machine gun fire raked the Americans, who were caught in the open, and sent them scurrying back up the hill. Parkin had to be carried. Multiple machine gun rounds had hit his thighs. A short time later, a low-flying German aircraft dropped an ominous "yellow smoke signal" onto Parkin's position, and enemy guns proceeded to blast the doughboys off the hilltop. It was, the major recalled, "the heaviest concentrated shell fire we ever experienced." Parkin's second in command, Captain Lewis C. Knack, had been killed by this point, and so, despite his wounds, the major continued to issue orders to the three 1st Lieutenants who could still function. He remained in command, directing the defense of Hill 378, until the bitter end, when a "large force of Germans" finally overran the major's position and killed or captured the remnants of his two companies.[19] For his conduct during this epic last stand, Parkin later received the DSC.

When read in tandem with the narrative that Parkin provided for the ABMC, *Serpents of War* offers the ultimate ground-level portrait of America's deadliest battle. The text helps us to understand the inadequate training and unrealistic expectations that, together with

19. Parkin, "Description of the Attack on Hill 378," 6–7.

forbidding terrain ideal for defense and miserable autumn weather, made the Meuse-Argonne so hellish for the citizen-soldiers who fought there, and it demonstrates just how formidable the doughboys' adversaries could be, even on the eve of the Armistice. Atop Hill 378, Parkin capitulated to enemy soldiers whose professionalism and skill, honed by four years of war, he could not help but admire. However, his experiences as a POW would soon reveal massive fissures within the Kaiser's army and leave little doubt that Germany was a crippled and exhausted military power.

Captivity and Aftermath

In many respects, Parkin's account of his capture, journey into Germany, and confinement in a prisoner-of-war hospital in Trier is the least convincing part of his narrative. Throughout this section of the memoir, he seems much too mobile for a man whose legs have been torn apart by 7.62mm machine-gun bullets. The sheer number of English speakers Parkin encounters also seems less than plausible (every other member of the Imperial Germany Army appears to have spent time in the United States), as well as the elaborate courtesy that the major receives in deference to his rank, often from some highly unlikely quarters.

Yet these suspect elements paradoxically add to the narrative's testimonial integrity. When defending the portrayal of war in his autobiography *Good-Bye to All That* (1929), a book widely maligned for inaccuracies, the British poet and novelist Robert Graves famously remarked, "the memoirs of a man who went through some of the worst experiences of trench warfare are not truthful if they do not contain a high proportion of falsities."[20] In other words, an honest portrayal of traumatic events, as processed at the time, will invariably confuse "rumours" with "scenes actually witnessed," unknowingly put forward false memories as genuine recollections, and scramble the timeline of what actually occurred.[21] One should expect such factual lapses, Graves maintained, in any truthful reconstruction of *what it is like to*

20. Robert Graves, "Postscript" to *Good-Bye to All That, But It Still Goes On* (London: Jonathan Cape, 1930), 42.
21. Graves, 42.

pass through extreme situations. Parkin's time as a POW was nothing if not traumatic. Indeed, although his narrative tends to gloss over his physical and psychological state once he was taken prisoner, it is easy to imagine the agony and terror he must have felt throughout his captivity. The major's physical pain was likely so intense that it warped his perceptions. In addition, despite Parkin's universally kind treatment from his captors, his circumstances placed his cognitive processes under extreme pressure. By surrendering, Parkin suddenly moved from a position of command and authority to one of absolute submission and helplessness, a shift so dramatic and upsetting that it may have distorted his sense of reality.

As a result, there is an almost hallucinatory quality to this section, which is filled with surreal images—Parkin lying next to a train track, so disconcertingly close to a passing locomotive that the railcars half-cover his body; a German soldier comically "stamp[ing]" around Parkin's stretcher to prove he is stronger than the captured doughboys who also helped carry the wounded major; another enemy infantryman's face half-blurring into the familiar visage of Conrad, the Parkin family's German-American gardener back in Pittsburgh. Indeed, it almost comes as no surprise when the major encounters a German strongman, again fluent in English, who "had travelled for years with Barnum's Circus in America." Anything seems possible in this funhouse-mirror portion of the narrative.

At the same time, however, Parkin offers clear-eyed insights into the state of the German Army at the close of the war, an army in political upheaval that had lost its will to fight. On his very first day as a POW, he notes the number of enlisted men who talk openly of a republic and of "throw[ing] out the Kaiser." And once a revolutionary government is established in Berlin, he witnesses acts of insubordination and contempt for upper-class officers that he finds utterly astonishing. At one point, for example, he notices a group of soldiers—"sloppy and indifferent, with hands in pockets"—who walk past "their officers without saluting or paying them any attention whatsoever." "Nearly all," he writes, "were bitter against the Kaiser and his advisors." Though Parkin delighted in Germany's defeat, one senses that the collapse in command structure that he observed offended some of his most cherished notions of military propriety.

Yet *Serpents of War* also shows that military discipline and efficiency remained in place within the *Deutsches Heer*, if just barely—the seeds of the later Nazi myth of an "undefeated" German Army in 1918. While recovering from his wounds, post-Armistice, in Trier, Parkin watches as regiment after regiment passes through the streets of the city en route to the other side of the Rhine, each led by a marching band and proceeding in perfect order: "It was evident that although the Germans were defeated and had suffered heavy losses, they still had many men and much artillery." Elsewhere, he notes that these troops carried "many flags and were decorated with flowers, wreaths, and greens. A strange sight to see retreating, defeated soldiers wearing the symbols of victory." Parkin's text remains silent on the issue of whether Allied forces should have pushed all the way into Germany and demanded unconditional surrender, as Pershing would have preferred. Chances are that the major, who had seen more than enough combat during his two stints in the Meuse-Argonne, would not have wished that outcome on anyone. Still, his account, likely penned in the 1920s, offers a rare American glimpse of a historical event that would, in the next decade, be twisted and misremembered to serve the ideology of the Third Reich.

The penultimate chapter of *Serpents of War* plunges us into a scene of post-Armistice chaos that stands in marked contrast to the German Army's orderly withdrawal beyond the Rhine. Parkin's journey from Trier to French-occupied territory in Lorraine captures the sweeping geopolitical impact of the Great War, as populations were displaced, international borders redrawn, governments toppled, and new nations formed. For example, the major's jam-packed train car, which might serve as a metaphor for Europe at this pivotal moment, contains soldiers and civilians of every description and nationality—French, German, British, Italian, and Russian, among others. Some of the passengers are released POWs, others German deserters (or are they now Frenchmen?) heading for their homes in Alsace or Lorraine, territories seized in 1871, soon to be restored to France.

After this turbulent glimpse of a continent remade by war, Parkin's memoir ends quietly and contentedly with his reabsorption into the AEF. From the town of Saargemünd, where he has the nerve to borrow money from a French General, he makes his way to an American military hospital in Paris, where he shows up without orders. Parkin leaves the rest of his story for the reader to imagine. Following surgery on his legs, he eventually received his orders to head stateside for demobilization, a seemingly happy warrior who had lived his dream of experiencing military history in the making. However, his wounds, it would turn out, went much deeper than the punctures in his thighs.

Once Parkin returned to the United States in the spring of 1919, his business ambitions shifted from Pittsburgh to Southern California, a mecca for Jazz-Age speculators and entrepreneurs. When the census was taken in 1920, he was living in Los Angeles with his wife, mother, and father-in-law, Ben Dangerfield, the "Candy King" of Pittsburgh, whose summer house on Hobart Boulevard, just south of the Hollywood Hills, served as the Parkins' residence. The household also included a Japanese servant.[22] Parkin worked for a time as a builder, then moved into real estate, where he enjoyed great success. By 1930, he owned a spacious house of his own on Hobart, as well as an oceanfront hideaway in the Balboa neighborhood of Newport Beach, where Parkin would often go to read one of the volumes in his extraordinary library and to brood in solitude.[23]

Despite his real-estate triumphs, the once-ebullient Pittsburgher became a haunted man over the years, plagued by "black moods" and prone to self-medicating with scotch.[24] In the parlance of the World War I era, he may have suffered from shell shock, what we would today categorize as war trauma. Yet where his response to war experience was concerned, Parkin often swung between emotional extremes, overcome with guilt and depression one moment, with pride and nostalgia the next. He never tried to put the war behind him. Never wanted to, in fact. He delighted in his hard-earned military honors, proudly displaying alongside his Napoleonic artifacts the Distinguished Service Cross and Silver Star that he received in a ceremony at the Presidio in 1923. He also regularly attended regimental reunions and remained in

22. United States Federal Census, 1920, Los Angeles Assembly District 63, Los Angeles, California, p. 14B, Enumeration District 176, Ancestry.com. Accessed March 30, 2022.

23. United States Federal Census, 1930, Los Angeles, Los Angeles, California, Roll 140, p. 22A, Enumeration District 185, Ancestry.com. Accessed March 30, 2022.

24. Walker, *Betrayal at Little Gibraltar*, 4.

contract with fellow survivors from 1st Battalion. Each year, on November 4, the anniversary of the battle atop Hill 378, he sent a dozen roses to Sergeant Major Robert MacCormack, a faithful companion during that bitter and uncertain moment of surrender and during the harrowing passage through the German lines that came afterwards.[25]

More than anything, though, it's Parkin's lovingly annotated book collection that testifies to the war's enduring hold upon him. As he struggled to understand his own traumatic experience, he immersed himself in the memories of other soldiers-turned-writers and, one hopes, drew at least some measure of solace from personal war literature. The war books he read, which included some of the finest military memoirs ever written, perhaps showed that he was not alone, that others who had passed through the inferno of battle likewise heard the call of accusatory ghosts and felt the same confounding mixture of contradictory emotions.

Eventually, Parkin's physical health went into "decline" for unspecified reasons.[26] One wonders whether the long-term effects of poison-gas inhalation, a common and often undetected malady among World War I veterans, caused his medical woes. Or whether the drinking increasingly triggered by his war memories began to catch up with him. Old friends and family members could see that he aged prematurely. In a photograph from 1937, featured in the society pages of *The Los Angeles Times*, Parkin poses next to his son and daughter-in-law, a dazzlingly attractive couple in swimsuits, at Balboa. It's a day of fun on the beach. Leaning on his son's shoulder, the lantern-jawed major holds a cigar and wears a jaunty sailing cap, but he is noticeably thin, almost frail-looking (earlier images show that he once had a stocky build), and his face is deeply lined for a man not yet sixty.[27]

His grandson, Pete Parkin, born in 1939, treasures two memories related to the major's service in World War I. Neither has anything to do with the dark side of Harry Parkin's war experience, something the loving grandfather was presumably adept at hiding when necessary. The first takes place in Parkin's relic-packed den in Los Angeles, a magical room with exposed ceiling beams that Pete, not yet six years old, found

25. Walker, 374.
26. Walker, 386.
27. *The Los Angeles Times*, July 25, 1937, p. 54.

enchanting. Here grandfather and grandson would "play" World War I and reenact the final moments of the battle atop Hill 378, crouching against the floor, as if it were the bottom of a trench, waiting for the bombardment to end and for the final German infantry assault to overwhelm the defiant doughboys. Pete also recalls that on V-J Day, Parkin rushed home to get his service revolver from the Great War. As part of the celebration, he wanted to send a few rounds into the air. But the action on his pistol was too rusty, and the gun wouldn't fire. More than three-quarters of a century later, his grandson still vividly recalls the old soldier's disappointment.[28]

Ultimately, Parkin's memoir speaks to the ambivalence toward war seen in his complex and interesting life. It is a mournful narrative that glows at times with happy memories, a proud tribute to courage that never lets us forget the terrible waste of youth, talent, and potential that military glory (if there is such a thing) demands. For this reason, and many others, *Serpents of War* is an instant classic; it takes its place among the World War I books that Parkin himself rated most highly, few of which explore the mysteries of battle—or captivity—with such anguished intensity or insight.

28. Interview with Pete Parkin, October 15, 2021.

Editors' Note

The original typescript of Harry Dravo Parkin's World War I memoir, bound in five volumes and housed in the Special Collections and College Archives Department of the Musselman Library at Gettysburg College, contains a number of repetitious passages. For whatever reason, Parkin sometimes told the same story more than once and sometimes reintroduced individuals multiple times. We have removed such instances of repetition, along with several lengthy digressions that detracted from the flow and forcefulness of the narrative. In addition, Parkin's original chapter organization was problematic with some chapters running nearly three-times the length of others. This too we have corrected. Most of the chapter titles in this edition are Parkin's; some we created, a necessary result of the new breaks between chapters.

The bulk of Parkin's text we have left unaltered. We have retained Parkin's original spellings, as well as his sometimes-eccentric punctuation, and we have not tampered with his sentence structure. For the most part, Parkin wrote well, and we have tried to stay out of his way.

Readers of *Serpents of War* should understand that this book is a war memoir—and thus a subjective account of often traumatic events as recollected by a fallible individual. The book should not be confused with a work of history. Our annotations, which we tried to keep at a minimum for the sake of readability, point out several places where Parkin's memory was in error. There are almost certainly others. Such is the nature of autobiographical writing, especially autobiographical writing that deals with war. In general, we believe that Parkin made a sincere effort to record the past as he remembered it, an effort that was at times heroic given the burdens he carried from his war experience.

S.T.
I.I.

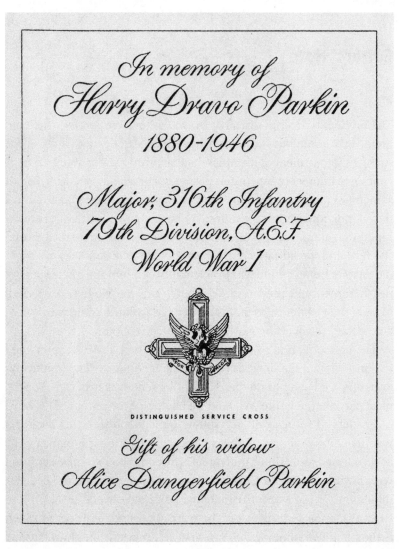

In memory of
Harry Dravo Parkin
1880-1946

Major, 316th Infantry
79th Division, A.E.F.
World War 1

DISTINGUISHED SERVICE CROSS

Gift of his widow
Alice Dangerfield Parkin

Book plate from the World War I memoir by Harry Dravo Parkin. (Courtesy of Special Collections and College Archives, Musselman Library, Gettysburg College, Gettysburg, PA)

1

Camp Meade

I first saw Camp Meade about August 26th or 27th, 1917. It made a very poor impression upon me. My good wife thought the place was terrible, and I agreed with her. The site was a sandy wasteland covered with brush and weeds and small woods. The roads were soft and muddy in places. Many cheap frame buildings were springing up all over the place. Carpenters and laborers swarmed everywhere. Trucks and wagons crowded the roads. All seemed confusion to the newcomer, but hundreds of buildings were rising. Lumber and building materials cluttered the ground. A new raw town like the descriptions of mining towns I had read. Not ready for us new officers, not by any means. We were at war with the world's greatest military power, and our country was caught in its usual condition of utter unpreparedness for war. So we have always been, and probably always shall be.[1]

We had motored from Pittsburgh to Baltimore in our Buick car, a gift from my Mother. We had a pleasant but uneventful journey. The only thing I remembered about it was that we heard George Cohan's famous song "Over There" sung so badly by some poor vaudeville people at Cumberland that we did not think it much of a song. It soon became one of the very best and most popular of the War songs.

It was my very strong desire to have my wife and son living as near me as possible. I did not know how much of life together we had left. Going to live in a strange city meant great sacrifices to my wife, but she felt as I did, and was willing to do so. She was always a very brave and

---

1. Camp Meade was named for the Civil War General George Gordon Meade and located eighteen miles southwest of Baltimore. It was built in the summer of 1917 as a mobilization and training camp for the 79th Division with troops arriving in September 1917. By the year's end, the camp grew in size to 2,900 acres and nearly 37,500 men. See https://history.army.mil/html/bookshelves/resmat/wwi/pt02/ch07/pt02-ch07-sec04.html#lg=1&slide=17.

helpful mate, and a loving and cheerful wife through all the days of the War.

We spent two days house-hunting in Baltimore. Many Army people were on the same quest, and, in consequence, houses were scarce. But, we finally found a beautiful place on Deepdene Road in Roland Park, one of Baltimore's nicest suburbs.[2] It belonged to Captain Gray of the Railroad Service of the Army Reserve. He had recently left home and was on duty in the South. The house was beautifully furnished, and we got it for one hundred dollars per month. The only trouble with the place was that it was on the farther side of Baltimore and on the farthest street from Camp Meade, but that could not be helped. I had to get my family settled before my duties at Camp Meade began. It was twenty-six miles to camp and many a hundred mile I drove that winter in blizzards and storms, rains and fog. My good wife returned to Pittsburgh to pack up what she needed and bring back our son and her cook, Anna.

At Camp Meade I reported to Colonel Oscar J. Charles, who was very pleasant and welcomed me to the Regiment.[3] He told me that he came from the Quartermaster Corps, and I wondered at the time that they did not give us a Colonel from the Infantry. The kindliness of this man did not last long. He believed in harshness and constant "bawling outs" to get results. He criticized all the time, but never praised our really sincere efforts and very hard work to perfect the Regiment. Soon he had not a single friend in the Regiment. Our loyalty was all to the Regiment and not in the least to him, our Commander. Had it not been that we were at war, and hence our greatest efforts needed to get the unit ready as soon as possible, that Regiment would have been a mess, with all the officers loafing and avoiding every possible duty.

When I first met the Colonel, he, knowing that I was the Senior Captain of the Regiment, offered me Headquarters Company. I had been

2. Roland Park was a planned suburb landscaped by the Olmsted brothers. It was an affluent community for the Parkins to live.

3. Colonel Oscar J. Charles was the first commander of the 316th Infantry. The 316th Infantry was one of four infantry regiments in the 79th Division. As a national army division, the 79th was created in the spring of 1917 to meet the emergency expansion of the army and mostly consisted of men drafted into service. Many of the officers were civilians who had been through a course of instruction similar to Parkin's training at both Plattsburgh and Fort Niagara, New York.

warned, by an old regular, not to take this company if I could avoid it. He told me it was made up of special troops, such as one-pounder gun sections, pioneers, signalers, the regimental band, and a lot of such stuff. He advised me to take a regular infantry company. So, I asked the Colonel to give me Company A instead. He seemed surprised, but granted my request without comment. I was very glad that I did not take Headquarters Company. It was all that it was described as, and I was much happier with Company A. All my training had been in the Infantry, and I felt that I knew something about that branch of the service.

The officer's quarters were not ready, so we slept all together in a barrack room on army cots without sheets but with blankets only. It was hot and the flies were thick, but we were by this time used to doing without the comforts of home; in fact, without many of the decencies of life. So, we just laughed and made the best of it. At mealtime the flies were simply terrible and settled on all the food. The bread plate and sugar bowl simply crawled. We ate very fast to get the food into us as clean as possible. Later on when the camp got settled flies were completely eliminated by screens and sanitary precautions and barracks and kitchens were clean and spotless.

For the first few days there were no duties and we were permitted to go to Baltimore to complete our equipment at the stores. Many of the items required by an officer could not be purchased. I had purchased most of mine from an ex-officer of the Guard, and so was better off than most. But I went to town anyway, as there was nothing else to do, and the camp was a dismal place to loaf in. After a few days our new Lieutenant Colonel Alden C. Knowles, the man who really made the Regiment, a good soldier and a just man, put the officers out at squad drill. We did not need this, for if we knew anything it certainly was close order drill, but we were glad to get something to do to pass the time. It looked very odd to see platoons of officers in their new spick and span uniforms marching about doing squads East and West, as they called it in those days.

In time our section of the camp was partially completed and we moved over there. It was called Section "T." We got settled in the long, low one-story building which was officer's quarters. We each had a small room to ourselves, about eight by ten feet, but it gave us privacy, which we had not had since entering the service. A small building behind our quarters was equipped with washstands, shower baths, and toilets. We had good spring cots, electric lights, and later, plenty of steam heat. With a few small rugs, a table and a couple of chairs, I made my room quite comfortable.

I never saw such wasteful construction in my life as went on in the building of our camp. Of course, it was a terrifically hurried job, and it was government work, and the attitude seemed to be that the government can afford anything. Great heaps of good lumber, cut in all lengths, rose all over the place. Each building was surrounded by a mass of nails and spikes. If a keg of nails was upset, no one stopped to pick them up. They were tramped into the mud. It was a dangerous place for auto tires. The buildings were simply slapped together. They were flimsy and of light construction, and roofed with tar paper. But, they did not go up fast enough to suit us even so.

After the drafted men arrived, the army retrieved most of this wasted material. Hundreds of kegs of nails and spikes were picked up and used. The scrap lumber was all used in building boardwalks and shelves and benches. In fact, so great was the need of this material that you had to watch your lumber pile carefully to prevent its being stolen by other companies.

I remember one morning, after about all of the scrap lumber had been used up, the Colonel came up to me at formation for drill, and seeing that my men were standing in the mud, said, "Captain you should build a boardwalk in front of your barracks for the company to fall in on." I replied that I wanted to do so but that the lumber was all used up. He insisted that lumber could still be found and that I must have the boardwalk. I took this to be an order, and consulted with my first sergeant, an old regular army man. Now there were still piled around the camp great heaps of good lumber that had not been used, but an order had been issued forbidding the use of this material. We were permitted to use only the scrap lumber. I had obeyed this order, but I knew that others had taken some of the regulation length planks and sawed pieces off it, thereby making it into scrap lumber. The Sergeant promised to take our half dozen carpenters and build us the boardwalk. I gave him no permission to use any of the good lumber. In a day or two we had a fine wide boardwalk the whole length of our barracks, and the company did not have to stand in the mud anymore. I thanked the Sergeant for the job, and the Colonel praised me for it, and the Sergeant only smiled, and offered no details. We all knew full well that it was built of regular length lumber, but no questions were asked. Anyway, most of that lumber was never used, and it remained in piles around the camp, exposed to the sun and rain and snow.

The most looked forward to event at Camp Meade by the regimental and other officers already there some weeks, was the arrival of the drafted men, the rank and file, who were to fill up the regiments of infantry, artillery, and the machine gun battalions, as well as the special and service units, such as Quartermaster, Ordnance, Ammunition Trains, Remount Stations, etc., etc. The Engineer Regiments took an especial pride in the fact that their men were all volunteers. It takes twenty-seven thousand men to form a complete Army Division, so we had a great mass of men coming, for whom preparations for their reception and care and training were fairly complete, all things considered. It takes about sixteen hundred officers to handle a Division.

An American Division, during the World War, 1917 to 1919, consisted of a Major-General, his Staff, a Headquarters of two Regiments, 3,600 strong each, commanded by Brigadier Generals. There are, hence, 14,400 Infantry in a Division, a brigade of Artillery having two Regiments, a Regiment of Engineers.[4] Each brigade of Infantry has its own Machine Gun battalion also. There are in addition many service and supply units, such as are named above, to which must be added hospital and sanitary units. Our Army Divisions were larger than those of any of the European Armies, and why I have never found out.[5] One

4. The 79th Division consisted of two infantry brigades—the 157th and 158th. Each brigade consisted of two infantry regiments and a machine gun battalion. So, the lineage of Parkin's regiment is as follows: 79th Division, 158th Infantry Brigade, 316th Infantry Regiment. The 316th Infantry was further subdivided into three battalions of four companies each. Infantry regiments in the United States Army consisted of 3,699 men at full strength.

5. The Commander of the American Expeditionary Forces, General John J. Pershing, set the size of American divisions at 28,000 soldiers apiece, more than double the size of their European counterparts in World War I (as well as the American infantry divisions that would fight in World War II). Pershing believed that larger units would have more

of our Divisions on a single road, which they never were, would be twenty-two miles long.

The day of the arrival of the drafted men came and we officers were all greatly excited. We were ordered to remain at our barracks while General Kuhn, the Division Commander, and his Staff met the long trains at the station, Annapolis Junction. General Kuhn shook hands with the first recruit to step off the train and said some words of welcome.

I remember well how the long column came up the dusty road from the station. The men were walking two abreast without order or step, as was to be expected. Most of them carried suitcases or bundles. With few exceptions they were poorly dressed. No sensible man would have worn his best clothes to the camp anyway. We looked them over with the greatest interest. Many thousands poured by us in the dust and under the warm sun. These men came mostly from the countryside and the small towns of Pennsylvania and Maryland. They were, on the whole, a good looking and sturdy lot. They were greatly interested and somewhat impressed by their strange surroundings, but seemed cheerful enough.

After many long columns had passed, one was finally halted in front of our Regimental Headquarters and we officers gathered there to look over our men, whom we must convert into soldiers to fight the Germans. Since I commanded Company A, I was called up first to receive my recruits. I remember a fine-looking big man standing in the column and I determined to have him, and I asked the Staff Officer to include him in my quota, which he did. This man's name has slipped my memory, but he proved to be as good as he looked and I made a Sergeant out of him, but finally lost him as he went away to Officer's School and became a Second Lieutenant. He was, however, of much help to me while he remained in my company.

On this date, September 19, 1917, my company received sixty men. I was to have in all two hundred and fifty men, and five lieutenants. We herded the new soldiers over to our barracks and assigned a cot to each man. They were glad to put down their burdens and let down.

striking power on the battlefield and remain functional for a longer period of time once they suffered casualties.

The rooms must have seemed terribly bare and unhomelike to them. Blankets and pillows were issued, and they made up their beds. I asked for cooks and four experienced restaurant cooks came to me. I was very lucky. Some companies had no cooks at all.

Trucks had dumped provisions at my kitchen, consisting of bread, beef, potatoes, etc. So, I had a Lieutenant take the four cooks to the kitchen and get dinner started at once. My men had a good meal that evening, and good meals as long as they stayed in that camp.

My five Lieutenants and I had a very busy day getting the men settled into their new home and getting their papers sorted out and arranged. It was very late when we retired, our new soldiers had been asleep in their strange beds for hours. There were many funny things said and done by the recruits, and we had to lead them about like a flock of sheep. There was, of course, no discipline or order, but it developed quickly and the men learned fast. They were much in awe of the officers. I saw to it that the recruits were treated firmly but kindly, and I never permitted any bullying or cursing in my company. I considered it unmanly to swear at men who could not swear back at you.

The next morning we lined the men up and I asked for those having military experience or training to step out in the front. Only three or four out of all that crowd of men stepped forward. One of these men had served in the regular Army. His name was Mansberger. I gave him several squads to instruct and he trained them well. The other three men were tried as Corporals, but did not make good. Mansberger became a Sergeant, then Mess Sergeant, and a very good one, although I never got over the idea that he was putting something over on me. He was reduced to the ranks in France for making trouble in the company. He was tried at Camp Meade for bringing liquor into camp, but got off; though, I always felt he was guilty. He finally met his death bravely in the battle of the Argonne Forest. A typical product of the regular Army. He knew his job, but got by with as little effort as possible. He knew how to soldier.[6]

Before the drafted men arrived, I had received three men from the regular Army. Corporal B----, who became my First Sergeant, was in

6. Charles Mansberger was from Pennsylvania, and was killed in action on September 29, 1918. He is buried at the Meuse-Argonne American Cemetery.

many respects a good soldier. I had later to reduce him to Line Sergeant for permitting open gambling in the barracks. He did not go to France with us since he had caught a venereal disease, and no man in this condition was permitted to go overseas. The other two men from the regulars were of no use to me as non-commissioned officers, for which purpose they had been sent, and upon my request they went back to their own regiment. B----, like Mansberger, had all the tricks of the regular, but both did a lot of good work in training the new men and forming the company, and I acknowledge my debt to them.

After dinner, on the first day, I had all the new men assembled in the large upstairs bunkroom and had them sit on the cots, and then I gave them a good talk. I told them that their new life in the Army would be very strange at first but they would soon get used to it. I impressed upon them the absolute need for obedience to all Officers and all orders, and the necessity for cleanliness and order. I said that we were all of us only temporary soldiers for the period of the War, and told them they would be proud all the rest of their lives of their war service, and for that reason they must be good and faithful soldiers and do their full duty willingly. I assured them that, while we must have first rate discipline in the company, I would see to it personally that they were justly treated and would permit no bullying in the company; and that any soldier who had a just complaint was to feel free to come to me, his Captain, and have his case heard. I made a sincere effort to cheer them up and make them feel certain that if they did their best they would be properly treated and cared for. And, I could see by their faces that I had succeeded. The meeting broke up quietly and I could see that they were pleased and reassured by my talk. I made this talk to each new group of men upon their arrival and I always felt well repaid for my trouble.

I was always strict with the men, but I always tried to be fair and just. Such, I know, is the correct attitude for an officer to take with soldiers, and the only way to win their obedience, respect and perhaps some affection, but the last must not be tried for, it will follow the other two.

When in ranks and at attention no man in my company dared lift his hand or turn his head. If his hat fell off, he let it go, and an officer picked it up and restored it to him. Nothing looks worse, than to see a military body of men violating the command of "Attention." It is the real test of trained troops: the manner in which they respect "Attention."

The first job with the drafted men was to get their Service Records started. This Service Record was a War Department form in the shape of a booklet in which each man's name, age and description, nearest of kin and other needed information was entered. Many other cards concerning each man were later filled out, until we got wearied of them. The fatheads at Washington seemed to have nothing else to do but invent blue cards, and red cards and purple cards. Paper work developed into a regular curse, and I had to keep a Lieutenant and a stenographer constantly at work in the company office to keep up with the flood of cards and foolish letters and requests for information. When we got to France, and out of the clutches of the nuts in Washington, we got clear of this paper work almost entirely and it was a great relief. All of these records were taken along with us in a specially built large wooden box and the greater part of them were never used there. Smith, the Company Clerk, spent his entire life in France guarding this box and moving it around the county.

Another of the first jobs was to get the men into uniform and this was a job that was never finished. Quartermaster trucks delivered huge loads of boxes to our quarters, all of which had to be signed for and contents accounted for. The loss of a pair of shoes would entail endless correspondence, and perhaps a charge against the Captain's pay. I put a Lieutenant in charge of this work and selected a recruit, who seemed intelligent and had experience as a store clerk, to assist him and act as Acting Quartermaster Sergeant. His name I do not recall, but he made good and did his work well and I appointed him Quartermaster Sergeant. The recruits were furnished absolutely everything from the skin out to overcoats, and it took a lot of clothing and a lot of record-keeping to outfit two hundred and fifty men. The campaign hats, the underclothes, the shoes, woolen shirts and socks all looked like good materials to me, but the uniform coats and breeches seemed made of cheap stuff, shoddy, and I cannot see why the Army bought such poor clothing. Also, the uniforms varied much in color. The overcoats were fine and heavy and of good wool.

There was a great deal of varied work to be done in equipping and organizing a company of Infantry. It was impossible for the Captain to attend to it all personally. I had five lieutenants and I intended that they should work hard and look after the different jobs, while I oversaw the whole thing, and made the final decisions, for I was responsible. There were finally four Platoons of sixty men each, under command of a lieutenant, and also a Headquarters detachment consisting of the cooks, orderlies, clerk, buglers, etc., under command the First Sergeant. The extra Lieutenant, the ranking one, was my general assistant, and in charge of the office work. The four lieutenants, who commanded the platoons, also had special duties. They oversaw the Quartermaster supplies, the feeding of the men, the care of the barracks, the entertainment of the men, etc., etc.

The training of the Regiment progressed very fast. The officers were keen and the soldiers were eager and willing. I remember Colonel Knowles and I were watching the platoons drilling one day, after the training had been going on several weeks, and he remarked that he had never seen recruits make such fast progress, and said he wished the regular Army could get such fine material in peace times. Even so, I could not help but compare these men with those that had attended the First Officer's Training Camp, who were, of course, the very pick of the educated young men of the country, and who made the most astonishing progress in military drill and duties that I ever saw in my life.[7] The drafted men could not compare at all with the candidates for commissions at the Officer's Training Camp, with some exceptions, but this was to be expected. Only a small percentage of the drafted men were college men, and most of these were soon sent to be trained as officers. The old European idea that it takes a gentleman to be an officer was almost 100% true in our own army.[8] The great majority of the old non-commissioned officers of the regular army, who were promoted to be officers in the World War Army were not successes as such. They

7. Parkin is referring to the first class of the Fort Niagara Officer Training Camp (OTC) that ran from May to August 1917. The camp consisted of 2,500 educated and enthusiastic young volunteers from largely affluent backgrounds, many of whom, like himself, ended up as officers in the AEF.

8. Samuel Hynes discusses class and rank in his study of American World War I pilots, *The Unsubstantial Air* (New York: Farrar, Strauss, and Giroux, 2014). He writes, "They were 'college men'—a phrase of the time that identified not only an educational level but a small elite class; if America had an aristocracy, they'd be in it," p. 11.

neither got along well with the other officers nor inspired a proper respect among the man. Captain Louis C. Knack, who was such an officer, was an outstanding exception. The other four officers of this type did not make good in our Regiment. They were harsh and unreasonable with the men.

A day in the new Army was a long and very busy time. First Call, or Reveille, was at six, then followed an hour to wash, have breakfast and clean barracks. Drill call came at seven and we took the men out on the drill grounds for four hours and a half. Frequent rests of ten minutes in every hour were given. Also, drill was varied by talks on Military Discipline, Military Courtesy, the Duties of the Soldier, Army Service Regulations, etc. The company would sit in a group on the ground and the officers, in turn, talked to them. We started back to barracks about eleven-thirty and had a few minutes to clean up, and then dinner, the main meal of the day, was served. The food was plain, but well-cooked and good and plentiful. An officer was present at every meal to see that all men were properly fed. When we got our share of the canteen profits, which I shall explain later, we were able to improve the food and chicken and even turkey and pies and cakes and many other good things were on the table. In fact, I believe that most of the men ate better food at Camp Meade than they were accustomed to in their homes, and they had better clothes and were much cleaner and in much better health. Many of them had never owned a toothbrush before. Also, they had regular exercise and good sleep at night. In fact, most of them in a month's time outgrew their uniforms—not fat, but good solid flesh and muscle.

After noon dinner there was a half hour to smoke and rest, and at one o'clock drill call again. This lasted until four-thirty, at which time the company was dismissed at barracks. A regular drill schedule was made up for each week by Lieutenant Colonel Knowles, and it was strictly adhered to. The drills were varied as much as possible so that the men would not get stale and lose interest. Close order or parade ground drill was followed by patrols, and scouting or grenade drill, or attack formations. A lot of time was put in building a bayonet course or run, and in building trenches—of these two things I will write later.

At five o'clock the Ceremony of Retreat was held. For this everyone must be neat and clean-shaven and have his rifle and equipment spotless. The men were carefully inspected. The Companies formed in front of their barracks, presented arms, the band played the National Anthem, and the flag, on the high pole in front of Regimental Head-quarters was slowly lowered. Always impressive to all. Supper followed at six, and the soldiers were through for the day, and could do as they pleased in or near barracks until nine when last call or Taps was blown and all must be in bed and quiet until six in the morning.

There was school for the non-commissioned officers, the Corporals and Sergeants for an hour five nights a week, seven to eight, conducted by an officer. It was, of course, on Military subjects.

But the officers, especially the captains, were not through with the day's work with dinner. There was French Class some evenings, and Military Tactics on other evenings. There were many orders on the captain's desk to read and learn, and many reports to get ready and pay-rolls to prepare. I made my Lieutenants do a lot of this work, assigning special work to each, but I was responsible and had to oversee all and do much of it myself. I got to bed as early as possible for I needed the sleep, but many a night midnight found me hard at it at my desk. But I enjoyed the army life and did not begrudge the long hours my duty took of each day.

We had good music, in fact, very fine music of a military nature. Our band was started with forty-five pieces, but later increased to sixty. There were many more applicants than could be taken, all professional musicians. I remember the first time the band appeared at Retreat. It could not march at all, but it could play well, and in a few weeks it was as fine a band as I ever heard. It played at Reveille and at Retreat and all parades. It also played in the officer's mess at dinner in the evening. Each company had the buglers for calls and commands in the field. These were at times assembled together and soon played well. We did not have them play with the band until after we went to France. It makes very inspiring martial music to have the buglers play with the band at parade. They swell the music and tone as well.

I cannot remember whether or not I have written elsewhere in these memoirs of the fine moral effect of military music upon tired-out or battle-weary troops; but this is an important matter in a War army, and so I shall risk repetition.

I remember that we were resting at Camp Normandie after our first experience of battle in the Argonne Forest. We were worn out physically and benumbed mentally from our terrible five days of driving the stubborn Germans, attacking their numerous machine gun nests, and enduring their accurate and awful artillery fire. Our losses had been very heavy and the memory of the torn and dead bodies of our comrades filled our minds. We were depressed and broken. An alarm might have sent us in desperate flight. The men were living in their small pup tents among the trees and it rained a great deal. No jokes nor laughs were ever heard in the camp. I was glad that we were out of the battle for a time at least, for we could do no more.

Some officer at Regimental Headquarters, it must have been Captain Glock or Captain Manning, for the Colonel and the Lieutenant-Colonel would never have had the idea, sent the band in trucks up to our camp. They set up their music racks among the trees and soon the whole place was full of martial and popular music. Men began to appear from all sides. A Y.M.C.A. Song Leader was with the band and in a few minutes he had several hundred men singing the army songs and laughing amongst themselves and at his jokes.[9] The band remained for more than an hour and left us greatly cheered up and encouraged. I saw this done several times during our stay on the Front, and I wished that we could have had the band every day when not actually fighting.

So greatly were the bands valued for their moral effect upon the troops that after our first battle, in which the bandsmen acted as stretcher bearers and several were wounded, an order from Pershing's Headquarters came out forbidding the musicians to go into battle in the future, and this was a correct and sensible order, and for the good of the Army.[10]

But I am far from Camp Meade in my thoughts and must get back. I regret now that I did not keep a day by day diary. I simply had not the time to do so, though I often thought of it. Hence, this tale will be

9. The Young Men's Christian Association (YMCA) functioned as an adjunct civilian organization to the US Army and was committed to providing wholesome welfare support and entertainment for men in army life.

10. Parkin is referring to General Orders 139 issued on August 24, 1918, stating that "The practice of using members of the band as stretcher bearers will be discontinued, except in cases of extreme urgency." It is interesting that he notes a strict interpretation of this order by his unit considering the urgency of his later engagements. See *United States Army in the World War 1917–1918: Volume 16, General Orders*, 426.

disconnected and rambling, but I will set down the things I remember.

More drafted men came to us at different times, but our work was never again so hard as it had been with the first lot, for we were not organized, experienced, and had a large group of partly-trained men to help us. To each new lot of drafted men I made the same talk I had made to the first group, and so tried to help them get started in their new and very different life. Strange to relate, I had to assemble my old men, after the second lot arrived, and give them, the old men, a good scolding, for they, as veterans, had started in with great glee to haze the already miserable and homesick newcomers.

Our sore-headed regular Colonel told me more than once that I was too soft and too good to my men, but since he also told me several times that I had the best company in the Regiment, and since I was the first Company Commander promoted to the rank of Major, I feel that my attitude towards my men could not have been very wrong. At any rate, it was my natural and only attitude towards them, and I, personally, found that they responded splendidly.

2

Our Voyage and Arrival in France

Sunday, July 7, 1918, was an eventful day in the history of the 316th Infantry, for it was on that day that our long and hard training at Camp Meade, Maryland, came to an end, at last, and we started upon our long journey to the battlefront. And, for many of us, this was life's last journey. But we did not think of that and were eager and anxious to go.

Good Dame Rumor had been busy in our ranks for months and the date of departure had been finally fixed in our minds many times only to pass by with nothing to break the regular routine of our lives. And so it came to pass that no one would believe anything at all about the date of our departure and, to raise a chorus of jeering laughter, it was only necessary to attempt to pass on a rumor about the date of leaving for France. I amused myself one day by starting such a rumor and for several hours it was told to me confidentially.

Major Herbert C. de V. Cornwell, Surgeon of our Regiment, knowing that I had my family living in Baltimore, and that I would want to send them back home to Pittsburgh before I left for France, had promised to let me have several days advance notice of our departure.[1] He said that he would have positive information, in advance from Medical Corps Headquarters at Washington, so that he might have all of his medical stores and equipment ready. This information would be confidential to him, but he was a close friend, and wanted to help me with my family. And, early in July, about the second or third, he took me aside and told me we would go on July 7th, but I must positively keep it to myself.

In the late afternoon of July 7, 1918, the four Companies of my Battalion, the First of the 316th Regiment, stood all ready to march down to the trains, on the sidewalks in front of their different barracks.

---

1. Dr. Herbert Cornwell was a prominent Harvard educated physician who before the war specialized on diseases of the nervous system at Presbyterian Hospital in New York City.

Although a Captain, I had for most of the eleven months at Camp Meade been Acting Major in Command of the Battalion. This was owing to the continued absence of our Major, Major Robert Meador, on detached service. He and Colonel Charles did not get along together and they were both glad to be separated. I had inspected the Companies. The men were neat and clean and fully equipped. They looked like good soldiers, and, now that the time had come to go, the great majority of the men were quiet and serious looking. I felt a great pride in them as I walked through their well-ordered and silent ranks.[2]

The inspections over and fully satisfied that we were prepared, I stood near Company A, my own company, waiting for the telephone message with my orders to march to the trains. Lieutenant Daniel Keller, Adjutant of my Battalion, stood nearby, saying "Farewell" to his wife. All the rest of us had made our "Farewells" and Mrs. Keller was the only woman present. They were both very brave about it, and concealed their emotions wonderfully. I wondered why they had not had this trying ordeal over before this and in the privacy of their home. Poor girl she was looking her last upon her husband, but if she had any premonition of this she was very brave and womanly and concealed her fears.

An orderly came hurrying from Regimental Headquarters bearing to me the order to march to the trains. Major Meador, who at this time was with the Battalion and in command, was away in Baltimore visiting his wife. Hence, I took command of the Battalion, and blowing my whistle for attention, gave the command "Companies Right by squads—Column Left," and we were off on the long and long-desired march to the battlefront in France.

The roads of Camp Meade were filled with troops on the way to the trains, and trucks loaded with the baggage of the regiments. I had a large suitcase containing my personal baggage. Not wishing to let it get out of my sight, for fear of losing it, I asked a very large Italian-American soldier of Company A to carry it, another man taking his rifle. It was very heavy and as we had a mile or more to go the sweat was

2. Parkin does not mention that many of the men who joined the 79th Division at Camp Meade were ultimately assigned elsewhere. According to William Walker, "seventy-two percent of the 95,000 officers and men trained at Camp Meade were transferred out of the 79th before it embarked for France," p. 86.

running down his face when we arrived at the cars. I thanked him and he said with a grin, "Captain, that case is a Son-of-a-Beech to carry!"

Each infantry battalion had a train to itself, composed of a number of ordinary day-coaches for the men and one Pullman parlor-car for the officers. The seats in the coaches were turned facing each other and three men, with their packs and rifles, were assigned to two seats. This did not give the men much room, but it was a great deal more room and comfort than they were to get on the trains in France. Transport officers at the station supervised the loading of the cars, and after the men were all on we officers went to our Pullman at the rear of the train. Major Meador did not show up. We pulled out at once, the men cheering wildly, every window full of heads. The Major overtook us at Hoboken, New Jersey, coming on the train of another regiment.

Many trains of our division had preceded us and the people along the line were now aware that soldiers of Camp Meade were off to France. All along the way were grouped thousands of cheering people. At every station and railroad crossing and in between. It seemed that we ran through a continuous cheering mass of people. Boxes of candy, fruit, flowers, cakes, came hurtling through the open car windows. Literally showers of it. These gifts flying through the windows of the fast moving train inflicted some painful bruises upon some of us, and shouts of laughter followed a man getting hit with a box of candy or a piece of fruit.

Baltimore was our first stop. As we pulled into the station we found a great crowd of friends and relatives on the platform, permitted by the railroad and military authorities to make a last "Farewell" to the soldiers. As our train came to a stop the soldiers in the car windows called out to the pushing throng, "First Battalion, 316th Infantry," and those who had friends and relatives in our unit crowded forward to the cars, the others making way for them. The men were not allowed off the train, but they were all in the windows and when any man's name was called, his comrades brought him to the window and gave him front place there. We officers got off and I told them to go along the train and help the people find their relatives and friends. Several poor dear Mothers came to me asking for their sons, and when I found out from them what companies the men were in they were soon with them. Hundreds of women and girls were lifted up by the crowd, all along the train, kissing and hugging the soldiers, and I could not keep the tears from my eyes as I watched these scenes of emotion and excitement. The situation was somewhat relieved and great laughter created by men carrying pretty girls along the cars who kissed dozens of smiling cheering soldiers.

We pulled out, after a fifteen minute stop, amidst tremendous cheering from the mass of people, the whole train roaring with return cheers. I stood on the car step as we slowly passed the closely-massed people who cheered, most of them with tears in their eyes. It was one of the great soul-uplifting moments of the War, and I have seldom been more moved.

We ran on through the night, illuminated by continuous bonfires, surrounded by large groups of people all the way. The gifts continued to fly in through the windows, all of which were open. A continued and noisy ovation. We stopped at Philadelphia, and here the crowd was even greater and the cheering louder than at Baltimore. And the same scenes were repeated, and there were the same anxious parents and relatives hunting for their boys.

After leaving Philadelphia we kept running through the crowds along the line, but as it got later in the night, or early in the morning, the people began to go home and the groups about the fires became smaller, but some of them remained practically all the way to Jersey City where we arrived early in the morning of July 8th, tired out with excitement and loss of sleep. Here we left the trains and boarded ferry boats which took us to the docks at Hoboken. "Hoboken or Hell by Christmas" became a saying in the Army in France. Meaning, of course, home with the War won by Christmas, or dead in the effort to bring this about. And we had the War won by Christmas, but mighty few of us were back at Hoboken by that time and I don't feel that any of those we left buried in France were in Hell either.

The whistles of other ferry boats greeted us and the few early passengers waved and cheered as we passed on the river. The troops were packed solid on the decks, but the trip was not long. We finally came to rest upon the cobblestones just outside of the docks. Although the men had been eating all kinds of food all night long, I thought that they should have a warm breakfast. There was a restaurant where the officers could purchase a good breakfast, but it was a small place and could not furnish even coffee for the soldiers. I carried with me some hundreds of dollars in cash of the mess funds of Company A, as did the other captains, and we offered to pay well, but we could get nothing. I finally got hold of a "Union News" boy, and from him purchased five hundred bars of Lowney's milk chocolate, two per each member of my company. It was the best I could do for the company, and in a very few minutes that seemingly large amount of chocolate was devoured, and I don't know to this day whether I charged up the fifty dollars I paid for this chocolate in the Company Mess Book.

Later in the morning the good ladies of the Red Cross set up counters on the docks and fed the troops plentifully with hot coffee and sandwiches and Red Cross buns. Soldiers are the greatest and most willing eaters I have ever known. They never refuse and would eat all the time, I believe. But a soldier on the move is wise to eat when and all that he can for he may find it a long way to the next meal.

We sat on our packs on the cobblestones most of the day, and but few people stopped to look at us through the bars of the high iron fence. Soldiers had become an old story to the good people of Hoboken. At noon a Battalion of Quartermaster troops dressed in overalls assembled in front of nearby docks. They had been loading ships. As they marched past us to lunch our infantrymen remarked upon their discipline and their right to be called soldiers in anything but a complimentary manner. The fact that the passing soldiers had been drafted into the Quartermaster Corps without having any choice in the matter made no difference to the Infantry.[3] Of course, it was not fair, but fighting men always have and always will look down upon their comrades in the services of the rear. A fine time my men would have had without the food and clothing and supplies these men of the Quartermaster Corps gathered and forwarded to them. The Infantry would admit that, but they will never grant these men equal standing as soldiers. The soldier who risks his life in battle feels that only a man who takes equal risks is his equal, and he can hardly be blamed for his attitude.

When the time came, in the latter part of the afternoon, to go aboard the waiting ships, we company officers were much concerned regarding

3. The US Army Quartermaster Corps bore the responsibility of keeping American soldiers clothed, clean, and fed on two continents. To supply a rapidly mobilized army of nearly four million men was a significant logistical challenge.

the accuracy of the records we had with us for each man. We had been so warned and threatened at Camp Meade by officers from the Staff at Washington. We were told that men and officers whose records were not absolutely correct and complete would not be allowed to board the ships and the guilty officers would suffer dire punishment. New and additional cards of record had been frequently introduced to us during the preceding winter. There was the yellow card, and the pink card, and the blue card, and the white card and so on up to the number of seven or eight for each man. One of the biggest fool things of the whole War.

And so each Captain and Company Clerk stood anxiously at the foot of the gangplank, with the box of records open for the inspection of the loading officers, who simply called the names of the men off as they came up in order and checked them off as they went aboard, paying no attention at all to our wonderful records. And, it made us sore. Such a lot of work, most of it of no real use. We had checked the names of our men a dozen times, in order to have them absolutely correct, but in spite of all this, one of my men corrected the middle initial of his name when the loading officer called it out. Of all times to do such a thing, and after all the chances he had to correct it. I told him to stand aside, when the loading officer looked at me severely, and was greatly of a mind to leave him behind, as he well deserved for his carelessness, and getting me in wrong after all my work. As the last man of my company went aboard, I was just about to tell the loading officer to mark off this man and send him to a Casual camp when the officer turned to the soldier, asked him his middle initial, corrected it on his list, asked him if he wanted to go, smiled at the soldier's eager "Yes, Sir," and told him to get on board. "You had a more correct list than most of them, Captain," he said to comfort me, and I followed my company on board feeling much better.

We sailed for France on the evening of July 9th. There was no attempt whatever at concealment of our departure. In fact, I do not see how there could be any. The four ships of our convoy, all of about 20,000 tons in size, the *Agamemnon,* the *Mt. Vernon,* the *Amenta,* and the *Orizaba* backed out of their docks in turn, their decks and rigging simply a mass of cheering soldiers, straightened out in the river, greeted by every whistle within a mile, and steamed down to the lower harbor where they assembled.

We had passed the previous night on board and were fairly well settled in our places before sailing. The evening before we had witnessed the departure of the giant *Leviathan*, largest of all ships, carrying the 315th Infantry and other troops. Great cheering and blowing of whistles occurred. She was so long and immense that there seemed scarcely room to turn her in the river. Many sturdy tugs worked furiously over her, but in surprisingly quick time they straightened her out, and with a hoarse blast of her siren, she moved majestically away on her journey. A bitter pill for the enemy this German built and owned vessel, greatest in the world, carrying thousands of soldiers over to fight their troops. My recollection is that she carried 12,000 troops each trip. No torpedo boats or rather, destroyers, ever escorted the *Leviathan*, because her speed was so great that no submarine could attack her.

The entire 316th Infantry, with the exception of "M" and Supply Company, was on board the *Agamemnon*. There was also a battalion of Engineers, most unwelcome intruders to us, and many Casuals, or unattached officers and men. We were terribly crowded and it was a most uncomfortable voyage. Fortunately, we had good weather and no rough seas, with sun most of the time.

But many of the men were seasick and very miserable, most of them for a day or two only, but a few all the way over. Poor fellows, they lay about the decks pale and green and utterly miserable, and we could not do anything to ease their suffering. My adjutant, Lieutenant Dan Keller, was sick most of the time, but he was very game and refused to give up to it. There were covered cans about the ship for the seasick, and on our inspection trips, poor Dan, had frequently to stop and use one of them. He was positively green at times and I urged him to go to his bunk, but he would not do so. Duty, with Dan, was first of all things. He was always a good and faithful officer and a pleasant companion, a perfect gentleman. His death, in the Argonne Forest, was a great and sad loss to me.[4] He had my affection and my respect.

4. Keller was a Columbia-educated officer from Lancaster, Pennsylvania. He married in the summer of 1917 before leaving for France the following year. He is buried at the Meuse-Argonne American Cemetery. For a detailed obituary, see https://www.google

Our ship, the *Agamemnon,* formerly the *Kaiser Wilhelm II,* [5] a German vessel, was of good size, about 20,000 tons I think, but she was loaded to full capacity, and even more, for after we thought we were full up, they sent on board some four or five hundred Engineers and this necessitated some of the men, and they happened to be my men, sharing their bunks with other soldiers, which meant that in these cases, one man slept at night and the other during the day. A very unsatisfactory arrangement, which led to much confusion and crowding and a mixing up of rifles and equipment.

The men of my company were five decks down and well below the water line. They were in cargo rooms about thirty feet square and ten feet high. These rooms were poorly lighted with a few bulbs, but the air was fresh and good, due to the forced ventilation. Bunks, built of steel pipe, three tiers high, filled all the space except that left for very narrow passageways. A man away back in the corner of such a room might well feel nervous about his chances of getting out in case of a panic, or even a disaster without a panic. Each man must keep his rifle and equipment in his bunk, or hanging beside it. The non-commissioned officers were distributed between the rooms a company occupied, and at night a commissioned officer was on duty in each room all night. The company officers stood watches in this work and they were helped out by the extra officers on board the ship, of which there always were a considerable number. These officers were armed with loaded pistols and their orders were to shoot down any man who tried to start a panic. One night one of my men had a nightmare and sprang up shouting, "The ship is sinking." The officer on duty hit him on the jaw and knocked him down, and quickly quieted the other men. The officer had a right to shoot this man, but he did not have the right to strike him, according to military law. Needless to say, we were all glad that he disobeyed the law.

I made a practice of going down into all of my men's rooms every night, about nine. I would work my way through the narrow passages,

.com/books/edition/Obituary_Record_of_the_Alumni/lbBGAQAAMAAJ?hl=en&gbpv=1&bsq=Keller.

5. The *Agamemnon* was formerly the German passenger liner *Kaiser Wilhelm II.* It was seized and put into US service as a troop transport after the declaration of war in April 1917.

dodging the hanging rifles and legs, back to the farthest corner and to the sides of the ship. I would talk with the men there to reassure them and let them realize that someone was interested in them. Soldiers appreciate such attention. A good captain is in many ways, a father to his men. A kindly but not a familiar father. There is a great difference.

These rooms occupied by my men, so far below the main open deck of the ship, were connected with the decks above by steel stairways of good width, and not by upright steel ladders, as might have been expected. With so many men below decks, ladders would not have permitted many to escape, in case of disaster. The stairways gave us a hope that many of us could get up reasonably quickly in case of need. Each room was shut off by heavy steel doors, which were kept closed, but never locked.

The feeding of some six thousand men on the ship was quite a problem, but the naval and quartermaster officers had evolved a solution which worked well and avoided confusion. All the tables and chairs in the main dining room had been removed and the carpets had been taken up. Serving tables had been set up at the foot of the stairway upon which the food was placed and behind which men stood to serve. Along these tables the soldiers passed with their mess kits and canteen cups, receiving the different foods as they progressed. They then went on into the main body of the room where eating tables hung from the ceiling. There were no chairs, the men ate standing up. It was purely a matter of eating for nourishment, not pleasure. When a man had finished he left the room by a staircase opposite to the one he had entered by, stopping on the way to wash his mess kits in cans of hot soapy water and rinsing them in clean cold water. In spite of every attempt to keep the dining room clean the serving tables and the eating tables would get slopped over with food. The room was unpleasantly warm and the odor was not pleasant.

Two meals a day were served, a rather late breakfast and an early dinner. Since the soldiers had no work to do, and could get no exercise, owing to the densely crowded decks, this gave them sufficient food.[6] I was frequently in the mess room, and the food seemed very good to

6. Not all ships transporting the division had the same fare. See *History of the 316th Infantry in the World War*, 20–21.

me. I heard no complaints from the men. Some thought they should have three meals a day, but it could not be arranged for so many.

Life belts had to be worn by everyone all the time. They were a great nuisance and very warm and we got very tired of them. We even slept in them. They were not the usual type. Ours had nearly all of the cork held upon our chests and backs. They were soiled and worn, and made us look slovenly. But we might need them desperately so we wore them constantly.

The bathing facilities for the soldiers were utterly inadequate. They consisted of a few shower baths. Very few men could use them. Some of my men, after a week at sea, complained to me about this. I spoke to one of the naval officers. He said he was sorry but could do nothing about it. He did not seem to have much initiative. I believe this is so of most naval officers. Those on our ship kept severely to themselves and seemed to think themselves better than the officers of the army.

Only one of the naval officers, a Lieutenant-Commander, was a good fellow. He seemed willing to do all he could to make our voyage as comfortable as possible. Perhaps he had enough rank to feel sure of himself, or else he was such a decent chap that even Annapolis could not ruin his disposition. I finally appealed to him and told him my troubles. He said he realized that the bathrooms were not sufficient. Between us we worked out a scheme to get the soldiers a good but a rather rough bath. We took them to the top deck by platoons, sixty men, had them strip off all of their clothes, gave out a lot of soap, and then had several sailors, from different angles, deluge them with sea water from fire hoses. The men enjoyed it and there was great deal of fun and laughter.

I have described the methods and arrangements for the care of the enlisted men during the voyage. Recreation and exercise for them might be said to have been non-existent. They were too terribly crowded for either of these things. All they could do during the day was to sit or stand about the decks and smoke and talk, and watch the other four ships of our convoy. They assembled several times at night in the large mess room, standing packed together and were entertained by other soldiers. Some of the entertainers were clever and the efforts were greatly appreciated, but no noisy demonstrations of approval could be permitted. It might be heard by a nearby enemy submarine. Slim Kalim was the cleverest and most popular of these entertainers.

He was a professional vaudeville actor, and he was in great demand. I stood on the balcony looking down on the sea of dimly white faces, showing faintly in the light of a few blue electric globes. The waves of subdued laughter came up to me. Poor fellows how easily they were amused, and what a responsibility was ours, the officers, taking them to a foreign land and into the most terrible war man had ever waged.

I have not written anything of the arrangements for the officers on the ship. We were considerably better cared for than were the enlisted men, as is always the case in the military service when possible. Officers occupied the cabins of the first and second class, and each had a berth to himself. Captain Manning and Captain James B. Montgomery, respectively Regimental Adjutant and Regimental Personnel Officer, and I had a small cabin on the main deck in which there were three berths. We three with our equipment crowded the small room uncomfortably, but it was clean and the beds were good. We had a washstand, but no bathroom. There was one porthole and during the day the air fresh, but as we were obliged to close the porthole at night, so that an enemy submarine might not see a light, the air became very bad, and we awoke in the morning feeling very dull and stuffy. We had to sleep in all of our clothes, and with our lifebelts and pistols strapped on. We took off only our boots, hats and overcoats. Consequently, we slept very poorly and in much worse air than did the men, far below us, whose rooms had forced ventilation.

The officers ate their meals in what had been the ship's library. We sat at small tables for six or eight and were waited upon by navy orderlies, young Filipinos, clean, quick young men dressed in white sailor's uniforms. The food was very good, and although the room was very crowded, the service was first class. There were bathrooms reserved for the officers, but there were so many of us that it was difficult to get a bath, and we often had to stand in line for the toilets. All in all, it was the most unpleasant voyage I have ever made on a ship. But "C'est la Guerre," we knew it could not be helped, and this was no pleasure trip.

The decks were common to all. No space was reserved for officers, nor was any recreation or entertainment possible, except the music furnished by a very good sailor orchestra in our dining room, during meals, and sometimes in the evenings. When dinner had been cleared away, we used to sit there around the tables smoking and talking, and having what drinks were obtainable. As I remember it, they were soft drinks and very few. Toast and coffee were served late in the evening. There was no privacy for the individual. You could not get by yourself and we felt this. Even in your cabin you had your roommates. In this respect, we were no better off than the soldiers, except that there were fewer of us in a room.

Every person on the ship was assigned to a certain lifeboat or raft and at the signal for lifeboat drill was required to assemble on the deck at the side of the boat or raft. The routes through the vessel for the soldiers occupying the many rooms were carefully laid down to avoid confusion and crossing of groups. There was no rushing nor crowding nor undue haste. Every day and sometimes more than once, the electric signal bells would ring and at once every man would go quietly and promptly to his station. It was rehearsed many times and always without warning, and we certainly got it down pat. The sailors would prepare and swing out the boats, and we would, in a very few minutes, be standing in ranks beside them. There were over seven thousand people on the ship and a place was provided for each of them.

The life-saving plan was quite different from what we had expected and entirely new to us. We were not to enter the boats and be lowered to the water in them, but we were to stand quietly in our places while the sailors lowered the boats, and when they were in the water, we were to go to the rail in single file and jump down into the water near our boat. Then, the sailors would help us aboard the boats, and those who could swim would help those who could not. All would be supported, in the water, by their life preservers until hauled into a boat. Officers with loaded pistols would enforce order and obedience, and shoot if necessary.

The scheme seemed a queer one to us, but it had been tried out with entire success on a transport that had been torpedoed on its way home, and not a life had been lost. It occurred to me that if, as I was rising to the surface, after my plunge, a soldier should light on my head, with his heavy hobnail shoes, having jumped down some forty feet, it would not be worthwhile to haul me into a boat, but I did not voice this thought.

And while writing of lifeboat drill I will set down the tale of the only submarine attack we experienced on the voyage. We had been escorted for the first three days by a squadron of destroyers. Then, for four days we proceeded without escort. For the last three days we were again escorted by destroyers, which had come out from France or England to meet us. How these small ships did jump and buck in the waves which scarcely moved us at all. And much of the time their decks were awash. Surely a beastly life. The day after they joined us we were sailing along, four ships abreast and one, the La France following at some distance, but in plain sight. Life-boat drill was just over when suddenly the alarm bells rang out again. I thought there must be some real cause this time. When I reached my station all eyes were upon the "La France," which was coming up at full speed, making a great bow-wave, blowing her whistle, firing her guns, and with a red flag at her fore mast. The destroyers, three of them, which had been in the rear, came tearing up at racing speed, making tremendous bow-waves. Running in circles, they crisscrossed in turn a spot in the sea, and dropped depth-bombs, which threw up great columns of water. Scarcely had the water fallen back when another destroyer raged over the spot and dropped another bomb. They must have let go a half dozen of them. If Fritz was there he certainly got a very hot reception, and it was officially thought that he actually was there. I turned to look at my men during this crisis to see how they were taking their first real danger, and I was comforted to note no sign of fear on any face, just the keenest interest and delight at the splendid work of the destroyers.

All of the ships had put on full speed, and the destroyers were soon left far behind, for a time only, as they soon regained their position in our immediate rear. The naval officers told us nothing at all, and we were left to our own conclusions. But the extremely quick and fierce attack upon the submarine, which we had witnessed, gave us a feeling of security we had not had before.

I came on deck one morning and there on our port side I saw a most astonishing and never-to-be-forgotten sight such as I shall probably never see again in this life. Ships, apparently without number, and of every known design and every size. Really a most astonishing and unexpected sight. A great fleet of supply ships, loaded with the sinews of war, slowly making its way to war-torn Europe. The surface of the sea, as far as we could see ahead, to the rear, and off to the south, was literally covered with ships. What a hunting ground for the German submarines. But alert guards, in the shape of long, lean gray cruisers, bristling with wicked-looking guns and inquisitive destroyers, some of which had come over to look at us, abounded, ready to pounce upon the hunters of their flock. Some of the vessels were large and imposing and some were small and rusty. Liners and tramps together, anything that would carry supplies. For hours we kept overtaking and passing the steamers of this great convoy. Perhaps the largest fleet that ever sailed together. The escorting war vessels stationed all along the fleet kept exchanging signals with our squadron. Here before our eyes we had evidence of the tremendous effort our country was making to win the War, and it added greatly to our assurance of final success.

Our ship carried guns, or cannon, for defense against enemy submarines. If I remember correctly there were four of them, two aft and two forward. They seemed large to us, and I think they were six inch or possibly eight in calibre. An alert crew of sharp young sailors stood constantly about the guns, their eyes fixed on the ocean, ready to spring into action instantly. All this gave us some small comfort. Our machine gun company had established posts with machine guns along the decks, and soldiers kept watch constantly. But they could not have been of much, if any use.

One morning a story became current that the ship next to us had run down and cut in two a Swedish schooner during the night. We could see scars upon her bow where the paint had been scraped off, and this confirmed the story to us. It was said that just before the transport struck the schooner, some of the crew of the latter cried out, "We are Swedes." Perhaps the poor fellows thought they were being run down intentionally. One or two of the crew of the schooner were rescued. The story had it that they clung to the bow of the transport, and were helped to the deck. The transport did not slow down, but kept on at full speed, and all the rest of the Swedes perished. Orders to the transport were not to stop for any other reason than a positive order from the flagship. It might have been part of a German scheme to torpedo a transport. Improbable as this may seem, it was possibly true, and the lives of six thousand men could not be risked, by stopping, to save those of a small crew of foreign sailors, or even American sailors.

During the voyage Col. Oscar J. Charles, the Commander of our regiment, attempted to square himself with his officers. However, many months of unjust and harsh treatment could not be wiped out now with a few honeyed words, and he failed entirely to arouse any response from his officers, who were summoned to his cabin in groups to hear his appeal for loyalty and teamwork. Little as I liked him, I could not help feeling sorry for the man. In my group I was ranking officer, and as such, had to make some remarks when the Colonel had finished his appeal, and I said what I could, in a general way, but my heart was not in it, and he must have realized it.

I was accompanied on many of my inspections in the evening by my first sergeant, Chambers. Although of no military experience before the war, he was a natural and very able soldier, and of the greatest help to me in handling the company of two hundred and fifty men. We used to stop on our tours of inspection and leaning on the rail, looking out over the dark sea, we would have long talks together, about many subjects. We talked as man to man, not captain to first sergeant. Chambers thought that most of us would be killed, and that the War would last long, and I agreed with him, but tried to cheer him a little. He was killed at Montfaucon on September 28th, and I felt a very keen and heavy loss in the death of this fine man and good soldier.[7]

July 18th, 1918, was a great day in the history of the Regiment, for it was on that date we finally ended our weary and crowded sea voyage, and came to the shores of beautiful France.

After making out land, low and dim, on the horizon, when first we came on deck, we watched it grow clearer and nearer, as the hours passed. For probably ninety-five percent of us this was the first view of the Old World, from which all of our ancestors came to the New World, now so far behind us. Could we have known what Fate held in store for us in that land ahead, we would have approached it in a more serious mood. But we knew not, and we were weary of the long voyage and happy to see France upon which the bright sun shone, bringing out the tall white cliffs topped by the clean green fields, with here and there a fresh white house with pretty red roof. High above the tops of the tall cliffs floated a huge sausage balloon. What purpose an observation balloon could fulfill, there on the coast, except to see and herald the approach of ships and convoys, we could not understand, and concluded that was the reason for its presence.

7. First Sergeant Lawrence Chambers, A Company, 316th Infantry.

The entrance to the harbor of Brest, for that was our port of debarkation, is narrow, exceptionally so. As we steamed slowly in, we met the monster transport, the *Leviathan*, majestically passing out to sea. She had left New York the day before we sailed, had crossed, unloaded, reloaded, and was now on her return voyage. Our ship was big, 20,000 tons, but as we came abreast of her she towered above us like a high steel cliff. And now occurred one of those rare and soul-lifting incidents of the War. A moment one never forgets nor ever loses the thrill of. Crowding her rails there above us were hundreds of wounded soldiers, their heads and limbs swathed in white bandages. A tremendous cheer roared up from our crowded decks, and thousands of hats waved frantically. Faintly down to us came an answering cheer, and crutches and caps were waved along the rails of the great ship. Back to them went another cheer, officers, soldiers, sailors, every one at the top of their voices, and they had passed on their way home.

The harbor of Brest did not seem large, but it was closely landlocked and a fine, safe anchorage for ships, with which it was crowded. War ships, destroyers, transports, and harbor craft, through which we slowly steamed, seemed to fill it almost to capacity. Rising above the harbour on all sides in tier on tier was the old city of Brest, picturesque and strange to us. Many great buildings of grey stone, some of them, no doubt, hundreds of years old.

But we had very little time to admire this fine old city, as we were to disembark at once. When we had tied up to our buoy, a landing stage was attached to us, alongside of which a steam lighter soon appeared, on which we were to go ashore. A very steep gangplank, without hand rails, was set up to a door in one of our lower decks. It was so steep that it was very difficult to negotiate, and especially so for soldiers heavily loaded with full packs, rifles, and equipment. Some of the men lost their balance and reached the foot of the gangplank in a clattering mess of self, rifle, and equipment. It became necessary to station soldiers on the landing stage to prevent some of them from sliding off into the water. One small soldier, entrusted with a package of Victrola records, lost his footing about half way down and simply plunged the rest of the way, his rifle and the records flung wild, but fortunately landing on the landing stage. And, strange to say, none of the records was broken, to the delight of his comrades, who had let out a groan when they saw them flying through the air. They would have been impossible to replace in France, and the soldiers greatly valued them. I came down the gangplank very gingerly, placing each foot sidewise and carefully on the cleats, and reached the bottom safely, but convinced that it was a mighty poor way to take men off a ship.

The large steam lighter was soon closely packed with standing soldiers, and we were taken to the shore and unloaded on a wharf piled high with American Army freight. We assembled in a freight yard in rear of the wharf. Col. Charles came to me there and turned over the command of the regiment to me, saying that he intended to stay the night in a hotel in the city. He directed me to march the regiment out to the rest camp, about five miles out of town. I was, at this time, senior captain of the regiment, and was given the command because the three majors were absent from the regiment on a special school detail, and the Lieutenant-Colonel, A. C. Knowles, was in charge of the debarkation of our baggage.

I had noticed other regiments of the division starting off to pass through the city of Brest, and had noticed that they had made no attempt to make any sort of a proper entrance into France. They did not use their military bands, nor did they display their colors, but kept these and the band instruments in their cases.

I felt that this informal and rather slovenly entrance into a country that we had come to help was all wrong. Our coming was to me at least too important a matter to be thus lightly treated. It was not military. The French would not have done it that way. And so I decided to march through the city with full military pomp and display. I knew that this would make a good impression on our men, and then one does not enter a foreign country at the head of a full regiment but once in a lifetime.

And so, when the regiment was formed and ready to move into the city, I ordered the band to the head of the column, and directed the band leader to play us through the town. I also sent for our colors, the national and regimental flags, had them uncased and unfurled and placed at our head. We entered and passed through Brest in full military pomp, the band playing constantly and the flags snapping in the breeze. The French people cheered us, and we went through with our heads held high, feeling like crusaders come to rescue a friendly country from its foes.[8]

On the sidewalk, looking at us with pride on his face, as we came up in perfect step to the fine band, I perceived Colonel Charles, our commander. Perhaps he had not expected me to come in in such fine style, but he could not resist the emotions of the occasion, and giving up his good bed in town, he came out into the street and fell in beside me, and marched through the streets with his regiment.

After we had left the main part of Brest we began to climb a long rather steep street, and the rain began to fall. The crowds were well behind us. The band put away their instruments, and the flags were encased. The command of "Route Step" that the men might march at ease was given. The glory was over and a wet march uphill only remained. I feel sure that Col. Charles regretted now that he had yielded to the pomp of war and joined us. He complained that his new boots hurt his feet, and he was getting them all covered with mud. He felt it was too late to go back to his bed. He finished the march with us and spent the night on some feed sacks, covered with a single blanket. Such is the price of glory

This, our first march in France, was naturally most interesting to us. We passed through several villages, after leaving the city, and also the Pontenèzen Barracks built of stone by the great Napoleon.[9] I had always been a great admirer of this great man, and it gave me a thrill to feel that I was now marching through his country at the head of troops come to help his beloved France.

We finally came to the rest camp. I had expected barracks of some sort, but we found only empty muddy fields. I remonstrated with the guide, but he assured me that this was the rest camp, and I told him it was a hell of a camp. Loud was the chorus of disapproval and disappointment. We were assigned a number of small fields, each surrounded by a high hedge. Night was coming on. We must make the

8. Oddly, this anecdote is not in the regimental history, which merely indicates "the Regiment debarked, and then began a weary, toilsome march through the backyard of Brest." See *History of the 316th Infantry Regiment*, 22.

9. Ironically, Napoleon's army built these barracks in preparation for an invasion of England.

best of it, and the best would be mighty poor. The soldiers each carried the half of a pup tent in their packs. So we set them to work putting up these shelters in straight company streets. Dusk came on before camp was made. Using my electric torch I showed some of the men, not long in the service, how to erect their tents. When they were all up the men put down their raincoats on the ground, and laid their blankets on these. They got in, two men to a tent, and lit their candles, and were cozy and comfortable. The officers had nothing. Not even a blanket. We were assured trucks would bring our bedding rolls and tents at once. They did not arrive until the next day. A cool, wet night under the hedges faced us. The distress of some of the officers was laughable. But Fate or rather the non-commissioned officers of my company were kind. They came to me and said they would double up three in a tent, and thus give us three tents for the six officers of the company. This was thoughtful and very decent of them. I would never have asked them to give up their tents to us, nor would I have taken those offered, if the occupants had not been provided for. We slept warm and dry and well, and awoke well rested.

Our first day in France was gray and gloomy, with rain and chill winds. But we were so glad to be off the crowded, smelly ship and in France at least that we were cheerful in spite of the weather. Food was brought out to us, and tents for the officers, and our personal baggage and bedding rolls arrived. We were soon comfortably settled in large tents and well fed, so things looked much better. We were greatly interested in the French peasants, who came to the camp to see the American "Soldats" and sell us things. Some of the young girls were very pretty. We saw no young or middle-aged men, except a few in uniform, home on leave. One good old French grandmother told me, through my adjutant, Dan Keller, who spoke French well, that if I would give her a good long rope she would permit us to get water from her well nearby. Such wonderful good water. She thought she saw a chance to get a well rope for nothing. Unfortunately for her the Army brought us plenty of water in tank trucks. Hence I had Keller, my adjutant, tell the greedy old beggar that we were greatly obliged, but did not need the water from her well.

Both Col. Charles and Lt. Col. Knowles left the camp of the regiment, and I was therefore in command, during their absence. A crusty old Colonel of the Inspector General Department appeared and was, of course, full of criticisms, and they fell upon me. I had not had time to get beyond the limits of my own battalion, and hence did not understand what he was crabbing about. Our own part of the camp had been cleaned up and seemed in good condition to me. But he took me down to the rear of the camp, and there, behind a hedge, he showed me an awful mess. The division which had preceded us had not dug any latrines, as we had, and the soldiers had covered the place with excretion. I explained matters to the inspector and pointed out our latrines to him. I said we had not made the mess and were not responsible. He replied that it was within the limits of our camp and that we were responsible that the whole place be clean, and he ordered me to clean it up at once. We had nothing but our entrenching shovels to work with, and I resented the job very greatly. I am not sure now, but I think we left it as it was, chancing the visit of another or the same inspector.

I got away, during the afternoon, and walked back to Pontanézen Barracks. They were of solid stone, in very good condition, and packed with American Soldiers. Framework of steel pipe filled the rooms, supporting bunks three tiers high. Napoleon's soldiers were never so crowded.

We were getting our first impressions of France and its people. We were greatly pleased with the beautiful green countryside and, at a distance, the pretty villages. But we were surprised and disgusted with the manure piles and the utter lack of sanitation. The French houses were built of stone, and they were as cold and cheerless as a tomb. Except for the purpose of cooking a meal they had no fires in them. And for this purpose the fires were very small. No doubt the people were used to the cold houses and dressed warmly. We, of course, got more or less accustomed to them, in time, but we never liked their chill interiors with the bad air prevailing therein.

The farmers seemed to be prosperous. Most of their houses and barns were built solidly of stone and had slate roofs. Some of the barns were quite large. But one of these farmers was evidently a very poor man. He came to me and complained that my soldiers were walking through his field of hay and tramping down his crop. He said it was his only field and the hay crop was all he had to live on. The field was small, not more than five or six acres, and if his statement was true he was indeed a poor man. I gave orders which stopped the soldiers walking through his field.

On July 21, at midnight, we left the camp. We took down all our tents and loaded up our baggage during the afternoon, to avoid the confusion of doing all of this work in the dark. The men's packs were also made up and piled along the lines of stacked rifles. Hence every man knew where all of his equipment was and could fall into ranks without delay. We had numerous fires to keep us warm and furnish light. The men sang and smoked and roughhoused each other. Midnight came and with it the order to march down into Brest to take the train. I called out the order, "First Battalion fall in," and the men greeted it with shouts. They were ready to go.

In a few minutes the four companies stood quiet and ready, the light from the fires glowing on their steady ranks. Military discipline had changed a riot of milling, shouting men, in a few minutes, into four well-ordered bodies of soldiers. Everything was packed, the camp site was thoroughly cleaned up, and now the fires were put out. At my command the battalion moved off and leaving the field took the hard road to Brest. As soon as we were well started, I passed the command of "Route Step" down the column, and the men began to smoke and talk and laugh. At "Route Step" troops are required only to keep their places in the column. They do not keep step and may carry their rifles as they please.

It was a dark and damp night. We passed through a number of silent villages, the people long ago in their beds. And I thought of the folks at home as we passed these dark houses.

It was cool and marching was easy. We entered the city of Brest and found the poorly lighted streets gloomy, with lights in only an occasional wine shop. There were no citizens on the streets to watch us pass. I looked back down the long heavy-laden column, the men's faces showing only when they came into the light of a shop or street lamp. Their heavy hob-nailed shoes made a sort of low rumbling noise in the quiet street. No other noise is like that of soldiers marching. A thousand soldiers moving in the night impresses one as a great force, not so much as a large body of troops, but as a mighty individual thing. It becomes a unit, a single thing, a force like a strongly flowing river.

3
In the Training Area

We arrived at the railroad yards of Brest at about two o'clock in the morning of July 21, 1918. When the men saw the freight cars, small wooden box cars with only four wheels, in which they were to travel, they greeted them with hoots and laughs of disgust and derision. At a later date, after long weary marches, they greeted similar cars with shouts of joy and relief.

We halted alongside of one of these dirty, beastly trains. I sent my adjutant, Lt. Dan Keller, to find a railroad officer and learn which was our train. He came back with a sulky first lieutenant. Keller said this officer had complained to him that no one seemed to be in command of my battalion. Such talk was utterly uncalled for, as we had just arrived and had halted in ranks, and made no trouble for any one. And so I spoke to the sulky young lieutenant sharply and asked him why he made such remarks. He made no answer and stood before me silent with down-cast eyes. I figured that he was tired out and overworked and let it go at that, and asked him which was our train. He answered we would take the one alongside of which my column stood.

Forty men, with their arms and packs and equipment and supplies of food were to go in each small car. It was an outrage on humanity to pack men in so for a long trip.[1] Twenty-five at most were all that should have been loaded in these cars. With forty men in a car they could not lie down to rest without being on top of one another. They could not even sit down all at once. There were no toilet accommodations of any kind whatsoever. Just empty, dirty box cars. We have much better cars for horses in the United States. The men were beginning to realize that

1. These were the infamous forty-and-eight boxcars which could transport either forty men or eight horses. The conditions were so cramped that "Private Doughboy decided that never again would he say a word against the B.&O. or even the W.B. & A." railways. See *History of the 316th Infantry*, 23.

France, as far as comforts and the decencies of life are concerned, was a century behind their own country. *And they never had cause to change their minds about this.*

However, being only a captain and acting major, I could not change the military transport system of France. Other American troops had endured it, and so could we. It was nevertheless inhuman and indecent to treat men like cattle.

I assigned the company commanders to different parts of the long train, and directed them to load on the men, forty to a car, without delay. This they proceeded to do, amidst the complaints of the harassed and crowded soldiers. It took the authority of the officers to get forty men into a car, as those already in asserted that there was no more room and crowded together most reluctantly. Boxes of provisions, bread, hard crackers, canned meat and beans, etc., were shoved into each car. A sergeant was placed in command and made responsible for the proper distribution of the food and the conduct of the men. The only water the men had with them was that in their canteens. They often ran out of water and suffered for lack of it on the journey.

When the last man was loaded I went forward to the front end of the train to the officers' cars. These would have made an ordinary traveler in the United States laugh. They were old, worn-out coaches of the Victorian period. Divided into compartments with six places in each. They had no corridors in them, and no carpets on the floor. The upholstery was worn and torn, and we found that the roofs leaked. I had with me Lieutenants Odum, Evans, Dyer, Swank, and Keller. Our locker trunks and bags were put in with us. We had very little room and must sleep upright in our seats for the next three nights and endure our crowded condition for four days of slow and tiring travel. There was, I believe, a toilet room in the end of the car, which one must reach along the steps on the outside of the car. We ate meals when the spirit moved us, using our locker trunks for tables, and having only bread, crackers, canned meat and beans. There was no possibility of cooking anything. Consequently one ate such food only from real hunger, never for pleasure. We also were short of water frequently. We could not wash our faces nor shave, and could only clean our hands by using water from our canteens and our handkerchiefs. Fine treatment for officers and gentlemen. We were a dirty and tired-out lot when we left that beastly train.

With the usual silly fuss, the blowing of fish-horns and squeaky whistles and much shouting, that it takes to get a train started in France, a matter of much amusement to all of us, our long rattling, jerking train pulled out of Brest, and we were off on a long, slow journey through Central France, a country beautiful beyond the power of words to express. Well worth fighting for, we thought.

We travelled across Central France from Brest to Vaux-sous-Aubigny, a small station near Is-sur-Tille, which place was not far from the ancient city of Dijon, a place of importance in northeastern France. As I have said we were on this cattle train for three nights and four days. I do not believe that we travelled in all more than four hundred miles, possibly five hundred, hardly more than a night's run for a good train in the United States.

We passed through St. Brieuc, Rennes, Laval, Angers, Chaumont, Tours, and many lesser cities. An extremely interesting journey, especially to those of us never before in Europe. We stopped one evening upon a bridge for a time. The view up the river, which here wound its way through a good-sized city, was very lovely. I think Tours was the name of this town. We had been told that the arrival of our division completed the first million American troops in France. The great numbers of our compatriots that we observed, as we journeyed along led us to accept this statement as true. The fields and towns and villages seemed to be full of American soldiers, drilling and marching and eating and working, all busy, very busy all the time. At a long halt in a railroad yard, our regimental band played a concert. A lot of men of an American railroad regiment gathered to hear the music. I heard one of them say to a comrade, "Gee, but it is good to hear an American band after all these months." When the "Marseillaise" was played all the Americans stood rigidly at the salute. I was amazed to note that the French soldiers present went on talking and smoking. Not one of them saluted. Apparently it was not customary to render honor to their national anthem.

The matter of attending to the duties of nature on the part of the soldiers became at times very serious. Some days stops were infrequent and very short. One day I requested the conductor, rather forcibly, to stop the train for a half hour. He did so, on the outskirts of a good sized town, and hundreds of the men got off in a field. In a few minutes, to my dismay, the locomotive blew its penny whistle, and the train started to move away slowly. The fool conductor saw what was going on. I was furious and thought I was going to lose about half of my men who had started running after the train holding up their clothes and shouting and swearing. I told Lieutenant John Swank to work his way along the slowly moving cars up to the engine, and shove his pistol into the engineer's face and make him stop, and stay stopped for ten minutes. This Swank did and we remained there until all the men were back in the cars.

On this journey the American soldiers had their first experience with French wine, and despite all the efforts of the officers they got hold of a lot of it. We had been a boozeless army in the United States, the most boozeless army the world had ever seen, but here in a country where wine was drunk as we drank water in our own country, and where every house sold wine, it was utterly impossible to keep it out of our army. Army headquarters had enough comprehension to appreciate the situation, and orders were issued, after we had reached our destination, permitting the troops to drink light wines and beer during certain hours of the day. Strong drinks such as brandy and cognac were strictly forbidden, but the soldiers drank what they pleased as there was no possible way to limit them. There was, however, surprisingly little drunkenness in our army in France. During our train journey we did not have the orders covering drinking, and we attempted to prevent the buying of wine by the soldiers. At every stop the French people tried to sell bottles of wine to the men, and while the officers seized and broke many bottles, the soldiers consumed a lot of it anyway. The officers with me had no wine. I thought it proper that we should set an example. Afterwards a high ranking officer of our regiment laughed at me about this, and told me that his crowd had plenty of it on the trip. Under the existing orders he should have refrained as an example to the regiment.

At one stop a train load of Allied wounded pulled in alongside of us. We regarded them with great interest. These men had been through battle. They were veterans. They had our great respect. What they had passed through, we had yet to endure. Green soldiers are always greatly impressed by the wounded. They were a very mixed lot: English, French, and colored troops. The lightly wounded leaned out of

the car windows and talked with our men. I remember one Scotch soldier wearing a kilt.[2] In answer to a question from one of my officers, he
said, laughing, "Yes, we have all sorts on this train, even n------." They
seemed a very cheerful lot and there was much laughing and banter
between the trains.

The remarkable beauty of the countryside of France, as we passed
slowly through it, was a source of constant pleasure to us. We were
continually crowding to the windows to see some beautiful view of the
charming landscape, or some pretty town, or fine old chateau in its
splendid park. Centuries of care and cultivation had helped nature in
the creation of all this beauty.

We arrived finally at the city of Is-sur-Tille. This place was a great
American army center. We stopped in a large railroad yard filled with
freight cars, and surrounded with great warehouses, packed with supplies for our army. Many quartermasters and railroad troops were busy
here. No fighting nor glory for them, nothing but hard routine work,
but, on the other hand, no death nor wounds either. Near the tracks
was a large American prison cage for offenders against discipline and
army regulations. It seemed to be well filled with a discontented looking lot of men.

Officers only were permitted off the cars. The poor weary soldiers
got no chance to stretch a leg. Most of the men of my Company A were
out of cigarettes. There was a YMCA or Red Cross canteen, I do not
remember which, at the station. Since I had plenty of money of the
company funds, I decided to buy two packs of cigarettes for each of my
250 men. I told a pleasant lady at the counter of my desire to purchase
500 packs of cigarettes, but said she, "Our regulations permit me to
sell an individual only two packs." I told her I wanted them for my 250
men, on the cars outside, who were out of tobacco and not permitted
to come off the cars and into the canteen. She expressed her regret
feelingly, but said orders were orders, and she could not do it. Could
anything be more fat-headed? Well, I raised a fuss and made a noise
and said I would write home about it, and complain to headquarters,
and got fairly unpleasant about it.

2. Presumably, this was a soldier of the 51st Highland Division, which deployed to the
Ardre Valley as part of the Second Battle of the Marne. It should be noted that the nearest
British army proper was far to the north of Parkin's position near Amiens.

I said, "If my men could come in here you would sell them each two packs, would you not?"

"Oh yes, indeed, gladly."

"Well, what is the real difference?" I asked. "There are the men in the cars, you can see them yourself. I will pay you and you have your own people distribute the cigarettes, two packs to a man."

Nothing doing. Finally my noise brought another woman from another room. She apparently had more authority or more brains and she agreed to my proposition at once, and the cigarettes were taken out and given to the men, who were very appreciative.

While we were standing at the station of Is-sur-Tille, a platoon of unarmed troops was marched on to the platform and halted near us. Their drill was good, and we noticed that each man wore on his left sleeve a gold charm, denoting six months foreign service. So we regarded these veterans with interest. I walked down the line and looked for wound chevrons, i.e. gold chevrons on their right sleeve. There were none, absolutely none. They were rear line or service of supply troops, and had not been at the front in battle. Necessary of course, vital in fact, but not to be rated with us, combat troops as we were. So we thought then, and still think. Some men sought service in this safe part of the AEF but the vast majority of them were assigned to it, and would much rather have gone to the front.

On July 24, our weary and long journey in the antique French train came to a most welcome and long desired end.[3] We reached the station of Vaux-Sous-Aubigny in the Department of Haute Marne in northeastern France. The nearest large city was Dijon. The poor cramped, dirty soldiers got out of their freight cars joyfully. After legs were stretched, and everything was off the cars, a meal out of cans (Ye Gods! How many such meals we were to have) was eaten, and then I had my battalion fall in on the road. We were all heavily laden with packs and equipment, and with a guide at my side, I set out to find our new homes, the villages we were to live in while finishing an already too long training to fight.

My guide, an American private attached to the staff in charge of the

3. The 79th Division deployed to the tenth training area near Champlitte and Prauthoy, near Dijon in France. By July 29, the division's units were in their billets stretching across thirty-eight villages and towns. There they trained for six weeks before moving up to the Meuse-Argonne Offensive.

training area, told me that my battalion would be billeted in the villages of Percey-le-Grand, and Percey-le-Petite, some six or eight miles away. The road was good and the countryside was green and beautiful, with here and there a red roofed, white walled village nestling among the tall trees. For the first few miles it seemed good to have a chance to stretch our legs and we enjoyed the march. The sun became warm, and our overcoats made us hot, and the packs weighed us down. Our long trip by ship and train had softened us some, and the march became a job. We passed some French peasants, but saw very few Americans. I gave the men more halts than marching regulations allowed. You are supposed to march fifty minutes and rest ten. Most of my marching had been done on horseback, and I was pretty well loaded myself, so I had a complete sympathy with what the men were enduring on this hike.

We arrived finally opposite Percey-le-Petite. The guide had told me that Percey-le-Grande was the better village and had better quarters, so I had decided to make it my headquarters. I therefore detached Company C under Captain Robert L. Fatzinger, and Company D under Captain Percy F. Burrage, the latter to be in command of the town and send them across the river to establish themselves at Percey-le-Petite. I went on a mile or two with Company A, under Lieutenant Burley F. Odum, and Company B, under Captain Louis C. Knack, and crossing the river, on an old stone bridge, we halted at the foot of a hill road, leading up to Percey-le-Grande, our final destination.

I halted the two companies here, and sent Lieutenants Swank and Keller into the village to find the mayor, get the billeting plan of the place, and arrange to lodge the officers and men. They came back in half an hour accompanied by the mayor, a small grey-headed man, who received us pleasantly, but could not speak any English. Lieutenant Keller spoke French fluently, so we got along very well. We discussed the billeting of the troops and having settled that, we marched up the hill into the main square of the ancient town. Many young children were out to see us come in, and a very funny, if somewhat shocking thing occurred. A very pretty little girl of eight or nine years of age cried out at the top of her voice, "Hurray, Geis Crise, here come the goddamn Yankees." The soldiers roared with laughter, but I was so astonished I could not laugh. Some soldier of another division which had preceded us in this town, the 28th Pennsylvania National Guard, I believe, had been perverted enough to teach this sweet little thing such profanity, which she repeated like a parrot.

I remained in the street until all of the five hundred men, composing the two companies, had been put away in their quarters. I always did this. Contrary to my expectations, the men were not taken into the houses of the people, but were put in out-houses, sheds and stables.[4] I did not like this at all, and protested to the mayor, through Lieutenant Keller, but the mayor said that such was the custom, and so the French troops were treated. I was not at all pleased, but could not change the arrangements. Many of the men got into the good graces of the people, later, and moved into the houses.

The men under shelter at last, we officers sought our quarters. The mayor took me to the house occupied by the last commanding officer. We had the best rooms in the town. Madame Robinnet was my hostess. A good looking brunette of about thirty-five. Her house was spotlessly clean. She showed me to a good, large room on the second floor, well-furnished in French provincial style, which means mid-Victorian.

I could have been very comfortable here, but upon opening the window, I looked down upon a large and steaming manure pile, the odor of which filled the room. I determined to stay the night and move on the morrow, if I could find a room not adjacent to the ever-present manure pile. Of this I was not at all sure, as the village was littered with these evidences of rural prosperity. That evening good Madame Robinnet gave us dinner, consisting of ham, eggs, bread, wine and coffee. All very excellent. She had plenty of sugar in large square cubes, something not expected in France. She said she had laid up a stock, as she knew the war was coming. She also had plenty of good butter, and her war bread was very good to eat. We paid her about a dollar each, and she protested it was too much. During dinner her husband, a tall well-built man, with bushy black beard and hair came in, and greeted us. He was a man of perhaps thirty-eight or so, seemingly perfectly healthy, and we all wondered why he was not in the military service. We learned afterwards that she had well connected relatives in Paris,

4. It is interesting that Parkin expected his men to be billeted in French homes as this was not the usual practice in France. Normally, if not at a large training or base camp, units would be billeted (or housed) on local farms where they would pay the farmers for use of their barns/land for shelter. Officers were usually put up in houses.

and this may explain her husband's presence at home, at a time when France needed every able-bodied man at the front. He certainly did not have our respect, and we saw but little of him. He seemed to keep out of sight most of the time.

The two rolling kitchens reached the village later in the day, and the men had a hot dinner. Company A placed their kitchen in a large shed, new and of the French army pattern, and the men ate there, seated on the ground. It was dry and protected. Company B was not in such luck, and had their kitchen in a small square off the street and in the open. Their men had to eat seated around on the cobble stones. The officers established a mess in one of the houses, on the main square, and had a dingy old room with a long table and benches. We got rations from the company kitchens, and had a cook and two orderly waiters. We were able to purchase very little to help out our rations but our food, though plain, was good, and plentiful, and well cooked, for I had a man named Gray, a restaurant cook in civil life in charge of our kitchen. He could get up a better meal out of army rations than any other cook whose meals I ate in the army.

The village of Percey-le-Grande interested us greatly and deserves a few lines of description. We were told that it had existed since the twelfth century, and doubted it not. The houses were built of stone, even many of the roofs were of large flat stones. The ancient wooden beams, squared roughly, and still very strong, seemed very old, indeed, to us. Certainly most of the houses were hundreds of years old. The main square was dominated by a good-sized church with a high steeple. Across from it was the mayor's office, occupying the second floor of a building, large for so small a town, the inhabitants of which numbered twelve hundred before the war. I used the mayor's office as my headquarters. On the mantel was the plaster figure, a bust rather, of a woman, representing the Republic of France. This I understand is found in every town in France. Here also was the government telephone station, our only connection with the outside world. The streets of the village were narrow and winding, and the houses were mostly built right on the side of the street, leaving no sidewalks, which was regrettable since the streets were always muddy and covered with manure, in spite of our daily efforts to keep them clean. The rest of the main square was bordered with houses, a few small shops, some stables, and there were a few trees on one side. It was not a pretty town, but it was quaint and ancient.

The people were all farmers. Each family had its portions of land surrounding the village. Young men were entirely absent. The old men and women, the middle-aged women, and the children worked the land, and they worked very hard, and very long hours. In the morning before we got up, and we had reveille at 5:15 a.m., and before it was daylight, we could hear their carts rumbling over the cobblestones as the peasants went out to the fields, and after dark we could hear them returning. This was their routing every day except Sunday, on which they enjoyed a deserved rest. The women and children went to church, and the men loafed about, talking and smoking. Everyone on this day dressed completely in black. Of young women there was also a complete lack. We were told that they were all working in the munitions factories.

Life in these small French villages would be terrible for the average American. There was absolutely no entertainment or diversion as we regard these things. Hard work, plain food, and sleep, with an occasional glass of wine in the near café, was all there was in life for these people. No music, no literature, no theatre, no moving pictures, and as far as we could see, no social gatherings, except in the church. The people had not even a daily paper. Their animals got about as much pleasure out of life as they did. An occasional government war bulletin, posted up in the square, around which they gathered, or a telegram announcing the death of one of their men at the front, were the only ripples on the placid stream of their lives.

The first Sunday morning most of the officers and hundreds of the men went to the village Catholic church. It was decorated with the usual awful religious figures and paintings. The singing of the choir, composed of women and old men, was terrible. There was no organ. When the collection came, the Frenchman with the basket had not enough success to satisfy one of our good Catholic soldiers, so he seized the basket and started over again, shaking it before each soldier until he contributed. In consequence, he got his basket well filled. This amused me greatly. After the priest got well into his sermon, we realized that he was trying to talk to us in English, to express his gratitude for the large offering. It was the queerest mixture of language ever heard in a church. Neither the French nor the Americans understood much of his talk.

As I have said, I was not satisfied with the first room assigned to me on account of the manure pile just below my window. Lieutenant Swank told me that he and two other officers were living in a fine house up at the end of the street. So I went with him to look the place over, and decided to move there at once. It was quite the most superior house in the town, and was the last on the street, the open country being next to it. It was entirely unoccupied by the owners, who were two maiden ladies of middle-age, who lived most of their years in Paris, and came down only for their vacations. They were both teachers in the Institute of the Legion of Honour, a school founded by Napoleon for the education of the daughters of the members of the Legion. It was in charge of Madame Robinnet, whose house I was leaving, and who was not pleased at my departure, saying that the town commander always used her room. Perhaps the previous commanders had been farmers, and did not mind the odor.

And so, I had my orderly move my baggage to the new place, which pleased me very much. There was a large living room, well furnished, a dining room and kitchen, neither of which we used, and several well equipped bedrooms on the second floor. We took the silk covered comforts off the beds and also the feather mattresses, and used our own bedding. We were careful not to abuse the furniture. There was a garden at the side of the house, which was "L" shaped, and a large porch, looking out over the long deep rear garden, and the fields beyond. Really a very fine and comfortable house, and well kept. We were certainly in great luck, and never again had such quarters in France. The toilet arrangements were ample but unique. In the bathroom stood large tin tub built over a large narrow fire box. A wood fire was built, and water carried to fill the large tub. In it was a wooden affair of slats to keep you off the bottom which, of course, was very hot. You could get a fine hot bath but you had to be mighty careful not to get burned. We enjoyed it greatly, but it made a lot of work for the orderlies.

After we had been some weeks in this pleasant house, I received a letter from the owners, saying that they would pay us a visit for two weeks, if it would not inconvenience us in the least. I replied offering to move out entirely, but they would come only on condition that we use the house exactly as we were then doing. So I was obliged to submit to their terms, and they arrived. They proved to be two extremely pleasant French ladies. They kept out of our way, and used the servants bedrooms and dining-room and kitchen. They could speak no English, but could write it perfectly, and we communicated by handing each other written notes. Dan Keller, my adjutant, who lived with me, spoke good French, and he talked with them quite often. He told them that I was a great admirer of Napoleon, and this pleased them. When they returned to Paris, we were sorry to see them go, and really missed them, and their ever pleasant kindness.

Our six weeks in Percey-le-Grande were extremely busy ones and our schedule of drill and military training was hard.[5] We got up at 5:15 a.m. and were out on the drill grounds, open country about a mile from the village from which the crops had been harvested, at seven thirty, returning to the village about four in the afternoon, with an hour's rest at noon for lunch, which the cooks brought out to us. From four to six the men rested, shaved, cleaned their rifles and equipment, brushed their shoes and clothes for the inspection which always followed retreat at about six, or sundown. Then dinner was served and the men had the evening to themselves, but for the officers there were classes of instruction or reports to make, which took many of the evenings.

We marched out of the old town in the early morning while the dew was still shining on the grass. Our drill ground was a high plateau, partly grazing ground and partly fields from which the wheat, and oats and hay had recently been harvested. A half hour of close order, or platoon or company drill in squad or platoon movement smartened the men up, and then various drills followed. We devoted a great deal of time to the new French method of attack. This was made in evidently extended formations. Ten paces between men, and twenty paces between the lines of men. Soldiers are hard to control and lead in this formation, especially in rough country, so considerable practice

5. Once American Expeditionary Forces units arrived in France they were transported to a training area where they received advance training in tactics under French or British instruction. Regular Army and National Guard divisions that had deployed earlier in late 1917 and 1918 received longer training behind the lines with veteran allied instructors. For new National Army divisions, such as the 79th, their training course was shorter and did not involve a significant course of trench rotation to acclimate men to their new environment at the front.

is necessary. Against machine guns and artillery no other formation is possible.

At times I had the two companies from Percey-le-Petite come over, and I maneuvered the whole battalion of four companies in the new attack formation against a line of hills, supposed to be held by the enemy. This was to me the most interesting and instructive part of our training as it was so we must fight the enemy. We also had scouting exercise and bayonet drill, and hand grenade drill, both with dummies and real live grenades. We put in a lot of time firing rifles at the target range, and worked hard to train the men who were not good natural shots, as many men are. The officers had practice with their pistols. Strange to say, though we were going to the front soon, and their lives might depend upon their ability to shoot, I had to "bawl out" some of the officers to get them to go out and practice with their pistols. What a queer indifference. The good shots among the men and officers labored long and painstakingly with the men who could not shoot. The military rifle has a bad heavy kick when it fires, and this makes many men afraid of them or gun-shy. Some of the men put their right thumbs around the small of the stock of the rifle, and then, in aiming, put their noses against their thumbs. The kick of the gun, especially when it was not held firmly against the shoulder, jammed their thumbs against their noses, and gave many a man a bloody nose. We taught them to put their thumbs along the small of the stock, not around it. We taught them never to jerk the trigger, which pulls the rifle off the target, but to take up the slack of the trigger with the forefinger and then gently squeeze it. This is called "milking" the gun. Before firing one should fill the chest with a deep breath, let out a little of it, and then holding the rest, get the sights on the target and milk the gun. This method gives the best results. Of course you must hold the rifle firmly against the shoulder, close your left eye, and keep the right eye open. Most beginners close both eyes at the moment of firing.

When we started our target firing, I was not satisfied with the results, and thought the men could do much better. So in the morning I had the two Companies A and B drawn up together, and I sat before them on my horse and gave them a somewhat vigorous talk on the value of rifle fire. I told them that we were soon going to the front lines, and that they might be subjected to a charge of German infantry at anytime. I said that I could not think of anything more discouraging to troops than to realize that they were maintaining a heavy fire upon an advancing enemy which was not effective and was not stopping them. "If you do not stop the enemy with rifle fire then, you must do it with bayonet and that is a nasty business, and unnecessary." I told them I wanted more interest, more intense effort, more enthusiasm in their rifle practice. "To be able to fire your rifle well may mean that you will get home safely after the war." The men were visibly impressed, and their work on the range became much better at once, and continued to improve. Bullseyes became frequent.

The regular army apparently had some surplus old colonels, which it did not want to entrust with command of troops, so they were put into the Inspector General Department, and became a nuisance to the combat troops while we were in the rear areas. We saw none of them in the front lines, which was one of the few blessings of that section. One day I was taking a rest in my quarters after drill, when an orderly from the officer of the guard reported to me that a strange colonel wanted to see me in the main square. I went down and reported to a fussy old, gray-haired colonel seated in a fine Cadillac limousine car. Not a speck of mud on him, and there never had been, nor would be. He hopped right on me, with both feet, on account of what he called the "very filthy condition" of my town.

"Very dirty, Major, inexcusably so, no excuse for it at all," and all that sort of talk. "Don't you ever clean the streets and this square?" he inquired, his fat face red with indignation, or on account of his tight collar, I was not sure which.

"Yes, sir, they are thoroughly cleaned every afternoon. The punishment squad goes over them every day with broom and shovel."

He seemed to doubt this, but I stood right up to the Old Beggar, and locked him squarely in the eye, for I was telling the truth. And just then the punishment squad, some twenty or thirty men, equipped with old wheelbarrows, borrowed from the villagers, and with brooms and shovels, invaded the square, and set to work vigorously to clean it up. The old colonel watched them for a few minutes in silence.

"And you do this every day, Major?"

"Yes, sir, every afternoon after drill."

"But how do the streets get so filthy between times?" he asked.

"A hundred or more cows, fed on green grass, are driven through the streets twice a day," I replied.

"Can't you keep some men constantly on duty cleaning up?" he asked.

"No, sir. My orders are to take every available man out to drill every day."

"Well, I am sorry, Major, but my duty compels me to report you for having a dirty town."

"Yes, sir," I replied, and stood at salute, as the old fuss-pot was driven away.

I returned to my quarters, filled with wrath at such lack of justice, and damned the whole lot, and wished them all captured by the Germans. General Kuhn, our divisional commander, told me, at a later date, when I related this occurrence to him, that he received many such reports from the inspectors, and threw nearly all of them into the wastebasket. He visited his towns himself and realized that we were doing the best we could to keep them clean.

I had another experience with this same "old inefficient." I was on field manoeuvres with a few officers and men, representing a skeleton battalion, and was advancing up a country road, when his car overtook me. He got out and asked me what my problem was. I told him I was part of a regimental attack upon a town, supported by artillery and that every battalion had the sector directly facing the town. He asked for my map, and wanted me to point out my present position on it. I did so. He looked at the map and said I was wrong. I respectfully stated that I was not, and showed him roads and paths nearby to prove it. He was not convinced until he appealed to his aide, who quietly said that I was correct. At that the Old Beggar went away.

Part of our training consisted of such divisional maneuvers. A skeleton division, which means that the units (brigades, regiments, and battalions) were represented by most of the officers and some non-commissioned officers, was taken out into the country for two days, and problems in the attack in liaison, support, and relief were worked out. We walked many miles and umpires were all over the place asking questions, checking up positions, and trying in general to get us officers in wrong. You had to know where you were and prove it on your map, what you were doing, what the general scheme was, and what your particular part in same was. Reports to the divisional headquarters were made upon you and contents noted upon your record there. So it behooved one to keep right on the job. This was the most practical training we had, and I enjoyed it and found it very interesting. It was as near as we could get to actual battle conditions.

Colonel Oscar J. Charles, our regimental commander, very nearly got me into serious trouble on one of these maneuvers and very unfairly at that. We were out on a divisional attack problem, and we had been given three objectives or points of attack. Our orders were to go on through to the third objective, where all the units would concentrate and the critique, or general talking over, would be held. This review was conducted by General Kuhn, the divisional commander, and his staff, and praise and censure was then given out to the assembled officers. Much could be learned at these talks, but many squirmed under sharp criticism, but it was fair and praise was generous where deserved.

We went on through the lovely countryside for most of the day, keeping in touch with the neighboring units until the middle of the afternoon, when we lost touch due to the fact that our way led for miles through a dense forest. Imagine our surprise, when upon coming out of the woods and arriving at the village, which was our final objective, we found absolutely no one there, except a few natives. We had expected to find hundreds of officers and men and many automobiles. According to my orders they should have all been there in the village or approaching it. I enquired the name of the village from the people. It was the right place, according to the written orders I carried, and I could not understand it at all. Perhaps I was away ahead of the others, so I decided to wait. A good old woman sold us some fried eggs and bread for lunch.

Still no one came. Not a single man. I had obeyed my orders, but had it been real war I would have been wiped out, as I was on the enemy's position, and I was utterly alone and unsupported. Sure that I was right, I waited on. The dusk of evening came on, and we were still alone. Finally I stopped a passing Y.M.C.A. Ford, and sent my adjutant, Dan Keller, back along the road to find someone and get me some information. Had I not been so sure that I had obeyed my orders, I would have done this sooner.

While waiting for Keller's return, we had a fairly good meal in a small cafe of the village. During the meal Lieutenant Lautenbacher, a very ugly and coarse sort of a fellow, amused us all very greatly by his attempts to flirt with a pretty French girl who waited on us. She would have none of him, and our laughter provoked him to greater but entirely unsuccessful efforts. At half past eight, Keller not having returned, I sought out the mayor, got billets from him in the spare bedrooms of the villagers and, tired out from our long hike, we all went to bed. I had a large room in the mayor's house, he was very nice to us, and I had just got settled upon a voluminous feather mattress, with which every French bed is equipped, when I heard the arrival of several trucks outside. Keller came in and reported to me that the orders had been changed, and the attack had halted upon the second objective, several miles in rear of us. These orders had been sent to all the regiments, but the runner from our regimental headquarters had never found me. They should have known this, because all officers are required to initial all such general orders when received and allow the runner to take the order back with him. Of course I had not signed any such order. Keller had brought two trucks and orders for us to return to our village. But it was late and we were very tired, so I decided to spend the night where we were and return early in the morning. Keller and his two drivers got beds, and we all had a good night's rest, returning to our own village for breakfast.

The next day I was in my quarters, after drill was over, when an orderly reported to me that the Commanding General was in the village square and desired to see me. I hurried there and found General Kuhn and his aide, my good friend Captain Harry Rapalye of Pittsburgh. I saluted General Kuhn, and he said, rather sternly, "So you are the major who got lost yesterday at the manoeuvres, are you?"

"No, sir," I replied, "I did not get lost."

"What, you did not get lost?" said the General, with a surprised look upon his face. "You were reported so to me."

"The report is not correct, General, I was never lost. I carried out my original orders and reached the third objective. I never received orders directing me to stop at the second objective."

"Is that so?" said the General, "We will have to look into this. Rapalye, make a note of it."

Courteously refusing an invitation to have dinner with me and my officers, saying his cook expected him home, and assuring me of a proper investigation of the report upon me, the good General went away in his fine big car, all the soldiers and officers in the square standing stiffly at salute, and my old friend Rapalye grinning at me through the window of the Cadillac. Rap told me afterwards that Colonel Charles had to explain and that he made a lame job of it and got his, as was proper. Colonel Charles tried to take it up with me, and I told him very plainly just what I told the General, and he dropped it quickly. It was an attempt at a very dirty trick, the results of which might have been serious to my reputation, for an officer who gets lost on manoeuvres would not be considered as fit to lead troops in battle.

All officers were ordered to get identification cards with their photographs on them. We were to report to a nearby village to have our photographs taken. No trucks were available, so I set off on a hot day, with most of my officers, to find the camera man. Arriving at the village all sweating, we regaled ourselves with cool wines. There on the wall of the café was a Napoleonic sabre, which I very much desired to purchase. But the landlady shook her head. Her grandfather had carried it in Napoleon's Army, and she would not take any price for it. I respected her for valuing the old sword so properly. It was the only thing I found in France which did not have a price.

The photographer did not come, and we had our long hot walk for nothing. When he did finally reach my battalion I was away at army school, and so I never did possess an identification card during my service in the Army. I never got into any trouble for not having one, but there could have been times when its possession would have saved me both time and trouble.

Near our village of Percey-le-Grande there was a small but perfectly medieval castle, which interested me very greatly. Dan Keller and I frequently took a ride on our horses after drill was over, and we often went by the old castle. The moat was empty of water, but still surrounded the place and was kept clean and in good condition. The draw-bridge and portcullis were in working order, and the former was in constant use. The battlements and towers and turrets were stained by time and weather, but in perfect condition. Sometimes we would ride clear around the walls, stopping at times to admire and enjoy the various viewpoints.[6]

Such a castle I had longed to be master of since my boyhood days, when *Ivanhoe* was my favorite book. And so we were one day sitting on our horses in front of the main entrance (I could not see enough of the place) when the drawbridge came clattering down, and out upon it walked the old Count, the owner. He took off his broad felt hat and saluted us with a low bow. We saluted him in return, and he asked if the American officers would not alight and enter the castle. We were delighted and followed him into the inner court, our horses' hoofs sounding on the drawbridge and through heavy walls. In the court an old servant came to take our horses. The old gentleman led us first up to the battlements. There he showed us heaps of large stones, piled up hundreds of years ago to throw down on the heads of the besiegers. And large iron cauldrons, which used to heat boiling oil for the same purpose. These had also been there for centuries. We looked down on the drawbridge through slits in the stone walls through which the defenders fired arrows upon the enemy.

We next went into a large attic, and the Count opened a large and worn leather trunk. From this he took out his old uniforms which he had worn in the War of 1871 against Germany. He was very proud of his military service, of course, and wanted us young soldiers to know that he had been a soldier too. We went on down through the large halls with a look into a room here and there. There was some fine old wood paneling and a lot of very old furniture in the rooms.

Finally we came to the grand salon of the castle. Several splendid windows, twenty feet high, lighted the fine large room. It was furnished in modern French style. On the walls were many military pictures, photographs, and paintings. There were also some flags and weapons. Several glass cabinets contained many curios, mostly of a military nature. It was room after my own heart. The good Count showed us everything

6. There is a small castle near Percey-le-Grande known as Donjon D'Isomes, but it consists of a single ruined tower and does not fit his description. A better candidate is the Romagna Commandery, a Burgundian castle located a few more miles from Percey-le-Grande, but still within easy riding distance; it operates today as a bed and breakfast.

and told us the story of many of the things. We came to two large photographs of two fine looking young men in uniform. They were hung with black crape and decorated with the Croix de Guerre.

"My two sons, all I had, both killed in this war," said the poor old Count, and his eyes filled with tears.

Keller and I felt deeply sorry for the fine old fellow and expressed our sincere sympathy in him. He thanked us and turned away and was soon smiling bravely. I was greatly touched by his terrible loss and his splendid courage. His wife had been dead some years. It would not seem that life held much for him now.

Talking cheerfully, he led us to some chairs near a window, and a servant brought us wine and cakes. And such wine. Tourists never taste such wine. It was a revelation to Keller and me. Aged and cared for years by experts in the art. We knew at once that we were honored with some of the best in his cellar, and we expressed our keen appreciation, and the Count was pleased.

Lieutenant Keller told our host that I was an ardent admirer of the great Napoleon and that I had a collection of Napoleonana. The Count said that he was also and seemed pleased to know that I was. He got up and, going over to a cabinet, he took out of it a small cross of the Legion of Honor.[7] Coming back to us, he bowed to me and presented the cross to me. Keller told me that this Cross had been given to the Count's grandfather by Napoleon the First personally and that the Count wanted to present it to me. I was much surprised and objected to depriving him of so priceless a relic. But he insisted and would not be refused, and so I accepted the cross with very sincere thanks. In insisting that I accept it the Count said that his sons were dead and he had no one to leave it to, and he felt very grateful to the American major, who was soon to lead a battalion against the enemies of his country. I carried this cross through the battles and through the days when I was a wounded prisoner among the Germans, and now it has an honored place in my collection of war medals. I enjoy pointing it out to my friends and telling its story.

There was very little amusement for the American soldiers in the

7. The Legion of Honor (*Légion d'honneur*) is a merit-based award for civilians and soldiers first created under Napoleon Bonaparte.

villages in France. Crap shooting took up much of their spare time when they had any money, which was usually only for a few days after pay day. This was a simple game of throwing dice on the floor. Orders were published against all gambling. But the poor fellows had nothing else to do in the evenings, and as long as the game was kept out of sight I was not supposed to know about it and did not interfere. Many an evening, when walking through the streets of our village, I heard the click of the dice, or bones as they were called, and the cries and curses of the gamblers, but officially I did not hear anything. I have little doubt but that there was plenty of gambling at headquarters from which these orders emanated. At my quarters we had an occasional game of poker, and then took up Red Dog. But this game always, from the very nature of it, got beyond control, and the stakes became too high.

In our division were many professional actors and entertainers and musicians. And so a troupe was formed to visit the many units and give them a show. This was most welcome, and we all enjoyed these evenings immensely. If the weather was fine, the show was given in the square. A rough stage was erected, and lanterns and candles furnished the light. If it was wet or cold, a barn was used. There were a few chairs down front, and the rest stood up.

We had the troupe in our village of Percey-le-Grand one evening in the middle of September. It was a pleasant evening, and the show was given in the main square of the town on a stage we erected at the side of the square. I invited the Mayor, and he sat with the officers on some chairs near the stage. He seemed amused at the antics of the performers and appeared to enjoy the music. Speaking no English, he of course did not get the jokes. A private soldier named Slim Kallum was the star of the occasion, and he could put over a song in fine style. Some of his jokes were rather strong, but the five hundred soldiers of the two companies stationed in the town roared and shouted with laughter and kept calling him back until he had used up all of his songs and stunts. Kallum was a professional actor and a good comedian. He took a crack at everybody and did not spare the officers. His imitations of some of the officers of the division were most laughable and well done. A trio of singers from our own Company A, professionals also, ran Kallum a close race for most applause from the soldiers. Their singing was excellent and they made a great hit. I was pleased to see the men having such a good time with so much hearty laughter and such keen enjoyment.

Leaves of absence were not permitted to officers or soldiers during the six weeks of intensive training in France. It was absolutely no use to even think of getting one. But such is the influence of the Jewish Church, even with the hard-boiled headquarters of the American Expeditionary Forces, that orders were received to permit all officers and soldiers of the Jewish faith to leave their regiments so that they might assemble in certain towns to celebrate one of their historic church festivals.[8] This order was a very great surprise to me, but I published it to the battalion, and we let the Jews go. I very much doubt if any other faith, unless it be the Catholic, could put such a thing over on the AEF. Some of these Jews had not yet rejoined their regiments when we received the order to move up to the front lines, and in consequence were lost for many days.

This matter of giving the Jews leave of absence unexpectedly brought me a lot of trouble. In fact it occasioned the only blot I know of on my military career. It brought to a head trouble which had been fomenting in Company A. The officer who had succeeded me in command of this company when I was promoted to major was an ex-regular army sergeant, and he was too severe with the men. There was considerable feeling against him, even among the officers, one of whom transferred to the battalion scouts to get away from him. I was about to recommend a change in the command of this company to the Colonel when the trouble broke out.

One morning when the company fell in for drill about two thirds of the sergeants and corporals were absent. A search for them in their billets and in the village proved fruitless. They were absolutely gone, and I was greatly worried and could not understand it. These men were the

8. Parkin's comments in this section reflect anti-Semitic attitudes shared by many Americans at the time (though he later praises the patriotism and courage of individual Jewish American soldiers). According to Nancy Gentile Ford, *Americans All!: Foreign-Born Soldiers in World War I* (College Station: Texas A&M University Press, 2001), various units in the US Army did, on occasion, approve special furloughs for Jewish troops so that they could participate in religious services. But not all appeals for faith-based accommodations were approved: for example, the quartermaster general refused "the Jewish communities' request for kosher rations for Jewish soldiers," 119.

best soldiers in the company, except the first sergeant, Chambers, and the few sergeants and corporals who remained.

I questioned first sergeant Chambers. He was a good man and faithful to me when I was his captain. He was torn between his duty and his loyalty to his comrades. He finally said that there had been much discontent in the company since I had left it and that the giving of leave to the Jews, and refusing it to all others, had made the discontented noncommissioned officers furious, and most of them had decided to take a day off without permission. He said they would be back that evening, he felt sure, and I did not need to worry too much about them.

First Sergeant Chambers told me that he did not know where the absentees were, and I believed him. These men were really perpetrating a mutiny in time of war, and they might be shot for their actions. The thing was a disgrace to the battalion and to me. This might cost me my command and send me home in disgrace. I had rather be killed in action. I was terribly worried, for such an occurrence could not be kept within my battalion. I sent the companies out to drill under command of Captain Knack and then started the search for the deserters. I had Lieutenant Keller, my adjutant, get on the telephone and call up all the other towns nearby to see if they had been seen, and this, of course, spread the news. I sent Lieutenants Naill and Swank out on my horse and Keller's to search the country and the villages. I called up my good friend Captain Manning, the regimental adjutant, and told him all about it and what I was doing to bring the men back and asked him to help me with the Colonel, who might raise the devil with me and probably would do so. And then, having done everything possible, I sat down by my telephone and worried, more I think than I ever had in my life, and was miserable.

About two o'clock that afternoon I heard a noise outside in the square, and going out, to my intense relief, I saw the absentees lined up, under the escort of Lieutenants Swank and Naill. They had been found in the tavern of a village several miles away and had come back willingly enough. I stood in front of them, and filled with anger, I gave them the worst balling out I was capable of, and it was enough to reduce them all, even the drunks, to a very humble state of mind. Then I ordered them all into the guard house and locked them up under guard. Next I had them brought into my office singly, and before a court of officers I questioned them all. They were respectful enough and all said they thought they should have leave of absence, if the Jews did, and made that their main excuse. All were worried when I told them they might be shot for desertion in time of war. I could not find out from any of them who were the ring leaders. Nearly all of them seemed not to have had any idea that the consequences could be so serious.

I made a detailed written report of the affair to Colonel Charles. Neither he nor anyone else in authority took the matter as seriously as I had expected. In fact but little fuss ever was made over it. I never heard about it from either brigade or divisional headquarters. I shall always think that my good friend, Captain Manning, our regimental adjutant, made light of the whole thing to the Colonel and the higher authorities and so saved me from a lot of trouble and possible disgrace. Our prompt recapture of the absentees helped the affair a lot no doubt.

Colonel Charles wrote me a letter, asking me to suggest a punishment for the offenders, which surprised me considerably. I would have liked very much to let the matter drop and release the men and let them keep their rank. I had come to regard the affair as a piece of foolishness which all concerned extremely regretted, and in which no real harm was intended, nor of which the possible consequences were appreciated. Also it would just about wreck Company A as a fighting unit to lose all these non-commissioned officers, and we were going to the front very soon. There would not be time to train others. However, I knew that such action, even if approved, and I much doubted if it would be, would seriously affect discipline in my battalion. These men must be punished, and the battalion must be impressed by their punishment.

And so I recommended to the Colonel that all of these offenders be reduced to the ranks and that they be scattered among the other companies of the regiment, outside of my battalion. Hence they would lose their rank and privileges and be separated from their friends. A fairly heavy punishment after all. The Colonel approved my recommendation. We were in the town of Tremont, on our way to the front, when his order reached me. The company was paraded in the street, the order was read to them, and then the men were degraded before the company by having their chevrons cut off their sleeves, and they were then led away to other companies, leaving all their friends behind. I did not attend the ceremony. I felt too bad about the whole thing, almost as a father with disgraced sons.

I thought, at first, that the matter of liquor drinking by the troops would be a serious one for me to handle on account of the way the soldiers abused this privilege during the first few days in our villages. Unused to wine, they poured it down like water, and, in consequence, over half the men were drunk the first two or three evenings. The guard house was full, and the drunks were all over the village. I cautioned the officers, some of whom took too much, and bawled the men out strong, and threatened to put sentries out to prevent drinking. And I made all the soldiers go to drill, whether they were sick from drink or not. They soon found out that they could not stand the pace, and, in a few days the drinking settled down to a common sense basis, and a drunken man became a rare thing among us.

We did not have a Y.M.C.A. canteen with us while we were undergoing the six weeks' intensive training in France. I presume they were not yet organized to serve all the troops. At Camp Meade we had a very good regimental canteen, where the men could purchase all kinds of eatables, smokes, and the many small things they wanted. And so they missed a canteen very greatly. Soldiers seem to want more sweets than the army ration provides, and they ate enormous quantities of candy and chocolate. In fact devoured all of this that could be brought to them. In a few days some itinerant merchants with wagons loaded with poor candies and fruits and cakes appeared in our villages. They did a rushing business, but the men complained that they were robbed by the excessive prices. I spoke to the Mayor about this matter, but he said he could do nothing about it, and the soldiers did not have to buy. This gave me an idea. When each wagon entered the village I had a sentry accompany it all during the stay. He had orders to prevent the soldiers from buying. And so they did no business. A day or two of this broke the prices in half, and then the guards were withdrawn.

All of the officers, except one to a company, were summoned one day to divisional headquarters to witness a demonstration of the French method of attack by Captain Van Dyke's company. It was well done, but I learned nothing new. I had done the same thing at Camp Meade with my company, under the instructions of French officers, and had been using this attack in my battalion, since being in France.[9] At this manoeuvre I met my good friend Alden C. Knowles, our old Lieutenant-Colonel and recently promoted to be Colonel of the 315th Infantry. He had always been the real head of our regiment, the man who made it what it was. Our own Colonel was not up to his job and was intensely disliked by everyone in the regiment. Colonel Knowles was very differently regarded, and while he was not greatly popular, he had many friends and he was respected for his character and his efficiency. A few of us higher officers knew him well and liked him very much. He was just and reasonable and he was a first-rate soldier.

Our new Lieutenant-Colonel, who had been our regular major, was a most polite gentleman, and a lovable fellow. I was very fond of him, but I could not respect him. He may have been a good soldier once, but liquor had got the better of him, and he was under its influence much of the time. The War Department must have had all of this on his record, and why they sent him to a new regiment, or to any regiment, I could never understand. Our Colonel knew his fault and kept him away from the regiment most of the time on detached duty. When he was with us I attended to most of his duties. Even at drills I gave the commands for him. He sat stupidly on his horse, and did not know what was going on. He should, at least, have been left in America when we went to France. The Colonel once confined him to camp for thirty days for drinking, but he was a regular officer, and they protected each other and covered up many things which should have been exposed. A new officer would have been bounced right out of the army for such offenses. I do not mention this officer's name.[10] It would do no good now to do so.

With two such officers at the head of our regiment, the loss of our only good regular officer was almost disastrous to us. And so I told Colonel Knowles that we were very blue, in the regiment, at losing him, and that he had left us in a devil of a fix. I told him that I was much

9. Some of the French officers that had trained the battalion in Camp Meade travelled with the division and continued instructing it in France. The divisional history indicates that the training was much more varied and intensive in France than it had been in the United States.

10. Major (soon to be Lt. Colonel) Robert L. Meador.

discouraged over our chances to make good in battle, and so were the rest of our officers.

Colonel Knowles tried to cheer me up, and said the regiment was good and would do its duty well on the Front. He hinted that there might be some changes among our officers in the near future, but he would not say anything definite, and, of course, he could not. Battle service quickly settled the status of the three officers I have been discussing. Colonel Knowles was recommended for promotion to brigadier general, and would have gone high, had the war lasted; the other two officers were both relieved of their commands for inefficiency and sent to duty in the rear.

4

The Army School at Langres

I was sitting, one evening, in my quarters in Percey-le-Grande, tired out by a strenuous day's training, when I heard the noise of a motor-bike coming up the street. This always heralded the coming of orders, and I wondered what was up now. I was soon reading an order directing me to turn over my battalion to my senior officer and report to the city of Langres to attend the army school there and take the special two weeks' course for field officers. I had expected promotion, but not a session at school. But I was not displeased as it would be a pleasant break in village life, and I would have the opportunity to learn all of the new things of the conduct of war.

That evening I called on good Captain Louis C. Knack, and made over the command of the battalion. Early the next morning I turned over to Lieutenant Odum, the company fund of Company A, together with all of the books, papers and cash. I had retained normal command of that company, although actually in command of the battalion. An hour's pleasant ride on the front seat of an army truck brought me to the station, where I had to wait a long time for a train. I fell into conversation with the band leader of the 315th Infantry, a pleasant educated gentleman and a musician of some reputation. He was en route to the army school for band leaders to take a course. Our army had schools of every possible kind in France. There were schools for horse-shoers, bakers, cooks, doctors, and for every type of soldier. We had been in camp in American nearly a year. Why was not all this school work finished there before we came over? Officers were constantly ordered away from the fighting regiment to go to school, and this in spite of the fact that these regiments had very few officers left.

The train for Langres finally arrived late in the afternoon. The band master and I got aboard and after a very short trip, not quite an hour, we reached our destination in the dusk of evening. An American soldier, on the platform, informed me that the town was on the top of the high hill, at the base of which we stood, and that I must hurry or I would miss the last train up. Telling me to leave my bedding roll and return for it in the morning, he seized my large heavy suitcase, and ran around to the rear of the station. The cog-train to the summit was already leaving the station slowly. We ran alongside looking for a seat. The cars were full, but the soldier threw my case in one compartment and I climbed aboard, rather out of breath. In my compartment were French officers, some French civilians, and opposite me two clean young American privates.

I thanked the bearded French officer beside me for making room for me, and then I asked the Americans what duty they were on at Langres. "Officers orderlies, Sir," one replied. He told me that they were serving American officers from the 26th Division, New England, I think. This division was serving in a British Corps, and like the British they had to put on "Side" and take orderlies with them.[1] Quite a bit of "Swank" for Americans, I thought. None of our officers brought orderlies along and never thought of doing so. I should have considered my orderly a nuisance, and as it turned out, they were really useless at the school I attended.

When we arrived at the summit, one of the American soldiers inquired if I had a billet. I told him none had been assigned to me as yet. "The town is very crowded, Sir, I am afraid you will have trouble finding a room tonight." And I certainly did. The soldier volunteered to carry my case and act as guide. Very kind of him indeed. We went first to the office of the school. Being late, it was closed. Apparently you could "Jolly Well" look out for yourself. The staff was not in the least interested in late arrivals, and I thought it pretty rotten treatment. We went to several hotels and two or three Y.M.C.A. places, but all were full and rather indifferent. Finally my guide took me to the medical school, hoping to find me a bed there. The adjutant was sorry but he did not have an empty cot. I was tired, disgusted and angry. I asked

1. The 26th "Yankee" Division comprised of National Guard soldiers from New England. It arrived in France in September 1917 and trained with the French Army. After fighting in the Spring Offensives, the division was placed under the French Sixth Army (not the British Army) for the Second Marne campaign. Later it fought at Saint-Mihiel and then the Meuse-Argonne.

him if I could sit all night in a chair in his office. At that he called in a sergeant and, after talking with him, told me that they had a broken cot they would repair and they could give me some blankets. This was real good of them for I had not the least claim upon them or this school. I thanked them very cordially. My guide left me then, refusing a generous tip I tried to press upon him, so I thanked him heartily.

I went into the darkened old town and got dinner. Where I got it and what it consisted of I do not remember. When I returned to the dormitory, for that was what it was, a long, high, old stone walled room, with a long line of army cots down each side, I found the place full of army doctors of all ages and ranks. A jolly, good-natured lot they were. Smutty stories were being told, and the room rang with shouts of laughter. Funny stories in truth but dirtier ones I never heard. Medical men do not take their military rank as seriously as do line officers. As a rule they are neither smart in their appearance nor in their manners, and they don't care much of anything about either of these things.

They made me welcome amongst them, and were surprised to see an infantry officer in their quarters. I explained why I was there. Soon the stories stopped and the laughter and talk subsided, and we all settled down for the night.

In the morning I had a good breakfast at the army mess shack in the courtyard. Hot porridge and eggs and bacon and coffee. This mess was run by the army Quartermaster Corps for the student officers. The food was very good and reasonable in price. I often ate here during my two weeks at Langres. It was in a temporary wooden building, not very large, and was run by army cooks and orderlies. This American food was a pleasant change from the French food we had to eat at all of the other places in the town.

The office of the army school directed me to the quarters I was to occupy. They were in a great brick barracks on the edge of the town, right up against the ancient city wall. It was an enormous building of many floors and entrances and was a barracks of the French army. In a good sized room eight of us officers were quartered. The walls were of brick and the floor of stone. Two large windows gave light from the courtyard. There was a large iron stove, but as it was August we had no use for it. A wash-room with showers, toilets and basins adjoined. The equipment of this room was severely plain but practical. The whole place had the atmosphere of a prison. The only furniture of our room consisted of our eight cots and bedding-rolls and locker trunks. It was a cheerful crowd I found there. Majors Atwood and Dodge of my own regiment, Majors Pepper and Langley of the 313th Infantry, two other majors not of our division, a captain of the 313th, and myself composed the group.

War laid a heavy hand upon this group of young soldiers. Two, Majors Atwood and Pepper, were killed in the Argonne Forest, and three were seriously wounded: Major Langley, the Captain of the 313th and myself. One, Major Dodge, was relieved of his command. The fate of the other two I never learned.

Some description of this interesting and quaint old town of Langres may not be out of place here. Built upon the extreme end of a high steep ridge it looks out upon the surrounding country and the view is superb. The countryside is laid out below almost like a map. Before the days of artillery Langres was as impregnable as a fortress could well be, and we were told that the city had not been captured by a hostile force since the days of the Romans. An ancient high stone wall completely surrounds the town and it is kept in its original condition. In this wall is an old gate built by the Romans. It is in an almost perfect state of preservation, but the carved figures upon it have been greatly worn away by the ravages of time and nature.

The main streets and squares were wide and open, and the buildings fairly modern French, but, to drop back into the middle ages, one had but to turn down one of the narrow winding side streets and there you were, back five hundred years, with the ancient houses, with their quaint doors of heavy iron studded wood and small windows, all about you. Overhead the upper stories, leaning out into the street, nearly touched each other across it. I used to delight to walk through these old sections of the town, and think of all the history they have seen in the making, and of the brave men who have gone out of these ancient houses to the wars, and of the courageous women who have remained behind in them, through all these centuries of time.

Antedating these medieval houses, and remarkably preserved, almost perfect in fact, was the front or façade of a Roman Villa. It formed the rear wall of one of the more modern buildings on one of the main streets. In building the new structure they had used this Roman front, as part of the new building, and had taken great care to preserve it. You entered the garden, in the rear, through an arched passage, and upon turning around you faced the original Roman façade. It had many fine pillars, carvings and statues, and of course windows.[2] A treasure beyond price to any community, and yet one German shell might have reduced it all to rubbish.

In another fairly modern building I found another almost unique and priceless example of ancient architecture. This time medieval. It was a circular staircase built entirely of solid stone entirely without support except where one end of each wide step fitted into the outer wall of the round tower and where the other end of the step, carved round to form a continuous high pillar, was set over upon another. Wonderful masonry work showing absolute exactitude and great engineering skill. In this day of steel such things are not built.

The United States Army School of Langres offered courses for officers in Infantry, in the Medical Corps, in the General Staff, and doubtless in other branches of the service, but of this I am not sure. The purpose of the school, of which all of the students were army officers, was to bring the officers up to date in all of the new and standard military subjects. When through with their term the student officers returned to their regiments and imparted the knowledge gained to their fellow officers and to the men of their units.

Having been recommended for promotion to major, although still a captain, I was sent to the special Field Officers course of two weeks duration. My fellow students were all colonels, lieutenant-colonels, majors, and a few captains like myself. We received our instruction through lectures, demonstrations, and field problems. A number of written tests were given us to enable the school to give us ratings on our work.

The lectures were given by experts in their respective services, all officers of the French, British, and American army. Most of the lectures were interesting and instructive. A British major covered the Intelligence Corps. He was a humorous beggar and mixed in quite a little profanity. An American lieutenant talked on gas and gas masks. He assured

2. This is likely the Renaissance House in Langres, which has a reproduced Roman façade. There is a Gallo-Roman Arch, without windows, as well as a Roman villa archeological site.

us that the German gas mask was punk, but the Germans seemed to get along with it. An American artillery colonel, an energetic, fine speaker, in lecturing on his arm, assured us that if we had enough artillery we would need no infantry to win the war. We did not believe this fellow entirely. A general of the Tank Corps tried to persuade us that tanks were the vital element for our victory. A French infantry major persuaded us, since we were all of the infantry, that our arm was the really important branch of the service and that we, and we alone, could win the war. Needless to say, the French infantry major got all the applause and appreciation.

Map problems were worked out on the blackboard and explained. The use of machine guns, one-pounder guns, trench mortars, and the handling of infantry in battle were all covered by the lecturers who spoke from battle experience and gave us the very newest and latest proved instruction. For officers soon to go to the front it was wonderful stuff and intensely interesting.

Our classrooms were rooms in large stone French barracks. We sat upon benches or rickety chairs. Never have I attended classes in which the instructor received such absolute and rapt attention.

Many days were devoted to practical work. The whole class, some several hundred, would be loaded into army trucks, sitting upon boards placed across the bodies of the trucks, a very rough vehicle, and taken out to one of the outlying forts of Langres and there we had actual demonstrations, with loaded ammunitions, of machine guns, one-pounder cannon, trench mortars, and the Browning automatic rifle. The accuracy of these weapons, in the hands of experts was astonishing.

An amusing but almost disastrous incident occurred during the demonstration of the Browning automatic rifle.[3] This weapon is a large repeating rifle fired from the shoulder. It has a considerable and

3. The Browning Automatic Rifle (BAR) was a new weapon debuted by the AEF in the summer of 1918. The son of its inventor, Val Browning, served in the 79th Division and was in France to see the weapon introduced within his division. The BAR was infinitely superior to the French Chauchat, the main automatic rifle issued to soldiers in the AEF. Manufactured by a French bicycle company, the Chauchat was prone to jamming and largely hated by its operators; some doughboys were issued a version designed to fire 30–06 American ammunition; tests later revealed that the weapon was incorrectly calibrated.

continuous kick, and to use it one must advance one foot and lean rather heavily against the rifle. Otherwise it will shove you all over the place. The class was grouped in a large half circle behind the American lieutenant, who was firing the automatic rifle. He used it very cleverly and cut down small trees and broke holes through a brick wall. A French general present was amazed at the results obtained. He was allowed to fire the automatic rifle, and not being properly instructed, it began to push him about, and the bullets began to come to the left, and all the officers then took to flight with much pushing and crowding. The instructor placed his hands on the French general's shoulder and straightened him out again, directing the fire upon the target. There was much laughter, but not until it was all over.

At one of the outlying forts a company composed entirely of American second lieutenants demonstrated infantry attack and the actual use of hand grenades. Most unfortunately one of these young student officers had his right hand blown off by a hand grenade, which he held too long, during this demonstration of the attack. He suffered greatly, but was very brave and excited great sympathy and admiration in our group. He was quickly bandaged and carried away and the attack went on.

Another day a platoon of the Blue Devils, the Chasseurs Alpins, demonstrated an attack upon a strong position, using machine guns, trench mortars, rifles and hand grenades.[4] These troops are very fine, and all were veterans of the front line. We stood nearby and watched them work up through trenches to the point of attack, which place they almost destroyed with real hand grenades and trench mortar shells, before the final rush with the bayonet. Such an actual demonstration teaches us more than any number of lectures ever could.

Some of our days were devoted to terrain problems or problems worked out on the actual ground. The instructor took us to a certain position, pointed out the positions held by the enemy, told us what troops we had. We spent some time looking over the ground and then a number of officers were called up to explain to the class their plan of

4. The Chasseurs Alpins are an elite mountain-fighting infantry unit in the French Army. Known in the Great War for their distinctive dark blue uniforms and floppy berets, they provided elite infantry tactical training to the AEF.

attack. At other times no one was called upon at the time, and we were required to make sketches of the terrain, and when we returned to our classrooms we wrote out a solution of the problem given.

We were even given some problems in handling corps and divisions. It seemed to me a waste of time for an officer of rank less than that of a colonel to study the command of such large bodies of troops. A temporary officer or a reserve officer would certainly never get an opportunity to handle a division or a corps. In fact, extremely few such officers ever got above the rank of lieutenant-colonel. All of our generals in France, except a few National Guard generals, who had too much influence with the powers that be to be kept out of France, were regular army officers, and none of these ever saw a full division assembled until the National Guards were called to the Mexican Border in 1916. It has been freely asserted, and I believe it is true, that the War Department sent the National Guard to the border not from fear of war with Mexico, but because they felt sure that we would be drawn into the World War, and they desired to have some troops, in addition to our small regular army, prepared for immediate service.

It was, of course, only proper that the regular officers should have all the higher ranks. They were trained commanders, but nevertheless many of them proved unfit for command of troops in battle, and even for command of the larger units before going to the front. Every officer who held a command on the Front, even that of a platoon, lived in constant fear of not making good, and being sent to the City of Blois for reclassification. The high command did not have too many officers in France for the work to be done, and it very wisely decided that if an officer could not command troops in or out of battle, he might be used for work of a different, yet very necessary character. A great many officers were relieved of their commands and sent to Blois. Here they were given staff work, or office work, or sent to labor troops to build roads or unload ships, and most of them did very good work in their new jobs.

We student officers were given a number of written tests as our course progressed, and while I felt that I knew the work and showed it in my test papers, I never knew what grades I received. A report was always sent to the commander of the student officers unit when the course was completed. Colonel Charles of our regiment never showed me this report nor spoke to me of it, so I presume he was satisfied.

Promotions in our large class of officers were very frequent. A great many received their promotions while at the school. It got so you had to look at an officer's shoulder straps before greeting him, or you might give him the wrong title. I was in hopes that my promotion to major, for which I had long been recommended, would reach me at Langres, but it did not, and I had to remain one of the very few captains in the class.

We ate most of our meals in a French restaurant run by the Y.M.C.A. and managed by a gray-haired New Yorker, who had never had any previous experience in such work before. Nevertheless, he did well at his job, and served us excellent meals at fair prices. He was a handsome, jovial gentleman and always had a cheery greeting and a pleasant word for us. Certainly a case of the right man in the right place.

Our work in the school usually kept us busy until four-thirty or five o'clock. We often spent the rest of the day, until dinner, in a large mirror-lined cafe of the usual ornate French type. Here we sat at the tables with our friends and talked over the school work and the war, while smoking and drinking wine or beer.

The shops of Langres were full of military equipment for officers. Musette bags, a sort of small canvas haversack, were a most useful thing to have to carry toilet articles, food, cigarettes, etc., and a thing that every officer wanted, as it relieved him of the necessity of carrying a soldier's pack, map and dispatch cases, boots, Sam Browne belts, canes, whips, raincoats, caps, all sorts of toilet articles, condensed heat burners, electric torches, etc. The prices were high, but the student officers thought they needed most of these articles, and trade was brisk. Much of it was later lost in officers' baggage, or thrown away by them as too heavy to carry in battle or on the march.

In one of the shops I found an illustrated "Life of Marshall Murat," King of Naples, Napoleon's greatest cavalry leader, and a romantic figure of those great times. It was a large book and beautifully illustrated in colors. It pleased me, and I knew it would greatly please my eight-year-old son, Harry. So I bought it and sent it off to him by mail. I was pleased to send him this gift, but felt that perhaps it was the last present he would ever receive from his father, and this thought filled me with sadness and my heart yearned for my dearly beloved wife and son.

Our two weeks of extremely interesting and helpful school work came to an end, and the class scattered to its various regiments. We officers of the 79th Division loaded our baggage into a truck and seated on top of it journeyed home through lovely rural France to our villages. I arrived in my village of Percey-le-Grande in the evening just as parade for retreat broke up. When I got down from my truck the square was full of soldiers of my own old Company A. I was glad to see them and had missed them and felt at home again to be amongst them all. Hundreds of heels clicked and hundreds of hands snapped up to smart salute. It was one of the happiest moments of my life. I returned their salute and said, "Good evening, Company A. I am glad to be back with you again," and many voices called back in greeting, and I felt greatly moved. I had shared the troubles and griefs of many of these men, and some of them I had praised and promoted, and some I had punished, but never had I refused to give one of them a fair hearing and just treatment within my abilities.

Perhaps the most thrilling of our drill periods after I returned to Percey-le-Grande was that devoted to practice with real hand grenades. We had put in many hours with dummy grenades, and the men had been well and carefully instructed. They well knew the dangers of a grenade. I confess that this business made me nervous. A careless man might kill or wound a whole group. The Mills grenade, "mark 8" this type was called, was about the size and shape of a large lemon.[5] To set it off you pulled a pin out of one end of it, and then you had five seconds before it burst. This brief time was used, of course, in throwing the missile to the to the spot where you wanted it to burst. The terrific explosion of these small things astonished all of us. One of the officers, who had attended grenade school, demonstrated their use to the rest of us and gave a final talk on the very serious danger in using them. Everyone was very careful and very serious. There were many accidents in our Army, but I am glad to say that there were none in my battalion.

At times, during this grenade drill, we would have an entire platoon of sixty men, standing well apart, so as not to interfere with each other, throw grenades together. The line of explosions there some thirty yards away was simply appalling. It certainly impressed all of us with the terrible efficiency of this weapon of offense and defense and increased our

5. The Mills grenade (or Mills bomb) was developed in Britain and introduced to the front in 1915. Parkin is likely referring to the Mills No. 5 Mark 1 bomb, but he could be referring to the later variations of the No. 23 or possibly No. 36 Mark 1 bombs.

confidence in our ability to meet the enemy. At the end of the practice my bugler, Harry Miller, with a long face, brought to me what looked like an armful of shredded wheat. It was the remains of his pack, which he had left on the spot where the grenades had burst.

A certain medical lieutenant attached to my battalion was simply terrified by the live grenades. So much fear did he show that I thought his conduct was unbecoming to a man, not to speak of an officer. He really made a fool of himself and lost everybody's respect. He was a large, fat man. I do not mention his name, either. To punish him, I called to him, and taking a dummy grenade out of my pocket, I rolled it along the ground to him. He was too terrified to move, and lay there trembling like a big bowl of jelly, and I turned away and left him to suffer, almost wishing it was real grenade The first night we were on the front and had experienced some shell fire, he put a sick tag on himself and was taken to the rear in an ambulance. They say he had pneumonia in the hospital. Perhaps he did, but fear and lack of manhood was what took him away from us, and I was damn glad he left.

On September 3, I received official word from Divisional Headquarters that I had been promoted to the rank of major. This was not unexpected, as the Colonel had told me, to my great pride and personal gratification and more than once at that, that I had the best company in the regiment, and that he had recommended me for promotion. Also I had recently passed the physical examination required of all officers recommended for promotion. Since I had been in active command of the battalion most of the time since the creation of the Regiment, I was entirely familiar with my duties. The battalion sergeant major brought me the message one morning while I was at breakfast. I had in my kit the gold oak leaves of my new rank. They had been given to me by my sister-in-law, Mrs. F. L. Arensberg, while we were at Camp Meade, and they were of solid gold. On my way out to drill, I stopped at my quarters and, taking the captain's double silver bars off my shoulder straps and off my cap, I put on the gleaming new gold oak leaves. That same evening I wrote the good news to my dear brave wife, and sent her a small gold oak leaf to wear, as was customary among officers' wives. I had two of them and needed but one for my overseas cap, but she would have received one any way.

I was host to the officers of my battalion at an evening party in our mess room in Percey-le-Grande. Captain Bob Miller made all the arrangements and gathered the guests. Sandwiches and drinks in plenty were served. Speeches of congratulations to me were delivered, the best of these came later in the evening, when the good wines of France had properly mellowed the officers, or comrades as they constantly asserted themselves to be, and which in truth we were and always had been. Lieutenant Sheridan made the prize oration of the evening, but rather ruined the effect by becoming maudlin in his cups over the approaching death in battle of many of us. Tears ran down his face, and his voice failed him. But the crowd roared with laughter during the saddest part of his speech and refused to have their high spirits dampened. All of that merry group were either killed or wounded, but we refused to think about our future fates that evening. Poor Sheridan, on the way home to his billet in Percey-le-Petite, fell into the canal and was fished out a soaking wet, but soberer man.

A little way outside of the village there was a small cemetery, closed in by a high wall, circular in shape. I used to walk out there, occasionally, just to be alone for a time. One wants to be alone now and then. It was not a cheerful place, but it was quiet and no one else ever seemed to go there. Here I was alone to think of my sweet wife and dear little son and beloved good mother. And while it made me sad to think of them, so far away, and realize that life with them was perhaps over, still I got some comfort from the thought of their love for me and mine for them. A half hour here with them in thought made me happier. It was the only way I could get close to them. Homesickness for these dear ones was my greatest trial during the war, and it is a terrible trial at times. I was glad to be so constantly busy, from early morning until late at night. Otherwise, I do not think I could have endured it.

5

The March to the Battle of the Argonne

On September 7, 1918, the First Battalion, 316th Infantry, received orders to be ready to move out to the Front, that mysterious and much talked of and thought of place, for which we had been preparing for many long, hard months. We were all, from major to lowest private, crazy to go, and all was excitement and loud talk and bustle of preparations. Little did we realize what was in store for us, and it is a good thing that we did not, else we had not gone up so willingly and so happily.

All that day, and most of that night we packed, cleaned up, threw away much that we wanted but could not carry, inspected and helped and got ready to go. Officers' trunks by order were to be left behind, and in them we packed all we could not take. Extra uniforms, extra overcoats, underclothing, packages of letters, many gifts for a soldier in the field from relatives and friends, useful and convenient, if they could not be carried had to be left behind in our trunks. My Adjutant, Dan Keller, had all the officers' trunks stored in the attic of good Madame Robinnet, where there were already many trunks left by the division which had been here ahead of us. Never since that day have I seen that trunk, nor ever expect to do so.

There was a great deal of heavy baggage to be left behind, and this was my greatest care in all the worry of preparing the departure. Large wooden boxes of company records and papers, and boxes of extra clothing, ammunition, phonographs and records, baseball equipment, which, when gathered together in one house, made an astonishing pile. I was told that Division Headquarters would send trucks for all this, but they did not come, and I did not feel at all satisfied to abandon their mass of stuff and perhaps be called to account for it later. Hence when we pulled out I left First Sergeant Chambers of Company A and several men to guard the baggage until the trucks came. Several days later, with great difficulty, they finally overrode us, and I was particularly glad to see Chambers, who was an excellent soldier and a very reliable man.

We were up early on Sunday, September 8, 1918, but in spite of every exertion it was nine o'clock before we marched out. I was glad no officers of the Divisional Headquarters nor our Colonel had entered our town that morning, or I would probably have been "bawled out" for not starting much earlier. All claims for damage to the village had been submitted, checked over, and sent on to Divisional Headquarters for payment. There were many of them, all small, for such things as broken windows, broken chairs, broken steps, lost chickens, etc. The French are indeed a patriotic people, and fond of the Soldat American, but likewise are they a thrifty people, and every franc counts.

At nine o'clock I formed up the battalion, and we marched out, with the Bugle Corps blowing full blast, amid the cheers and hand wavings of our good friends of the village, with whom we had spent a strenuous, but happy six weeks. As I sat on my horse watching the companies march by, with Dan Keller beside me, good Madame Robinnet passed, in her best black dress on her way to church service, and she bade us goodbye and bon voyage. I let Captain Knack take command of the battalion, and remained behind with Keller, for a final inspection. My wagon train, for which I was also responsible, followed my battalion, and consisted of five wagons, one for each company, and one for the officers' bedding rolls and suitcases, four rolling kitchens, and one water cart.

It took Keller and me about two hours finally to set all things straight at Percey-le-Grande and then we set out at a fast trot to overtake our column. Our persons and our horses were loaded with equipment, hanging all over us, and as we trotted along we flapped and banged like Christmas trees run wild. This we had to get used to. Field glasses, pistols, canteens, helmets, saddle bags slapped and bounced as we urged our horses along the fine white road.

About noon we overtook the battalion eating a cold lunch, on the roadside, just beyond the town of Champlette. Soon we were on the road again on our long weary pull for the town of Pierrefaites, our destination for that day, and twenty-six long kilometers from Percey-le-Grande. A long march, but we were in good condition, and our orders were to pass the night there, and I was determined to make it.

The men suffered from the heat, as the sun shone bright and warm. Each man had on his helmet, overcoat, wool uniform, wool shirt, and carried his full pack, with blanket, half shelter tent, food, extra shoes, extra socks, extra underclothes, canteen full of water, his belt full of ammunition, his bayonet, his mess pan, knife, fork and spoon, his first aid packet, all strapped on to him, or hung on to him by belts and straps. It was a heavy load they carried, sixty pounds at least. Many, contrary to orders, had additional weight on them, but at every halt, they began to discard this extra stuff. Books and small packages, and sweaters and knitted helmets, wristlets and mufflers, knitted by loving hands at home, were thrown into the ditch at every halt, and gathered up eagerly by the French peasants, many of whom were warm that winter in knitted goods not intended for them. But no man threw away any of the proper equipment. The officers and sergeants enforced strict orders against this.

My first official visitor on this march was Captain William Scott, of Divisional Headquarters, who was in a motorcycle sidecar. He was an old friend from Pittsburgh and Fort Niagara Training Camp.[1] He was out on the road checking up the marching battalions of the divisions to report on same to General Kuhn. I had a short chat with him while the men marched by. He seemed surprised that I was making for Pierrefaites, and told me I had still a long way to go, but I assured him I would make it before we slept that night.

My next visitor was Colonel Charles also in a sidecar. He was very anxious to be assured that I could make my appointed destination that night, and I promised him I would get there, and with all my men. He told me to nurse them along, using all the halts I thought necessary, and to be sure and arrive at seven in the morning at the entraining point at Le Ferte-sur-Amance. As this place was only four kilometers beyond Pierrefaites I felt sure I could make a start at five in the morning and be on time, and so assured the Colonel I would do. He left me looking very much worried, as he always did.

We marched on down the fine hard road, and the heat of the sun was

1. Fort Niagara was home to two Officer Training Camps in 1917 for aspiring officers. The first course, which ran May through August, was Parkin's class. He joined 2,500 men from Pennsylvania in training, many of whom were also from affluent families. See https://nystateparks.blog/2017/10/10/training-the-doughboys/.

occasionally lessened by light showers of rain, a relief to all of us. We passed through many quaint old French villages, the people standing in their doorways to watch us and return the greetings of the trudging soldiers. Old men and old women and children and young women, and occasionally a soldier or two home on leave, but no men of military age. France had all of her manhood under arms. How it must have encouraged these brave people to see these long columns of sturdy young men passing up to the Front to help France and strike at the invader of their beautiful land.

After leaving one of these towns I met my next official visitor. A fine khaki-colored Cadillac touring car stopped on the roadside, and an aide, alighting, requested me to come to see the Brigade Commander, Brigadier General Noble.[2] We never knew in what mood we might find this officer. At one time he was courtesy and kindness personified, and at another he was pompous and arrogant. Rumor had it that his mood depended upon the condition of his flask, and this rumor was generally accepted in the brigade. Today he was much out of humor. "Major, how many men have you left on the road?" was his greeting to me.

"None at all, Sir, I have them all with my column." He expressed surprise and almost doubt.

"How do you do it, Major?"

"Sir, I have a strong rear guard, under orders not to leave a single man behind. When a man gets exhausted his pack is put on a wagon and when a man collapses he is put on a wagon for a few miles. I have been with the rear guard most of the march, and feel confident we have not left a man behind."

The General congratulated me and said I was doing better than many other commanders, some of whom had left the roads full of exhausted men. This time I got praise from him and not censure, but I was not always so fortunate.

General Noble left me and rode on down the road I had passed over. Shortly afterwards his car overtook me. I noticed several doughboys

---

2. Brigadier General Robert H. Noble (1861–1939) was a career army officer. A graduate of the United States Military Academy, he served in the Indian Wars and in the Spanish-American War, the latter as a staff officer. He served extensively overseas before then taking command of the 6th Infantry Regiment in the Pancho Villa Expedition. He came to the western front with the 5th Division in May 1918.

hanging on his running boards. He called out to me in an angry voice.

"Major Parkin, you assured me that you had left no men behind, and I found these men on the roadside in your rear."

I felt somewhat nervous and could not understand it. Approaching his car I looked at the men and saw, with relief, that all of them wore the collar ornaments of the 313th Infantry, which had passed over the road ahead of us. We had seen quite a few of them on the roadside. I called the General's attention to their collar ornaments. He looked at them and ordered them roughly off his car. I had difficulty in keeping a smile off my face.

It was now getting late in the day and as the men became more weary, more frequent halts became necessary. The military rule in marching is to march fifty minutes and rest ten. But in a march of such length and with the men so heavily loaded this rule cannot be adhered to unless a commander is willing to lose a considerable portion of his men, who fall out. This I was unwilling to do, so I suited the halts to the necessity of the occasion.

The work of the rear guard now became very hard, but it was done efficiently, if a little roughly at times. Kindness often helps a tired out soldier, but when it is not effective sterner measures must be resorted to. More than one man who would not listen nor obey was strenuously jerked to his feet and roughly ordered to get on his way, which most of them did. But this was only done to men who, although tired, were apparently able to make further effort. Often the wagons had to be stopped and an exhausted man lifted on to them. I was with the rear guard almost all of the time after noon, walking and leading my horse. First Lieutenant Joseph E. Dyer of Company A commanded the rear, and he was ably assisted by First Lieutenant Norman A. Bussey of the Medical Corps, whom I had there to judge the condition of the men who fell out. Some of those who fell out were very plainly falsing exhaustion even if very tired. Such men got a warm reception from these officers, were jerked to their feet and sent back to their companies with small sympathy. I watched all this, and saw that these officers were using good judgement, in their difficult work and handling the situation well. It was due mostly to their efforts that I finished this hard march and brought every man of my thousand to the trains the next morning.

My next and last official visitor on this march was General Joseph E. Kuhn, Commander of the division.[3] A finer soldier and kinder gentleman never wore uniform for any country. When General Kuhn's car, a fine limousine, met us, I was riding at the head of my men, and this was one of the few brief periods of that day that I was at the head of the column, having been there but a short time. It was raining and I had my rubber rain cape on, a most useful and comfortable garment for a mounted officer. I rode up to the open door of his car, saluted him, and was about to get off my horse, as is customary, when meeting a superior officer who addresses you, when he told me not to dismount. In the car with him was my good friend Captain Harry Rapalye, his aide, and an old Pittsburgh and Fort Niagara friend. We greeted each other. The General said, "Major Parkin, I promoted you recently because I had confidence in you. Now, Sir, on a hard march, where is the proper place for the commander?"

"With the rear guard, Sir, and I have been there almost all the time."

"Correct," said the General, clapping his hands together with a loud noise, which made my foolish French horse jump and slide around in the mud. The General repeated this action frequently, apparently not noticing how it made my horse jump and flounder.

He was greatly pleased when I told him I had not lost a man so far, and had me explain how I managed the march to succeed in this. On learning my destination, he seemed surprised at the length of my march, and concerned as to whether I would get there, telling me it was still quite a journey. I promised him to make it if I had to march half the night. He congratulated me upon the success of my march, but after watching my men file by he said, "Major, your men are too heavily loaded, their packs are much too large, they are carrying unauthorized articles beyond their regular equipment. Did you receive my order to prevent these men from doing just this?" I said I had, that I had issued it and directed the officers to enforce it, but had not personally inspected

3. Major-General Joseph Kuhn (1864–1935) graduated first in his class from West Point in 1885. An engineering officer he taught at West Point before serving in the Spanish-American War and then in the Philippines. He had extensive experience as both an engineer and an observer of foreign armies at war before US intervention in 1917. At that time, he was president of the US Army War College before taking command of the 79th Division.

the men's packs. I told him that we were fast losing this extra stuff and felt sure that we would drop most all of it today.

The General told me that he had followed the route of our Third Battalion from Chasigny, and was much angered to find the roadside littered with men who had fallen out. He even took my good friend Major Atwood back over the road, in his own, car, to show him the men he had lost. He told me that he had been strongly tempted to relieve Atwood on the spot, but his reputation and previous good work saved him.

After some advice and good wishes the General left me, and as it was almost evening we halted to eat some of the cold food we had with us. Captain Knack and I shared a can of corned beef and a box of crackers. We had stopped in a beautiful part of the road. It was lined on both sides with fine tall trees, the rain had made all the countryside green, and the setting sun threw wonderful colors over it all. Tired as we were, we both noticed and admired the beauty of the end of the day. But night was fast coming on, and we had but little time for the beauties of nature.

Riding to the head of the column I directed Lieutenants Swank and Naill, in charge of my scout section which led the march, good, reliable little men, both of them, to be very careful not to run away from us in the dark, and to keep in touch with the leading company in their rear. To watch their map carefully, especially at crossroads, and to inquire at every group of houses, and of any peasants for the village of Pier-refaites, our destination. I told them that I must march with the rear guard, where our troubles would be greatest. Feeling sure that my advance was in good hands, I signaled my good little bugler, Harry Miller, who was always near me, and the call of attention, and of forward put the column in motion again for our last and hardest pull of the day.

I sat on my big black French horse at the side of the road, and watched the battalion march past in the dusk, speaking to an officer here and there, and cautioning the men to keep closed up and not to fall out, as they might be left behind and lost. When the rear guard came up I joined them and dismounted to give what help I could. Things went very well for half an hour and then we began to find men on the roadside. We helped them up and urged them on, from some of the most weary we took their packs and put them on the wagons, and some of the men themselves we put on the wagons. When the stragglers became too numerous to handle I would have the halt sounded and give them a short rest. We met no one on the road and I got no advice or help from my superior. No doubt they had long ago finished their days work, and were comfortably under shelter from the rain which came on again. As the hours passed the men became so weary that we spent as much time resting as we did marching, and I began to despair of ever getting to my destination.

During one of the halts I rode to the head of the column and found one of our army trucks in a small village. Here was a ray of hope, and I asked the driver where we were and how far it was to Pierrefaites. He replied that he did not know, and was lost. He had come from the direction in which we were marching. I was provoked at his seeming stupidity and talked to him rather roughly, I fear. Some of the men had scattered among the houses of this village and were sheltering from the rain wherever they could. We had a hard time getting them back to the road, and went on our weary way.

After another hour of this continued struggle to keep the column moving, during which the efforts of the worn-out rear guard of necessity became harsher and more drastic, I was sitting in the mud on the bank at the roadside when I heard someone coming down the column asking for the Major. I called out and soon a soldier from the advance stood before me and gave me the most welcome news that our destination was just ahead. This was a great relief to me, and I mounted and rode on down the road and found Swank and Naill at a small group of houses, a peasant from one of which having just told them that it was the much desired village of Pierrefaites.

Looking about in the dark, I could see but a few old houses, too few for a company. I sat in the rain undecided for a minute. My officers and men stood around in the mud looking to me for orders. It was plainly up to me and I wasted no more time. To the right and left were open fields of beets, protected by high wire fences. Ordering some of the men to cut a way thru the fences with their wire cutters, I led the first company into the muddy field, my small belt electric torch giving me but little help. One after another I led in and placed the other three companies, and ordered the shelter tents put up at once. Some of the men dropped in the mud, and it was with difficulty they could be got to put up their tents. Then back to the road I went and cutting a way again through the fence, I put the wagon train in the opposite field. Good Captain Louis C. Knack came up to me and said he had found a large shack, big enough for all of his company and perfectly dry. Could he use it? He certainly could, and into it he packed all of his weary men. I rode around looking for others, but Captain Knack, an old campaigner, who knew best how to look after his men's comfort, had found the only one.

In a short time the other three companies had their shelter tents up in long rows, and in each a candle gleamed. With their raincoats under them and their two blankets and candles lighting the tents, each pair of the men, for they each carry half a small tent, soon were comfortable and warm. The field took on the appearance of a comfortable camp, and I knew the men would be warm and would get no more rain on them. We had arrived at nine-thirty, and before ten all of the men were under cover.

I had asked my adjutant to see if he and I could get shelter in one of the houses. It was a great bother to get our tents and bedding rolls out of the wagons, and I did not want to bother the weary men to do so and set up my tent. He found me and said he had arranged it. Seeing that the men were all settled, I did not put on any guard. I told the Captains to be ready to march at four-thirty and followed Dan Keller, my adjutant, to our quarters. We put our weary horses in a shed, taking off their saddles and giving them hay, and then entered this tiny house. Here we found a man and his wife, who treated us kindly and gave us most welcome hot coffee. We went upstairs and found two clean beds, an unexpected joy. I expected to sleep on the floor or sit out the night in a chair. It was a typical small peasant's house. The stone walls and rough beams had no covering. There was heat only in the kitchens, and then only at meal times. The upper floor where we slept reminded one of a hay loft. But the two single beds were clean and comfortable, and the bed linen was spotless and fresh, doubtless newly made up for us, and we slept in our dirty clothes, taking off only our coats and boots.

It never occurred to me that night, too tired as I was, to inquire into things, that we were using the only two beds in the house. But such was the rather astonishing fact, as I learned from Lieutenant Keller in the morning. This hospitable French peasant, and his no less hospitable wife, had given up their own beds to us, and had sat up all night in chairs.

We slept like logs, and immediately, so it seemed, the old peasant was shaking me by the shoulder. It was four o'clock and still dusk outside. We were soon eating a hasty but good breakfast of eggs, bread and coffee. Our orderlies had found and saddled our horses and we rode out to the battalion to find the companies packed up and forming line in the field.

The rolling kitchens were steaming, but as breakfast was not yet ready I decided to pull out and halt for it later. I instructed Lieutenants Swank and Naill with their scout detachment to form the rear guard and help the wagon train out of the mud on to the road. We set out in the early morning light. It was cloudy and very damp and muddy. No bright sunrise to cheer us. To my surprise we first passed through a large straggling village. Pierrefaites proved to be a good sized place, in which all of my men could have been sheltered. We had but reached the outskirts when we camped. In the dark and rain we could not see, and had mistaken the first group of houses for the village. But it did not matter much. The men had been fairly comfortable and had had six hours' sleep, and seemed much refreshed and fairly cheerful.

Leaving the village behind we began to descend a long winding hill road. A passing truck informed me that the entraining station at La Ferte-sur-Amance was at the foot of the hill a little more than a kilometer away. As we now had plenty of time, I halted for breakfast, the first hot meal the men had had since we started yesterday morning. Instructing Captain Knack to allow the men a half hour for breakfast, and then to bring the battalion on, I told him how far our destination was, I rode off down the hill to the village and on to the loading platforms. Here I found Colonel Charles and reported to him, telling him where my men were. He seemed glad and relieved to see me. When my men arrived they halted in the mud near the platforms, unslung packs and waited in the rain and mud for some hours. Sunny France indeed. Rainy, muddy France we thought a much truer name. Nearly every day it rained, and rarely were we free from our very close and annoying friend the mud.

The Third Battalion, under Major Atwood, loaded on to the tiny

French train first. It was their first experience in such work and there was, of course, some confusion and blundering. This was to be expected. My Captains and I stood by and watched carefully, learning all we could as our turn came next. The Colonel was everywhere fussing and butting in, and hindering very considerably the Majors' efforts. Two hours was allowed for each battalion to load. They just about made it. Just as they pulled out Atwood came up to me and smiled and said, "Now it is your turn to catch it Old Man." He swung on to his train as it passed and waved me a pitying farewell.

But I had profited by his experience and had learned something. While they were placing my cars I called the company commanders together and assigned each a task. Captain Knack was to load his men and then the large pile of provisions, the latter on flat cars. Captain Burrage would load his men and our horses. Captain Fatzinger would load his men and our wagons. Lieutenant Odum of Company A, in command of same, also had a task, which I have forgotten. As soon as the cars were placed we began at once to load on the men, forty with all their equipment, to each small box car.

I had been at the station getting the ticket or bill of lading for my battalion and wagon train, which ticket I still have. It set forth the number of men, officers, wagons and horses. The officers had an ancient passenger coach, which leaked at different places, but we did not complain. It was much better than marching in the rain and mud. We traveled northward on the Paris-Belfort Line, and passed thru the beautiful and historic Marne Valley. We passed many trains coming down from the Front loaded with tired and dirty soldiers, who did not hesitate to let us green troops see their genial contempt for us. That night about ten o'clock we reached our destination at Revigny in the Department of the Meuse. It was raining hard and we were all tired. In my innocence I thought the kindhearted railway officers would not expect us to unload in the dark and rain. It seemed outrageous to ask it. Soon an officer hammered on our door and asked for the commanding officer. "You must unload at once Major and clear out of the yards, as other trains are just behind you and will need the platforms."

So we got out, and down came the beastly rain in sheets. The captains had the same tasks as when loading, but it was a harder job, on account of the dark and we were allowed but few lights as the Germans might bomb the place. Our first warning of the Germans. We were near the Front, so we thought.

While we were unloading in the rain, struggling with our wagons and horses, to my intense anger a truck train came down the platform alongside of my train and completely blocked our work. I jumped on the drivers hard, but they referred me to their captain. I soon found him and ordered him to get out at once. He demurred saying he was there to get the baggage on the other side of the platform. He regretted to interfere with me, but meant to carry out his orders. In fact he verged on impudence. Then I lit into him good and plenty, ordered him to move at once, told him to be d--- careful how he spoke to me, his superior officer, giving him my name and rank, and asked his name in order to report him for disrespect to a superior and a few other military crimes. The Captain seemed to think better of it, apologized, and pulled back his trucks at once. Perhaps I was over conscious of my lately acquired dignity as Major, having been such but six days, but anyway I took that gentleman down a bit and got rid of him.

Nearby I heard a major arguing with the railway officers about unloading. He refused flatly at first to unload in the dark and rain, saying he would do so at daybreak. They told him he had been there an hour and in one more hour they would pull out his train. He thought better of it later and began hurriedly to unload, and in the midst of it, they backed out his train with half of his men and baggage on it. Such cursing and shouting of protests, all to no avail. Away went his train and half of his outfit, leaving him in a devil of a mess, which probably cost him his job.

Well under our allotted time, we were unloaded, the wagons loaded and the companies formed. Before we marched out I called Lieutenants Swank and Naill, gave them a lighted lantern, showed them where the town of Tremont where we were going was, told them to lead off and not get me lost. We studied the map a while, and then we set out on another wet night march.

After marching for three or four hours my men began to fall out in large numbers. The train ride, packed in as they had been, had been no real rest. I knew I had not much farther to go, and I did not want another long struggle, like the previous night, so I halted in a large village, called the company commanders and told them to let their men scatter among these houses and barns for a couple of hours rest until daybreak. At the order the men scattered, at once, and in five minutes not a man of the thousand was in sight. Every shed and barn and dog house must have been filled with them. Dan Keller and I rode up a side street and finding a large barn, we opened the door, took in our horses, were about to climb into a wagon full of straw, when we saw it was full of sleeping soldiers, then we pulled down some straw in a corner on the floor, and lay down with our overcoats over us and slept.

We were awakened at daybreak by voices, and got up to find, to our surprise, a group of Italian soldiers, examining our horses and about, no doubt, to examine our saddle bags. When we got up they stepped back, not having seen us before, but did not offer to salute or address us.

This town was full of Italian infantry resting.[4] I was surprised to see them in France. Were France, England, and Belgium so hard pushed that they must bring over Italian troops? But the facts are that these countries sent many times more troops to Italy to help her than she ever sent to France. But we did not know this at the time, and thought it a bad sign for the condition of the Allies in France.

We returned to the main street, and there found the rolling kitchens steaming and the smell of coffee and slum (meat and vegetable stew) in the air. Many of my men and officers were gathered around them eating. I had the buglers sound mess call several times, and the rest of the men came running from all directions. I thought that would rout them out and it did.

There were many Italian soldiers and some officers in the street now and they stared at my men with much curiosity, and were no less scrutinized by my soldiers. The Italian officers offered us no military courtesy and we gave them no salutes. Such was the good effect of the hot meal that we marched out of that village; the men roaring, "Pack up your troubles in your old kit-bag" at the top of their voices. Very

4. The Italian Second Corps was involved in the Second Battle of the Marne. They suffered significant casualties blunting the German offensive.

different from our weary slovenly entrance. I rode back to see if all the men had gone and discovered only one straggler, who when he saw me scurried off down the road after the column at top speed.

After leaving this village, we began to climb long steep hills, and our faithful friend the rain descended upon us in generous and continued sheets. The singing died out rather abruptly, and we were reduced to silent foot slogging. Fortunately the way to Tremont, our destination, was not long, about three kilometers. On the way we passed American machine gun companies marching in the opposite direction, units of our own division, which was arriving and concentrating about Tremont. These machine gun companies were very short of mules, and had one mule pulling several carts, hitched together, with the men helping to pull them. Why they should be approaching the Front so short of mules I could not understand. We were fully equipped in all things, except that the men of our regiment machine gun company had no revolvers for defense in close action, actually fighting the Argonne Battle without any means of defense except their machine guns. As they did not have rifles they were personally unarmed in this battle, and would have been entirely defenseless in hand to hand combat, which fortunately they did not experience, but what assurance had they that they would not do so?

We entered Tremont almost seven in the morning, being the first unit to reach that place. It was a large village, with a number of fine large private homes, built by natives who had made their fortunes elsewhere, and who had returned here to live for a part of the year, at least, as the French often do.

We hunted up the Town Major, an excitable little French lieutenant, who was in charge of the billeting of troops here. When he discovered that two battalions, ours and another to follow, were to be billeted in his town he immediately blew up, and got tremendously excited. Never before had he had to billet more than one battalion. It was impossible. Such waving of hands, such furious talk, such a fool attitude about a job that he had to do anyway. I let him blow off a lot of steam, and then told him to get busy at once and get my men out of the rain. We got our list of billets, a sketch showing the streets and houses and how many men to go in each. I put Lieutenant Swank in charge of settling the men and officers in their houses and in an hour the whole battalion was under cover, the companies housed together by streets, so that they could assemble promptly.

In the midst of this work the Brigade Commander, General Noble, arrived, warm and dry in his car. Apparently out of humor, he called me to his car. He asked me if I was in command of the town. I told him I had not been so designated. "Are you the ranking officer present?" I did not know that, our Colonel might be in town, he was due here. He asked where his own quarters were. I told him I did not know about any quarters except those of my own battalion, which was not yet completely quartered. I had only just arrived and had been completely busy getting my battalion settled. I gave him to understand that his quarters were none of my affair. He had plenty of aides to locate them. It was really not in the least any of my business. He was unreasonable and cross and said, "Think up, Major, think up, don't think down all the time." Such utter rot. My job was to think about my battalion and about it solely and only, and he knew that mighty well. I left him to find his own quarters.

Expecting a similar fuss with our Colonel, I found out where his quarters were, after finishing with my men (I would not have done it before), and when he arrived I had him taken there, reporting to him myself the facts of my journey, and that my men were all quartered and comfortable. He seemed pleased and was very pleasant.

My own quarters were in the City Hall, which was a combination mayor's residence and municipal building. It was a large building on the hillside, overlooking the town, and I had a large room on the third floor, well-furnished and comfortable, but I did not have a fire and it was raining and chilly.

We arranged an officers' mess, with a French woman at the house where Lieutenant Joseph Dyer lived. She was an excellent cook and we fared very well. About six officers were in on this mess. The first night we entertained Colonel Charles, Major Cornwell, and Captain Manning at dinner, as they had not as yet arranged for their meals. Another guest at this meal was Y.M.C.A. Secretary D. M. "Judge" Kimbrough, a man who was to become one of my closest and dearest friends.[5] He had

---

5. Donald M. Kimbrough was a chancery court judge from Mississippi. He was also a professor at the University of Mississippi School of Law, a position he returned to after his service in the YMCA at the front. Michael Landon, *The University of Mississippi School of Law: A Sesquicentennial History* (Jackson: University Press of Mississippi, 2006), 52–53.

such a wonderful genial smile, and seemed such a fine character that I was greatly attracted to him at once. He said that he was assigned to our Second Battalion but after we talked awhile, he accepted my invitation to transfer to my battalion, which was soon arranged.

One of his most important services was to keep his little canteen supplied with candy, cakes, cigarettes, tobacco, cigars, writing paper, and many other little comforts for my men. The importance of these little luxuries to men deprived of all other good things of life was very great, and helped the spirits of the men, very greatly.

We remained in Tremont three days, during which we rested and had no drill as the skies were full of airplanes, many of them Germans, and we did not want assemblies of soldiers to let them know the town was full of troops, and perhaps bring down a bombing fleet upon us. Groups of men were strictly forbidden, and all walked close to the houses, and kept nearly all the time in the houses. On the 13th, orders to move came, and we were told we would travel by French truck or camion train. We sent off our wagon train and our horses during the day, and also reduced our personal loads as much as possible. A large room was filled with surplus and unnecessary things, and it was all left behind.

At evening a long train of camions came into the town, war-worn and battered looking, very high, and very large, each manned by two Chinese in sheepskin coats.[6] Silent, queer looking men with an odor all their own. This was our first view of such war transport, and we found it very interesting. The train stopped, when half through the town, extending for a long way on each side, and we hastily loaded in the men, twenty-two to each camion, and the men were terribly crowded to get that number in. About fifteen in each would have allowed them some comfort, but our men were fast learning that comfort is a rare thing in war.

Seeing that most of them were loaded and the officers were finishing up the task quickly, for they gave us but little time, I walked up to the front of the train, where I was told I would find a seat in a touring car.

6. These drivers were not Chinese. They hailed from French Indochina and would today be described as Vietnamese. Their presence here is one of many reminders in Parkin's text that France fought in World War I as a colonial power with territory in Africa and Southeast Asia.

Just as I neared the head of the column a shrill whistle sounded, and the trucks began to move. So I climbed into the nearest one, and found a few officers in it. All night we rode through the darkness, bumping and jolting on the hard boards. Captain Ben Hewitt and I stretched out on the dirty floor, side by side, with a blanket over us, and slept in spells, but we got no real sleep. The only town I knew we were passing through was the large, partly ruined town of Bar-le-Duc. Practice makes perfect, of course, but it seemed a wonderful thing to us that these Chinese could drive those great trucks, at good speed, with no headlights and only the small red taillight of the truck ahead to guide them, keeping very close together all the time, and yet never touching each other.

In the very early morning we reached Blercourt, and I was ordered to unload and get under cover as quickly as possible. I was to march on a short way to the ruined village of Dombasle, our first war wrecked village, and here our first taste of shellfire and bombs. We got our men off the trucks quickly and formed for the march, platoons in column of twos, on the side of the road, with a long interval between the platoons, which formation was the one used at the Front, as it did not show the men on the road so much to the enemy airmen, but which scattered my battalion over a long stretch of road.

After we started, a billeting officer, an Englishman in our service, took me ahead, in his Ford car, and showed me the town of Dombasle, a poor and ruined place, with scarcely a roof in it. Then he took me back to my column, and as we were marching up, Captain Manning, adjutant of the regiment, came up in a Ford, stopped, and told me that I could not stay in Dombasle, as the place was wrecked and offered no shelter. He wanted me to halt until he got my place changed, but I told him I must get off the road as soon as possible, and, if he got me different orders, he could overtake me with them. He did not do so, and I marched on to the town. Poor Manning, new to the French, as were all of us, thought the town unfit for troops. Many worse places we had later on, and glad enough to get them. But I received orders again and marched through this town on up nearer the Front, putting part of my command in dugouts, our first experience with them, and part in the woods in shelter tents. We were now near Camp Normandy. Captain Knack and I did not like the dugouts, which were damp, dirty, and smelly, and inhabited by large rats, so he found us a small shack, with beds made of chicken wire, most uncomfortable things, but it had good air, and we had it cleaned out.

Our camp was about two miles behind the actual Front lines and was a station for reserve troops, but we were to move up and relieve the French troops. In fact the 315th was to take over the Front lines that day, and during this day we heard our first enemy shells. They shrieked over our heads very high up and burst in and around Dombasle. We were glad we were not there, and laughed to think that pompous old General Noble was getting his first taste of shells, and getting it good too. Major Cornwell told me afterwards that it got so hot that he and the Colonel took refuge in a deep ditch from the shells, which annoyed them very considerably.

Nearby, hidden in the woods, were French batteries of the "famous soixante-quinze" guns; we pronounced it "Swas-and-cans."[7] These wonderful guns had saved France many times in battle, the clouds of their shells crushing and demoralizing the advancing hordes of Germans. Our own artillery used these guns, and an artillery Captain told me that the French record was sixteen shots a minute, but his men had raised the record to twenty-one shots a minute, and had done it by reloading the gun at the pause in its recoil, before the gun starts back to the gun carriage. It seemed incredible that men could work so fast, but I give the story as told. These 75s were the only guns that could keep anywhere near our advance in the Argonne.

As we heard them this day in the woods they had a most unusual sound, unlike any gun I ever heard before. It is best described as a short, quick metallic bark, very sharp with a brassy tang to it. This Front country was most interesting to us, and we spent the day getting acquainted with it. Across the road from our woods, where our camp was, there lay a very large French military graveyard. Thousands of graves, laid out in endless rows, mute evidence of the terrible and prolonged fighting which had occurred in this section. As I came up the road, I had noticed

7. French 75mm field guns, the best weapons of their kind. These were effective against attacking infantry and proved extremely reliable at the front. They were much less effective against fortified positions. World War I era film footage confirms that American artillerymen could, in fact, do exactly what Parkin describes here—reload the gun during the split second when the barrel was extended backwards in its recoil position.

a large purplish sheen on the hillside, and could not imagine what it could be. I found on approaching closer that it was the sun shining on the decorations of all this mass of graves. Each grave had a large red, white, and blue cockade, with long streamers to it, all made of painted tin. The rattling of these decorations in the wind, at night, was a weird and ghostly sound. Poor France, how many of these large graveyards we passed on our marches, always in respectful silence.

6

On the Front Line

On this day, September 14, 1918, we saw our first aeroplane fight. High over our heads, two considerable groups of aeroplanes waged battle with each other, and the rattle of machine guns was continuous and fierce. As they whirled and fought before our astonished eyes, many shells burst around them, some with black smoke and some with white. We understood the black smoke shells were German and the white French. Both sides seemed to us to shoot indiscriminately at the whole mass. We expected to see many aeroplanes drop, but not so. Only one fell, turning over and over, and we let out a gasp of sympathy for the poor fellow, but having fallen some distance, he straightened up and returned to the fight, and soon both sides drew off.

Nearby our miserable camp was a large collection of fine stone huts with windows and porches. Only some of these were occupied by French officers. I had Dan Keller ask a French officer if we could not use the vacant ones, but he was told they belonged to a different camp, and it was impossible. It did not seem very hospitable to us, but doubtless it was best for us to remain in the camp to which we were assigned, but it did not seem proper then. Our plain wooden shack was not fit for an American cow, but we later on lived in much worse, or in none at all.

In the afternoon I received orders to march back through Dombasle to another camp further to the rear. Why we should move was not explained to us. It later proved one of these most annoying mistakes that are frequently made in war. After dark I set out down the fine road, through the ruined village, and on to our new camp some distance further on in a large wood. At Dombasle the road forked, and to be sure all were coming Keller and I dropped out by the roadside to watch the men pass. Two companies only passed, and the road was empty. I had lost half of my battalion. I was much provoked, as I had warned the captains to keep in touch with each other. Ordering Keller to gallop to the head of the column and halt it and wait for me, I set off down the road at a gallop, and at the crossroads took the other road and soon overtook my two lost companies, plodding peacefully along behind a French Battery. I am afraid I said some stiff things to Captain Fatzinger, for I was angry. He claimed the battery had cut in ahead of him, and he thought we were just ahead of it. Of course this was no excuse, and I told him so rather bluntly.

After uniting my battalion we went on and reached our camp without further mishap, but in the blackest time of the night. Keller, who had been there before, was of the greatest help in getting the men into the various large shacks, which were scattered throughout the wood. Plain bare things, their only quality was that they were dry. They were all filthy, the French camps being always disgracefully filthy and messy. Our first task always was to clean them up so that they would be fit to live in. The French Army knows nothing of cleanliness and neatness as we know it. There are no braver soldiers, but there are much cleaner soldiers, and it is a quality well worth while in war, especially appreciated by the people who come after you.

It took a long time in the pitch black darkness with only a few electric torches, to get the men into the shacks, but I always made it a rule in France never to think of my own comfort until all of my men were cared for. This night I found some of my officers thought otherwise, and I told them that in future they would provide for themselves only after their men were provided for. There were plenty of very neat little officers' shacks, of one or two rooms, and the best one had been reserved for me, and I had Keller put in one nearby. In the morning we surveyed our camp and found it a very comfortable, pretty place, much better than the one we had left. I had been told that my wagon train, which I had not seen since it left me at Tremont on the 11th, would join me today, but as it did not come I sent some officers out on bicycles to hunt for it. We were now completely without food of any kind. The Colonel arrived, and I told him we had nothing to eat and that our wagon train had not joined us. He said he would see that we got food, and hurried away. He was good at such things, and in a couple of hours a large truckload of food reached us, and it was most welcome.

At length our missing wagon train arrived, found and brought in by that hustling young officer, Lieutenant John Swank of my scout section, and soon the rolling kitchens were steaming, and we had a hot dinner. There were considerable vegetable gardens in this camp, but the French camp staff would not allow us to take anything from these gardens. It was apparently a permanent rest camp, or camp for reserve troops, and it was well built and equipped with stoves. The officers' quarters were very comfortable and fitted with rough furniture and beds. But our stay was not to be long. That evening a divisional staff officer arrived in an automobile with orders for me to move again that night. He showed me a map and gave me a choice of my old camp, or Camp Normandy. I chose Camp Normandy, knowing it could not be worse than my old camp, and hoping it would be better.

We set out at dusk back up the road to Dombasle. It was a moonlight night, and I warned the men that if aeroplanes came over us not to look up at them, as their white faces would betray our position. We had not been on our way long when I heard aeroplanes over us, and immediately a large bomb with a brilliant red flash burst in the field near the column. It was our first bombing attack and startled me considerably. I halted the column and moved it off the white road onto the grass, so that we should not make such a target. To my dismay I saw that the whole thousand greenhorns were gaping at the sky, the long line of white faces showing very plainly in the moonlight. I rode down the line, handing out pungent, forceful remarks, which soon put those faces down under the helmets where they belonged. Several other bombs burst near us and scared us all I think, then machine gun fire broke out above us, and the German airman was driven off, to our great relief. On a nearby road I noticed a French battery standing under the bank at the roadside, absolutely motionless. Even the horses seemed to know the danger and were quiet.

I do not feel that I have adequately described the awfulness of these bombs and their effect upon green troops, nor do I feel that my pen is capable. First you hear a heavy thud on the ground followed instantly by a blinding, shattering crash and brilliant flash of red, which momentarily lights up the vicinity. The shriek and whiz of flying pieces follows, and you cannot help ducking and shrinking. Your ears are shocked and you stumble and are confused. You are so demoralized by a close explosion that you do not know at once whether you are hit or not. You cannot help think of how terribly you will be mutilated if a piece of the bomb strikes you. Every soldier feels that if he must be hit, he wants it to be a clean bullet wound and not a tearing mutilating wound from a piece of bomb or shell. I was badly frightened on this occasion, but responsibility for my battalion helped me master my fear. Doubtless the men were badly frightened also, but except for a swerving off the road near the point of explosion, they gave no evidence of their terror.

As we passed through the town of Dombasle-en-Argonne, an American truck train attempted to cut through my column and block the road for me. I quickly rode to the point of contact and putting my horse across the road in front of the trucks, ordered them to stop. A transport officer came up and got mad and disputed my right of way. I was passing the crossroad before he came up and I had the right of way as he knew or should have known, and I would not give it up. The leading truck started and nearly hit my horse, and then I got mad but kept my horse right in front of the truck and spoke to the transport people in the good old Army style, which seemed to quiet or awe them, I am not sure which, but they waited until my column all passed. I had many such fights for right of way in the night marches in France, with both French and American units.

When I had finished my fight with the truck train in Dombasle and my men had passed, I was about to follow them when an officer who had been standing by the road spoke to me. I had not noticed him before. It was General Noble. I saluted and got off my horse, making some apology for the manner in which I had been obliged to talk to hold the road.

"That's all right, Major, when you have a job like that to do, do it right. I don't blame you in the least. You were in the right," said the General.

He asked me some questions as to my cause for moving, and I explained it to him, mounted my horse and trotted off up the road after my battalion. The moonlight was very brilliant, I remember, and almost as clear as day. There was much traffic on the road, as this was a main artery for this front, and all the movement of troops and supplies goes on at night. Artillery, troops, all French, passed us coming down, and also long trains of wagons and trucks. In spite of long years of war the French soldiers were still a gay, cheerful, and chattering lot, and I was much amused by the greetings exchanged between them and my men. Once in a while a staff car, or a dispatch carrier on a noisy motorcycle, would tear past us without lights, using the center of the road where they had very little room, but wonderful to see and they never seemed to hit anything or anybody.

We passed our old camp and the large ghostly graveyard near it. Most of those resting therein had marched up this same old road, hopeful of surviving the dangers of the battle to which we were getting nearer at every step, but soldiers do not think long about such things, each hoping that it will be the other fellow who will get hit and that he will come through.

We arrived at our new location, called "Camp de Normandie," in the very early gray of a chilly morning. It consisted of a large group of cheerless shacks built of wood and tar paper or corrugated iron, these last being half round in shape, called elephant huts, and dry and cozy, really the best and warmest huts in France. But these shacks were only for officers, and the men must use the very large and deep dugouts, about thirty feet deep. The camp major, a middle-aged fat French sergeant, showed us over the place. The dugouts were dirty, musty, and to us, new to such things, entirely unbearable. Water dripped from the ceilings and covered the floors with pools. We went down endless, muddy, wet wooden steps, steep and slippery. The bunks were filled with mouldy straw and rags. Electric lights were provided, but we could not use them as the engines were not running. Candles would not help much in utter darkness. The bunks were built in tiers right up to the ceilings.

This was our first view of front line shell-proof dugouts. It seemed a horrible, unhealthy place to put my good clean American boys to live. We were not yet ready to accept all the conditions of life at the Front, and since the French sergeant said that German shells had been very infrequent of late in this camp, I decided to let my companies camp above ground in the clean green woods, using their pup tents, but camping as near as possible to the dugouts to which the companies were assigned so that in case of heavy shell fire the men could go below ground as quickly as possible. The officers were assigned to the huts, and I had the largest and best in the center of the camp. It had four small bedrooms leading off a large center room, which was used as a living room, office and dining room. This hut was lightly constructed of wood, giving no protection at all from shells, as were all of the others.

Two officers lived in the woods with each company, using shelter tents. The officers of the companies took turns at this. All through the war part of the officers were constantly right with the men at all times. We never left them alone, not that we did not trust them, but because it was our duty to look after them constantly.

My hut was furnished with rough furniture and beds and had a large stone fireplace, where we often had a fire in the evening. There was a porch with benches, and board walks led all over the camp, which was fortunate as the place was very muddy. My staff officers lived here with me, Lieutenants Keller, Swank, and Naill. We were all good friends and made an agreeable and happy family.

Judge Kimbrough found a large shack nearby called a "Foyer de Soldat," and here opened his canteen and sold supplies of all kinds he could get to the men. He never lacked customers. We had trouble getting the waiting line of men to stand close under the eaves of the building so as not to be seen by enemy airmen. The Judge lived in his shack but took his meals with us and spent some of his evenings with us, but we could not get much of his time. He felt that he should devote practically all of it to the men, with whom he was justly very popular and much thought of. Many a down-hearted fellow the Judge cheered up and helped.

In this camp we had our first experience with gas attack alarms, most of them in fact nearly all were false, and many amusing things happened in consequence. We experienced no gas waves, and the alarms were started by an occasional gas shell, the effect of which was always very local. But orders had been given to pass along all gas alarms. This was done by the sentries and military police grinding Klaxons.[1] If a gas shell fell anywhere behind the front trenches, the nearest sentry started grinding his Klaxon, and for miles in both directions the noise was continued, and at first all hastily put on their masks. It was ridiculous and utterly useless, but it was the natural result of a fool order and green troops. Half the time the "all clear" signal was not passed, and

1. A hand-wound siren.

some of us sat for hours half smothered in the masks, when there was no gas within a mile of us. I remember passing Capt. Knack's hut, and he came out with his mask on and asked when the "All clear" signal had been passed. I told him about an hour ago. He had been sitting all this time with his mask on and was entirely disgusted with the gas alarms. I had a good laugh at his expense. It did seem ridiculous.

Another time Dan Keller, during an alarm, went to sleep with his mask on. One makes such a queer sucking noise breathing with one on. This noise awakened me, and I woke up Dan, whose head and face were bathed in sweat, and I had a good laugh at him also. Captain Feuardent, the French officer attached to our regiment, was much disgusted with such a terrible fuss about gas and said he had never seen troops so nervous and fearful over it. The horrors of gas had been so drilled into us that it was no wonder we at first made fools of ourselves over it. We learned soon how and when to use our masks. The alarms the first few nights were so frequent that we finally ignored them altogether, which was perhaps not wise but much more comfortable.

During these days we spent at Camp de Normandie, the 315th Infantry, now under command of our old Lt. Col. A. C. Knowles, had been in the front trenches having relieved the French troops. Since we were to relieve this regiment in a few days, I received orders to take my company commanders and visit the section I was to take over in order to familiarize myself with it. This was always done by officers of the relieving regiment when possible. We went up one morning for this purpose, and as we went along through the woods and fields we were simply amazed at the quantity of artillery we came across. Living so near it, we had been entirely unaware of its existence, except those batteries near our camp. Of course it was all moved in at night and was so cleverly camouflaged that it was practically invisible until you came right upon it. The art of camouflage had been developed to a fine art, and the results obtained are astonishing.[2] It is necessary to hide the guns from the enemy airmen, to protect them and also keep the enemy from learning of an artillery concentration on the front. Out in

2. The use of air reconnaissance during the war proved that necessity was the better part of invention. Gun crews knew the risk of aerial spotting and photography came with the potential for deadly enemy counter-battery fire, so they concealed their locations from observation.

some open grass fields were placed whole batteries of light guns in gun pits, the whole being covered over so cleverly with camouflage cloth screens, as to be entirely invisible until you were within a few yards of it. Some we only discovered by hearing the men's voices as we went by.

There were guns of every size and shape from the immense naval guns, manned by French sailors, the great howitzers of huge bulk down to the little 75s. They were packed in close in such numbers that we were continually coming on them and at times had to hunt a path through them. Shells of all kinds and sizes were piled all through the woods in enormous quantities, covered with green branches and cloth. The ditches on the roadside were full of shells, seemingly miles of them. Gun pits had been dug by the gunners for nearly all of the guns, and on the roadsides in the banks great square places had been cut out of the earth, into which great guns had been pushed and set up for firing. Even to our inexperienced eyes here was positive evidence of a coming attack by our army, and on a great scale at that, for these guns were not here for defensive purposes. No such number would be needed for that

Half way up to the front line we came upon a large collection of stone huts, built into the hillside, and so protected largely from German shell fire. In one of these, very comfortable and well housed, we found Col. Knowles, who received us very kindly and showed us maps and gave us directions and advice as to reaching his front line. After a short rest here we went on to the trenches, avoiding some high places which our guides said were under observation by the enemy. By the side of our path ran a ditch filled with telephone and electric wires. There were a great number of them. A shell falling in this small ditch might cut them all at once, but being collected so, it was not a long job to repair the whole lot. Occasional shells fell on the sector near enough for us to see the effects, and we saw dirt and stones thrown up and holes dug in the earth.

Reaching the rear section of the actual front line, we looked about us with great interest. So much had we heard and read of this much desired and much hated place. Your mental attitude depends upon your place in the war scheme, on whether you are going up for the first time or going up again.

We were on the Avocourt-Malancourt Sector of the Argonne Forest Front. This was a quiet sector, no fighting nor raiding had been going on for months, and only occasional shell fire disturbed the absolute peace of this front, which in other days had seen terrible fighting between the French and Germans, especially bitter had been the struggle for Hill 304, which was on our front. Other divisions had weeks of this experience on a quiet front and training there under French instruction. Our division had but a few days and no front line training.

I was taken to the P.C. (Post of Command) of Major Patterson of the 315th, whom I was to relieve. He was an old Pittsburgh and Fort Niagara friend and he received me cordially in his little shack, which consisted of two white-washed rooms, a table and chairs in the front room, and two beds in the back room. It had a half round corrugated steel roof, not shellproof, but the entrance to a large deep dugout was right at his door. Nearby was a hut where his meals were cooked. Major Patterson complained that he had been bothered to death by visits of groups of officers from the division who expected him, at any hour of the day or night, to explain the maps and front to them and provide them with a meal. Knowing that I was to relieve him, he very willingly went over all the maps and orders with me in great detail and gave me all the information he had. These maps showed the entire trench and defensive system and the locations for machine guns, supply and ammunition stations, points of rally, strong points, routes of communication, location of troops in front trench and reserve trenches, in fact all that a commander of the section would need to know. There were also maps of the enemy's trenches and confidential information as to the troops in them, their numbers and condition of morale, all obtained by the intelligence service. It seemed very complete and wonderful to know so much about the Germans, but I guess they knew just as much about us.

Major Patterson gave us a guide and we set out for the front trench. We were most anxious to stand at last in the very front trench. We went up a long communication trench or boyau as the French call it. It was very deep, the sides well above our heads, and we walked the entire way on duck-boards or boardwalk. At places where the sides were lower we looked out over the fields and saw great wide barriers of rusted barbed wire running across the front in endless lines. Here and there we mounted steps in the side of the trench and looked out over the fields from machine gun and observation positions. All avenues of approach were well covered by these very efficient looking little guns, whose crews lay near in the trench, and many boxes of ammunition were stacked nearby. Now and then we passed small ammunition dumps, full of boxes of hand grenades and rifle cartridges. In another place in pockets in the wall of the trench we saw shovels and picks and tools of all kinds. First aid stations for the wounded were ready and equipped. Finally, after a long walk, we stood in the goal of our ambition, after many months, the front trench.

We were told that the French had wrested these trenches from the Germans, and some trenches led towards the Germans, blocked only with twisted masses of rusted barbed wire. That did not seem sufficient protection to me, but it had to the French, who had fought here, so we must be content with it. I was told that it was not dangerous here to look over the top if only one at a time did so. I mounted on the step and looked out over No Man's Land, my first view of this terrible land, of which I had heard and read so much for over four years.

It was desolation itself. Ominous, dread inspiring, it held me silent and deeply impressed. Broken trees, bare shafts of trees, broken rusted wire, shell holes, weeds, a torn and broken and utterly wasted place.[3] On a slope some two hundred yards away the German trenches were pointed out to me, but all was quiet and still there. I could not see a man. But doubtless we were seen and watched, and I had an uncanny feeling that I was being observed as I stood there.

We, new soldiers, were all impressed by the front line and made our long walk back to Camp de Normandie in silence for the most part, each thinking of what we had seen and what the front might mean to us.

Back at camp I received word that the entire regiment would concentrate in and around Camp de Normandie. We must provide quarters for many more officers. I gave up my fine big hut to Col. Charles and the regimental staff, not through any desire to deprive myself, but because the Colonel gets the best quarters always. My own officers doubled up

---

3. Parkin joins a long list of other war memoirists in describing the desolation of No Man's Land as seen for the first time. Years of artillery bombardments, attacks, and the detritus of stagnant living, meant that the closer one got to the front, the more likely that you would be affronted by a poisonous environment where quite literally men moldered into the shell holes.

in the huts, some sergeants were put out of huts, and ordered to pitch their tents. Dan Keller and I assigned all of the huts to the arriving officers, and they got settled without any trouble. The Colonel was much pleased with the hut I had given to him, as he well might be. Lt. Col. Robert Meador, who could not endure Col. Charles, remained with the Second Battalion in a nearby camp. He avoided Col. Charles as much as was possible.

On the evening of September 24, 1918, I moved my battalion out of Camp de Normandie and up into the front lines, relieving the First Battalion of the 315th Infantry under Major Patterson. We went in very light, leaving our packs, blankets, and everything we could spare, piled in heaps in the woods of Camp de Normandie under a guard. We never got much of this stuff back, as the Germans shelled the place heavily, destroying most of it, and looters, French we thought, stole most of what was not destroyed.

As it was dusk I rode my horse up to the lines. We moved in without loss, as there was but little shell fire. Judge Kimbrough, who had a lot of "Y" supplies in his hut, stayed behind to look after them, but I knew from his attitude that he wanted to go with us. Threading our way through the artillery, we reached the station of the reserve company, and here I left Captain Burrage with Company D as my reserve.

We went into the trenches west of the village of Esnes and of Hill 304. I reported to Major Patterson, and my captains, who knew the ground, having been there before with me, took their companies forward to relieve Major Patterson's companies. He and I sat in his hut for an hour, talking and waiting for the relief to be reported as completed, when I would take over the command. The report came in that the relief was accomplished, and Major Patterson went off to the rear, riding my horse back to Camp de Normandie. Just as he was leaving, we stood together watching his men march past, and the shell fire became fairly heavy passing pretty close over our heads. It confused his men a little, and the column got disordered some.

We were all of us in danger from these shells, but he kept his head and spoke sharply to his men, restoring order among them. I remember he said to them, "What do you think this is, a Sunday School picnic?" It wasn't, and we all knew it wasn't. These men were all new to shell fire and ducked every time a shell passed, and there is no more natural and yet no more foolish thing to do. The shell you hear has passed you, except when you hear a certain shell noise, a loud fierce hissing sound, and then is the time you want to drop flat or throw yourself into a trench or dugout, for that shell is coming right at you and will strike very near. You soon learn to understand shell noises at the front and can tell by the sound of the shell just after you hear the report of the gun whether it is going high and is harmless, or whether it is coming low and in your immediate vicinity. I cannot exactly explain the difference in the noise, but the droning sound is high and harmless and the shrill hissing shriek is low and dangerous. I have often seen groups of soldiers standing together with the noise of shells filling the air, and they entirely indifferent, and then suddenly you see them scatter and fall flat, and very quickly a shell bursts near. They have heard it and know it is coming.

My hut was called P.C. Copinard. Below it in a great deep dugout was a large telephone exchange, where a dozen operators sat before a large switchboard. It did look queer to see all this so far below ground, it was so entirely unexpected.

I understood that there was a thin line of experienced troops from a National Guard Division stretched along my extreme front. We were not entirely trusted as yet, being green troops. This night I had an experience which I do not understand to this day. We had been warned of German spies and had been ordered to be extremely careful in talking to strangers. A man was brought to my P.C. dressed as a private soldier, but wearing an officer's arms and equipment. He said that he commanded the battalion of National Guard troops stretched across my extreme front. For some reason I was suspicious of him. He began to ask me a lot of pertinent questions about the division, the impending attack, the hour of same, and other important things. I evaded his questions, and he learned nothing from me. He got angry over it, and I asked him to show me his papers and identify himself. He said he had no papers with him. In fact, he could not present any proof whatever of his identity, and I got more suspicious than ever and almost had him arrested. When he left me I had him followed, but my man lost him in the front trenches, so I did not get proof of him by that method, but rather more suspicion.

On September 25, I was visited by a number of parties of officers, all wanting to see my maps and all full of questions. Among them was my friend Major Pepper of Philadelphia, with whom I had been in Officers' School at Camp Meade and at Langres.[4] He was a very fine type of gentleman and a very good officer, as well as an esteemed friend. As he went away he called back some joking remark to me. Little did he know that tomorrow was his last day on earth. The next time I saw him was late in the afternoon of the next day, September 26, advancing with my men in support of his regiment, the 313th. I met two men carrying a stretcher. They stopped for a rest, and I went to look at the officer on the stretcher and was grieved to see that it was my friend Major Pepper. He was unconscious, and his face was almost purple, his eyes were turned back. I took his hand and spoke to him, but he was beyond talking. He was evidently very dangerously wounded. He was a large man and his bearers were exhausted. They asked where the nearest field hospital was. I did not know, but told them to go on to the rear. They said the surgeon had told them his only chance was to get to a hospital for an operation. I was shocked at his terrible condition. They went on, and I saw them stop soon and both bend over him, and I believe that he died then.

On the evening of September 25, I came out of my bedroom in my hut into the front room and found an officer lying on the floor there half asleep. To my surprise it was my friend Major Allen.[5] I knew him first at Plattsburg Training Camp in August 1916, where he was regimental surgeon, being a major in the Medical Corps Reserve at that time. He was very popular and efficient. I met him again at Camp Meade. He had transferred to the infantry, and I think he was in the 314th Infantry. I roused him and offered him my bed for a rest. He said he had been walking all day and was very tired, but only wanted to rest a while on the floor. Dinner was brought in, and I gave him a good hot dinner, for which he was very grateful and which he very much enjoyed. He did not know that it was his last dinner in this world. Poor fellow, he

4. Major Benjamin Franklin Pepper, thirty-nine years old, came from a prominent Philadelphia family and left behind a wife and three children. He was killed by a gunshot to the head at the front of his men. His adjutant, Francis Patterson, was killed next to him.

5. Major Alfred Reginald Allen was a University of Pennsylvania trained neurologist who joined the army reserves in 1915. He was in First Battalion of the 314th Infantry and is buried at the Meuse-Argonne American Cemetery.

was killed the next day, bravely leading his men in battle. He was regarded as one of the brightest officers in the Division and was much respected and liked. He had been an instructor in the machine gun school at Camp Meade, something very different from medicine, which had been his profession. Both he and Pepper would have reached high rank had they lived, and had the war gone on. They had more brains and ability than nine of ten regular officers I knew and quickly mastered the military profession. I never heard the details of his death, but hope I shall someday. Strange that I should entertain both of these brilliant young majors, good friends of mine, the day before they died, but yet when one remembers that it was on the Front and in battle, it is not strange but rather pathetic. What a shame to cut off thus abruptly two such splendid young men.

On the afternoon of September 25, 1918, I was summoned to Col. Knowles' P.C. for a conference on the attack of the morrow.[6] I had been out in the trenches and the messenger had trouble finding me and consequently arrived somewhat late at the conference, which was held in Col. Knowles' mess shack. All the battalion commanders of our Brigade, as well as the Lt. Colonels and the Colonels were present, seated at the mess table. Brig. General Noble presided, and I made my explanations and apologies to him, which he accepted kindly. He explained and described the plan of the attack for the 26th, and I thought he did it very well if somewhat generally and briefly. Our plan of attack was that used by the French. We were to advance in very open formation, the men ten paces apart and the lines or waves twenty paces in advance of each other. This would save loss by shell and machine gun fire, but it scattered the men very much and made it very hard to handle and control them, especially in wooded country, and we found this to be true in the battle.

The General explained the attack in general and answered questions, but said he would leave the details to the regimental and battalion

6. Plans for the opening phase of the Meuse-Argonne offensive were kept secret to maintain the element of surprise. Thus, Parkin and his fellow battalion commanders were unaware of the exact day/time of their attack or against what position they would be called to assault. The disadvantage of this approach was that attacking battalions did not have time to substantially train their men for the specific tasks they were called upon to do.

commanders, which was proper and correct. This was not always the method, and we sometimes received sheets of orders in such great detail and so voluminous that we did not even have time to read it all. Some Divisional Headquarters tried to do all the thinking even for the lieutenants and sergeants. They tried to arrange minute details even for small trench raids, things which we at the front knew better than they at the rear did and could have arranged and thought out better for ourselves. Such undue supervision and over-direction angered us and also even made our work harder for us.

For the attack tomorrow the Colonel told me that I was to have half of Company F as "moppers up" to follow my leading company and clean up the trenches and dugouts. I was to have a platoon of the regimental machine gun company and a one-pounder gun, all under my command. I also had a few squads of pioneers from the headquarters company to cut wire and help out in trench construction. So with all these extra troops and my own four companies I had nearly twelve hundred men to lead and direct in the battle. How all these units worked out I will describe in my description of the battle.

I was ordered to follow the 313th Infantry, which would lead on my half of our sector at a distance of 1,000 meters as support.[7] They would lead for two days, and then we would pass through them and take the lead ourselves. So the first two days our trouble should be shell fire mostly.

We were informed that the 37th Division would advance on our left; they were from Ohio. On our right the 4th Division would advance. The 314th Infantry would lead the 315th Infantry for two days. The formation of the division proved to be a mistake. A brigade should be echeloned in depth for driving attack. We had our brigades just the opposite. The 157th Brigade consisting of the 313th and 314th Infantry was at the front, and the 158th Brigade, consisting of the 315th and 316th Infantry, was in support. Each brigade should have had a regiment in the lead and the other in support. The regiments were shifted between the brigades during the battle to bring about this formation, and

7. The 313th Infantry "Baltimore's Own" was under the command of Colonel Claude Sweezey.

this led to much confusion. We changed our brigade not our position.

The attack was to be prepared by a tremendous artillery fire from twenty-three light batteries, twelve heavy batteries, and twelve heavy trench mortars, all these in support of our division alone.[8] After going over the plans thoroughly and getting an understanding of the, we separated back to our various commands. On the way back to my P.C. I met Lt. James Anderson with a few wagons loaded with food for our men, and I told him where to dump it. Unfortunately this food was not packed so that men could carry it properly, being in large boxes and cans and mostly uncooked. This was a serious error on the supply department's part. Consequently we went into battle with but little food and that mostly crackers and bread. You can't carry cans of beans and tomatoes and slabs of bacon, and it would be no use anyway, as you have no chance to cook it in battle. We should have had prepared and ready-cooked battle rations in small packages. There may have been such things, but we never had them. The Germans did, for we found them on their dead bodies and ate all we could find. The American pack has no place to carry food anyway. It is supposed to be rolled in your blankets, but we left our blankets behind. The small pack has a place for mess outfit, but no room for food. A little can be carried in the mess pan, but not enough to help much. Our troops should have had a haversack in which to carry food as the French had.

Col. Charles directed me to inform the National Guard Commander on our front to draw off, after dark, and move his men out. I sent this order to that officer and received a reply that it would be impossible for him to comply, as his men were scattered along a wide front, and he could not collect them in the dark. By this time regimental headquarters had moved up to my P.C., and Col. Charles and Capt. Manning had occupied my hut with their various aides and staff, leaving me and my staff without quarters. We did not mind, we were so busy and excited that we did not need quarters. I informed the Colonel of what the commander of the guard troops on our front had said, and he ordered me

8. The overall preliminary bombardment for the opening phase of the Meuse-Argonne was to be the largest cannonade to date in the history of the US Army with over 2,780 artillery pieces firing for three hours on the German positions before the infantry attacked. More shells were expended than during the entire American Civil War.

to go down to the telephone exchange and inform Divisional Head-quarters. This I did. Shells were falling rather heavily about us when I went down into the dugout, and I was glad to get below ground, as I was not yet accustomed to them and they frightened me consider-ably. Divisional Headquarters told me by phone to pass through the troops on my front when I advanced, and I started upstairs again. It was a most unusual and interesting sight to see this large telephone exchange, away down there underground, with the many operators busy with their phone calls, just like in a city exchange, the whole place dimly lighted by candles, the men working just as calmly as if in a city exchange in spite of the distant crash of bursting shells and the knowl-edge that a large shell might crush in the dugout on top of them, leav-ing them to a miserable death.

As I neared the top of the steps, the noise of the shells seemed to be much worse, and I hesitated, fearing to go out among them. But I soon realized that this was a poor attitude on the eve of a battle and that my chances of making good were small if I did not take hold of myself. So I put aside fear, a thing I had to do many times, and went out of the dugout and back to my P.C.

As soon as it was dusk I had parties of men sent out on my front to cut roads through the wire for my advance in the morning. This was a very nervous job for them. Part went as wire cutters and part as guards to protect them. Lts. Fox, McKeen, and Burdick were in charge, and they did their trying and dangerous work well. Several times during the night the different parties were on the point of firing into each other, thinking the other party were Germans. These men were out all night and got no rest before going into the attack.

About eleven o'clock the Germans put down a heavy barrage on the American lines away off to our left. The fire seemed very heavy and restricted to a fairly small area. We concluded that the Germans were preparing the way for a local raid on our lines, doubtless to get prison-ers and information. We wondered how these soldiers over there were standing all that shell fire, and if the Germans would be able to break into their lines.

The officers received maps of the Argonne Forest with the sector of our advance marked on them by Capt. Glock in blue pencil. The famous town of Montfaucon was right on our front and its capture was our first objective.[9]

Just before dark I had the pioneers sent me from Headquarters Company instruct a number of my men in the art of wire cutting. The pioneers seemed to know but little about it. To my great disgust the wire cutting tools proved but poor things. They were too small to give proper leverage and worse than that they were of soft steel, the edges turned and worn smooth, and it was very hard work to get results with them.

At eleven o'clock the heavy artillery in our rear opened fire on the German lines. It was our first experience with a heavy artillery preparation. We were simply overcome by it. Such a tremendous tumult of noise we had never experienced. The roar of guns was continuous and awful. It is impossible to give an idea of it. The skies were continually lighted up by the great white flashes of the guns. We could hear the hundreds of shells hissing and shrieking high over our heads on their way to the German lines. Surely there would be nothing and no one left there to resist us. The German shell fire ceased entirely. At two thirty the smaller guns and the 75s near us joined in, and now the roar and tremendous noise of all these hundreds of guns grew greater and greater until it was not a mere noise but a continuous roaring thundering, the intensity of which bewildered and confused us. It was the greatest concentration of guns in all the war and the most terrific artillery preparation man ever attempted.

9. Montfaucon was an impressively held defensive position that commanded from its heights the entire valley below. The Germans had built an artillery observation post there and reinforced it with multiple trench lines, pillboxes, and machine gun nests. German defenses by 1918 were constructed in depth, so that attackers would take substantial casualties moving from position to position before then suffering a counterattack.

7

In Support in the Battle of the Argonne

For hours this awful roaring continuous tumult continued, and finally we even got somewhat accustomed to it. It gave us confidence to feel that such a preparation was being made for our advance, and to know that we had such artillery to support us when we advanced.

Major John B. Atwood, commanding our Third Battalion, was to go forward on the right of our regiment, and I, with the First Battalion, was to move on his left. We arranged details together and agreed to keep in touch and help each other as much as possible. I did not have the position of the 313th Infantry, which regiment I was to support, clearly in my mind, and this oversight on my part nearly got me into trouble, but I managed to get my battalion in its right place and to start at the appointed time. About three o'clock I started up Boyau 6 to find the 313th, my men following me two abreast. I reached the front trenches and found Col. Sweezey of the 313th in a dugout and told him I was support him at 1,000 meters. He wanted to know why I was right up with his regiment and ordered me to go back to my proper distance.

So back down the trench we went and reached the end of it just as day was breaking, and I saw Atwood's men advancing, I ordered Capt. Knack to climb out of the trench to the left with Company B and take the lead; then as Capt. Burrage with Company D came down the trench he did the same thing, following Knack. Capt. Fatzinger reported just at this time with Company C—he had not been with me on the march up the trench. The half of Company F under Capt. Hewitt had followed Capt. Knack, and I then moved forward with Company C and my machine gun platoon and one-pounder gun. I was now in correct position alongside of Atwood's battalion and had thus got out of some confusion into proper formation in a very few minutes. I was greatly relieved because for a time I felt that I had got things mixed up.

Just after we got started properly, a staff car appeared full of officers and watched us through their field glasses. I was indeed glad to be well straightened out and moving forward in good shape. I did not have Company A with me at this time as it was regimental reserve and under Col. Charles's orders. We crossed a small open valley just behind the front trenches, and as I passed through it I climbed over a small knoll and had a good view both to the right and left, and here I saw the most inspiring sight I think I saw in France. As far as I could see to the right and left were great numbers of American soldiers advancing on both sides of us in endless lines. There seemed to be no end to their lines. It was a wonderful sight, and it made us feel better to know there were so many of us going forward all together and at the same time. It was the men of the 37th Division I saw to the left and those of the 4th Division I saw to the right. It made us feel that we had plenty of help in this attack.

After we passed through the open valley we ascended a slope and came to the front line trenches. Here on the ground white tape had been stretched to show the companies of the 313th where they were to form in the dark for the start of the attack or the "Jump Off," as they call it in the army. Passing over the trenches we entered No Man's Land, and our troubles began. We immediately came into a mass of undergrowth, twisted wire, broken trees, shell holes half full of water and mud. To keep our formations in such terrain was utterly impossible. In most places it was useless to try to break a way through. Also the men lost sight of each other and could not keep in touch. Soon we were broken up into small parties going single file by a path, or through the easier places, or in groups advancing by a narrow road here and there. Often I saw officers upon stumps or tree trunks trying to direct the advance of their men by the easiest ways. Keeping formations in such country was not possible. We had been warned to avoid paths and roads, as they would be under machine gun fire, but we had to get forward so risked the machine guns, which we had heard ahead firing at the 313th Infantry for some time. Uniforms and leggings suffered greatly from the briars and barbed wire. Many of the shell holes were thirty feet in diameter and twenty feet deep, and the men had to go around these, thus crowding up on those to the right and left. The compass was our only guide, our direction was 258°, and all the officers and sergeants constantly referred to the compass to keep our advance in the correct direction.

It was not long before we came upon the dead of the 313th, killed by machine gun fire. The sight sobered us all and brought us a greater realization of battle. We had to halt frequently, as the 313th was delayed or held up by the machine gun fire, which frequently broke out in deadly rattle.[1] The wounded of the 313th had been coming back for some time, each wounded man supported and helped by one or two comrades. Wounded men were a new thing to us, and it seemed terrible to see them in their bloody bandages. We soon learned to accept them as part of the day's work. Some German prisoners came back through our lines, escorted by some smiling and very proud men of the 313th. A general crowding over to the road to see these prisoners occurred, and I must confess I went over myself. They seemed very content to be prisoners, looked well dressed, very strong looking men, somewhat older than our men averaged.

I stopped some men who were cutting off their shoulder straps and searching them for souvenirs, which we Americans were always after all through the war.[2] One of the prisoners was wounded in the stomach by a bayonet thrust, so the guard told us. He was in a bad way and was carried. We got the men back to their formation and went on with the advance.

During a halt Capt. Knack and I were sitting with some others on a small bare hillock when machine gun bullets began to whiz past us very close. It was almost amusing to see every one roll off that hillock with great haste.

Lt. Howard Kates took a Browning automatic rifle and several men and went forward to get that machine gun. He went running and leaping over the logs, utterly regardless of his danger, and I was told that

1. Both of the regiments leading the assault on Montfaucon faced stiff resistance between their jumping off point and the German intermediate line stretching from the Bois de Cuisy to the west and the ruined villages of Malancourt and Haucourt to the east. The 316th Infantry followed behind the 313th as they approached the heavily defended German line at Redoute du Golfe in the valley below Montfaucon.

2. German shoulder straps (also known as shoulder boards) were popular souvenirs and provided important information about the enemy. Each strap was decorated with the number of a German regiment or, in the case of Guard Regiments or other elite units, ornate cyphers.

he did wipe out the gun. I admired his courage and indifference to danger. We had been under German shell fire for some time, but it was not heavy, and so far had caused us no loss. It did worry us however and caused some scattering and ducking among the men. Shell fire is always harder on the morale and the nerves than on troops physically, and so it makes troops much harder to handle and command.

After passing through No Man's Land, we encountered alternate open fields and patches of thick woods, and the going was somewhat easier and we could form our men and handle them better. The 313th had wiped out most of the machine gun nests, but some had not been found. When well concealed in the woods it is very hard to discover them. They are covered over with branches and leaves and cannot be seen or located until you come right upon them. The sound of the machine gun only indicated their location, and this was very deceptive and extremely hard to follow. Our leading companies cleaned up quite a few of them, but not without loss.

During one halt we had stopped near a road which was under heavy machine gun fire. When the signal was given to advance, Capt. P. F. Burrage got calmly up and proceeded down this road, totally indifferent to the bullets, which flew around him. His men followed without hesitation, such an example could not be resisted. The woods were so thick here that the road was the only means of advance.

Lt. Col. Meador came up from the rear to see how things were going to report back to the Colonel. We were at the time under fairly heavy machine gun fire, but he came calmly up the road and joined us where we were sitting in the ditch and did not seem to notice the flying bullets. I told him about our advance and that we were frequently held up by the 313th, which seemed to be having a hard time ahead, as the roar of machine guns was very heavy up front.

At another halt my staff and I had an experience which seems rather funny now, but did not then. A German sniper in a tree, and there were many of these left behind by the Germans, had fired some bullets very close to us as we sat on the ground, so we moved into a small shell hole, which was not large enough for the four of us, myself, Lt. Keller, Lt. Fouraker, and Sergt.-Major MacCormack. This sniper was a pretty good shot and fired very close every time one of us moved. We were most uncomfortable and getting fairly mad about it. No one seemed much afraid. When I saw the advance begin again I knew we must get up and go on, and I feared this meant the death of one of us. So I thought out a plan. I gave each a direction to run in at the count of three. I counted, and we all sprang up together and ran in different directions. The German sniper was so confused at so many targets, all going in a different direction, that he did not fire a shot, and we all got away.

About German snipers, I would like to include here a few lines. We always regarded it as a mean, contemptible way to wage war. It was more like real murder than war. Snipers never stopped an advance nor won a battle and hence are, in reality, useless in winning a war. I have always thought it took a mean, sneaking man to make a sniper. Our men hated them and killed them ruthlessly like dogs. But it must take great courage to remain behind after your army is driven back and keep on killing men in the midst of the enemy, knowing that you have but the slightest chance to escape death, as you are bound to be discovered sooner or later.

These German snipers dressed in loose green clothes and hid up in the branches of the trees. Their specialty was officers, but as officers dress like the men and often carry rifles, the sniper has but little chance to pick them out. Unfortunately for me I had a fur collar on my overcoat and I wore French boots instead of legging, and this was the cause of so many bullets missing me by so little during the first two days. At one time I was so angered by several bullets passing close to my head that I snatched a rifle from the hands of a man near me and emptied its six bullets into a tree top nearby, hoping to get the sniper, but did not see him fall out. Good Capt. Knack standing near me laughed at my rage. Where the snipers were thick there was a continual uproar of rifle fire, our men firing into the tree tops all about us in answer to the snipers. Every now and then a German would fall out of a tree, turning over and over and hitting the ground with a dull thud. They got no sympathy, and the fall of a sniper was always the signal for a cheer from our men.

During an advance this first day we passed over three different lines of German trenches. All of these defenses had been subjected to concentrated artillery fire, and it was very apparent that this fire had been heavy and accurate. The trenches, especially those of the first line just beyond No Man's Land, were pounded and smashed out of all resemblance to defenses, and the freshly turned up ground looked as if it had been mixed up and intermixed by giant hands. Mingled with the earth were the remains of wooden supports, beams, duck-boards, arms, helmets, clothing and all the general wreck of a once occupied position. Cartridges lay in heaps and were scattered all over. From the mouths of broken dugouts poured out an ill-smelling gray smoke, showing that our moppers up had been busy throwing hand grenades into them to wipe out enemy skulkers who would not come out and surrender.

Towards afternoon the German shell fire got heavier, and the machine gun nests and the snipers became more numerous, and in consequences our progress became more difficult, and our losses heavier, but still our task was light compared to what it became when we took the lead. In some machine gun nests the Germans were captured surrounded by great piles of cartridges with their guns cold. These men were always taken alive. Apparently they knew they were abandoned and left behind and were not willing to sacrifice themselves for merely making difficult our advance. In other nests the machine gunners fired to the last minute and then jumped up and tried to surrender, with the American dead lying right in front of them. Very rarely were they taken alive in such cases, nor should they be. It is hard to grant mercy to people who have slaughtered your comrades to the very last moment.

In our first day's advance we passed through No Man's Land, the Bois de Malancourt, crossed the Golfe de Malancourt, an open space heavily wired and entrenched, and entered the Bois de Cuisy where we passed the first night.[3]

On this first evening I had some adventures all by myself. When we had halted in the late afternoon, I was with my staff at a group of German shacks and dugouts, which seemed a very good place to pass the night. I was tired out, having had no sleep the night before, and having carried a heavy load on my person all day. There came to me a runner from Col. Charles ordering me to report to him in the rear. So I passed

---

3. As indicated, the 313th had great difficulty in taking these positions. Colonel Sweezey of the 313th reformed his regiment at dusk at the northern edge of the Bois deCuisy under the shadow of Montfaucon looming distant in the horizon. With dusk falling, he ordered the attack continued at great cost, a final assault that was met with stiff resistance.

my command to Capt. Knack, and leaving my heavy fur overcoat and equipment with my staff and wearing only my pistol, I went back a long way to the road where the Colonel had been, but he was not there.[4] This provoked me greatly. I did not feel that he had a right to ask me to leave my command during battle, and if he had he should have waited for me or left a guide to take me to him.

The runner was very tired and asked me if I could find my way back to my P.C., and I told him I could, but found later that I could not. So many paths and woods looked alike that as I made my way forward I got lost and confused. The light in the woods was fading and finally I was lost. The snipers were still shooting, answered by our men, and bullets flew through the trees. As I might meet Germans at any time I walked along quietly with my pistol ready in my hand. I was very tired and very nervous.

Suddenly I fell hard and flat on the path, tripped up by a wire stretched across by the Germans, a few inches from the ground. I did not realize at first what had happened to me and thought I was shot or knocked down. I got up, and my nerves were not helped any by this accident. Every turn in the path presented possible danger; even our own men might shoot me in the dusk. Suddenly rounding one turn I stopped, and my heart seemed to die within me. I could not move, and my pistol hung useless by my side. I thought my end looked me in the face. There in the path, very close, was a machine gun pointed at me; a German sat behind it, his fingers on the trigger; another knelt at one side, feeding the cartridge belt to it.

How long I stood thus I will never know. I wondered that they did not fire, and then I realized that there was something peculiar about these men, and I found myself leaning over them. Both were dead and cold and rigid and partly collapsed but still in their positions. What a feeling of relief came over me. I passed on, not thinking then to push these dead men over. No doubt they frightened others who followed me along that path.

I came out on to a wide road and here found many of our wounded, wrapped in blankets, having had first aid attention. They seemed

4. This is indicative of the communications difficulties throughout the day up and down the line.

cheerful and were attended by hospital corps men. Here they must lie until ambulances could get up to them. I gave some of them cigarettes, but most had some. I spoke to several of them. Going on, I entered another wood and at a turn in a path found two freshly killed American soldiers, the blood still welling from wounds in their heads. As I stood looking at them a bullet passed by my head so close as to feel hot. I looked up the slope and saw an American soldier behind a tree, working the lever of his rifle. He had fired at me, and he doubtless had just killed the two men I had been looking at. I was furious and called out to him roughly, using some profanity I fear. So angry was I at such merciless and criminal slaughter and my own narrow escape from death, and so overwrought were my nerves that I was tempted to shoot this crazy fool.

A medical officer interfered and apologized for the man, telling me that they had a first aid station there and had suffered much loss from the German snipers, who had shot down their stretcher men. So they had stopped several soldiers and asked them to protect them. These men had had many narrow escapes and had got very nervous and excited, and he feared they were shooting at everything that moved in the woods near them. I told him about the two freshly killed Americans in the path where I had nearly been killed. Warning the man to cool down and shoot more carefully, I was about to go on when they brought in a captain of the 313th I knew slightly, but whose name I have forgotten. He was shot through the stomach, but seemed in no great pain. He expressed sorrow when told about Major Pepper and others who had been killed and did not seem to realize his own bad condition. He turned on his side and seemed to faint. The doctor said, "He is dying and will never speak again." Saddened at this sight I left them.

As I went along in the increasing dusk I kept inquiring for the 316th, but none of the men I met seemed to know where the regiment was. Many groups of German huts looked like the one at which I had left my staff, but all were deserted and empty. I felt several times that unfriendly eyes were looking at me from the mouths of the dugouts, and this may have been the case or it may only have been my nerves. In one instance I believe it was so. As I approached one group of huts I heard voices and saw the smoke of a fire. Sure that I had now found my friends, I called out to them and hurried up. There was the fire burning but no one was in sight. They must have been Germans who fled into the dugouts when they heard my voice. Convinced of this, I did not remain there long.

Occasionally I came upon the dead, lying singly or in groups. There were not very many as our losses on this first day were not heavy compared with the days that followed. But it was very uncanny finding them thus in the darkening woods, when one was alone and one's nerves were highly strung, and I felt very much alone then among them. They lay in all attitudes, and most of them had a surprised look on their faces. Their faces had lost their natural color and had taken on a yellowish green tinge.

The wounded had practically all been gathered up by now, here in the rear, but I came upon one poor little Italian-American soldier lying in a shallow shell hole, covered over with a raincoat. He was shot through the chest and seemed very weak and in a bad way. I leaned down to talk to him and try to encourage him a little. His voice was very weak, and he asked me not to leave him there alone. I could not stay, but promised to send some stretcher bearers after him very soon, and going on, I fortunately met two of them nearby and led them back to the wounded man, who was very grateful to me. It was a relief to me to see him carried away from that lonesome place in the woods. I was not yet hardened to the awful sights of battle, as I became later. One had either to get hardened somewhat and accustomed to such things, or one would become mentally unbalanced, as I saw more than one man become.

I came out into an open field and there found Company A, my own old company, which was regimental reserve and in the rear. I was glad to see them after my lonely march and spoke to the men. An orderly came to show me where regimental headquarters were, but I told him to tell the Colonel I would go forward to my battalion as I felt I must be with it during the night. Going on I fell in with Company A, under Capt. Kelley of the 313th Infantry, which was moving up to the front. I do not understand, even now, how this Company of the 313th was so far to the rear, even if it was regimental reserve of the 313th, unless it had got lost. I walked some distance with them, in the dark, and finally up in the Bois de Cuisy, close up behind the 313th, I found Company D of my battalion, which was my leading company. I struck their most advanced post, which was in an old German gun position, and here I found Lt. Fox and Lt. Burdick, and I was very glad to see them. My other companies were behind them in the woods, as was my staff. It was too dark to attempt to find my staff now, and it would have been dangerous, as one might be shot. I had found my battalion and was in the place where I might be needed most if anything happened, so I decided to remain for the night where I was.

It was cold and raining, and I had no overcoat nor raincoat and began to feel the weather. All of the men had on both overcoats and raincoats, so I borrowed a raincoat from one of them and put it on. It kept me dry, but did not keep me warm. I talked with Fox and Burdick for a while about how things were going, and they told me the 313th was having a very hard time to capture Montfaucon, which was now just ahead of us. They said the rattle of machine guns had been terrific. We sat for a while in some small dugouts not big enough for one to sit upright in. In fact they were mere holes in the walls of the gun pit, probably used by the Germans for shells. But it was warmer in there than outside, and one was protected from the rain. We had very little to eat, just a few crackers and some canned salmon.

After a while the rain ceased, and as I felt very much cramped in the hole and very tired, I went out and stretched out under a bush on the wet ground, with nothing around me but the thin slicker, or raincoat, and tried to get a little sleep, but did not and only dozed for a couple of hours. I was very cold, and the ground was very hard, and it seemed that either my pistol or my water bottle must always be under me to add to my already great discomfort. All around me, under the bushes, were my men trying to get some rest. It was a most miserable and trying night, and I thought the dawn would never come.

During the night I heard movement around me, and someone close to me said the 313th had moved off our front and were concentrating to the right to attack Montfaucon in the morning. There was now nothing between us and the Germans. I got up and found Lt. Burdick, who told me he had heard the same thing and had put out outposts on his front in consequence.

More than once during this night I thought of what would happen if a German attack had burst upon us in the utter darkness. One could not have told foe from friend, nor could the officers have much chance to rally and lead the men. Utter and awful confusion would have resulted and friend would have killed friend.

Morning dawned dull, gray, and discouraging. Wet and raining. The woods were soaked and dripping wet. No steaming rolling kitchens stood nearby with hot breakfast ready, as the good people at home doubtless thought they would. They were far in the rear, unable to come up on account of the terrible roads. For breakfast we had what little was left of the crackers and canned salmon and bread we had carried over the top with us.

We looked about us and found ourselves in a fairly open woods, crossed in all directions by paths and muddy roads, made by the Germans, who had been here nearly four years. Dugouts of heavy construction were here and there among the trees, sign posts in German at the crossroads, and some wooden huts, mostly broken by shell fire, stood close to the paths. Water pipes with spigots were found throughout the woods, but we could get no water from them for our canteens, as the shell fire had broken the pipe system, or the Germans had destroyed it themselves. This had long been a quiet front where exhausted troops from the hard fighting in Flanders had been sent by the Germans to rest up in these quiet, protecting forests. We found many evidences of the comfortable quarters they had built for themselves, but most of it now was broken and open to the rain. German steel helmets were found in piles, also many other parts of their equipment, such as rifles, bayonets, shovels, belts, clothing, cartridges in great numbers.

At daylight I saw my other companies among the trees behind us and was greeted by Captain Knack and other officers. My staff came up, and I recovered my good warm overcoat, which I put on at once. Lt. Col. Meador, who had worn it during the night, said it was the warmest coat he had ever worn, and he offered me a hundred dollars for it, but I would not have taken any price for it under the circumstances.

Lt. McKean, who had been very ill, but who had refused to go to the hospital, during the first day had become much worse and was in danger of pneumonia. He had to give up now and was carried to the rear on a stretcher. His face was highly flushed and he had a high temperature. This brave young officer had shown much courage and tenacity.

I went forward to the edge of the forest and found Col. Sweezey of the 313th there, sitting in the gutter by the road using a field telephone.

Near him lay a small wounded German soldier, covered over by blankets. He did not seem to suffer much and was much interested in us. He had been kindly treated and was in no fear whatever. All of our prisoners seemed satisfied and happy to be done with fighting. I never saw any of our men treat them unkindly.

I spoke to Col. Sweezey and told him I was right in his rear. He told me that he was attacking Montfaucon, which loomed up in front of us through the heavy mist on its high hill, at once, and I assured him of my support. I stood on the edge of the woods and watched his companies line up and disappear into the thick mist, which was a good protection to them, as they must cross a wide, open field in approaching the town. They had had a hard and bloody time of it yesterday in trying to storm this formidable hill and had suffered heavy loss. All of their three majors were down—Major Pepper was dead, Major Langley was wounded, and I do not remember whether the third major was killed or wounded.[5] But it certainly looked as if the majors did not last long in battle, not very encouraging news to me, a major myself.

Soon after the leading companies had entered the mist, German machine gun fire broke out ahead of us, and I have never heard such a terrific roar of machine gun fire. It was awful and sounded like the cataract at Niagara Falls. To think of human bodies facing such blasts and such sheets of flying lead. It is a wonder that any of these men lived to enter that town. Had it not been for the mist, most of them must have been struck down.

I reported to the Colonel that the 313th were attacking Montfaucon and received orders in return to close up on them and give them close support in this attack. As I was right up in their immediate rear I had my leading company follow their rear company, and soon my entire battalion was in motion. We went down the slope through the open fields into the valley, Capt. Fatzinger, with Company C, leading the way. In the valley we halted for a considerable time while the 313th fought its way with great gallantry through the town of Montfaucon. The sun came out and the mist evaporated, one of the few, if not the only time we saw the sun in this battle. There ahead of us in an immediate front

5. The third was Major Israel Putnam who was killed by gunshot wound to the head at the front of his men as they attacked Montfaucon late in the afternoon on the 26th.

loomed the famous town of Montfaucon, a stronghold held by the Germans for nearly four years, and one of the strong points of the Hindenburg Line. It stood up very high above us, and its buildings looked very white and lean in the bright sunshine.

I looked ahead and saw Capt. Fatzinger's company right up with Col. Sweezey of the 313th, available for his use if he needed its help. But he did not ask for the help of any of my companies, and the 313th stormed Montfaucon and captured it without help from any other unit, and they must be given the entire credit for this military feat. While waiting in the valley before this town, my men were out in the open fields. It happened that when we halted my staff and I were just crossing through a small stream, which had cut a deep channel, and we were thus in a sort of large trench and here we remained. Soon German shells began to fall in our immediate neighborhood, and some of the men of the company just in front of us began to run back to our shelter. This would not do, and I stood up and ordered them back to their places. As it did not seem fair for us to have cover while they were out in the open and to set them a proper example, my staff and I left our trench and moved out into the open field. I would not have any of my men ever say that I took shelter from shell fire and ordered them to remain out in the open.

We moved on up the slope and passed through a great deal of rusty wire partly broken up by our artillery fire, but not all by any means. The 313th had made a good job of cleaning up the town, at least I must say that we entered with very little loss and received but little machine gun fire. I passed by doorways and dugout entrances and once again had that uncanny feeling that unfriendly eyes were looking at me, and it must have been so, for the next day a number of German machine gun nests were discovered and the men captured. They had not been firing on our men for some considerable time.

We went up one of the main streets, the men keeping a sharp eye out for the enemy with rifles ready. Personally, the only Germans I saw in this town were some prisoners who came back from the 313th. There is on the top of the hill the ruins of a large white stone church, and I passed within a few feet of it as we progressed. Reaching the level streets at the top of the hill we halted again. I went forward and saw Col. Sweezey standing near a tree. The shells were falling thickly around him. Capt. Fatzinger and Capt. Hewitt of my battalion had their men right

up with the 313th now. I felt that I was giving the 313th as close support as it was possible to give. Col. Sweezey saw me, but offered me no
orders nor suggestions. He had captured the town. It was now early
afternoon, and he was preparing to attack the Bois de Beuge, which
lay north of the town across a wide open valley. I was close enough to
assist him if the enemy counter-attacked him.

Realizing that he had the situation in hand and seeing my two leading companies under cover on the northern face of the hill towards the
enemy, where they could help Col. Sweezey, I went back a little ways
to my staff and established a P.C. in a cross street up against a ruined
house, where I could be easily found and where I had a little, but very
little, protection from the shell fire which was getting very heavy. The
Germans, knowing we were in the town, were trying to blow it to bits.

Not far away was the large stone house used by the Crown Prince
of Germany to observe the attacks on Verdun. Our men found in this
place a very large telescope, which the Prince had used to watch his
brave men miles away. He had this house so full of concrete and railroad rails to protect him from shells that there was not much space left
in it. The 3rd Division, which relieved us in the Argonne, sent this great
telescope to West Point with a plate on it stating it was captured by the
3rd Division. General Kuhn heard of it and took the matter up with the
War Department. The plate on the telescope now reads, "Captured at
Montfaucon by the 79th Division, presented to West Point by the 3rd
Division."[6]

The shell fire continued heavy all afternoon, and the roar of machine gun fire up front was heavy at times. I had reports back from my
front companies and several times went forward to see personally what
the situation was. The 313th was tired out and had suffered heavily, and
they made but little progress that afternoon, and while they made a
lodgment of some of their men in the Bois de Beuge, they did not succeed in capturing it. But I felt they had done enough and thought our
turn to lead was about due. And it was. Towards evening Col. Sweezey
with two officers came through our street. His face was drawn and

6. According to William Walker, this "multistory telescopic periscope," long displayed
at West Point, was featured in *Life* magazine in 1941 but disappeared soon after and has
never been seen again. It may have been lost to a scrap-metal drive during World War II,
p. 385.

haggard. He had endured two of the hardest days of his life. Since the shell fire was so heavy I thought he was hunting a place for his P.C. where there was some protection. I asked him if he was and offered him mine.

"P.C. hell," said the Colonel. "I want to get in touch with division P.C. and have your regiment relieve mine tonight instead of in the morning. We are all shot to pieces."

He went on towards the rear to get a telephone.

Dusk soon settled over the ruined town, and as things became quieter, except for the continued shell fire, we settled down to try to get a little rest. Owing to the shells, which flew close over us we had to get in close to the stone wall we were behind.

The street at the base of the wall was piled up with broken stone which the shells had knocked down. It was on this broken stone that we sought to find a comfortable place to lie down. It was the most uncomfortable bed I ever enjoyed. Some shells burst in the ruins just across the street, so we did not want to lie down any farther out in the street than we had to. Occasionally a shell would strike the top of the wall behind which we lay, and a shower of stones would drop upon us. The helmet was a good hat in these conditions.

A group of German prisoners with several guards had halted in the street near us. The guards and some of our men stood around in a friendly circle with these prisoners, and they talked together in German. One of our sergeants, seeing one of these prisoners with a heavy gray blanket, took it away from him and brought it over to me. I was glad to get it as it was very thick and warm, much better than ours, in fact better than two of ours. I shared it with Capt. P. F. Burrage, who was with me, and it gave us both a great deal of comfort that night there on the wet stones and ground with no other protection.

Burrage was a brave and heroic gentleman. During the first day's advance in the Argonne he had become very ill and seemed threatened with pneumonia. He had alternate chills and high fever. He became weaker as the advance went on, but he would not give up and go out of battle on account of sickness. The second day he was much worse and looked very pale and weak. In his condition he was risking his life by not going to the hospital. He was always a very quiet, steady man. He made no complaint now, but everyone could see his bad condition.

This night he was worse, and I made him get under my warm blanket with me. The ground was so wet and cold that we really never got very warm, but it was much better than out in the open. Capt. Burrage was shaken in his fits of chills so that he shook the blanket. I talked to him about his condition and asked him to go to the rear to hospital. He said he would hand over the command of his company to his ranking 1st Lieutenant, but he wanted to go out tomorrow with it in the attack anyway. I had to yield to such splendid courage and sense of duty.

Early the next morning just as we began our attack, Capt. P. F. Burrage was struck in the back of the head with a piece of shell and seriously wounded. Months after I heard from his wife that he died in hospital and that she had received a letter from the nurse who cared for him, telling her of his death. I recommended him for a posthumous award of the Distinguished Service Cross, and I sincerely hope his wife received it.

I was not to pass much of the night on those awful stones. A runner came down the street, calling my name. He took me back some way to a sheltered place on the hillside, and here I found Col. Charles, Col. Sweezey, Major Atwood, and others. The order for us to take over the front line at once had arrived. Col. Charles read it to Atwood and me by candle light under the protection of a blanket held over us. Col. Sweezey gave Col. Charles the information he had for him about the front and the position of his men. Then Col. Sweezey got into his bedding roll bed, which had been brought along for him. Col. Charles seemed confused and undecided what to do. He kept asking Col. Sweezey questions over and over. Finally Col. Sweezey, who was tired out, spoke to Col. Charles very sharply and said he had already given him all the information he had. Then Col. Charles subsided. Col. Sweezey had endured two awful days and in the first place gave Col. Charles a proper report on the situation. He had my sympathy in the matter.

Major Atwood and I assured Col. Charles that we would take over the front line at once, and he seemed relieved by our attitude and directed us to proceed at once to do so. As it was very dark and shells were falling as well as rain, and as our men were somewhat scattered, it was a very difficult task for us to accomplish, as Atwood and I agreed, but we did not tell the Colonel so. As a matter of honest fact, no formal relief was made until daybreak on account of the difficulties I have mentioned. My men were partly mixed up with the men of the 313th, and when I reached the front line I agreed with Capt. Kelly, who commanded the 313th there, all the majors being killed or wounded, that we had better not attempt to move any men in the darkness, but leave them as they were until morning. We had plenty of men in position to resist attack, should it come before morning. So I took over the command from Capt. Kelly and let it go at that for a few hours.

Before I left Major Atwood, we agreed to keep in touch with each other and help each other all we possibly could. We were to advance our battalions side by side. Poor Atwood, that was the last time I saw him until I stood and looked down on his dead body three days later, although he was killed early the next morning.

That night, September 28, 1918, when I went forward to take over the front line, I found considerable difficulty in finding the commanding officer, Capt. Kelly. It was so dark that I could not see at all, and I stumbled and slid and fell over things. I could hear voices around me and finally found a man who could take me to the P.C. He led me through some streets and wire and took me at last into a long narrow dugout, dimly lighted by a couple of candles. Along the wall, on a bench, sat a number of officers and men, trying to sleep and get a little rest.

Capt. Kelly greeted me and was very glad to know that I came to relieve him. He said they were all shot to pieces and had suffered heavy losses. I sat with him and talked the situation over and asked him many questions. He seemed more cheerful than I would have expected. Of course the fact that he was being relieved would help his spirits or any other man's under the circumstances.

Capt. Kelly looked at my fur collar and my boots and said, "Major, I fear you won't live long tomorrow."

I asked him why.

"Your fur collar and your boots will show the German snipers that you are an officer. With the fur collar they will think you are a general. Better throw away that coat."

I was unwilling to do that because it was so warm, but I did not want to be conspicuous. So I turned the fur collar inside my coat and plastered my boots with mud, and the captain thought my appearance all right then. He advised me to take a place in line with the men and carry a rifle, which I did for a while next morning, but found the rifle a nuisance to me and dropped it. I had messages to write and receive, and the field telephone to handle at times. I could not be bothered with the rifle.

We sat together there in the dugout for some time, probably two hours or more, waiting for daylight. The noise of the bursting shells outside continued all this time, and occasionally a very heavy one shook the ground with its explosion. As we sat in the dugout I became very thirsty, having had but little water all day. I asked Capt. Kelly if there was any water near. He said there was a little spring which dropped slowly at the other end of the dugout, but doubted if they could spare me any. In fact seemed rather unwilling to let me have any. So I said to him, "I am in command here now, and I intend to have my canteen filled."

He said no more about it, so I gave my canteen to one of his men and asked him to fill it. It took some time, as the water flowed very slowly. When I got the canteen back I greatly enjoyed a long, cold drink and kept the rest for the morning. We were always instructed to save our water in battle as much as possible, as we might find ourselves lying wounded with an empty canteen, and a wounded man suffers terribly if he does not have water. During the Argonne Battle I gave away most of my water to the wounded I passed, as I could not resist their fervent appeals for water. I consequently never had very much water with me.

When dawn came at last, did the good cooks hurry up with plates of hot cakes and sausage and steaming cups of coffee to fit us properly for the day's battle? They did not. The rolling kitchens were miles in the rear, and many of the cooks were fighting in the ranks, rifle in hand, and against express orders to the contrary. They refused to go home to their women folk and say they had cooked all through the war and had not been in a battle at all.

Those of us fortunate enough to have any left munched some crackers and chocolate, and a few had cans of food of different kinds. For the next three days we received no food of any sort whatever from our supply people, and we were reduced to eating what little we found in German knapsacks. This consisted of small flat round cans of what seemed to be a mixture of mashed potatoes and ground cooked meat. It was very good and we wished we could find more of it. We found some cabbages in small German gardens near their huts and dugouts, and more than once I was glad to eat this cabbage raw.

As a matter of fact I ate very little during the five days we were in battle, and I did not seem to need food nor miss it much. My mental and nervous condition was such that my bodily wants were forgotten and did not annoy me much.

The Parkin family in Baltimore before his embarkation to France. Captain Harry Dravo Parkin is in his AEF uniform and his son is wearing a child's officer's uniform to match his father. *From left to right*: Captain Harry Parkin, Alice Mary Parkin, and Harry Dravo Parkin, Jr. (Parkin Scrapbook)

Three trainee officers on the target range at Fort Niagara, New York. Parkin is on the left joined by Captain Dodge in the center and Captain DuPuy on the right. Captain Charles DuPuy wrote his own memoir of service entitled *A Machine Gunner's Notes from France* (Pittsburgh, PA: Reed & Witting, 1920). (Parkin Scrapbook)

Captain Albert Haan in hospital in France. Haan was a company commander in the 126th Infantry and was wounded in action on August 29, 1918. Parkin met him in hospitals in Paris, Savaney, and Brest before they were shipped home together on the *Saxonia*. (Parkin Scrapbook)

Regimental Post of Command near Verdun used by Colonel George Williams and Major H. D. Parkin when they commanded the 316th Infantry. Parkin writes of this image: "These shacks were half demolished by shell fire when we used them in November 1918. Note the railroad rails in the back-ground. They were set on end, close together to form a protection from shells. The Germans built this place. [. . .] Forty feet underground there was a large four room dugout, which was shellproof." (Parkin Scrapbook)

Major H. C. de V. Cornwell, Regimental Surgeon, 316th Infantry. Parkin wrote in his scrapbook: "Picture taken under heavy shell fire. The rifle in picture was driven into a tree by bursting shell." Parkin admired Cornwell characterizing him as a "courageous and efficient officer, good comrade, beloved and respected." (Parkin Scrapbook)

Lieutenant Daniel Keller served as the Adjutant of the 1st Battalion, 316th Infantry. Keller was killed by a shell on September 29, 1918, near Boise 268 in the Meuse-Argonne Offensive. (Parkin Scrapbook)

American infantry in a shell hole on top of Hill 378, also known as "Corn Willy Hill." Parkin laconically annotated this photo in his scrapbook: "This hill was the key point of the whole front. It was captured by the 316th Infantry after heavy losses." (Parkin Scrapbook)

Private First Class James A. Gallagher. Gallagher was in Company A of the 316th and served as a runner for 1st Battalion Headquarters. He gave this photo to Parkin with the inscription: "To Major Harry D. Parkins [*sic*]. My War time Commander and Comrade." (Parkin Scrapbook)

MAJOR WILLIAM SINKLER MANNING OF THE WASHINGTON BUREAU OF THE NEW YORK TIMES, Killed in France in the World War, Is Laid to Rest in Arlington National Cemetery in the Presence of His Father, Former Governor Richard I. Manning of South Carolina, Mrs. Manning, His Six Soldier Brothers, General Pershing, and Practically the Entire Body of Newspaper Correspondents in Washington. (*Times Wide World Photos.*)

Newspaper clipping of Major William Sinkler Manning's funeral at Arlington National Cemetery, attended by his father Governor Richard Manning of South Carolina and many other dignitaries including, General John Pershing. Manning's death was a particularly hard blow for Parkin, who saw him as both a close friend and a courageous officer. (Parkin Scrapbook)

Post-war studio photographs of Major Harry Dravo Parkin in his uniform and wearing his fur-lined custom-made officer's overcoat. Of special note is the Distinguished Service Cross medal that dates this photo to post-1923. (Parkin Scrapbook)

Wounded soldiers of the 316th Infantry being evacuated from Hill 378. Regimental aid stations were set up near the combat zone to provide first aid and to triage soldiers before they could be evacuated on ambulances like the one in this photo. (Parkin Scrapbook)

Post-war photographs of Major Harry Dravo Parkin showing clearly his 79th Division "Cross of Lorraine" patch and his overseas stripes. On the breast of his custom-made officer's tunic is his Distinguished Service Cross as well as his World War I Victory Medal with two battle clasps, for the Meuse-Argonne and service in the Defensive Sector. (Parkin Scrapbook)

Signal soldiers with carrier pigeons in wicker baskets at the front. Note the rifle sitting next to the basket. Parkin wrote of this image: "Carrier pigeons in baskets ready to go over the top with the troops. They were always taken when possible. The safest surest messengers." (Parkin Scrapbook)

"A *posed picture* to show trench fighting," wrote Parkin. "These men would have their equipment on consisting of cartridge belt, bayonet, canteens, small pack, and gas mask, all of which are lacking, if they were in actual battle." (Parkin Scrapbook)

Field kitchen of the 315th Infantry, 79th Division. The ability to provide men with a hot meal was one that commanders like Parkin worried about, as there was a direct connection between food and morale. (Parkin Scrapbook)

First aid station for the 316th Infantry near Hill 378. These German-made corrugated iron huts are similar to those mentioned in Parkin's memoir. These small huts were repurposed by medics in the 316th during the final phase of the Meuse-Argonne Offensive. (Parkin Scrapbook)

Captured German soldiers holding loaves of bread. Parkin recalled that these soldiers were captured by the 316th near Hill 378 on November 4, 1918. He wrote in his scrapbook: "I remember the tallest one very well. He asked me the way to the rear." (Parkin Scrapbook)

The ruins at Montfaucon proved to be a formidable defensive position. Parkin marked this photo as his Post of Command on the night of September 27, 1918. "Here we lay all night on broken stone under heavy shell fire." (Parkin Scrapbook)

The temporary graves of Major William Manning and Captain Lewis Knack on Hill 378. Both men were killed in action in the attack on Corn Willie Hill. Subsequently, their bodies were repatriated to the United States. Both officers are now buried at Arlington National Cemetery. (Parkin Scrapbook)

Captain Percy Burrage. Burrage worked for The Prudential Insurance Company before training at Plattsburg and joining the 79th Division. He was wounded in the attack at Bois de Beuge and died on September 30, 1918. (Parkin Scrapbook)

German dugout near Hill 378. Dugouts like these were concrete reinforced and specifically designed to resist punishing shellfire for the defenders who lived underground. (Parkin Scrapbook)

Ruins of the church at Montfaucon. After four years of shelling little remained of the monastery and the ruined village surrounding it. (Parkin Scrapbook)

View of Death Valley to the north of Verdun in the eastern section of the
Meuse-Argonne Offensive. This open terrain was where the 79th Division
fought their last battles of the war. (Parkin Scrapbook)

8

Leading the Attack

In the dim early morning light, as I came out of the dugout, I saw soldiers everywhere among the trees of a nearby orchard and among the half-ruined huts around us. Officers and sergeants were busy collecting their men, who had got scattered during the night. Major Atwood's men and mine were badly mixed, but after some confusion and running about the companies were formed in the gray morning light, and Atwood's companies marched off to the right to form for the attack on our right flank. It was still too early for the German artillery observers to see us, and also we were mostly hidden from sight by the trees and huts. My companies D, B, and C, having formed, and I having assisted the company officers in hurrying the men to their places (Company A was still regimental reserve and not under my command), I led them down the slope to the road which here passes right along the foot of the hill. Here I stopped and directed Capt. Fatzinger of Company C to lead his men out into the open meadow, throwing them into the open attack formation as he advanced. This he did at once. Already the German shells were bursting in the meadow, the Germans having seen Major Atwood's men forming there for the attack. As my men came into the open the shell fire increased and soon became very heavy. We were now experiencing the heaviest and worst shell fire we had yet endured.[1]

Company B under Capt. Knack followed Company C out into those awful bursting shells, which began to strike on the road and in front and back of it. They came so thick and burst so close with such awful noise and whistling of fragments that I thought the end had surely

---

1. After the fall of Montfaucon, the Germans increased the concentration of their bombardment as they knew the allied positions, points of concentration, and direction of attack. The Germans also had time between the 26th and 27th to reinforce their defensive positions.

come for me and my staff: Lt. Keller, Lt. Fouraker, Sergt.-Major Mac-Cormack, and Cpl. Euwart, my faithful orderly. During one of the worst storms of shells I lay down on the road with my staff, who were already lying there by my order. But up and down the road on both sides I could see shells bursting right in the road, so it seemed useless to lie there as there was absolutely no protection. I could not expect Company C to advance over the road while I was lying flat on it, so I stood up and truthfully I did not see how I could last long in such a smashing storm of shells. The air was hazy with dust and smoke from the shells, and out into this with a field telephone in his hand and a very worried look on his face walked Col. Charles all alone. He stood there looking forward toward the Bois de Beuge, which we were advancing to attack.

We might endure a reverse here, as the 313th and one of my companies had failed to capture it the evening before, and the Colonel was worried. He took no notice of the shells, which were killing and wounding my men and smashing down the trees and huts around us. I could not help but admire his cool and steadfast courage, and whatever else I may say of this officer, I want to state now that he was a very brave man in the face of terrible danger.

I went over to Col. Charles and spoke to him. He asked me if I wanted any special artillery support, as his field phone was connected with the artillery. I then asked him to have the artillery shell the Bois de Beuge for twenty minutes. We were forming to attack these woods now about a quarter of a mile in advance of us. The Colonel feared some of our own men might be in those woods. I told him I was the leading unit of attack and there could be none of our men there, and if there were a few from some other unit it was better to chance killing them than to leave the Germans undisturbed to kill a lot of my men with their machine guns. I urged him most strongly to call for a barrage on these woods. An artillery major and observation officer came up, and I appealed to him to help me get those woods shelled, but the Colonel could not decide (that was his great trouble), and the woods were not shelled that morning, and I lost a lot of good men in taking them.

Off to the right, coming from the direction of Major Atwood's battalion, I saw through the haze of the shell smoke a man hurrying in our direction. Almost, it seemed, he dodged the shell explosions, and it did not seem possible that he would get through alive. But he did, and as he came up to the Colonel I recognized my good friend Lt. Joseph Horne. The blood was running down his face from a cut on the top of his head caused by a shell splinter, which had cut into his steel helmet just enough to give him a slight wound. The helmet certainly saved his life. He threw it away and picked up another. Lt. Horne brought a written message to the Colonel from Major Atwood, the last he wrote. It said, "For God's sake get us artillery support. The German shells are wiping us out." And so it seemed from the heavy shell fire we saw on his position, but the Colonel did nothing that I know of.[2]

Lt. Horne returned through the shell fire to Major Atwood, who was in a shallow shell hole. He had got his men formed a few minutes before I did and was waiting to advance with me. Lt. Horne later told me that Maj. Atwood rose on his knees to look towards my battalion. He sank back saying "Oh!" and was dead when he touched the ground. A bullet had passed up his left nostril and through his head, coming out at the top of his head. I saw his body two days later, on our way out of the battle. His face was not disfigured at all, and there was just a little blood at his nostrils. When we found him he was still in the little shell hole, lying there with his helmet over his face. His pistol and belt and field glasses were gone, but nothing else had been taken. I took his wrist watch and small Bible and some papers, all of which I gave to his mother in Pittsburgh.[3] Chaplain McNary and I searched his pockets and took everything we thought worthwhile. We did not have much time, as the regiment would be moving on at any minute, nor did we have any tools, except a couple of trench spades.

Nearby was a shell hole. There was water in the bottom of it, and the ground was yellow clay and soaking wet. I did hate to put the poor fellow into this place, but there was no help for it. It was all we could

2. The situation for Major John Atwood's battalion was particularly dire as they came under fire by machine guns, mortars, and powerful Austrian 88mm field guns. Atwood's message is even more desperate in full: "Being fired upon at point blank by field pieces. For God's sake get artillery or we'll be annihilated." Atwood received support and was able to advance. For a good account of this action, see Gene Fax, *With their Bare Hands* (New York: Osprey, 2017), 277.

3. John Baird Atwood was from a prominent Pittsburgh family and educated at Shadyside Academy and Princeton, Class of 1905. He has a memorial at Allegheny Cemetery in Pittsburgh and a memorial archway dedicated to his memory at his college alma mater. He was posthumously awarded the Distinguished Service Cross.

do, and we did not want to leave him there unburied where he had already lain two days. We had a few men with us, and they gathered the bodies in the immediate vicinity. They brought in the body of Lt. Albert C. Wunderlich and the bodies of six privates, whose faces I did not recognize. We placed the eight bodies, two officers and six privates, in the bottom of the shell hole (it was not deep), in a row, put their helmets over their faces (they were all dressed in overcoats), and shoveled the wet earth over them. How I did wish for a few boards or even blankets to cover them with first, but we had nothing and could get nothing and had very little time to do anything. Capt. Louis C. Knack, who was with us, stood with me by the grave, and good Chaplain McNary recited the burial service. We turned away saddened, such a miserable grave might wait for each of us.

But I have turned aside from the story of my battalion, which I left moving out into the open fields just north of Montfaucon to attack the Bois de Beuge.

Company C, under Capt. Robert L. Fatzinger, led the attack, followed by Company B, under Capt. Louis C. Knack. I followed Company B with my staff, some runners, and half a machine gun company, all of us spread out in open formation. Company D, under Capt. P. F. Burrage, brought up the rear. I did not have Company A under my command at this time as it was Brigade reserve and was kept in the rear.

We were now leading the attack and began to suffer heavily at once. From the Bois de Beuge German machine guns swept our lines, and the shell fire never ceased but got heavier and more effective as we advanced down the slope to the small creek at the foot of the slope leading up to the woods. Word was frequently brought to me of this officer killed and that one wounded until it seemed that we would soon have no officers left. It seems vain to attempt to describe the terrifying effect of heavy shell fire on troops exposed on in the open. It is a frightful ordeal to the most seasoned troops, and it was even worse to our new troops. Nearby you would see a brilliant flash, a shattering crash follows, the earth trembles, you see men staggering in the smoke, and hear awful cries. Hours of this with the immediate proximity of death is enough to unbalance men mentally, which it often does. As we advanced, the Germans laid down a barrage in front of us. We would not go back, we could not stay where we were, and as each line neared this line of bursting shells, it ran through them as fast as possible. When we came to it we set our teeth and plunged through, blinded, deafened, and choked with the shell bursts. Many figures lay on the ground, but on coming through I was relieved to see all of my staff still going forward near me.

On we went and as my leading company neared the woods ahead, the roar of machine guns became even louder. At the foot of the slope we had to stop a few minutes as the companies ahead made slower progress into the woods. I saw Lt. Norman L. Botsford going forward with his platoon. His face was pale, he limped, and blood was dropping from a wound in his right buttock, which looked serious enough to me to tell him to drop out and go to the rear for medical attention. He protested against doing so, saying he was the only officer his captain had left, so heavy had been our casualties already. I could not order him back in the face of such spirit and devotion, but I could and did recommend him for the Distinguished Service Cross. Near me on the ground lay a soldier whose head had been cut in half by a piece of shell, and I saw another whose head was completely taken off. Such sights are very trying on one's nerves and courage in battle.

As I climbed the slope to the Bois de Beuge, I came upon a group of officers and soldiers near the railroad track, all of whom were strangers to me. I asked a captain what outfit they belonged to, and he said the 37th Division, which was on our immediate left. They had been driven into our sector by heavy shell fire. I knew it was not their first battle, so I said, "Captain, I suppose you are used to battle by now."

He replied, "Major, you can never get used to it, and each succeeding battle gets harder to endure."

I found later that this was the truth. Your first battle is the easiest to go into, at least, because you do not realize what you are about to endure. This captain had on a German officer's belt and Luger pistol in addition to his own. The Luger pistol was regarded as one of the prize souvenirs of the war, and I envied him its possession.

During the advance we had come under machine gun fire frequently. These bullets coming in a steady stream make a very wicked, shrill hissing sound. When this now familiar sound is heard, every one drops to the ground, or at least stoops low for a few seconds at least, and stooping low was really the worst thing one could do as machine guns are most always placed low, and their bullets fly low, and hence instead of exposing one's legs only, one exposes one's more vital parts by getting down. You should either lie perfectly flat, or keep erect on your feet.

I entered the Bois de Beuge with the men of the machine gun company assigned to my battalion. We passed through it in single file using the paths. The woods were so thick that it was impossible to tear your way through. In the woods we met very little enemy fire as the companies ahead had pretty well cleaned them out of Germans. At one place I saw officers firing pistols into dugouts and men standing by with their rifles at the ready. The men were now scattered and the attack formation all broken up.

I was informed that Capt. Fatzinger of Company C had been badly wounded, and that he was lying nearby in the woods. I made a brief search for him, but could not find him and went on with much regret, for he was a close friend and a good officer, and I had suffered a double loss. I was told afterwards that he had stopped to consult his map and was leaning over looking at it when a German arose out of some bushes near and shot him in the back. Sergeant Grover C. Sheckart, who was with Capt. Fatzinger and devoted to him, was so infuriated that he rushed into the bushes, drove out the German and another and killed them both with his bayonet. Sergeant Sheckart was of German parentage, but nevertheless he was the best German killer in my battalion and an extraordinarily brave man, who has been decorated with the Distinguished Service Cross, which he most worthily earned and which I had much pleasure in helping him get. I will have more tales of Sergeant Sheckart's bravery to tell later.

We came out of the Bois de Beuge into open fields, and here the officers left got the men back into formation as well as possible and advanced again, immediately coming again under very heavy shell and machine gun fire, which quickly dotted the ground with dead and wounded. The German defense in the Argonne Forest consisted mostly of artillery and machine gun fire; there was not much infantry on our front at least. But against such defense and such heavy concentrated fire infantry suffers very heavily, and as they say in military language, "is soon consumed." We were fast being consumed. I took twenty-two officers into this battle and brought out five only: Capt. Knack, Lt. Fouraker, wounded in the hand; Lt. Hurly, wounded in the ankle; Lt.

Clovine; Lt. Jos Dyer; and Lt. William Dreher. Of these, Lt. Hurley did not come out of the battle with us, having gone to the hospital. He rejoined us later at Verdun.

In the open fields again north of the Bois de Beuge, which we had just captured, we reformed our men again and went on toward Woods 268, which lay across our front. We were now entirely exposed to the fire of the German artillery again, and in full view of their artillery observers, and they shelled us accurately, continuously, and heavily, and I was going to say without mercy, and this is certainly the truth. Fortunately they used mostly high explosive shells, which penetrated the wet ground deeply and which explosions were therefore largely localized, and one had to be very near to the explosions, as many were, to be injured. Had the Germans used shrapnel, which bursts twenty feet above the ground and showers it with steel fragments, our losses would have been much greater. From the woods ahead and from the flanks also came streams of hissing bullets from the German machine guns. These little guns are the poisonous vipers of modern war and hated like snakes by the infantry, who crush them out without mercy at every opportunity, but in front of each crushed machine gun next is always a number of your comrades, dead and wounded, except in rare instances.

In spite of continuous loss we kept up a slow but steady advance and reached Woods 268. This afternoon we had sunshine for a change, and I think it cheered us all a little. Clearing this woods, which was large and very thick, was a slow matter. Such a task is largely a matter of almost individual effort, as the officers can see and direct but few of the men, who work through the woods in small groups and even alone, opposing the rifle and automatic rifle to the machine gun. It was late in the afternoon when we reached the northern edge of Woods 268. We had been largely confined to the paths in this woods, on account of the extreme thickness of the underbrush, which it was impossible to tear one's way through. Looking out from the edge of the woods I saw an unusual sight, to which Capt. Ben Hewitt called my attention. There on a knoll in the open field not more than five hundred yards away was a German field piece of artillery, which had just ceased firing. Around it an excited group of German gunners were busy. Our men were firing at them, but in the excitement seemed to be making poor practice. A team of six galloping horses came tearing over a rise, swung into place very neatly behind the gun, which was quickly attached to the limber. There was a wild scramble among the gunners to climb into their places on the gun and limber, and away the whole unit went at full gallop, bumping and bouncing, and were quickly out of sight and all this time under a hail of bullets. I could not help admiring their work and also hoping that some of our bullets would wreck the whole thing, but I really believe I was glad to see those brave men get away with their gun.

Our position here was high, and looking back on our left I could see the troops of the 37th Division considerably behind the point of advance we had now reached. From what I had seen of the position of the 315th Infantry on our right, before entering these woods, I believed we were ahead of them also. As our orders were to keep our place in line and not get too far ahead or behind the units on our flanks, and as doing so would only bring a concentrated fire upon us, it being now late in the afternoon, I decided to pass the night where I was. No food, not even a piece of old bread, not even water, no blankets, absolutely nothing to give us courage and strength for the terrible ordeal of the morrow. Nothing but the "will to do," and our own sense of duty and self-respect to carry us on and help us in the attack we all knew we must make in the morning. It rained most of the night and shells fell, and we lay in the mud under the dripping bushes, cold, weary, wet and hungry with the thought of tomorrow's battle and wounds and death to wear down our courage.

About five o'clock a runner brought me an order to report to the Colonel, whose P.C. was now at the south end of the woods we were occupying. As things had quieted somewhat and seemed fairly safe for the time being, I went back through the woods accompanied by my faithful orderly, Corporal Euwart. I had before this established a line of outposts on the edge of the woods, under an officer, and had placed some machine guns there also. The officers had placed all the men they could gather in position to help the line at the edge of the woods and resist any attack the Germans might attempt. I turned over the command to Capt. Knack, told him where I was going, and told him to exercise his own judgment in the command until I returned. Going back through the woods I noticed several wooden shacks or huts left by the

Germans and a large number of the wicker cases they use to carry their artillery shells in, showing that the woods had long been an artillery position for them. Well it never would be again, if we could prevent it.

I found Col. Charles with his staff at the other end of the woods, about a quarter of a mile or more behind my front, or it may have been nearer a half mile. This was the closest the regimental P.C. had been to us so far in the battle. The Colonel asked me many questions as to how the battle was going and of my position for the night. I assured the Colonel that all was as well as could be and that I felt sure that I could hold the woods, in the rear of which we then were. He seemed reassured, and I made him a report of my losses in officers showing him that they had been very heavy.

I noticed that Capt. Feuardent, the French officer attached to regimental headquarters, had several men busy digging a small trench in the ground. As soon as it was finished, he got into it and stayed there, inviting the Colonel and others to join him. We had been out in the open so much that this action on his part seemed strange, if not too cautious to me. But shells were falling all around us, and Capt. Feuardent, wise with long battle experience, was simply taking cover against useless exposure to enemy fire. He was as brave as any when need arose, but he did not expose himself needlessly and in this instance probably saved his life. For I had scarcely finished my report to the Colonel, when a shrapnel shell burst directly over us and stunned us all. When I recovered I saw the Colonel sitting on the ground holding his right hip with his hand, with an expression of great pain on his face and calling "tourniquet, tourniquet." We all thought him badly wounded, and two medical officers rushed to his assistance. They took his breeches down, but could find no blood and no wound. A piece of the shell had hit his water canteen, smashed it and bruised his hip.

He felt the water running down his leg and of course thought it was blood. It was quite a shock to him and a narrow escape. This occurrence became quite a joke in the regiment, and all the men knew of it. Had the Colonel been popular it would not have been so much of a joke. Many a long, weary, wet night march, thereafter, was eased by a roar of laughter caused by some man calling out in a loud voice, "tourniquet, tourniquet."

But there was a fatal and a very sad result from the explosion of this same shell. Sergeant-Major Harold H. Bair,[4] regimental sergeant-major, who was standing near the Colonel, was struck in the right thigh by a large piece of this shell and died in a few hours as a result. I was very close to him and saw it all. He lay on his stomach clasping his face in his hands, calling out, "Oh Christ! Oh Christ!" His face was contorted with agony. One of the medical officers left the Colonel and hurried to Bair. He turned him over to find his wound, and there in his right thigh, half-way down to the knee, was a large, open and awful wound, the flesh torn open just like raw beef and the blood gushing forth in great quantity. The doctor took off Bair's belt, and making a tourniquet of it around the upper part of his thigh, he drew it as tight as he could, stopping the flow of blood considerably, but by no means entirely. He, the doctor, looked up at us and shook his head sadly, and we understood that there was no chance for the Sergeant-Major. The frightful shock and loss of blood would kill him. He was made as comfortable as possible and wrapped in a blanket. It was not thought worthwhile to put him through the agony of being carried back to a field hospital.

A very sad part of this story is that Sergeant-Major Bair had only just rejoined the regiment, not more than a half hour or so ago, I was told. He had been sent to the officers' training school at Langres, I believe it was, and was there working for a commission when he heard that his old regiment was going into battle. He refused to have it go in without him and resigned his position, gave up his chance to be an officer, which every good soldier wanted very much to become, and hurried to rejoin his old comrades, only to meet death with great suffering, just as he had caught up with them.

Shortly after Sergeant-Major Bair was wounded, evening came on and the battle lulled and shells became infrequent, while just previously the shell-fire had been very heavy. I was greatly surprised to see Capt. Knack, followed by a lot of men, coming back through the woods in the immediate rear of which we were. I hurried up to him and asked what was wrong that he had given up our front line, which I considered so necessary to maintain. Here now was the whole front backed up upon Regimental P.C. He said that the German shell-fire got extremely

4. From Hanover, Pennsylvania.

heavy on the front edge of the wood, and he could see no use staying there wasting men's lives; so exercising his own judgment as I had told him to do, he had ordered a retirement for a short ways into the wood. Of course he did not know Regimental P.C. was up so close to him. Capt. Knack was no coward, but a fearless soldier, who was thinking more of his men than himself.

The Colonel came up and was much worried to have his front back on his headquarters. I told him I would take my men back to the front of the woods at once and reestablish them there for the night. It was no small matter to gather the scattered men, in the woods and the dusk, but all the officers helped and soon we led them back through the darkening forest, all alert and watchful, with rifle and pistol ready, for we did not know if the Germans had advanced into the woods. It was a nervous, anxious march, but we regained the north edge of the woods without finding any Germans in them and soon had the men in line among the trees and several machine guns placed with them.

I stood on the edge of the forest and looked out over the open fields and small patches of woods we must advance over and through tomorrow. Everything was so quiet and peaceful like a countryside at home in the evening. Not a gun cracked nor a shell burst, nor was there a German in sight, but well I knew that that beautiful countryside was full of enemies and machines of death.

The regular night rain set in, as we finished placing the men, and added to our other discomforts. Lt. Keller, my adjutant, and I searched for a thick bush to protect us from the rain and finally settled for the night under a bush, lying on his rain-coat and covered over with my rain cape. But soon the bush got soaked, and the rain dripped on us, making us damp and uncomfortable. We slept fitfully and very poorly and got little real rest. Empty stomachs and anxiety make poor sleep persuaders. We were lucky to be alive and so tired and miserable, with perhaps but a short time to live, and poor Keller was killed early in the morning. During the night, in the intense darkness, I heard someone calling my name through the woods. I answered and Lt. Lautenbacher of Company C asked where I was. I tried to direct him, and by frequent exchange of calls he finally found us, after much stumbling and crashing through the undergrowth. And when he did finally reach our miserable bed, he stumbled over our feet and fell full length upon us, with his weight of some two hundred and twenty-five pounds. There was a scramble to get ourselves separated, and strange as it seems now, much laughter among us at our ridiculous position. He got up finally and apologized and gave me some orders from the Colonel relative to the attack of the morning. I have forgotten now just what they were. Poor Lautenbacher, he was to die also tomorrow.

The miserable night finally passed, as all nights must, and the dawn came in the woods damp, gray and sullen. No sun to warm and cheer us. Again, for the fourth time, the rolling kitchens with their good hot soup and stew and coffee were many miles to the rear. I don't believe there was a dry crust among us all, and few had even a mouthful of water.

We were to advance at seven to keep in line with the units on both sides of us. Why we never made a night attack and thus escaped most of the enemy's fire, I do not know, but it was doubtless due to the unavoidable and terrible confusion which generally occurs in a night attack, and here in the mixed woods and open fields it would be practically impossible to direct and control troops at night. It was very difficult to do so in daylight.

While the companies were forming in the woods for the attack, gathered and placed by the surviving officers and sergeants, who were now very few, the sergeant in charge of the one-pounder gun, a very heavy piece which his men had carried for three days, the wheels being useless in such country and long ago abandoned, came to me and said they could carry it no farther as the men were done up. He also reported that of all the quantity of shells they had started with, there were but sixteen remaining.

From the edge of the woods I had noticed ahead of us and off to the front a small clump of trees, from which machine guns had been firing at us over the open fields between. I pointed out this enemy position to the gun sergeant and ordered him to bring up his gun and fire his sixteen shells into the clump of trees. Laboriously the weary men carried the heavy gun to the edge of forest, and the sergeant carefully figured the range and sighted the gun. I stood by watching his work. His first shell burst just short of the trees, the second plumped right into them, and rapidly he fired the other fourteen shells, all of which burst right amongst the trees, which were his target. I had seen these one-pounder guns demonstrated at the School at Langres, and I knew it was a wonderfully accurate weapon in the hands of a good gunner.

I watched the target with my field glasses, and when about half of the Sergeant's shells had burst among the trees, I saw a lot of Germans issue from the rear of the clump of trees and run away toward their rear as fast as they could. The gun crew soon saw them and were much elated at the success of their work. There was no more machine gun fire from that woods for some considerable time. As soon as the last shell was fired, the Sergeant ordered his crew to scatter away from the gun and told me that the German artillery observers would see the flash of it, and their shells would soon fall near the gun. He was correct. In a few minutes they came and burst very near the gun. One of these shells killed my adjutant, Lt. Keller. The gun was abandoned there, and we never saw it again.

To return to our attack on this morning of September 29, 1918, all of my companies had led the attack on different days except Company A, and now it was their turn. Company A, under Lt. E. M. Sanborn, had been acting as regimental reserve for the first three days of the battle, but the Colonel had sent it back to me, knowing how my battalion had suffered heavy losses. But it reported at only half strength, having suffered much from shell fire and having lost many men by details from it and by men lost and straggling due to the thick woods and the darkness.

I therefore directed Company A to lead the attack, and forming in the woods they went out into the open field beyond and immediately came under a terrific shell fire and machine gun barrage, the worst fire and hardest test of courage they had ever endured. I watched them go on through this awful fire and could see their ranks thinning out at every step. I stood at the edge of the woods to watch the other companies form and follow out into the hell of shell fire. Company B under my good old friend, Capt. Knack, came next and went bravely and coolly out into the shells. But for two of them the test seemed too hard. I saw them drop to the ground and let their company go on without them. I went over to them and ordered them to get up and follow their company.

They looked at me with frightened eyes, but did not obey my order. Company C was coming up, and I did not want such an example to deter them. According to army regulations, disobedience on the field of battle must be punished at once by death. I should have drawn my pistol and shot them both. Too many men were being killed, and I had not the heart to do such a thing anyway. Picking up a heavy entrenching spade from the ground, I hit each of these two terrified men a resounding whack on the seat of his breeches, putting my back into the blow, and was about to repeat the treatment when they jumped up and made off at full speed after their company, fearing the spade more than the shells, or more probably brought back to their proper state of mind by such heroic treatment. Probably these men had done well so far and would in the future. The terrors of battle break down many brave men. Army regulations permitted me to shoot these men under the circumstances, but army regulations never permit an officer to strike a man, under penalty of court-martial, but I was too much wrought up at the time to have regard for regulations. I don't believe they ever lodged a complaint against me.

Company C passed me and went on after Company B. The shell fire grew worse and was simply terrible. I thought we were going to be completely wiped out. The ground was covered with dead and wounded men, and for the latter there could be no immediate help, and they must lie there amid the bursting shells which tore great holes in the earth and finished many a poor fellow.

Company D came out of the woods last and did not advance very far when the entire advance came to a stop. So heavy was the fire from shells and machine guns and even trench mortars that men simply could not endure it, and the survivors lay flat on the ground to get what little protection they could. I was greatly distressed at the failure of my battalion to advance further and with my own responsibility for our success. We must get forward. Such had been our teaching and the essence of all our training. I ran about among the men urging them to get up and go forward and did get many of them to rush forward in small groups. But in the main my efforts were vain, as the terrific fire was more than human beings could endure, and our losses were becoming awful. Nearly all of the remaining officers were dead or wounded. The unit on our right, our Second Battalion, was somewhat protected from German shell fire by the woods it advanced through. The unit on our left, a regiment of the 37th Division, was not up in line with us and was protected by a ridge in its front. This left my battalion the main target for the German artillery and machine guns. We were in the open, absolutely without protection, and they poured on us a concentrated fire, which was more than we could advance under, nor do I believe could any troops have advanced under such a fire.

Such was my anxiety about my responsibility that I had no thought of my personal safety—sometimes there are greater things to think of. I was walking about in the open fully exposed to that fire for ten minutes I suppose, perhaps longer, trying to get the men forward, but beyond being knocked down by the concussion of an exploding shell and being very slightly wounded in the right shin by a very small bit of shell, I suffered no harm whatever, and now, when I think of that awful shell fire, I wonder that I ever came through it alive. Once a small bomb, probably from a trench mortar, came bounding along the ground, jumping from side to side, the fuse sputtering and crackling, and actually passed between my feet and exploded beyond me.

For the time being, at least, our advance was stopped, but we had no idea of retiring, and I expected we would go on when the fire lessened or we received help in some way either from our own artillery or from more infantry sent in.[5] But we never did advance any further on this plateau, but were withdrawn and advanced in the afternoon on our right, through the woods. But that part of my story comes later. There are still many details of this terrible morning that I must record here. They form a story of death and heroism which I feel a duty to set down.

The death of Lt. Daniel Keller, my adjutant, a close friend and efficient officer, was a great shock and a great loss to me. I had left Lt. Keller and Lt. Fouraker, my gas officer, at the edge of the woods, while my companies were forming for the attack early in the morning, and had gone back into the woods a little way to see what delayed one of my companies from coming out. When I returned to them, Lt. Fouraker was standing with his hand wrapped in a bloody handkerchief looking

5. Parkin's lament that the infantrymen of the 79th Division received no help from artillery is a familiar one in the literature of the AEF. Despite the best efforts of engineers, who braved enemy shellfire while rebuilding roads, it almost always took longer than expected to haul artillery pieces into new positions.

down at Lt. Keller, who lay on his face on the ground. He told me a shell had burst very close to them and had wounded him in the hand and got poor Keller he feared.

I turned Lt. Keller over on his back and saw a large hole in his chest, near his left shoulder, from which the blood was pumping strongly. It looked like an awful wound to me, and I feared that he could not survive it. I spoke to him and asked him if he felt badly, and he said, "No." The shock had numbed him so that he was not suffering except in his breathing. Quite a large piece of the shell had entered his lungs apparently. I knew his only chance was to get to the first aid station, back in the woods, some hundreds of yards away. I stopped two wounded men, on their way back, and ordered them to carry him with all possible speed to the first aid station. They picked up poor Keller, one taking him under the arms and the other holding him under the knees, and carried him away as fast as their condition permitted. Just as they left I put Keller's overcoat over him and leaning over said something to try to encourage him and bade him goodbye. "God bless you, Major," was his reply to me, and we gripped hands at parting. I never saw him again. The surgeon told me that he was in a stupor when he reached the first aid, and that he died in that condition.

Capt. Benjamin H. Hewit of Company M, a very fine officer and a beloved comrade, also gave up his life on this morning.[6] He had been assigned to me with half of his company as "moppers up" to clear our trenches we captured. He came to me early on this morning and said he had so few men left that he had sent them to one of my companies. He asked how he could best be of service to me. As Company A had very few officers left and was to lead the attack, I asked him if he would go out with it, not in command but just to help Lt. Sanborn all he could. He very readily agreed, and I sent him out to his death unknowingly. Capt. Fatzinger of Company C told me afterwards, or rather wrote me, that he came upon Capt. Hewit sitting in a shell hole, very white in the face, and with his arms crossed over his breast. He had been shot through the chest by a bullet. His only hope was to have immediate

6. Like most of the officers in the regiment, Hewett was a Pennsylvanian. He was educated at Lehigh and Purdue Universities before he went through OTC with Parkin at Fort Niagara. His local paper reported his death as a German atrocity for shelling the wounded. See Walker, *Betrayal*, 172.

attention, and some of Capt. Knack's men who were near carried him off to the rear. Just before they reached the edge of the woods, a large shell struck full upon the group, and with the exception of one man who had his left arm torn off, the group was absolutely wiped out of existence. Of Capt. Hewit and three of his bearers absolutely no trace was left, and a hole in the ground marked the spot where they had been obliterated.

Lt. Phillipus Miller was badly wounded in the elbow and suffered for years in hospital and will never have the full use of his arm. He was able to crawl away to the rear and get attention at the first aid.

Lt. E. M. Sanborn suffered six wounds on this day and was very lucky to survive his terrible experience. He remained with his men until wounded several times. On his way to the rear he received two more wounds, and at the field hospital received his sixth wound from a piece of shell while lying on a cot.

My scout officer, Lt. Richard Y. Naill, was severely wounded in the hand on this memorable morning and did not recover until after the Armistice. I missed his valued services very greatly.

Lt. Ivan L. Lautenbacher of Company C was shot through the chest this same day and mortally wounded. He died very soon in the field hospital. The last I saw of this gallant officer was in the dusk of the evening. He was placed in a large chair and four men put poles under it carried him off, shoulder high, to the field hospital. Poor fellow, sitting up there looking like the Sultan of Zanzibar borne high, he was being carried to his deathbed.

To return to our situation on the open plateau, our advance finally stopped or rather was crushed by the intense, concentrated fire of the enemy. Convinced of the utter impossibility of getting forward for the time being at least, I took refuge in a shallow ravine and lay down flat upon the ground, for the protection was very slight, the ravine not being very deep. Here I found Capt. Paul Strong and Lt. James Cragg, who were in charge of one of our companies supposed to keep us in liaison or communication with the 37th Division on our left. The terrible fire had driven them to cover also. I was now very much worried and concerned over the situation of my battalion and very desirous of talking it over with my ablest adviser, Capt. Louis C. Knack, and in my great anxiety I must have expressed my thoughts, for Sgt. Gover C. Sheckart of Company C, who lay near me, with great bravery and entire indifference to his personal safety, went out of the ravine to the front of the plateau under the heavy fire, found Capt. Knack and brought him back to me.

We talked our situation over and Capt. Knack agreed that to try to advance farther under such a heavy fire was a useless waste of life. So having his advice I was more content to wait until the fire slackened or we got assistance or support from other units in the line to our right and left. So far we seemed to be well in advance of them.

"But," said brave Capt. Knack, "if we can't advance we will stick it out and not let them drive us back," and stick it out we did, there in the open, through most of that day.

While we were lying there in the shallow ravine, Capt. Knack, Capt. Strong, Lt. Cragg, and I, and Sgt.-Major McCormack, the shells fell heavily and some of them very close to us. Any second one might wipe out our entire group. We could not lift our heads, so close over us flew the stream of machine gun bullets, and under such extremely dangerous circumstances we were shaken with laughter by an occurrence which struck us as very funny. Some of the shells which fell just behind us threw up huge clods of wet earth, and some of these fell on our backs and legs and shoulders, thumping us heavily and almost knocking the wind out of us. The sounds of the thumping and the expressions on the faces of those so hit seemed comical, and we all laughed over it more than once. Perhaps some of this laughter was due to nervous strain, but most of it I think was not. One of Capt. Knack's men crawled back to him with a message, and while they were lying on the ground with their heads close together talking, a bullet struck the man in the head and killed him instantly. His body gave a convulsive shudder and he had "gone West." I lay within a few feet of him when he was hit. It was but a momentary shock to us—we had become hardened to such things—and his body lay there in front of us, disregarded. Any one of us might soon be as dead as he.

Just in rear of us was a small clump of bushes, and I was thinking of crawling into them, as they gave some slight protection from enemy observation at least, and had turned partly around with this intention in mind, when I saw a shell hit right in the midst of the bushes and wipe out the whole lot at one blast. Had I had my idea few minutes sooner my career would have ended in that explosion.

While we lay in this ravine I kept wondering why the men of the 37th Division on our left did not appear in the open fields in that direction. I spoke to Capt. Knack about it, and Sgt. Grover Sheckart, a man with no fear in his make-up, got up without any orders and went off to the left, along the top of a low ridge with the bullets knocking up the dust and dirt around him, fully exposed to the enemy machine-gunners and utterly indifferent to the hail of bullets. We watched him with great admiration for his bravery, but with a tense fear that he would fall at every step. He stopped on the top of the ridge and stood there, looking away to our left rear, and then turned and hurried back to us again through the hail of bullets. Throwing himself down beside me, he reported that the infantry of the 37th were climbing the rear side of the small ridge in force, and would soon show on top of it. I thanked him and also rebuked him for so endangering his life. He did not seem to feel that he had done anything unusual.

Very soon long extended lines of infantry topped the low ridge to the left of us. There seemed to be a great many of the khaki-clad soldiers, but no sooner did they show on the top of the rise than the German artillery, doubtless waiting for just this event, simply deluged them with shells, turning all their guns away from us. So thick were the explosions and bursts of shells that we could scarcely see any men on the position. They retired back of the ridge, unable to stand such punishment, and it is no reflection upon their courage that they did retire, as the concentrated shell fire was more than men could endure. They came up bravely several times afterwards, and were each time literally blown off that ridge. They did not occupy that ridge while we were on our position, and we remained out in front with our left flank unprotected.

During one of the intervals between the attempts of the men of the 37th Division to capture the low ridge on our left, one of the most exciting incidents of the battle occurred. To my great surprise a company of German infantry rose up from the ground on the German slope of the ridge on our left—we were far enough in advance to see both sides of the ridge the 37th Division was having so much trouble taking—and started off to their rear in a leisurely manner and in good order. We had not seen them before and no doubt many of the bullets which had so harassed us had come from them. Their insolence in marching off in such a manner right in full view of us astonished and angered us. Perhaps they thought we were wiped out completely. They very soon learned differently. All over our position officers and men arose and began firing rifles at the Germans as fast as they could work the bolts. The excitement caused a too rapid fire, which was not as effective as it should have been. I picked up a rifle myself and emptied it several times. The Germans must have been four or five hundred yards away when we first saw them, and their dignified withdrawal became a hasty retreat when our bullets began to fly around them. They soon disappeared from view.

I remember distinctly one German soldier on the flank of the retiring company nearest us. When I first saw him he was marching along leisurely with his big pack on his back and his rifle on his shoulder. When the bullets began to fly around him he walked faster and then began to run awkwardly. I was firing at him slowly and carefully. Suddenly he stopped abruptly and fell down on his face. Whether he was hit or only taking cover will always be a question.

9
Another Lost Battalion

It was now getting on toward the middle of the afternoon. We had not advanced further, but neither had we been driven back. Any movement on our part brought down a deluge of shells. We were accurately spotted by the German artillery and machine gunners. It occurred to me to remain quiet until dusk and then make an advance under cover of the darkness, at least as far as we were now able to see the country in front of us. Knowing the terrain well minimizes the difficulties of a night attack. But I did not get an opportunity to carry out this purpose. A runner from Regimental headquarters reached me, crawling on his hands and knees, with an order to report back to the Colonel. The message was imperative. Without delay I gave over the command to Capt. Knack with directions to hold on until he heard from me, and I started back with the runner and Corporal Euwart, my orderly. Twice before we reached the woods we heard the shriek of approaching shells and each time threw ourselves flat on the ground. They burst so close that I finally entered the woods with my head ringing from the explosions and my face covered with the dust of them. Even for three men moving the Germans sent a volley of shells.

Going back through the woods, still harassed by the bursting shells, I passed the regimental first aid station, where the wounded were being gathered for medical aid. Many of the badly wounded lay about on the ground, among whom Major Cornwell and Lt. Burke and the other medical officers worked bravely and industriously in spite of the shells which fell all about them. I saw Lt. Eastman M. Sanborn standing there with a hospital man putting bandages on his wounds, of which he had four or five. He was smoking a cigarette and grinned broadly at me when I greeted him. I did not see my adjutant Lt. Keller and had not time to look for him. When I reached the regimental P.C. at the rear end of the woods, I found there a group of officers: Col. Charles,

Lt. Col. Meador, Capt. Fitzpatrick, Capt. Manning, Capt. Glock, Capt. Montgomery, Capt. Goetz, all of whom belonged to regimental headquarters, and Capt. Feuardent and Lt. Castel, French officers attached to our regiment. Capt. Feuardent being an old timer on the front and not believing in taking any more chances with shells than was necessary, was once again sitting in a small trench he had had dug for him.

I reported to Col. Charles for orders, and he requested a list of my losses in officers, which I made out for him. It was long and included all of my officers except about six. The Colonel informed me that the 313th Infantry would pass through us soon and that I was to form up the available men and officers left in the neighborhood and follow the 313th in support. I sent word to Capt. Knack to bring back what men he had left.

The officers I had for this advance, as well as I can remember, were as follows: Capt. Louis C. Knack, Capt. Paul M. Anderson, Lt. Hurley, Lt. Fitzharris. There were several others, but I do not recall their names. We set to work and gathered up all of the men we could find in the neighborhood and formed them into three companies in the open to the right rear of Woods 268. Here we were protected from observation by the Germans and comparatively free from shell fire. I counted roughly some 380 officers and men.

We waited for the 313th Infantry to come up and pass through us to the attack. While waiting here I saw two sights I shall not soon forget. Off to our right rear, beyond the Sector of the 315th Infantry in an open field, I saw a regiment of the 3rd Division advancing in perfect order in widely extended open formation. They came on beautifully and seemed to have a great many men. Soon the German shells began to burst amongst them, throwing up huge bursts of dirt and smoke. The holes in their formation caused by these shells seemed to fill up automatically, and their steady advance was not interrupted in the least. It was a beautiful, thrilling military spectacle. I do not know what regiment it was, but they deserve great credit. The other sight was gruesome and ghastly. Two men came up to our medical officer, leading between them a man who had been injured by the blast of an exploding shell. His clothes above his waist had been completely torn off his body. His head, face and body down to his waist were jet black, and red blood was running over his chest from a wound in his shoulder. He was the most awful looking wounded man I saw in France, and yet he did not seem seriously wounded and could walk with assistance. Our doctors took charge of the poor fellow.

Before we gathered and formed our men for the attack I noticed something which rather amused me. Shells had been falling in considerable numbers in our neighborhood, and a great many of the men had crawled under the bushes and undergrowth along the edge of the woods, apparently feeling that they had some protection overhead. Of course they were just as exposed to shell fire as we who were out in the open, and it did seem humorous to me to see them sitting in there, looking out at us. They might as well have held up a raincoat for protection from shells.

The 313th Infantry came up in open attack formation and in good order and seemed to have a lot of men left. There were no officers of field rank with them (officers of rank of major or higher), and they were led by Capt. Colly Burgwin and Capt. Kelly. They passed through us and went on through a heavy shell fire into the Woods No. 250, called by us the Bois de Cunel.

I waited a short time, and as the 313th Infantry machine gun company did not move forward, and feeling sure that we now had out designated depth of 600 meters between us and the 313th Infantry, I signaled to Capts. Knack and Anderson, and my three companies advanced against Woods 250 in support of the 313th Infantry according to my orders. We passed through the machine gun company and came out into the open under observation of the German artillery, which immediately deluged us (no other word so expresses the storm of shells which struck us) with heavy shell fire, and our losses started at once.

The bursting shells were so numerous and so close that I thought our advance would be broken up at once. The air fairly rocked. The fumes filled our mouths and nostrils, and the flying pieces of shell seemed to fill the air with their shrieking and whizzing.

Feeling sure that we could not endure such heavy devastating fire for long, I signaled with whistle and shouts for double time, and we started to run for the woods, now about fifty yards ahead of us. Our feet were large and heavy with clinging masses of soft mud, and we ran on slowly and heavily, stirred to our greatest efforts by the many close-bursting shells, which took steadily from our decreasing ranks.

Men will do strange things in the face of close death. Running and stumbling, confused by the shell bursts, and expecting to be torn apart by one at any instant, I was amazed to come upon a soldier with his clothes down, there in the open field, simply engulfed in bursting shells, attending to duties of nature. As I passed I shouted something at him, but he refused to be disturbed either by me or the shells.

We reached the most welcome shelter of the woods at last, out of breath and somewhat stunned and confused by the shell bursts so close. Being now out of sight of the German artillery observers, we suffered less from the shells, although they still came among us in considerable numbers.

Just at the edge of the woods Lt. Fitzharris was killed instantly.[1] The poor boy lay on the side of the forest road on his face, so quickly changed from a live, active and keenly intelligent young officer to what now seemed only a shell. Looking down on these bodies of my slain friends and comrades, I could not bring myself to feel that this was all for them, that they had ceased utterly to exist. They did not seem to be there any more, just their bodies, their unimportant parts left with us. They had gone on to some place. Thoughts of a hereafter are thus impressed upon one very forcibly upon the battlefield. I can never believe that physical death ends all for the fine, intelligent characters I have seen cut off thus abruptly from the physical part of life on the field of battle.

Queer what thoughts one has at such times. Not only did I feel and think the things I have mentioned about poor Fitzharris, but I have always retained the mental impression of what fine new French field boots he was wearing, and I remember his new well-filled musette bag. We left him there, after making sure that he was dead and beyond all help. It was a week at least before American soldiers occupied these woods again, and there in the rain and utter silence of the woods Fitzharris and his dead comrades lay alone.

We advanced through the forest, obliged by the density of it to keep mostly to the forest road. Knowing the 313th Infantry had preceded us, I did not much fear enemy machine guns. Soon we reached a spot

1. Joseph Christopher Fitzharris was from Philadelphia and was a graduate of Lehigh University. He served as the Third Battalion Intelligence Officer.

where the road forked, going off at right and left angles. Except for some few stragglers, who could give me no information, and for the dead and wounded, we never saw anything of the regiment which had preceded us into the forest. The fork of the road going to our left more nearly followed our compass direction of 258°, so I led my men along it. I cannot to this day understand why we never found the 313th Regiment in that woods. They must have taken the road leading to the right at the fork, and when they received order to withdraw, as they did during the afternoon, they must have gone to the rear through the right or eastern half of the woods.

I had been informed that some units of our division had attacked the woods earlier in the day and were still within them. About half-way through I came upon the remnants of this force, which had had a hard time. The 313th Infantry had passed them to their right, I believe, for I found dead officers and men of this regiment later on in the day, lying in the woods on their right front, but they knew nothing of what had become of that unit. The group we came upon consisted of Capt. John Somers, Lieutenants Murdock, Horne, and Bliss, with some thirty or forty men. They were lying among the trees at another crossroad. I took over the command of the whole party, and as the shell fire again became very heavy, allowed the men to take what protection they could among the trees and made no attempt for the time being to advance, not knowing then where the 313th Regiment was, nor where the Germans were.

To add to our already too many troubles, shells began to fall amongst us from our left rear. Actually our own artillery, away back in our own rear, either French or American guns, began to shell the woods in which we lay. No doubt orders had been sent to them earlier in the day to shell the woods, before we captured them, and were so long reaching the artillery that now, complying with their orders, they were killing their own men. This often happened during the war, as communication during battle was so difficult. We were much disgusted and angered at having to endure this extra punishment from our own guns. The Germans were already giving us plenty.

During this heavy shell fire we made no attempt to advance, but lay flat on the ground, taking what cover we could from the trees and logs. When the shell fire lessened some we advanced through the woods very slowly and cautiously, expecting all the time to get into touch with the rear of the 313th Infantry. We came upon a very large German shack there in the dense forest. It was built like an ordinary frame house of one story and had a kitchen, a large combination dining and living room, a hall-way, a number of good sized bedrooms, and a large porch.

Here the German officers had lived in the greatest of comfort. The living room was well furnished with tables and comfortable large chairs, and an upright piano stood against the wall, some German music upon it. The interruption of life here was apparently very sudden.[2] A half-eaten meal of meat, potatoes, cabbage, and bread still remained on the table, the chairs thrown back as if hastily vacated. Books and parts of personal equipment littered the room. Many souvenirs here, but we were too weary and heavily laden to take any of them along.

I walked down the hall and looked into the bedrooms, which were clean and comfortable. On the beds were good heavy gray German blankets. The beds had not been made up, but they looked clean and inviting to weary men who had been sleeping on the wet, hard ground. Officers' coats and caps hung on the hooks. I would much liked to have taken a cap, but had no place to carry it.

In the kitchen was a large iron stove, crowded with pots and pans in which we found food. And there, tacked on the wall, was the menu for the day. I took it down and put it in my pocket, but lost it later. In the kitchen yard were many fine cabbages laid out on the ground in regular lines, all clean and ready to cook. We ate some of this raw, miserable food for half-starved men. Rabbit pens filled part of this yard, and there were great piles of empty beer and wine bottles against the wall of the house. We always found these three things where the Germans had lived: cabbages, rabbit pens, and great numbers of empty bottles.

On the porch were rustic comfortable chairs, and the porch railing and pillars were of the rustic type. Excellent and careful carpenter work was everywhere in evidence.

I would have much liked to pass the night in these wonderful quarters, but it was not a good position for defense. Nearby were several large and deep dugouts, into which some of our men had disappeared.

2. These officers left in haste to fight against the 313 Regiment, who attacked their eastern flank.

The light was fading in the woods and the dusk was falling. Further advance was not wise, and I decided to retire a little ways to the road which crossed the forest and there take up a position for the night. I called the officers together—we had spent only about ten minutes in the shack—and instructed them to gather the men and retire to the road, taking up a position on the south side of it. I told Capt. Somers to put out outposts on the road leading toward the Germans, which crossed the road we were to occupy at right angles, and also to place pickets on each end of our road where it left the forest on both sides. This would protect us on our front, our right, and our left. I did not fear for our rear. The forest was so dense that the enemy must approach us by one of these roads, but if he did attempt to reach us through the woods we could easily hear him and prepare a reception for him.

While the officers were getting the men into position for the night I did some scouting in the woods in front of our position, accompanied only by my faithful orderly, Corporal Euwart. At the end of the road leading to the right edge of the forest I looked across an open field to another forest and there among the trees saw a group of good sized buildings, above which flew a large Red Cross flag. These buildings were a little in rear of our position. I saw men moving amongst these buildings and judged them to be Germans, although I could not be sure even with my field glasses, so poor was the light. I learned afterwards that this place was "Madeline Farm," which had checked the advance of the 315th Infantry. Here they suffered heavy loss and were withdrawn before they succeeded in capturing the place. So the men I saw were Germans. I cautioned the officer in charge of this outpost to be very careful and pointed out the position of the enemy to him. Corporal Euwart and I next proceeded very cautiously along the edge of the road leading north from our position, taking what cover we could.

We came to the northernmost tip of the woods and stood there among the trees, looking out over the wide expanse of open fields. There, slightly to our left and in full view and within a half or three-quarters of a mile away, lay the town of Romagne, our final objective. Between us lay open fields and no more forests. An advance would be fairly free from machine guns, but terribly and for a long time exposed to artillery fire.

I thought as I stood there that if I had fresh troops with me or proper support for my weary half-starved men, I could easily pass those fields in the dark and surprise and capture that town. It did not look like much of a task to me, and to take our final objective would be an achievement worthwhile. But apparently I was already well out on a point considerably ahead of our troops on either side of us. There were no signs of the 313th in the open ahead of us. Even if I had gone on to Romagne and captured that place, the probability is that I would have been cut off and captured, for my division, unknown to me, had already received orders to retire to a good defensive position preparatory to being relieved. There would have been another lost battalion in the history of the AEF.[3]

While I was standing there at the end of the path on the edge of the woods—I had stepped out from the trees for a better view as there seemed to be no Germans near us—to my great surprise two German soldiers appeared on the top of a small knoll within fifty yards of us and stood looking off to our left towards the front of the 37th Division. They were ordinary sized men and were unarmed and were wearing their round caps instead of their steel helmets. Their attitude and dress indicated that their fighting for the day was over. I had a good look at them, and I was not tempted to shoot them down. The evening was so beautiful and peaceful after the hell of the day that it would have seemed wrong to start killing again. Corporal Euward stood perfectly still looking at them and made no move to shoot them. Perhaps he felt as I did. Suddenly they saw us there so near them, where they had certainly not expected to see an enemy or they would not have so exposed themselves in full view. They dropped out of sight very quickly, apparently jumping down into a trench.

Immediately after the disappearance of the two Germans, a rocket arose in the dusk from their position. No doubt a warning signal to their friends that the enemy was near. I would guess that these Germans passed a very nervous and anxious night, knowing we were right up on them, if they did not retire, as they probably did. Corporal Euwart and I went back along the road, keeping in the edge of the forest as much as possible. We came upon our outpost under Lt. Paul Eckley,

---

3. Parkin's reference here is to the famous 'Lost Battalion' which consisted of companies in the 154th Brigade/77th Division under the command of Major Charles Whittlesey.

and I told him of the presence of the Germans so near. He had about twelve men with him. I relied upon him to protect us, as he was a very good and very keen young officer.

Reaching our position on the road crossing the woods, I went off to the left edge of the trees to see what was on that flank. It was now almost dark, but off there in the open fields some two or three hundred yards I could very dimly see men moving and what I took to be a motor truck or two. They were pointed out to me by the officer in command of the outpost here. He had seen them when the light was better. They were Germans, and they were digging and preparing a position, no doubt, for machine guns. We could hear their voices.

The enemy were on both sides of us about level with our position and on our immediate front. If some of them came in behind us we would be completely surrounded. But the Germans apparently did not know our position, and I very much doubt if those on either side of us knew we were there at all. What a chance to surprise and clean them up that night, but I was alone with only a few tired and nerve-wracked men and no help anywhere near me.[4] Jumping one of these three parties of Germans would warn the others, and I did not have enough men to attack them all at once. It was a wonderful opportunity, but means to take advantage of it were lacking.

I returned to my main position at the crossroads and found the men placed along the rear side of the road among the trees with a support group on the road in rear of the center. This was as well as they could be placed, and the dispositions had been made by that fine old soldier, Capt. Louis C. Knack of Company B. We had no machine guns to support us and must depend upon our rifles and bayonets. I did not expect nor much fear an attack by the Germans in these woods. It might come, but I did not think it would. I felt that we were reasonably secure unless we were cut off, and I did not fear that much as there were plenty of our troops in our rear, so I thought. As a matter of fact there were none near us, all having retired to a point more than a mile in rear of us, but I did not know it then, or I should have lost no time in retiring also.

Being still mystified about the disappearance of the 313th Regiment

---

4. His battalion was also far to the front of the units on either side. An attack with a greatly reduced force came with significant risks.

and wishing Col. Charles to know my position and that of the enemy, as well as desiring orders for the next day, I sent off Lt. Goetz to the rear to find the Colonel and carry out these missions. After he had left I sat there on the edge of the road with some of the officers, and a discussion of our position arose. Every one of those officers thought that we should retire back out of those woods upon the rest of our regiment. Even Capt. Knack was of that opinion. They all regarded our position as most dangerous and thought we would be cut off.

I combated these opinions by saying that we could defend ourselves for the night and in the morning the whole division would be advancing again, as well as the 37th Division on our left, and they would soon come up with us and we could go on. If we retired back out of the forest into the open fields we would again in the morning have to endure the terrible artillery fire we had endured in advancing into the woods, and I thought it useless and a waste of life to do so again. But I got no support whatever in my opinion. As I was in command, I decided to pass the night where we were and so stated, ending the discussion. I was responsible and I would exercise my own judgment. Capt. Knack's was the only opinion which shook my decision at all, but I felt I should hang on even against his judgment.

A runner came back from our front outpost calling my name softly. He told me that Lt. Eckley said that his men were jumpy and nervous and that he requested ten more men for his outpost. I sent the ten men out to him under another officer to keep him company. Twenty-two men made really much too large an outpost, for they were supposed only to warn us of the approach of the enemy and retire upon our position, but under the circumstances I made no objection. Strange to say, I was on this night more free from fear and anxiety than I had been since entering the battle, and most of the rest seemed to be just the opposite. Our situation seemed to exhilarate rather than to depress me.

We had been sending back wounded men ever since we entered the woods. There were quite a few of them, and the carriers had depleted my force too much, so I stopped it. Near us on the edge of the road lay a half dozen of these poor fellows, who had been made as comfortable as possible, but some of whom suffered dreadfully. Sending them back was against our orders anyway. We were to do what we could for the wounded and leave them behind us for the hospital corps to pick up.

We sat there on the wet ground along the road, tired out, but not free to sleep. No breakfast, no lunch, no dinner that day nor the day before, nor the day before that. The first day of the battle had practically used up the food we carried in with us. We had been practically without food for three days. Some may have had some bread, and some some crackers, but the great majority of us had nothing to eat and had had nothing for two or three days. Personally I did not seem to miss food much during the battle, but this was my fifth night without but very little sleep, and I was beginning to feel the strain. Smoking in our position was most dangerous, so I had ordered no smoking after dark, and so could not smoke either.

Capt. Knack and I were discussing as to who should try to get some sleep while the other kept the command, when we heard someone coming along the road from our rear and laid our hands on our pistols. The steps came nearer and nearer, my pistol was out and ready, when a voice began to call my name softly. I answered. It was Lt. Goetz come back to us from the Colonel, and he carried astonishing news. We were far out in front of our division, all alone amongst the enemy. There was no help within a kilometer of us, and he brought me orders to retire at once. I was certainly most surprised at his news. I sent out runners at once to draw in our outposts and ordered the men to form in the road. While all this was being done, Lt. Goetz told me his story.

He had gone back through the woods and across the fields to the place where we had left the Colonel and regimental headquarters. When he arrived there he was astonished to find it occupied only by the dead. Not a living man of all those we had left was there. He did not know what to think of it, but knew he must find the Colonel. Back to the rear he stumbled on in the darkness and finally after a long walk was challenged by outposts and found himself with the regiment. He finally found Col. Charles, who said he had sent messengers to us when he received orders to retire, and as they had heard nothing from us and we did not come back, they had decided that we had been wiped out by the enemy. The Colonel directed Lt. Goetz to hasten back to us, give us orders to retire at once, and guide us back to the regiment. He had had difficulty in finding his way to us in the dark, and a less intelligent officer might not have succeeded at all.

When the wounded heard that we were going to retire they feared they were going to be left behind there in the woods to the enemy and began to voice their distress. So I went over to them and leaning down told them who I was and promised them that not a man would move out until they had been carried to the rear. This quieted them, and they thanked me. Some bunks were torn out of a nearby shack, and the wounded were placed on these, and four men carried each of them. One man who had been shot through both ankles shrieked horribly in his great pain when they moved him, and the men stopped, but I made them move him onto the litter as we could not avoid it. His poor feet were almost cut off and hung down, seemingly held only by shreds. I heard afterwards that he lost both of his feet.

All the outposts having reported in and the wounded gone ahead of us, we started two abreast on our march to the rear. Every man was quiet and kept his equipment from rattling. We had just left the rear of the woods when a Star-light burst in the air on our left, and we halted and stood fast in the brilliant light. The Germans had heard us. When the light burned out we went on, but had to halt again when the light flooded the fields about us, but they did not fire upon us. A Star shell, or Star-rocket, throws a brilliant white light for hundreds of feet about it.[5] Everything is lit up as plainly almost as by daylight. The thing to do when such a light bursts is to throw yourself flat and lie motionless. The next best thing is to stand absolutely still until the light fails. Our column of nearly two hundred men had not time to drop flat. The only thing to do was to be absolutely motionless. Moving objects always draw fire. Fortunately, in our case, the Germans who fired the light were not very close, and we drew no fire. But it is nerve wearing to stand out in the open under a bright light, expecting a machine gun to open on you every second.

We went on stumbling through the black darkness, which was always much worse after the Star-rocket went out, and came at length to the place where the Regimental Headquarters had been, at the rear end of Woods 268.

Since we were leaving all this space open to the enemy, I halted and ordered some of the men to leave the ranks and look around for any

5. These were Very lights, or flares, fired by the enemy at intervals to look for enemy activity.

wounded that might be there. But we found none, only the bodies of the dead. I saw one figure, lying on the ground, wrapped to the shoulders in a blanket, and thought I had found a wounded man. I leaned down and looked into the face and recognized our regimental Sergeant-Major Bair. I spoke to him, but got no answer. I touched his face, and it was cold as stone. Poor fellow, he was dead and had been left behind. Back of us in the dark woods, left there alone with their dead comrades, lay I knew the bodies of my good friends and comrades. Lt. Keller, my adjutant, Capt. Lukens, and many others. I hated to leave them there unburied on the cold, wet ground, their comrades gone so far away from them, and their bodies to be rifled by the enemy. But no living man that I knew of was left behind us. I would willingly have fought the enemy for time to remove the wounded and would never have retired until all of them had been carried back. To tell the truth I was not pleased at our retirement. This giving up of ground that had cost us so dearly was against my ideas entirely.

We resumed our weary march across the dark fields, occasionally passing the lonely dead. As we neared our lines we came to a water pipe which was running water in good quantity. Most of the men were famished for water, so I halted to let them fill their canteens. I felt fairly safe now, although we might still be attacked by the Germans. My acting adjutant, suffering from overstrained nerves, got much excited over the danger of our position and carried on so that I was obliged to settle him down by threatening to send him to the rear and relieve him of his position. He was near the breaking point, but rallied himself and gave me no more trouble. It took much too long to fill all of the canteens, and I told the rest of the men they must share in what water had been taken or find water behind the lines. We could not wait there longer. We were challenged, as we neared our line, but Lt. Goetz, who had gone on a little ahead, satisfied the guards.

As we entered the lines I had him count the men in our column. There were one hundred and sixty of us left out of three hundred and sixty men with whom I had entered the woods that day. The other two hundred were killed, wounded, lost, sent back with wounded—at any rate they did not return with me. I knew that many of them would never again march with me.

At this point, we passed through many machine guns placed to cover the front with their fire and thus protect our position in case of attack by the Germans. It has always been my conviction that in battle we used our machine guns too little. The machine gun company was left in the rear of the regiment, and the idea seemed to be that it was a defensive instead of an offensive unit. The higher authorities always seemed to fear so much that the machine guns would be put out of service. We of the front lines got very little help or support from them. I sent for them many times and hardly ever had them on the front line with me. This is not the proper way to use machine guns in battle. They should be freely at the disposal of the firing line commanders.

As I have said, we entered our lines through many machine guns, all placed to sweep our front. The regiment had retired to the ridge just north of the town of Montfaucon, which ridge we had captured early in the morning two days ago. So we gave up the fruits, except this high ridge, of two days' hard and bloody fighting, which cost us hundreds of men killed and wounded. But it was necessary to be in a strong position when relieved, in case of attack by the enemy during the relief. As a matter of fact there were no strong positions between this ridge and the point of our farthest advance.

I directed Capt. Knack to assume command of my few men, only one hundred and sixty left with me now. I should like very much to have a list of the names of this heroic one hundred and sixty men, for they stayed with me through all the hell and trial of the battle and were the real true heroes of the regiment. No quitters nor slackers in that list, but only real, true, brave soldiers.

My orders were to report to Col. Charles upon reaching our lines, and I went stumbling through the dark woods, hunting for him, inquiring of every man I came across for the regimental P.C. At length I heard Capt. Manning's voice and finally reached him where he lay in a roadside ditch, protected somewhat from the rain by the heavy underbrush. Here were all the survivors of regimental headquarters, sleeping there in the mud. I asked Manning for the Colonel, but he replied that the Colonel was asleep and tired out and that he, Manning, would take my report, which I gave him in very brief terms. I asked Manning why they had retired and left me out there in the front alone. He said they had not done so, but had sent at least two messengers to me and in the confusion of retiring in the dark did not know, and could not find out, whether I had rejoined or not. Apparently Manning felt he had done his duty by me and was surprised to learn, when Lt. Goetz had so informed him, that I had not received my orders to retire.

I felt that my welcome back to the regiment, after the experiences I had gone through, was most casual and unappreciative. I had expected the Colonel and his staff to give me a real welcome, some commendation, and perhaps make a bit of a fuss over me. We had been practically lost to the regiment and in great danger of being surrounded and cut off, and our return and my report caused about as much excitement as that of the officer of the guard at Camp Meade, who would report, "All well and no change."

Capt. Manning asked me if my men had been put on the line of defense, and I told him that Capt. Knack was in command and they were all on the front. Manning told me that we would be relieved tomorrow and sent to the rear to reform and get a rest. I was glad to hear this. Four days of battle had taken nearly all of my officers, killed and wounded, and my men were exhausted and disorganized. It had been a very severe test for new troops, in battle for the first time, and I felt that we had done well and come off with much honor to ourselves, entirely inexperienced of the Front, as we were, when we went over the top.[6]

So my first battle, an experience I had looked forward to through many long, weary months of preparation, was practically over, and I was still alive. Many, many times during those four days I did not see how I could come through it alive. So many were killed and wounded beside me, and the shells had fallen so close and so thickly, while the whizzing of the streams of machine gun bullets had seemed so near that to avoid them seemed impossible. Capt. Manning's news that we were through with our part of the battle, for the present at least, filled me with a deep sense of gratitude and thankfulness to God that I had been spared and brought through safely.

6. His pride and optimism stand in direct contrast to the first impression of the 79th Division's conduct formed at Pershing's headquarters. The division was criticized for its inability to take Montfaucon the first day and then to break the Kriemhilde Stellung beyond, failures that allowed the Germans to reinforce their positions and that brought the entire American offensive to a standstill. Pershing and his staff believed that cowardice and incompetence were the causes of this poor performance in battle. This stigma persisted, but has been corrected by historians since. See William Walker and Gene Fax's studies for revisionist accounts of the 79th Division.

I found my way back to my men, and Capt. Knack and I lay down on the wet ground among the bushes to get some much needed sleep. He had got hold of a blanket somehow. He had an almost uncanny way of finding things for our comfort. We got down on the wet grass and pulled the blanket over us. Just as we were settling to sleep Lt. Jos. Horne came along tired and miserable, and we took him in with us. Actually the three of us there on the soaking ground with only a blanket over us were warm and comfortable. Our three bodies made enough heat together to keep us all warm. There was no shell fire and no noise, and we might have had a very much needed, good night's rest had it not been for a wounded man near us who was horribly and pitifully wounded.

We had become conscious of a terrible groaning and moaning near us and went over to see if we could be of help. There on the ground was a fatally wounded man, the most pitiful and awful sight I think I ever saw. I can never forget it. We made a light—someone had an electric torch. He lay on his face in the mud, and his face and head were thickly coated with it. He was shot through the head. Major Cornwell, who was nearby, told us that nothing could be done for him and that he was really unconscious and not suffering pain and must soon die. Near him was a blanket, which had been placed under him several times, but he would always move off of it.

We could do absolutely nothing for this poor fellow, whose condition wrung our hearts. We put the blanket under him again, and good Capt. Knack tenderly wiped the mud off his face and head. Such a terrible thing to see and remember. Constantly and without ever stopping, he moved his head from one side to the other with the regularity of a pendulum, groaning terribly and continually all the time. For hours he kept this up. Why could not nature let go of life and let him be at peace? It was almost impossible to believe that a man who groaned and moaned so terribly was not suffering frightfully. Northing I saw in the war so wrung my heart in sympathy. I felt that the doctor should have had the right to help the poor fellow by hastening his passing. A medical corps man remained with him. We could not endure the sight longer standing there helpless. We returned to our blanket, but sleep was gone from us in spite of our great weariness. Towards morning the awful groaning ceased, and we knew the poor fellow was at peace at last.

During the night we were disturbed by movement through the woods by soldiers near us. I got up to see what was the cause of all this noise. Some of the men I questioned said they had orders to move off to the left. I asked them from whom they got such orders, and they replied that they had heard them from other soldiers. Feeling sure that this movement was all wrong and without reason, I ordered the men to stay fast in their present positions, and to pass on the word to stand fast and not move. We were on the proper defensive position, and there was no sense in such a move. Any such orders should have come to me and been given out by me. Such rumors and consequent mistakes often happen in war, and sometimes have serious results.

I have omitted any mention of the sumptuous repast we enjoyed just before composing ourselves to our well-earned rest, of which we got very little. While I was seeking a soft place on the ground assisted by Capt. Knack, my orderly, good faithful Corp. Ewart, came to me and whispering low in my ear said he had obtained some food. As we had not eaten for two days or more, this was indeed good news. I did not ask the good corporal where he obtained said food, and I would not have cared had he stolen it from General Pershing himself. This treasure of food consisted of a small can of salmon, called "gold fish" by the soldiers, and a small box of hard biscuits or crackers, just enough food to provoke our hunger, but we were to get very little of it at that. Corp. Euwart gave me the food and turned away, but I made him sit down on the ground to share it with me. We got the can of salmon open and how wonderfully good it did smell and how quickly the odor spread through the woods. Before we got the box of crackers open we had been joined by five officers, all half-starved. I regretted their presence exceedingly, much as I valued these brave gentlemen. So I was host and tried to be cheerful about it too. We seven dined off that great mass of food. Each had two biscuits heaped with salmon. I do not like salmon—I hardly ever eat it—but I never tasted better food in my life. I could have eaten about six cans of it myself.

10

Relief

The morning of September 30, 1918, dawned gray and chilly; no sun came up to cheer us and warm our cold bodies. But we felt cheerful anyway, for we were to be relieved today, and our first battle was over. We were glad to be alive and felt that we had done well in our first fight. We got hold of some jam and biscuits on this day and it appeased our hunger some, but was poor food for hungry men who wanted meat and bread and coffee. It was quiet day for us, very quiet compared with the four preceding days. We remained scattered along the front and through the woods. It was not wise to gather together as the occasional shells might strike a group. No fires were permitted as they would mark our position. Montfaucon loomed high just behind us in its towering position on its high hill. A deep, wide valley lay between us, and in it we knew lay unburied comrades. Chaplain McNary was there busy with a detail of men gathering the dead for burial. Capt. Knack and I got permission to attend the funeral of Major Atwood, which I have already described.

On our way back to where he lay we passed some German knapsacks, which we examined. They contained many letters from home, and some photographs of women and children. Valued treasures which some German husband and father was now missing very greatly. Captain Knack picked up a fine heavy German blanket and took it with him. It was a great comfort to us that night, when we lay out on the cold ground. We were walking over ground where three days before we had endured and survived terrible concentrated shell fire, which I had not expected to survive. How peaceful and quiet this meadow now, and what an awful place it had been on that morning.

It was cool and rainy during the afternoon, and a warm, dry place to rest in was not to be found. I had my post of command in a little clump of trees where a depression in the ground gave me some protection from the cold wind. We knew that we were to be relieved that afternoon by the veteran 3rd Division.[1] We kept looking off to the rear for signs of the relieving troops, but could see none. The hill upon which Montfaucon sat covered the rear from view, and doubtless the 3rd Division was behind it now. In the middle of the afternoon and very suddenly coming through Montfaucon and down over the hill appeared many long lines of American infantry, all in single file and with good distances between the men. I had wondered how they would come in, but had not thought of this formation, which was a very good one to avoid loss by enemy shell fire. The whole country in our rear seemed to be full of moving men in long lines.

The excellent German artillery observation saw the relieving troops as soon as we did, and shells began to fall among them very soon after they appeared. We watched the shells bursting over them and between their long lines. They suffered some loss, but came on steadily, closing up the occasional gaps. The shell fire was not very heavy, and their losses, as far as we could see, did not amount to much. I wondered that the Germans did not shell them more heavily. When the leading files of the lines reached our position, they halted and the officers were taken forward and shown our front lines, and the situation was explained to them. Although called a Regular Army Division, the "Third" was such in name only, being composed as were all others except the National Guard Divisions, of new temporary officers and men from the draft. I heard some of the men tell my men that they were replacements and that this was their first battle. Their men wore the heavy full pack. We had only a light pack, having left our pack rolls containing our blankets and shelter tents at Camp Normandy. The full pack is too much of a burden for men to carry in battle, and I was surprised to see the men of the 3rd Division carrying theirs.

It took some time to effect our relief and replace our men with those of the 3rd Division. As my companies were relieved and came back out of the woods I had them formed up just in rear of the forest in open attack order, in order to go out to the rear and avoid casualties by shell fire as much as possible. When all four companies were formed, the

1. The 3rd Division fought with distinction at the Second Battle of the Marne in July 1918.

Colonel ordered me to move out, and I sent off my companies at intervals well apart, and the men well spread out. Capt. Knack and Chaplain McNary and I were near each other during this retirement, leaving with the last of my companies. Capt. Knack said, "Wouldn't it be hard luck to get hit now, going out, after coming through the battle?"

Shells soon fell among us, and a few of my men were hit, but no shell fell near our group. Capt. James Montgomery, regimental personnel officer, while coming out with Capt. Manning, regimental adjutant, was hit in the hip by a piece of shell and rather badly wounded, but recovered after the war. He had come all through five days of battle up to this last minute only to be wounded then.

Passing through the ruined town of Montfaucon, where we had endured such a terrible night of shell fire, I got separated from my men and had some difficulty in finding them in the rear of the town, but after much weary walking succeeded in doing so. I was surprised to find long columns of transport, artillery wagons, trucks, etc., immediately in rear of the town. I did not expect to find them up so close to the firing line and do not think they should have been. A forced retirement in haste would have made an awful mess of things, with all the roads blocked. The drivers looked at us, fresh from the battle as we were, curiously, and made many comments on our rough and weary appearance. No wonder. Unshaved, starved, weary and unkempt, we presented a most woe begone appearance. Along the road and at the crossroads, I noticed heavy, stout, concrete pillars, so close together that a wagon could just get between. I could not understand their purpose, but was told later than they were placed there by the Germans to impede the progress of the tanks of the enemy.[2]

Here in the fields back of the hill of Montfaucon many troops, units of the 3rd Division, were coming in, and units of the 79th Division, ours, going out. Here also were the tents of a large field hospital, which had suffered much from shell fire. One of my officers, Lt. Sanborn, was in this hospital when it was under shell fire and received a wound in his hand. The 3rd Division halted some of its units near this hospital,

2. Though he rarely mentions them, French tanks were used in the assault on Montfaucon and the Kriemhilde Stellung in support of the advancing 313th and 316th Infantry.

which was a great mistake, for the German artillery in firing at them often hit the hospital.

The Regiment assembled, and Col. Charles led us back towards the rear. My battalion led the way, and I walked with the Colonel. We talked but little. We were both tired out, and my thoughts were full of the battle and the good comrades I had lost. So few officers were left to us, another battle would finish off what few we had. The Colonel had been told that our field kitchens were waiting for us with hot meals cooking and ready. But he did not know where they were and kept asking everybody we met for them. We never found them and passed by within a quarter of a mile. The cooks finally gave us up and fed any soldiers that came along and threw out the rest. I do not know whose fault it was that we missed this hot meal, which we so terribly needed.

We marched on and on and on until I was so weary and exhausted that I thought I must fall into the ditch by the roadside, and the men could scarcely keep on their feet. Every time we halted the men dropped down in the mud of the road and the ditches. Evening came on and still we plodded wearily along. We came upon a long truck train standing in the road blocked by the traffic. It was full of wounded. Their calls for water were pitiful in the extreme, and many of us climbed into the trucks and gave these poor sufferers the last of our water. Here were our wounded, some of them hit five days ago, and they were not yet back to the hospitals. Capt. Fatzinger spent fifty-two hours in one of these trucks. Many of these poor fellows died who would be alive today if they could have got to the hospitals and had proper attention. All this suffering of the wounded was in a large sense unavoidable. There were but few roads, and the Germans had mined and shelled these almost out of existence.[3] Our engineers worked like beavers under shell fire to repair the roads and did wonders. But these few roads had to be used first of all to bring up artillery and ammunition and food and troops in order to win the battle and keep the attack going forward. After all these had gone up, and only then, could the wounded be taken back.

Darkness came on and still we struggled on. I passed a wagon which

3. The key aspect here is the fact that the underdeveloped road network was insufficient to support such a large offensive. Heavy rains compounded the congestion and difficulty moving supplies up the line and wounded down it.

was full of loaves of bread, and men were chopping up the loaves and handing them out to the passing hungry men, who seized them eagerly. They gave me a quarter of a loaf, and I ate it all and felt better. We halted again and I told the Colonel my men could not possibly go any farther. They were leaving the road and lying down in the fields. The Colonel said we had to go just a few hundred yards further. So we roused up the exhausted men and went on and soon left the road and placed our men on a hillside, where we all lay down on the wet, muddy ground, so glad to stretch out our weary worn bodies. The soft, wet grass seemed a bed fit for a king. Capt. Knack and I took in with us Lt. James P. Cragg, who was so cold that his face was blue. We put him between us and placed a heavy German blanket, which I had carried all the way, over us, and we slept well and all through the cold night. You reach a stage of physical exhaustion in war in which you could sleep well on a pile of broken rocks. The average civilian has not the slightest conception of what the words "physical exhaustion" mean, nor have they any idea of what exertion the human body is capable of under the stress of necessity.

October 1, 1918, I awoke in the dull gray of the morning and found my body so stiff and sore that I could get to my feet with difficulty. I was greatly refreshed by the long sleep and soon got over my stiffness by stamping up and down. Capt. Knack lay on the ground nearby with his overcoat, which he had taken off, wrapped about his head and shoulders. He always claimed that one could sleep much warmer by using the overcoat in this way. Being an old experienced campaigner he surely ought to have known. Capt. Knack claimed that Lt. Cragg and I had taken all of the protection of the heavy German blanket and that he had had no good of it. Hard luck for the good captain. We did not realize that we were doing so.

I stood there in the early misty morning, looking down the hill side, crowded as it was by hundreds of men of our regiment, survivors of our first battle. Many still lay upon the ground in all attitudes, sleeping the sleep of complete exhaustion. It looked like a hill side that had been charged over by infantry, which had left behind a thick carpet of dead and wounded men.

Our position was now fairly well to the rear, but exposed to full view as we were on the hill side, we might have been caught by long range artillery, or bombed by enemy airmen, so we got the men into column and were soon on the road again, going farther to the rear. Our share in the present battle was evidently over for the time being at least.

This day was a day of long, continued and weary marching. Cold and weary from our days of battle, for one night on the wet ground without blankets as the men were does not suffice to restore and re-fresh men exhausted by five days in battle without food or blankets, we set off along the muddy roads. These roads near the front were in terrible condition from shell fire and hard use. We passed thousands of engineers laboring sturdily on the wrecked roads, filling shell holes with trees, rocks, dirt, and even dumping wrecked automobiles into some of the largest craters to help fill them up. I saw many of these engineers lying in the gutters and thought them at first to be dead men. I discovered, however, that they were exhausted men who were being allowed a spell of sleep, as the engineers had been working night and day without ceasing for some days trying to get the roads in shape to handle the traffic which it was absolutely vital must pass up to the front with ammunition and supplies if the battle was to go on.

The road was jammed with traffic. Long lines of trucks moved slowly past us up to the front and many wagons drawn by horses. We used too many horse-drawn vehicles in France for a nation as modern as we are.[4] Thousands of trucks were kept in private business at home, all of which should have been seized and sent over to the Army, and I cannot see why it was not done. If wagons and horses could be carried over in the ships, then trucks could have been taken over instead of them. My regiment never had anything but horse-drawn transport, and we were always very short of horses, so much so that they even took horses from officers, battalion commanders who needed them to handle their units properly. I never gave up my horse and refused more than once to do so. Being the only major left in the regiment after our first battle, the other battalions were commanded by captains who had to walk with their men. I suppose they humored me, as my rank entitled me to a horse. I understand that the Colonel and his staff gave up their horses, but then they had a Dodge car to ride in and did not need them.

4. With poor roads and heavy rains, horses and mules were better suited to getting supplies up the line than trucks, depending upon the circumstances. The European armies all relied extensively on horsepower for their logistical supply.

Our progress was slow and our regiment was stretched out for a mile or more as we had to go much of the way in a single file, threading our way through the traffic or walking along in the gutters. This day I had to walk, as my horse was in the rear with our wagon train, which we had not seen for a week. During one of our many halts I came across an engineer captain working on the road, whom I had dug trenches with at Camp Meade, Maryland. We were glad to meet again and shook hands cordially. He was a fine chap, and I regret that his name has slipped my memory. We talked a while and he told me the German snipers in the trees had killed many of his men. The fire at times got so bad that he had to take men off the work and send them out to shoot the snipers. He told me one story worth repeating. The brother of one of his sergeants had been shot dead in the road beside the sergeant, who was infuriated against the snipers in consequence and went into the woods with a rifle to try to kill some of them. When the sergeant came back to the road he met an engineer escorting a German sniper who had surrendered to him. The sergeant, who was ordinarily a mild enough man, rushed up to the prisoner in a fury and drove his bayonet through his chest and killed him on the spot. Such was the bitter feeling against the hated snipers, who were considered as mere murderers, that all those present approved of the sergeant's act, and the officers did not reprimand him for killing the prisoner.

We did not come out of the Argonne by the route we had followed in our four days' attack, which of course we made in a direct line following the compass direction of 258 degrees across fields and through forests. We came out by a roundabout route, following roads no doubt guided out by the route that would least interfere with the troops and traffic going in. It was a long hard day's march, and we all became exceedingly weary towards the end of it. We passed through several demolished towns seemingly full of our soldiers, and from their steaming, rolling kitchens some of our men got some food, but not many of us had time to get any. Some parts of the roads were reduced by traffic to a condition of thin gray mud several inches deep, through which we slopped our weary way. I noticed several large groups of German prisoners in one of these towns hungrily devouring huge loaves of our good army bread. Much better bread than they had eaten for years. Trucks loaded with food passed us frequently, and in response to shouted requests from my men, they threw off to us as they passed many loaves of bread and hundreds of boxes of hard tack, all of which was quickly picked up by the hungry men and soon devoured.

In the latter part of the afternoon we came into familiar country and recognized the trenches from which we had started our attack six days ago. What we had gone through since that morning which seemed so long ago. It seemed that we had been in another world. Here in the trenches near Avocourt, I had left my bedding roll, and my orderly, faithful Corp. Euwart, recovered it for me next day, and I greatly enjoyed the comfort of sleeping in it again.

We were very weary from our long march, but word came that we must keep on the Camp Normandie, where we had lived in the huts before going up to the front lines. So we made another effort and went on to the rear, passing many of the heavy guns still in positions along the roads and in the woods which had supported us in our first days of attack. The line of attack was now too far away for them to assist it and the miserable roads made it impossible to move these great guns across No Man's Land. The smaller guns were gone ahead and were now up near Montfaucon, where I had seen them on our way out. The great piles of empty shells about these batteries showed how tremendous had been the expenditure of ammunition so far in the battle, which had really just got started.

In the evening we reached Camp Normandie, and it seemed like coming home. Near the huts which had been occupied by the officers I halted by the road side and watched the tired men straggle by, telling each company commander to place his company in the woods where it had been and have the men get their packs and blankets and shelter tents from the dump where we had left them under guard. Unfortunately this camp had been heavily shelled during our absence and many of our packs had been destroyed by the shells, and the guards, driven to the dugouts by the shells, claimed that the French had stolen a lot of our equipment also. This, of course, could not be proved. The men had to do the best they could with what was left.

When the last company had passed, I turned to the huts and was much provoked to find them all occupied by the men of a truck unit. They were respectful enough, but said their orders were to occupy the huts, and of course I could not blame them nor could I turn them out. In one hut I found a couple of my men, Capt. Burrage's company clerk and another man left by him to care for and guard the company records. These men had a soft time of it while we were in battle, and so I ordered them out and told them to use their shelter tent, and I moved in and was most glad to get the warm dry hut after all of our wet, cold nights on the ground.

Into this small hut with me I took Capt. Knack, Lt. Fouraker, my gas officer, Sergeant-Major Robt. S. MacCormack, and Corp. Euwart, my orderly. All these good, faithful men, who had gone all through the battle with me, I wanted to share what comforts I had. We were much crowded, but I would not have permitted one of them to sleep out in the rain. We seemed a little closely bound family which shared everything equally. Capt. Knack and I slept on the rough wooden bed, and under it on the floor MacCormack and Euwart slept, while Fouraker made himself comfortable on a sort of shelf on the side of the hut.

We had something to eat, and Capt. Knack made us some hot coffee over a lamp or candle. We rolled in soon after and slept the long, solid sleep of worn out men for ten hours or more. In the morning we were much refreshed. The other officers had also had a hut, the men of the truck unit having doubled up to let them have it. After breakfast I went to see how my men fared. This was the first time I had left it to the company commanders to carry out my orders for the men's comfort for the night without overseeing it myself. For once I was too worn out to do my duty entirely. I found that most of the men had slept on the grass under the trees and bushes, too utterly tired to put up their shelter tents. The long lost rolling kitchens had found us and the men were enjoying hot coffee and a hot meal again. During the day the camp was put in order, and the tents were put up among the trees, where they would not be seen by the enemy airmen.

In the afternoon the men were cleaning their rifles, some of which in spite of orders had not been unloaded. Corporal Green of Company B was walking by a group of men busy with their rifles when a rifle went off, and the bullet struck the corporal in the head, killing him instantly. I reached the spot just after it happened, and the poor fellow lay there in the path on his face. I had seen many men killed in the last few days and had become hardened to the sight, but this death, this useless waste of a fine young life, shocked me greatly. I was greatly angered and lectured the men severely on such almost criminal care-lessness. One man nearby was accused, but he stoutly denied it. As there were hundreds of dirty rifles near, and no one would admit it, we could not prove who had killed the corporal. And it could not have helped if we had found the man who did it. It was purely a most regret-table accident.

The evening before, after we had got settled in our hut, I went to find Judge Kimbrough in his Y.M.C.A. hut, and we were delighted to see each other again and to know that each other was still alive. He told me that I looked bad and older, which was probably true as a result of my battle experiences. During our absence the camp had been frequently and heavily shelled and the good Judge had been driven to the dugout many times. But his hut had not been hit, and he had most of his sup-plies left, not having sold much to other troops. We sat and talked for some time, telling each other of our experiences in the five days we had been separated. Never have I been more glad to see a friend, and I was much pleased to have him again with my battalion where he was of greatest help to me in many ways. The next day my men crowded to his hut and bought cigarettes, candy, chocolate, cakes, and other things the soldier loves, and most of them got writing paper from him to write home to the folks.

October 2 was spent at Camp Normandie continuing the much-needed rest and hot meals. The Colonel sent us the regimental brass band, which I was glad to have to cheer up the men. I told the leader to play light, cheerful music, and we stood around among the trees and listened to the good music for more than an hour. It is wonderful how military music will brighten up weary soldiers and put the pep back into them again. We all felt better for the concert. The band had been in the battle as stretcher bearers, I was told, but they were never allowed to go in again. An order from headquarters at Chaumont forbade it, as bands were considered too valuable in keeping up the soldiers' morale to risk the musicians, who would be hard to replace, in battle. Easy on the bandsmen, to be sure, but good for the service on the whole. On October 3, we rested at Camp Normandie also, and the companies were checked over and lists of the dead and wounded and missing, as far as was possible, were made up. On this day our genial and well-liked YMCA song leader, Kenneth Clark, arrived with his little organ and gathering the men about him had a rousing song fest in the forest.[5]

Three days thus we spent at Camp Normandie resting and eating hot food and cleaning arms and getting the men equipped as well as possible. These three days restored us greatly, although we could not forget those terrible days of battle and the good comrades we had lost. But few shells fell on our camp during these days. The Germans were too busy with our friends up front to give us much attention.

Before closing the story of our battle in the Argonne Forest, I want to tell of two tank incidents which occurred. During the afternoon of the third day, September 28, as we were advancing through the woods, most of my men and officers (in fact nearly all) concealed from my view by the trees and undergrowth, in other words out of my immediate control as often happens in battle, there came running up to me a breathless soldier, who cried out, with great excitement, "Major, the German tanks are advancing against us, and they are very close to us."

My heart froze within me from a great fear which took hold of me. I remembered that at the military college at Langres we had been told that there were but two effective defenses against tanks. One was artillery for direct fire at them, and the other was to dig wide trenches for them to fall into. We had no artillery and certainly no time to dig wide trenches. Lacking both of these defenses, we had been told that the only thing possible was to stand up like men against them and not be driven back, an awful thought at such a time. What could mere men do against armored tanks with machine guns in them? As we stood there I felt that it was all over with us, and our minutes of life were numbered. My courage returned somewhat, as the tanks did not appear through the trees to annihilate us, and I asked the man where he had seen the tanks. He took me forward a little way to the edge of the woods and pointed out some large objects moving some considerable distance away. My field glasses soon proved that they were German trucks moving off to the German rear, and they were nearly a mile away. There

5. Kenneth Clark was a composer of college songs and jingles. Educated at the Kiski School and Shadyside Academy in Pittsburgh, Clark went on to Princeton where he composed popular songs for the glee club such as "Princeton That's All" and "Princeton Forward March." He was remembered in his *NY Times* obituary for his fun-loving songs and also for his book *Bottoms Up*, a compilation of drinking songs published under the pen name Clifford Leach.

being no woods between, we could see them a long way. They were off to our left and out of our sector. I made a few pithy remarks of a rather intense nature to the messenger. He had given me one of the worst scares of my life. He brought me no more information during the battle. I did not miss him greatly.

Later in the afternoon of this same day, September 28, 1918, in fact it was almost evening, there came to me in the woods several French officers. They were dressed in black leather coats, gray breeches, and black leather leggings. Their insignia of rank, the small gold bars usually worn on their lower sleeves, were placed upon the breasts of the leather coats. They explained that they were officers of a French Tank Squadron, which was nearby in the woods. They had been sent on to me by Col. Charles, who sent me a message to use my own judgment in cooperating with the tanks.

I was glad that the Colonel had left the situation to my judgment, for it was late in the day, my men were exhausted, and scattered through the dense woods, and our losses had been very heavy. We had reached the northern edge of the forest and must now go forward through the open fields, where I knew we would come under very heavy artillery and machine gun fire. I did not intend to attempt those open fields that day and wanted the night to reorganize and gather my scattered battalion before doing so. Our advance for that day was over in my judgment. These brave Frenchmen had come to help me make an attack. They said they would precede me out into the open fields and help my advance and also protect me from the enemy in the woods on our right front. I explained to them the condition of my battalion and told them also that it was too late to cross the entire width of the open fields before us, which was a distance of at least a mile, with the town of Romagne showing there at the other side. Night and early morning would find me in the open fields with no protection from the enemy observers, and we would be crushed by artillery fire before we could get formed for attack in the morning. I earnestly requested them to wait until morning.

I was most anxious for their assistance when I could make some proper use of it. They could not be persuaded to stay with me until morning. Why I do not know. They had ample cover for their tanks there in the woods. They insisted on getting back to the rear that night.

I presume they had orders to do so. They left me, and a little later I was much surprised to see them issue from the forest into the open in front of us. The tanks did not attempt to go far, but crawled about in the field near us. I had not seen them in action before, and we watched them with great interest.

To our astonishment each of these monsters was preceded by an officer on foot out in the open absolutely unprotected. They walked along, testing the ground with their canes in the coolest possible manner. Certainly one of the bravest things I ever saw. They were subjected to some, but not much, machine gun fire. The Germans, no doubt, thought it no use to waste bullets on them and also they did not want to give away the positions of their machine guns. But there was some machine gun fire, and these brave Frenchmen walked out in the open absolutely indifferent to it. We expected them to fall every minute and voiced great admiration of their bravery. The German artillery observers spotted the tanks very quickly, and shells began to fall around them. At this the officers retired to the tanks, which turned and made for the woods.

One of them had been going along the edge of the woods at our right front, firing into it at the machine gun nests there. This tank and another, which was farthest out in the open, were doomed and never got back to the forest. The shells were dropping fast now about the tanks hurrying back to cover. Suddenly one of the tanks farthest out was squarely hit by a shell, and to our astonishment great tongues of fire poured from it. We would never have expected such a fire in a thing built entirely of steel. It was the gasoline and oil burning. To our horror not a door of that tank opened. Not one of the six men in it survived.[6]

While we were still suffering from the shock of this horrible disaster, to our dismay another tank not far from us, which had almost reached the protection of the trees, was hit by a shell and started to burn fiercely. But to our relief, a door opened and four of the six men of the crew leaped out and ran for the woods. The two others were doubtless killed by the shell. By this time the other four tanks had reached the forest,

6. The Schneider CA-1 was a six-person tank introduced in 1917. French unit Groupement IV assisted the Americans at the Meuse-Argonne. As this section of Parkin's account makes clear, tanks in World War I were death-traps, not war-winning weapons. It took a number of key technological and tactical developments during the 1920s and 1930s for tanks to become reliable, faster moving, and more effective in battle.

and we saw no more of them. But out there in the open remained the smoking, wrecked tanks, the sepulchers of eight brave men, looking like great monsters in the fading light.

To resume my narrative, interrupted by these two stories of the tanks, we received notice, or rather orders, on October 3, 1918, that we would that evening leave Camp de Normandie. Our rest and refreshment here had been of great help to us, and our minds had recovered largely from the terrible strain and trial of battle and the near and often presence of death. I spent the day getting my battalion ready for the road and arranging the loads of our few wagons. For my company and battalion records, my officers' bedding rolls, and Judge Kimbrough's YMCA supplies I had but one wagon, the other three being loaded with food, ammunition, spare rifles, and other necessary supplies. We had now on hand the bedding rolls of the officers who had been killed and wounded. What to do with them was a problem. We opened those of the officers who had been killed and took out the smaller personal effects, which were meant to return to the relatives. Also all letters and papers. Chaplain McNary and Judge Kimbrough took charge of these things, which were put in separate bundles with the name of the owner on same. The blankets, clothes, boots, etc., were partly distributed to the surviving officers, but most of this equipment was abandoned there at Camp Normandie from necessity.

The bedding rolls of the wounded officers were not opened and were taken along with us. I do not know what finally became of them, but part of them I understand were finally recovered by their owners, who either returned to the regiment or had them sent to their hospitals. Under the stress and strain of war on the Front, personal property of those absent does not and cannot have the protection afforded to it under ordinary conditions. My own personal baggage after I was wounded suffered like that of the others, and I recovered only a part of it.

We were all ready to move out at dusk when orders came directing that the wagon train take a different route. Owing to these late changes in my orders I was a little late in starting my march. This was another great source of worry to unit commanders. Orders often reached us late and sometimes changes in orders never reached us. There was often good reason for this, but that did not help us, who were responsible, any. I had scarcely got well started upon my night journey and was riding along alone at the head of my men when a runner overtook me with orders to report back to Col. Charles at Camp de Normandie. After all my worry and troubles in getting away, this order provoked me a great deal. I gave over command to Capt. Knack and told him to keep on going and galloped back through the mud and darkness to find the Colonel. He was not to be found in the camp and had left, after sending for me. Perhaps he got tired of waiting for me. This provoked me still more. It was not the first time the Colonel had so treated me. I set off after my troops at a gallop, risking myself and my horse for the road was full of automobiles, trucks, and wagons, many of which I grazed past in the darkness. Recovering my place at the head of the column, I settled down for the night's march. As usual it rained, but my rubber cape and steel helmet kept me dry and warm.

This night we came upon something entirely new to us, and we thought we had seen about everything on the Front. We were wrong. While riding along in the dark I became conscious of a glare in the sky in front of us, which gradually became brighter and stronger, until at the end of an hour's marching this countryside around us was so illuminated that we could see everything quite clearly. Major Cornwell and I could not figure it out at all. Searchlights would not make such a tremendous light, nor did we think it could be caused by a fire, unless a whole town was ablaze. At length, reaching the top of a long grade, we came right upon the mystery. At the opposite side of a large, flat, smooth field stood lined up a considerable number of trucks. Dynamos on them were running at high speed and making a loud drumming or humming noise.[7] On the front of each truck were several large brilliant electric lights, which brilliantly illuminated nearly all of the large field. We understood at last. It was a landing field for aeroplanes which were out on a night flight, and all these lights were to show them the place to land when they returned.

We marched on, soon accustomed again to the dark night, Major Cornwell and I talking over many things as we rode side by side. I remember we discussed life and death quite a lot, having of late seen much of both. We overtook the Colonel's car at a cross-roads. In it were Lt. Col. Robert L. Meador now in command of the regiment, Col.

7. A "dynamo" is an electric generator.

Charles having gone to the hospital as a result of the wound in his canteen, and Capt. William S. Manning, adjutant of the regiment.[8] Capt. Carl Glock, Regimental Intelligence Officer, was also with them. These two latter gentlemen were among my best friends in the regiment.

Capt. Manning gave me the direction of the march over the crossroad, and letting the column march on, Major Cornwell and I pulled up beside the car for a brief chat and to get orders. We were all glad to know that Col. Charles was no longer with us and hoped he would not return to the regiment. Not a very nice thing to say, perhaps, but the utter truth nevertheless and purely his own fault that the entire regiment felt so about him. If ever a leader of men completely failed to win their loyalty, respect and devotion, this unfortunate officer did so. And I think that being constituted as he was he could not help it. I have seen him make deliberate efforts to recover his proper position with his men and officers and then do something that offset all of his efforts at once. The march that night was helped along considerably by gales of laughter caused by some wit calling out, "Tourniquet, tourniquet."

Our march of this night of October 3, 1918, led us through Bantheville, Sivry la Perche, not a light nor any evidence in these partly ruined towns of any life in either place. We crossed the Blercourt Road and on to Nixeville, finally reaching the Bois de Nixeville, tired out, wet and muddy, in the very early hours of the morning. I remember the ever present rain was coming down unusually heavily as we halted in the ankle deep mud on the forest road with the dripping trees standing thickly on both sides of us. There pulled off a little to the side of the road stood the Colonel's Dodge car, and as I rode up Capt. Manning leaned out and told me that we would pass the balance of the night here. Cheerful prospect for weary men. Dripping trees to sit under and wet, muddy ground to rest upon. Not a shack nor any shelter in sight, no fires to warm and cheer the men permitted, as there had always been in other wars. Enemy airplanes would see them and report our presence, both to their long range artillery and their intelligence officers.

Sitting there on my horse in the heavy rain, I felt a great sympathy for my weary men, who must pass the miserable hours until daybreak

8. Colonel Charles was relieved of command.

in such an inhospitable place, but there was no help for it, so I gave the order to fall out, and in a few minutes all of the men were off the road and crashing about in the bushes, seeking a spot to settle down in. Their officers had disappeared with them, and I was left alone in the road with Major Cornwell. We rode along it for a short ways and came to a long open shed, and our hopes of shelter rose, but coming closer we found it packed full of horses and harness. Some French wagon outfit was before us.

Dismounting, we tied our horses to posts and left them there in the rain, all of our equipment still upon them. This was no way to care for horses, but in this situation it was the only way to care for them. My flashlight showed a room built onto the end of the long shed, and opening the door we entered to be greeted with a terrible odor of foul air and manure. Two cots, one in which French soldiers swathed in dirty gray blankets were sleeping, and a large pile of empty sacks just about filled the small room. One of these soldiers, awakened by our entrance and recognizing our uniforms, sat up, waved us out with his arm, and said roughly, "Get out," which was all the English he had. Such treatment angered me, and I answered him just as roughly. He lay back upon his cot and said no more. His comrade did not take any notice of us. I sat down upon the pile of dirty sacks and told Major Cornwell that we would pass the rest of the night here. But he refused. The welcome we had received and the smell was too much for him, and he said he would prefer to stay out in the rain, and out he went.

But I thought I could stand the bad air because it was dry and fairly warm, so I remained. Again the unfriendly French soldier sat up, looked at me, and I turned my light upon him, expecting some trouble with the fellow, but to my surprised he pulled off one of his blankets and held it out to me. This was better. I was warm enough in my heavy wool-lined overcoat, and I refused the blanket and thanked him. He subsided again and took no further interest in me. I began to find the strong odor oppressive and most unpleasant and hearing voices outside, got up and went out. There I found Major Cornwell and Lt. Burke of the medical corps busy with some rubber and woolen blankets, making a bed upon the steaming manure pile in the rain. At their invitation I got into their unsavory bed with them, and we three passed a comfortable balance of the night. Our bed was soft and warm, and we had a good rest.

We awoke early to find a dull, gray, wet morning. Most discouraging and disheartening weather. We had been awakened by the talk of the French soldiers, busy with their horses in the shed near us. Throwing back our blankets reluctantly, we got out into the mud, refreshed and rested but still capable of hours of sleep. Corporal Euwart had found my poor soaked horse, and I saw that he had taken the equipment off its weary back and was rubbing him down with some hay.

Breakfast was now the question of the hour. I had food in my musette bag, but a cup of hot coffee was my great desire now. I knew that our rolling kitchens were somewhere nearby, and I set out to find them. They were in the open at the farther end of the wood and were already surrounded by hundreds of hungry men, standing about patiently, waiting for breakfast. The cooks told me that hot coffee was all they were preparing, as the men had food with them, and that on account of the lack of water they feared they would not have enough of that to go around. There was water in the neighborhood, and I bawled the cooks out for not making sure of plenty of hot coffee for the men. That much they could and should have made sure of.

I knew that good Captain Knack would make coffee for himself in all probability, as he always carried the necessary materials in his bag, being an old campaigner of many years' experience, so I hunted him in the woods and sure enough found him in the act. He had a can of condensed heat, and sitting on top of it was his canteen cup, from which came the savory odor of good strong coffee. We were close comrades and shared all that we had, so I knew I would be welcome, as I was. Soon I made a good breakfast of a large cup of extra strong hot coffee with sugar but no cream, and crackers and corned beef. Many a cup of fine coffee did my good old friend make for me on the Front.

Capt. Louis C. Knack of Company B, First Battalion, 316th Infantry, to give him his full title, and I were sitting on the ground at the edge of the woods smoking, having finished our breakfast, when I saw Col. Meador's Dodge car come out in the open and stop, and word was passed for me. I went over, and Col. Meador told me he was going ahead to a village to see if he could get some eggs. Being next in command, I understood that he was turning over the command of the regiment to me.

Sometime later a runner came through the woods calling my name and reaching me said that General Nicholson, our brigade commander, was back in the woods at regimental P.C. or the spot on the road side where Col. Meador's car had been standing. I went back along the muddy road to the P.C., and there found the General sitting upon the stump of a tree, considerably stirred up at not finding any one there to meet him. I saluted and he asked me peevishly where Col. Meador was. I told him, and that I was present in command of the regiment. He said that I should in that case have remained at the P.C. In that he was correct. He asked me if Col. Meador before he left had turned over the command to me. I told him he had. The General wanted to know if the Colonel had actually done so in the military phraseology. I said he had not, but there was no doubt in my mind of his intent to do so, since he had hunted me up and told me he was leaving the regiment. The General seemed to want to get something on the Colonel, and I did not help him any.

Then the Brigade Adjutant, Major Pleasanton, took up my chastening and asked me if I had not been late in starting my march the evening before. I admitted that I had been a half hour or so. He wanted to know why, assuming a very superior air with me. And then I took the air out of him by telling him that it was entirely due to the very late arrival of orders from Brigade Headquarters, as the Colonel had told me, which changed our plans of march just at the time we were about to move out. Hence it was really his own fault for not getting the orders to us earlier, and he knew it and subsided very considerably. General Nicholson heard it all and smiled a wide smile to see his adjutant put it all over himself, instead of over me, as he had intended doing. They had no orders for me and soon departed, saying that march orders would reach me later.

October 4, 1918. We remained the most of this day in the Bois de Nixeville. It did not rain much, but the sun did not come out, and we did not get dried out much. We had in the regiment now but 1,858 men left out of the 3,600 we took to France. Our first battle had cost us very dearly. Not all of these missing men were dead or seriously wounded. Quite a number of stragglers, men who had got lost from us in the Argonne Forest and had served through the battle with other commands as often happened, and men who had been only slightly wounded returned to the regiment later on.

In the latter part of the afternoon marching orders arrived, and since Col. Meador had not returned (they had found a good place to eat in the village ahead), I proceeded to get the regiment together and on the road to move out. Col. Sweezey of the 313th Infantry sought me out and complained that I was filling up the road with my men and preventing him from getting away and said that he was to leave first. I was much surprised to see him and learn that his regiment was also in the woods. So I rode along the road and ordered my men off to the side to let good Col. Sweezey, a soldier I always liked and respected, have the road so that he could lead out.

Now followed another long and weary wet night march. We proceeded by way of Lempire, Dugny, Aucemont, where we crossed the Meuse River through Dieue and Genicourt, where we found the 313th installed and eating a hot meal from their rolling kitchens, much to our envy, and finally reached the half-ruined town of Rupt-en-Woevre at midnight. Here the regiment halted, all except my own battalion, which had to go on three miles farther to a cantonment in the woods, there not being room for all of us in the town. We had marched nine hours and were worn out. One march is much like another and so having described others, I will not go into details again, except to say that this one seemed to weary us more than most others we had made. During one of the short halts, I remember I was so tired that I lay down full length in the ditch by the roadside, utterly indifferent to the water in which I lay. At the halts some of the men would fall down in the road and had to be dragged to the side to avoid being run over.

When we halted in the main street of Rupt-en-Woevre, Col. Meador came to me and told me I must go on, as I have said, for another three miles, and I told him that my men simply could not do so. He said he was sorry for me, but that it was his orders. I was so tired and felt so keenly for my men that I fear I insisted more than was proper on staying in the town. He said that he had to go to General Nicholson yet that night and report, and I had better rest my men a little and try to finish out the march. This I finally agreed to do. After a half hour's rest we dragged our weary battalion out of the town and managed finally to reach our cantonment, throwing ourselves down most any place in the filthy shacks and going off at once to sleep.

We awoke late and first of all looked over the camp and got the men properly placed in the large wooden barracks and the officers in the small huts nearby. The buildings were full of refuse of all kinds, left by the French troops, who certainly do leave the filthiest camps I have ever seen. All this mess was cleaned out at once, and the men were made as comfortable as possible, having first of all a hot breakfast before being required to do anything.

This cantonment was in a beautiful little valley a couple of nights' march back of the St. Mihiel Front, to which I knew we were now on our way. The French had built large wooden barracks and many small and comfortable shacks with beds, tables, chairs and fireplaces, and windows. It was a rest camp for their troops. High up on the hillside I had a neat small shack to myself. In front was a little terrace, and it was surrounded by the trees. It had only one small room with a bed, a table, and chair, a fireplace and in the back a small dugout for one only. It was a fine comfortable little place, but I was too lonely there, so was in my shack only to sleep, being with Capt. Knack and the other officers during the day.

October 5 was a day of much needed rest and cleaning up for all of us. In the afternoon I rode into Rupt-en-Woevre, a place half ruined by shell fire, to see Capt. Manning about some business of the Regiment. We all knew by now that Col. Oscar J. Charles had been officially relieved of the command of the regiment, and the satisfaction of everyone was not concealed. We knew Lt. Col. Meador would not get the regiment, and also that we would get a new colonel who might be a much better man.

I was talking to Capt. Manning at Regimental headquarters when a divisional staff car stopped out front, and to our great surprise Col. Charles got out and came hustling in, calling out a greeting, "Well how's everybody?"

Apparently he was very glad to get back to the regiment, which was only natural, for the regiment was our only home in France, and we felt very lonely over there when away from it. The situation was very strained and embarrassing to us all. Here was a colonel who had been relieved of his command and apparently did not know it. There were several divisional staff officers in the car with him who must have known it, but they must have been afraid to tell him. We all looked at each other and did not know what to say, after getting up and returning the Colonel's greetings. But Capt. Manning saved the situation by taking the Colonel aside and asking him if he had not received the order relieving him of the command. He said he had been in hospital and had not. Capt. Manning got a copy of the order and gave it to him. He read it and his face went gray and drawn.

I feel sure all present felt really sorry for the Colonel. It was a great blow to any man's pride. He did not stay but a few minutes longer, said goodbye and went out and away to Divisional Headquarters in the same car he came in. He was sent to Blois for reclassification and assignment to other duties in the army, as had been thousands of other officers who had not shown a fitness for command of troops on the Front.

General Joseph E. Kuhn, divisional commander, told me after the war that when Col. Charles reported to him after being relieved of his command, he said, "General, I have learned a lot in my first battle."

General Kuhn replied, "I am afraid you learned it too late, Colonel."

October 5, 1918. I rode back to my battalion, had a frugal lunch, and then inspected my men's billets. They were as clean and comfortable as could be expected. I had dinner with my officers after we had the ceremony of "Retreat" there in the woods with only our buglers for music. This formation had been ordered. During inspection at retreat I found a number of men without arms or equipment and asked them where they were. They were men who had been only slightly wounded or had been sick and had only just returned from the hospitals. They said their arms and equipment had been taken away from them and had not been returned when they were discharged. I instructed their company commanders to equip them from the extra supplies we had on our battalion wagons. I fear that some of these men were slackers in the last battle, but it would be very hard to prove that, and we soon had other things to think about.

In the evening I was in Capt. Knack's shack, smoking and talking with him and Lts. Dreher, Dyer, Clofine and Fouraker, all the officers left out of the twenty-six the battalion originally had, with the others dead, wounded, and ill. There were so few of us now that we felt very lonesome if we did not stay together. We had a good fire and some candles, and the room was warm and cheerful. Quite a contrast from recent nights out in the rain and mud, and we thoroughly appreciated and enjoyed the cozy comfort of the place. The fact that our men were also under cover this rainy cold night was an additional cause for satisfaction. We had been enjoying ourselves for an hour or so and congratulating ourselves upon such a night of comfort, listening to the rain beating upon the window panes when there came a knock upon the door, and in came a rain-soaked French officer and two of his men.

He saluted us smartly—the French officers are always very military—and I thought what a picture he made there in his faded, wet and muddy uniform, the rain gleaming on his helmet. You may find many faults with the French, but you will always respect them as soldiers. He addressed us in French, and we answered in English. Lt. Keller, who generally interpreted for me, was dead, back there in the Argonne Forest. But my Italian-American orderly, who spoke French, was nearby, and in a few minutes he was giving me the most unexpected and unwelcome information that this French officer was consumed with regret to inform the American major that the Americans must vacate the camp in behalf of a French infantry regiment now marching towards us, which had orders to occupy the camp for that night. He was the billeting officer out ahead of his regiment to arrange such matters.

I was somewhat astonished that he would ask such a thing of his allies on such a night and told him politely that he must find some other place for his regiment as we proposed to stay right where we were. On his insistence I told him plainly that I was there by orders from Divisional Headquarters and could not move without orders from that source and that I did not intend to ask for any such orders. He asked me what he should do. I told him to find some other place or do as we had been doing recently, sleep out in the open. The poor weary officer left us with a look of despair on his face, and we saw no more of him. Had there been room I would have gladly shared our quarters with the French, but there was not, and I would not have turned out my men for the personal guard of General Pershing without orders to do so.

Sometime after the French officer left us, I said good night to my officers and climbed up the hillside to my own cozy but lonesome little shack. Just as I reached it I became aware of the sound of many airplanes approaching and soon the dark sky above was full of the loud humming of German machines. You can tell them from ours by the sort of interrupted hum of their Diesel engines.[9] Ours sound steady and continuous. I wondered what they could want in our locality. Had they come to bomb us out?

As I stood there looking up but seeing nothing and expecting to see the angry red flashes of their exploding bombs on the camp below in the valley, I was suddenly greatly astonished to see bursting out along the top of the ridge across the valley from my position the glaring shafts of a number of large searchlights, which began lacing the dark sky in all directions, searching for the hostile machines which they now and then picked up out of the darkness, the airplanes shining like silver in the brilliant glare of the searchlight. Immediately upon the discovery of an enemy in the sky, artillery fire crashed out from the same ridge, and I could see the anti-aircraft shells bursting high up in the air. And so it went on for some time, a wonderful and thrilling sight, intense and most interesting to me. I forgot all about the danger of bombs in my excitement. It was something like a gigantic Fourth of July celebration.

Gradually the hum of the motors became lower and more distant as the enemy made off in the distance. I did not see a machine hit and do not believe one was. For a short time the white beams searched out the sky, and then were suddenly extinguished and all was quiet and dark and peaceful. The whole affair began and ceased so quickly that it all seemed like the passing vision of a disturbed mind.

October 6, 1918. Orders had been issued that the companies should engage in squad drill for a good part of this day. Not that proficiency in squad drill would make our men any better soldiers on the front to which we were going, but it was thought at Division Headquarters that such drill with all of its details enforced would restore discipline and efficiency in the men. It was an idea taken from the British I believe. It may have worked all right with the British temperament, but it did not with the American. Instead it disgusted and irritated our men and officers and all seemed useless and absurd under the circumstances. I stood and watched the squads marching around among the trees and shacks, stumbling over the uneven ground and continually getting in each other's way, and I realized that the drill was doing no good but

9. Parkin is in error here. German aircraft were not powered by Diesel engines.

only harm. If I had had the authority I should have stopped the whole absurd performance and have let the men have a second day of rest, for the long night marches ahead.

In the afternoon I was summoned to regimental headquarters, where I found nearly all of the surviving officers of the regiment, many of whom I had not seen since before we went into the battle of the Argonne Forest. Many familiar faces were absent, never to be with us again. Considerably more than half of our officer strength had been lost in our first fight. How would we ever have veteran trained officers of battle experience? Another battle would probably take off the rest of us.

General Nicholson came in and addressed the officers, and to our complete astonishment and anger he gave us a thorough bawling out for our conduct during the battle of the Argonne Forest. He accused us of everything but cowardice. It was a most unjust and unfair arraignment of a new regiment in its first battle. I was thoroughly incensed and was more than once on the point of correcting some of his absurd and unfair statements. Lt. Col. Meador, whose place it was to defend the reputation of the regiment, being its commander, said nothing, but stood with hanging head, by his miserable attitude giving the old general who had not been up at the real front line once during the battle encouragement to go on. His main criticism was based upon the number of stragglers in our rear and the excessive number of men who carried back the wounded. There may have been truth in this part of his criticism, I cannot say as to that. I and all the other officers were up at the extreme front all the time, doing our best with the men we had.

After the General left the room, Lt. Col. Meador, whose place it was to have defended us and told the general the truth but who said nothing, to our disgust weakly said to us, "Well I guess we are not so bad." Splendid encouragement to officers angered and humiliated unjustly. I thought, "God help us in our next battle if we don't get a new leader." This man carried a bottle with him always and was generally under the influence of drink. His mind had become completely befuddled and his nerves were gone. He was a courteous and kindly gentleman and unafraid in battle, but not nearly as competent to lead men in war as Col. Charles was, and he as I have said was entirely unfitted. Capt. Manning told me that when Gen. Kuhn had questioned him concerning Col.

Meador's efficiency and demanded a plain answer, he had told General Kuhn that Meador was an imbecile.

I am telling the plain, untarnished truth about men and events in this tale. Some of it is very rough stuff.

After the meeting of our officers broke up, we stood around for a while, expressing our indignation at such an unjust, undeserved rebuke to each other. I think we all of us were greatly hurt and amazed at receiving criticism when we felt that we had earned praise. No general ever did more to injure the morale of one of his regiments than did Gen. Nicholson on this day.

I returned to my camp much disheartened and very low in my spirits. I felt that the lives of all those fine officers and men of my battalion who had been killed had been wasted. I was warned before leaving that we might move out for the Front that night. When I reached my camp I directed my officers to prepare to march. After dark the order reached me to move and shortly afterwards, in the rain as usual, I sat on my horse by the roadside watching my battalion entering the road for its night march. Col. Meador came up in his car and asked why I was not well on my way. I told him that I had only received his order a short time before. He seemed surprised that I had not had it a considerable time before. At any rate I was off in plenty of time to make the distance so I did not bother to find out why the order was delayed. That was his business and not mine anyway.

We marched a good part of the night. The road was not crowded nor was its condition bad. Once I remember coming to a place where the road split. There was no sign post to help me. This fork in the road was not shown on my map. No military policeman was present to answer questions. I halted, being the leading unit of the regiment and was in a quandary as to which way to go. The road leading to the left seemed to me to go more in what I thought was our general direction, so I decided to take it. I was lucky for I took the proper road. Other officers were less lucky and lost their commands for going wrong under similar circumstances.

We marched through Mouilly to the Grande Tranchee de Calonne Road, several kilometers behind the front lines. The entire regiment concentrated in Le Chanot Bois, near Dommartin la Montagne. Col. Meador, Capt. Manning and I had been here a day or two before, locating our place to spend the night, but I must confess it was very hard to find the place in the dark. The men and officers, except for a few small shacks, had no shelter from the rain except the trees and bushes. Judge Kimbrough and I crawled into our battalion wagon, which had stayed with us, and crowded in between the baggage and the canvas top, we spent a dry but most uncomfortable time until morning came.

October 7, 1918. On October 7, the regiment remained in La Chanot Bois. The woods were wet and muddy and the men sat around on the logs and in the grass. There was no complaint, as we were used to it by this time. I found several fires on my rounds and ordered them put out at once. They were a comfort to the men, and I would have been most pleased to permit them, but their smoke would give away our position to enemy airmen and might bring a shower of bombs down upon us.

11

The St. Mihiel Front

I had found regimental headquarters in a fair sized but very filthy shack. On our arrival it was too dark to see much, and everyone was too tired, but today a couple of orderlies had been busy cleaning out the refuse left by the French. As was customary when taking over a new front, a party of officers was sent forward to the new lines to get acquainted with them before taking the regiment in. Col. Meador, Capt. Glock, and Capt. Manning went in the Colonel's Dodge car, and I rode on the front seat of a truck which was filled with company commanders. We went along the famous Grande Tranchee road, which paralleled the front line part of the way and was very close to it.

After traveling a short distance, we came up an open place in the woods in which the Germans had built a beautiful house in the style of their Black Forest homes. Large overhanging roof, the walls of logs, and the trimmings of green and white. A beautiful building, neatly and cleverly made. Doubtless the headquarters of a German general. Around it were flower beds and walks and little fences. The style of the whole place was rustic, the porch furniture and the railings all being most cleverly done out of small tree trunks. I did not see a more charming place in France. Set among the trees with all the green about, it was a picture most pleasing and pretty.

We found an American brigadier general established here with his staff. One of his aides introduced us all, and he was most kindly and pleasant. I have forgotten his name. Breakfast was just ready. Col. Meador and his staff had theirs in the house with the General, and a most excellent one it was, they afterwards assured me. I was overlooked in the invitation, and the General apologized to me for the mistake. However, the rest of us had coffee and bread and syrup at the cook's shack, and we satisfied our appetites fully.

We were given guides here and went on to the front. We passed numbers of French soldiers, and I was impressed by their neat, clean appearance. They were entirely free from mud and dirt. Their equipment of brown leather was clean and bright. Their helmets shining. They must have been new troops. We saw very few soldiers so clean and neat on the front, and that is why I mention them. At one place we heard a fine military band, playing in the woods off to the left of the road. A few enemy shells passed over us, one of them rather close, which broke off a small limb of a tree, falling near our truck. The driver put on his brakes and looked at me in a startled manner. Apparently he was not used to shells. "Step on it," I told him, and he lost no time getting out of that vicinity. The officers all laughed at the way he tore along.

Going down a long hill through a very narrow winding road we reached a small village of stone houses. Here there seemed to be a good many American soldiers. We entered a large bare house and met a colonel of the Marine Corps, who was in command of one of the regiments we were to relieve, the 101st Infantry of the 26th Division. A French house is bare at best, but more so when used as an American headquarters. Except for a few cots and chairs and tables the place was unfurnished. A cheerless, chilly forlorn house, its only comfort a smoky fire and a roof and windows intact, keeping out the rain and wind and keeping in the penetrating chill which all these old houses have.

We stayed with the Marine Colonel for a short time, discussing the general situation on this Front and learned that outside of considerable shell fire, which fell at all hours of the day and night, and frequent night raids by both sides, the place was considered quiet.

Evidently the higher military authorities did not consider a drive by the Germans on this front as even probable, for we were to relieve the regiments holding the line by battalions. Thus we, the 316th Infantry, took over the length of front previously held by the 101st and 102nd Regiments of Infantry.[1] We placed two battalions in the line, each taking the trenches of a regiment, and had one battalion, the Third, under Capt. John Somers, in reserve in our rear back in Le Chanot Bois.

1. The 101st Regiment consisted of soldiers from the Massachusetts National Guard and the 102nd those of the Connecticut National Guard. Both regiments were in the 26th "Yankee" Division.

We learned that we were taking over the Troyon Sector, which lay in the northeastern sector of the territory taken from the Germans by the St. Mihiel drive. Our position was about twenty kilometers southeast of Verdun. Montfaucon was twenty kilometers northwest of Verdun. Our last battle was on the front a night's march north of Verdun, hence all of our military operations were in the neighborhood of this famous city.

We were given guides and set out to visit the positions we were to occupy. Arriving there I was greatly impressed with the strength of the position and felt that no great force would be necessary to hold it, especially in view of the fact that we were assured of ample artillery support and the assistance of a machine gun battalion, as well as some trench mortar batteries. The main line of resistance ran along the crest of a high wooded cliff called the Cotes de Meuse, which averaged about one hundred and fifty feet in height. The front slopes were very precipitous and in most places heavily covered with underbrush. To scale such a position under the fire of machine guns alone would be extremely difficult, if not impossible. Such was the strength of the place that I never felt the least uneasiness over an attempt by the enemy to take it.

From the top of the cliff we had a wonderful view of the country side. In our immediate front lay a wide flat valley, in which on a clear day we could count twenty-six villages, most of them partially ruined. At the foot of the range lay Herbeuville, Hannonville, and Thillot. Farther out were Saulx and Wadonville, about five kilometers distant from our main line, and in these towns was a line of outposts about a kilometer from the German front line.

Each battalion kept one company on outpost duty. They were too far out from support, but the Germans had placed their lines well out in the valley to offset somewhat the great advantages of our much higher position on the cliffs. To observe and keep in touch with them it was necessary that our outpost line be very near to them. We would not give up our fine position on the cliffs, which could be easily defended by a few troops, hence the very unusual position of an outpost line far out beyond any hope of help from the main body, other than that given by artillery fire, and of this they gave generous and frequent assistance. In fact we were informed that the troops on outpost duty here were doing "Forlorn Hope" service. In case of attack they were to hold on to the last man without hope of help in order to give warning and time to the main line. No plans for retiring were made for them. Such had been the orders of the regiments we relieved. We all thought this unnecessarily hard and a needless waste of life, for the outpost line could not hold on long anyway. The orders were changed for our regiment through the efforts of our adjutant, Capt. Manning, and lanes of retirement which would be free from our own artillery fire were provided.

Beyond our outposts, the German lines lay in Marcheville, St. Hilarie, Butgneville, and Harville all strongly wired and entrench. Thirty-five kilometers away on our right front lay the city of Metz. Some claimed that on a very clear day the city could be seen from our main line, of course with the aid of field glasses.

All of this information we obtained from the major commanding a battalion of the 101st Regiment while sitting in his P.C., a large wooden house built and furnished for a German general, the finest, most commodious headquarters I ever saw on the front in France. Its only disadvantage was that it was situated almost at the foot of the cliff, on top of which was our main line and thus between my main line and my outpost line. Also it was completely exposed to the artillery fire of the enemy and in full view from his lines. To offset these disadvantages, it was exactly in the center of my section, and so far back from the outpost line that warning of an attack would be received in ample time to retire up a long flight of wooden stairs, which were close to the house or shack, to the main position above. We never had to do this in the month we were here. Also, as a protection from artillery fire, there was in the hillside close by a large concrete-lined dugout of several large rooms, to which we could retire. Only a few times were we obliged to do so, and last but by no means least, there was the great comfort and convenience of the place to consider, and for these reasons we were willing to undertake any risks involved in living here. Our greatest danger was from being captured by small raids, which might slip through at outposts.

Such an unusual headquarters merits a detailed description. The house, a one-story affair built of wood and covered on the sides and roof with tar paper, which made it warm and comfortable, was placed right up against the foot of the cliff, part of which had been dug away to accommodate it, thus giving complete protection from the French shells, for when the German general occupied the place the cliff was between him and the enemy lines. At one end of the building was a room about fifteen feet square, which I occupied with my adjutant, Lt. Joseph Horne. It was furnished with two beds along the rear wall, a telephone table by my bed, a large square table in the center of the room, where we ate our meals and carried on our office work. There were two more small tables by the wall and a number of comfortable chairs.

A fire place of carved marble, doubtless taken by the Germans from some French house, served to heat the place and give some distinction to the room. On the walls hung two large fine mirrors in gilt frames, likewise purloined from some French home. It was surely the most home-like, comfortable room I had occupied in all of France and I was glad that the German general had been so particular of his abode on the Front. A narrow hall led from this room to the other end of the building. On the rear side was a kitchen, equipped with stove and tables, and a bunk room for the men. On the front side of the hall were two rooms for officers, furnished like mine but smaller. The other end of the building was taken up by another bunk room for the soldiers and had a large stove in it. There was an entrance to the hall from the side of the house, and in my room a door opened on to a small porch. All of the rooms were lighted by French windows, also apparently from a French house. We were greatly delighted with our new quarters.

I have forgotten the name of the major who received us in this fine shack, for we never called it a house. He entertained us at lunch, which we enjoyed, being always very hungry, and it was all very good. We went over the whole matter of his section with him, I being especially interested since I was to have command of it. His maps not only showed all of his own trenches in great detail, but also the trenches of the enemy in equal detail. Secret information he gave me, in form of orders, told what regiments of enemy troops opposed us, showed their exact position, gave their strength, the condition of their morale, and a short history of each. It was almost astounding to see how much he knew about the enemy. All this of course was obtained through the secret services of France and the United States.[2]

2. This is likely speculation on his part. Intelligence came from many different sources and this information could easily have come through aerial observation, desertions, and captured soldiers.

One regiment opposed to us was described as much depleted in numbers from battle service, having only about fifty men to a company instead of two hundred and fifty, but it was a Prussian regiment, their morale was reported good, and we were warned that they were aggressive fighters who would give us trouble. The other enemy regiment on our front was reported to be of small account as a fighting unit. Its morale was very low, and we need not fear it much. It was an Austrian regiment. The amount and variety of information each army obtains concerning the other on the front is simply astonishing and is concrete evidence of the splendid heroic work of the Intelligence and Secret Service departments.

After getting all the information we could on our new sector and arranging to move in the next night, October 8, we bade au revoir to the hospitable major and made our way back up the hill to our cars. I rode home in the Colonel's car with Lt. Col. Meador, Captain Manning, and Major Cornwell.

On the evening of October 8, in the ever present rain, we made the short march up to the front and relieved the 101st and 102nd Regiments. I took the left of the sector with the 1st Battalion, and Capt. Paul Strong took the right of it, with the 2nd Battalion. We were about a half mile apart in our P.C.'s and had not enough men to join up a solid front between us. But I did not get in to my positions without some troubles. In the first place the guides sent out to meet me got lost and led me in by a wrong road up a long hard hill. Not until we finished this hard climb did they realize their error and so reported to me. I rated them soundly. We had to retrace our steps in the mud and rain and in turning back got mixed up with a wagon train coming out, and in the darkness there was much confusion. Orders could not be shouted as they would doubtless bring down a shower of enemy shells. By riding about considerably and personally directing the men and wagons I finally got my battalion out of the mess it was in and back down the hill again.

Coming in by the right road net time I sent off my four companies to relieve the four in the positions. Each had a guide, and the company commanders had been with me on my previous visit and so should be able to find their proper positions. I decided to let them try anyway, as it was not my work to lead each company in. They all succeeded and without undue delay. I had Capt. Knack, the only captain left with me, since he was the most experienced officer I had, go out on the extreme front with Company B and relieve the outposts beyond the town of Saulx. This was the most difficult relief to effect, being so near the enemy, and it was the last reported complete. I left my horse with my orderly, Corp. Euwart, on top of the cliff, and attempted to find my own way down to my P.C. I found this very difficult and finally came to the telephone station on the crest of the cliff. No guide had been provided for me, and I wandered about in the inky darkness trying to find the road leading down to my P.C. but was unable to do so.

I finally found some wooden huts in a quarry and going in found myself in the telephone central office for this front. It was still manned by the operators of the division we were relieving. Shells fell with great frequency on this position, and these men had no adequate overhead protection from them. But they must stick by their very important work in spite of the shells so that communications might be maintained. They seemed a very cheerful lot and did not worry any over their perils. Several were working at a large switchboard, answering constant calls and making connections. Their only light was from a few dim candles. Asking my way down, I was respectfully told that a line man was going down in a few minutes to repair a line and he would guide me to the P.C.

My guide was soon ready, having packed up his bag of tools and with a joke for his comrades we left the warm hut and went out into the cold rain and the mud. It was absolutely dark outside, without even a star. I could see nothing, but my guide knew his way. Stumbling along, we came to what he warned me was the top of a long wooden stairway, which led down the face of the cliff to the P.C. I was hunting. Even yet I could scarcely see at all. The steps wound back and forth across the face of the cliff. Here and there parts of the railing were gone, and steps were frequently missing. Several times I narrowly missed a bad fall. The guide went slowly and warned me of most of the bad places. The descent seemed endless, and I thought we would never get down. My equipment was heavy and encumbered me greatly. At length we reached the bottom and stood on solid ground again, to my great relief. There nearby loomed a large shadow, which my guide said was my destination. Thanking him warmly for his kindness and trouble, I entered the shack and found my friend the major whom I was to relieve.

Thoughtful man, he had some hot coffee and something to eat for me, which was most acceptable.

We sat there by the fire, smoking and talking, waiting for the reports from the different companies that their relief was complete. As fast as his companies were replaced by mine they pulled out from our sector and marched away through the night to assemble at a designated place, where he would meet them. The three companies on the main line of resistance back of and above us were soon reported as relieved. We had to wait an hour longer for the report that the outpost company, away out there in front, was replaced by Capt. Knack's company. I felt sort of guilty to sit there by the fire in the comfortable hut and know that poor Capt. Knack and his sturdy, weary men were trudging along out there in the rain and mud, so close to the enemy. But it could not be helped, and I knew that I could reply upon him to do the job right.

After what seemed a long wait, during which it was hard to keep awake, the phone rang and the major got his report that his outpost company was starting in. I spoke to Capt. Knack, who said all was quiet and all the men placed, out in the rain and mud. He himself had a good hut, but did not expect to be in it much, this his first night on a new front. In a half hour we heard the relieved company tramping by our shack up the road, and the Captain stopped in to report to the Major, who now getting into his short heavy overcoat strapped on his equipment and wishing me good luck and giving me a hearty hand-grip in good-bye went off cheerfully into the night, on his way to go into the great drive we were making in the Argonne Forest, from which we had just come. Thankful that we did not have to do so, I turned in on my bunk and with my heavy overcoat over me slept the dead sleep of a tired man and was not awakened until morning had come some hours ago.

During the day my staff gradually arrived at the shack. Lt. LeRoy Fouraker, my gas officer, shared the large room with me and acted also as battalion adjutant until replaced in a few days by Lt. Joseph Horne. Judge Kimbrough, and Chaplain McNary, the Catholic chaplain attached to my battalion, shared the next room. Another room was occupied by an artillery lieutenant who was stationed with me as liaison officer for the artillery on the main position above us to give me the artillery support I needed. I forget his name. He spent his time poking up the fire and whistling all day long, but was quick by telephone to get me artillery fire whenever I wanted it, any time of the day or night. Lt. Fouraker roomed with him while Lt. Horne was with me. The cook and my mess orderly took possession of the kitchen and gave us very good meals during our stay on this front, getting their supplies from the different company mess sergeants. They had bunks in the room next to the kitchen. In the large room at the other end of the shack was Sergeant-Major Robert S. MacCormack with a half dozen or so battalion runners, my mounted orderly, Corporal Euwart, and some others.

We understood that it was the intention of those in high command to keep our division on this front, the Troyon Sector, St. Mihiel Front, for some considerable time, probably two months at least.[3] We held this line from October 8 to October 24, and all of this time the 316th Infantry and the 313th Infantry were in the front trenches, while the 314th Infantry and the 315th Infantry were far in the rear in village west of the Meuse River, exposed to no danger except possibly that of longest range shell fire. It was understood that the time of front line service during our stay here would be equally divided between the four infantry regiments of the division, two of them being on the front at a time. This, of course, would have been only fair and reasonable. About the time we of the 316th Infantry and 313th Infantry expected to be relieved to go back to the villages in the rear to rest, reorganize and refit for about a month's time, the entire division was pulled out of that front and started on the road to Verdun to go into the drive again. Consequently we lost our turn for rest and reorganization in the rear, and I was highly incensed over it, for my men needed that change very much, and we were not in proper condition to undergo at once the terrible strain of battle. This was stupid work by the divisional staff.

I cannot give the account of our stay on this front by dates, that is the day by day, as I do not have the data, but I must write it in a general way.

On the first day I was visited by the major in command of the artillery on the ridge above, which was supporting us. This outfit was from Georgia, and I must say from the way they handled their guns

3. After their ordeal at the Meuse-Argonne, the 79th Division was transferred to a quiet sector to reconstitute their ranks and to acclimate the men to life at the front through trench duty.

that they were good and knew their business. The artillery major was a very pleasant gentleman and most anxious to give me complete and full support. He asked me to call upon him at any time of the day or night and as frequently as necessary. He had an abundance of ammunition, so that in case of doubt as to whether I needed artillery fire to ask for it anyway. Better to waste shells than risk not giving support to the outpost line at a time when it was needed. Also he had only forty-two horses left out of one hundred and forty-five, and he could not possibly haul away his store of shells in case he should be moved. I called upon him many times, and he always responded promptly and vigorously.

I feel sure now and did then that most of these alarms from the outpost line were false, but I felt sorry for the men away out there near the enemy, and I never failed to send the shells out beyond them when they were called for. The rapidity with which that battalion of Georgia artillery could fire its guns simply amazed me. The reports were as rapid as those of an automatic pistol. Within two or three minutes after I had asked for fire, over the phone, I used to go outside to listen. The air above me would be full of screaming shells on their way to the Germans and then very shortly, away off in the darkness, I could see the flashes of the bursting shells.

The artillery major had the Croix de Guerre.[4] I asked him how he had gained it. He smiled and said it was given him for coolness under shell fire. He asked me not to laugh. I did not but he did.

"Swell artillery officer I would be if I could not be cool under shell fire," said he.

However the decoration was on a good man, a first-class fighting man. The Croix de Guerre was intended to be given very liberally, and it was. I have heard that Germany intended to give the Iron Cross to one in every twenty men. I know they did give it very liberally. We held our decorations too closely, much too closely.[5] I heard a story of the Croix de Guerre. One of our officers was sent to find a certain French officer and objected that he could not as he did not know him.

4. The Croix de Guerre, or Cross of War, is a French decoration for valor. It can be—and often was—bestowed on soldiers of other nationalities fighting in France.

5. American military officials were especially selective when it came to the awarding of the Medal of Honor. The War Department maintained that this decoration had been bestowed far too liberally during the Civil War.

"That's all right," said his superior. "You can't miss him, he hasn't got the Croix de Guerre."

The living conditions of the men were miserable. The outpost company spent the night out in the open fields mostly in the rain. During the day they had a ruined village to stay in where they could have poor protection and very little comfort. It was damp and they had no fires. Two of my companies were placed in open trenches with absolutely no protection save that given by holes they dug in the trench walls or in the ground just in rear of the trenches. These were always damp and clammy. The reserve company was in a small woods on top of the ridge, and here there were quite a few small dugouts. These also were wet and muddy and ill ventilated, not fit to keep a valuable pig in. The men had hot food from the rolling kitchens twice a day, but they did not have dry beds, nor dry clothes and shoes.

One day I received a message from regimental headquarters that my outpost town of Saulx would be raided by the enemy that night in force, and I was directed to withdraw my outpost lines back some distance and place them in the fields in rear of the town so that the enemy would have his trouble for nothing. I went out to Saulx accompanied by Judge Kimbrough and Corporal Euwart to arrange the matter with Capt. Knack, who was in command out there. It was quite a walk, being about five kilometers. But the road was good and the day was fine, so we did not mind it. As we came near to the town we separated and had intervals of fifty yards between us, because the enemy had been firing shells even at individuals going out to the outposts. Usually two shells were fired. They did not take more than two chances at snuffing out a man's life. It was not worthwhile to waste more shells to get one man, but we would not even waste that many on one man. Corporal Euwart was leading and sure enough just before he reached the edge of the town he got his two shells. One burst in a field near him and the other on the edge of the village. We all started to run for the ruined houses for cover. The Judge and I arrived very close together and I shared his two shells, both of which burst near us as we got among the first houses. A large piece of shell struck a wall with a loud whack just above the head of Lt. Hurley, who stood in a doorway laughing at our undignified approach and at me, picking myself up from the mud where I had fallen in my haste, but we all laughed at him for the manner in which he ducked when the piece of shell struck near him. There we were, all four of us, laughing at the near approach of a nasty death.

I found good Captain Knack in his dugout, and we picked out a new outpost line in the fields behind the town, which his men would occupy when dusk fell. During the day they left only a few scouts out, and the others remained in the town to rest and eat their meals. The enemy did not stir during the day, as the fields were open and our artillery had the ranges down pat and could easily see them from the top of the ridge.

While Captain Knack and I were standing talking in the street, just as I was leaving, a sergeant who was a stranger to both of us came up, saluted, and asked me if it was true that we were going to evacuate the village. We do not answer such questions quickly on the extreme front. I asked him who he was and what he was doing there.

"I am in charge of a radio section of the signal corps in this town. We are out here to intercept German radio messages and have been here over a month," he replied.

His papers and general attitude convinced me as to his identity, and I told him we were leaving the place only overnight as we had warning of a German raid for that night. He said he guessed he would stay. If our men, who had been there some time, had not located his section, he did not think the Germans would, especially in the dark. Their presence with all their apparatus was entirely unknown to us. It was a plucky thing to do, and I admired his courage. As it turned out there was no raid that night; either the information we had was false or the enemy changed their plans. Capt. Knack and his men had a most uncomfortable night out in the open, for it rained hard, and the poor fellow caught a bad cold, so when he came in the next evening I made him stop off at my shack. We gave him a hot meal and a good warm bed, as well as a good hot drink of cognac. He was much better the next day and insisted on going back to his men in the wet woods.

One evening I was out at Saulx and had decided to go out with the outposts to see them placed. I wanted to see for myself what conditions the men spent the night under. The small groups were leaving the town just as dusk fell, and I was walking out with Lt. Jos. Hyer in command of Company A. I had planned for some time to do this, but I was to be disappointed again, for a runner overtook me with an order to report back to regimental headquarters that evening for an important conference. It was at least three miles to headquarters and perhaps nearer four. I was tired and muddy, and it started to rain. This order disgusted me entirely. I would have to walk half the way and ride the rest of it on my old French horse. But orders must be respected. After a weary walk through the mud and rain, I arrived at my P.C. very tired and still disgusted, to be gladdened by the information from Judge Kimbrough that the order was canceled by phone, and I need not to have arrived until morning. I threw my weary body into a chair before the fire with an exclamation of joy. These frequent conferences were a great trial to the commanders of the front line, and many of them were not worth the time and energy they wasted.

We were greatly annoyed and harassed by continual calls for reports from regimental headquarters. Reports on our strength, reports on equipment, reports on our sick, reports, reports, almost every day until we got entirely sick of them. I suppose most of them were necessary, but they were an awful trouble. My sergeant-major and adjutant spent nearly all of their time collecting information and making up reports. I was frequently scolded over the phone for not getting in this or that report.

Sketches of our line of defense were wanted. They already had perfect drawings of them, left by the division we had relieved, and we had made no changes in the lines. Brigade headquarters demanded a detailed finished sketch in the daytime without getting killed, and it could not be done at night. I sent in two different sketches showing our approximate positions. They would not do. Must be absolutely definite and show every post and every man. Such a demand was ridiculous. General Nicholson raised the devil with Capt. Manning, our regimental adjutant, over this sketch, and my good friend Manning begged me to help him. So I got a draftsman, had him in my shack at a table most of a day, and he made a beautiful, detailed sketch of the outpost line, a fine drawing showing every post, every man, and covering every square yard of ground. It was truly a pretty thing, most of it imaginary, but it pleased the General very greatly.

One day Lt. Col. Meador and Capt. Manning visited me in my P.C., their first visit to my shack. My good friend Manning, on seeing the exposed position of my P.C. out in front of my main line of defense and at the foot of the ridge next to the enemy, began a strenuous opposition to my remaining there. I insisted on remaining where I was. I was entirely persuaded that the Germans would make no attack on this front. They were much too busy holding their other fronts against the Allied drives. Our only real danger was from a small raiding party, which might slip through the outposts. We numbered about a dozen all told and could defend ourselves. Also there was artillery stationed even below us near Herbeuville.

All these things I told the Colonel, but Manning, and entirely for my sake, persuaded the Colonel that it was very unsafe for me there, and I was directed to prepare another P.C. in rear of my main line and move to it as soon as it was ready. I selected a position for the new post of command in a little open spot in the woods up on top of the ridge and started Capt. Knack's company to work digging a large dugout. I told him confidentially that we would not be there a great while longer, as we had been promised our turn back in the rear and also that I did not want to move, so he was to take his time on the job and not get the place ready any sooner than he could avoid. He understood and put a few men to work. As they had but few tools and were not pushed, they made but slow progress and finished only the entrance to the dugout. I gravely inspected the work frequently and as gravely reported on it to the Colonel when asked as to its progress. As far as I know, neither he nor Manning ever saw the place. General Nicholson kept them too busy with his incessant demands for reports.

One day, while riding my horse along the crest of the ridge just in rear of my main line of defense on my return from a visit to regimental headquarters, I had a curious experience and a narrow escape from death. There were two routes for me to take, one by road well in the rear and protected from enemy view by trees and camouflage screens, and the other much shorter and more direct by path much of which was exposed to the view of the enemy. The German gunners often threw shells at small groups of our men and had even done so to individuals at times. I knew this, but we had got used to taking our chances with the shells, so this day I took the shorter and exposed route. As I was trotting slowly along thinking of different things, I suddenly became convinced that someone was watching me and that I was in danger. I put spurs to my old French horse and urged him into a reluctant canter. I had traveled at this pace but a short distance, when I heard a medium-sized shell burst not far behind me, and turning in my saddle I saw that it had struck squarely on the path and just about on the spot my horse would have reached had he kept on trotting. I have never had the least doubt that this shell would have killed or wounded me if I had not hurried my pace. The enemy gunners had seen me with their glasses, had estimated my rate of progress and had set their range to get me with one shell. It was excellent artillery practice and had I not that curious and unexplainable premonition, they would have succeeded in making a marvelous shot and another war widow.

Upon our arrival on the St. Mihiel Front we received a warning from one of the officers of the regiment we relieved which saved us many lives. It also exposed another artillery trick on the part of the Germans. No doubt our own artillery practiced these same stunts and thought them clever business, so I do not hold them against our friends the enemy.

Company A relieved another company on the left of the main line of defense, on top of the ridge. They went into trenches which were situated about one third way down the face of the steep slope. Just above them on the crest, or rather just below the crest, where they had protection from artillery when used by the Germans, was a line of partly demolished wooded huts, which would still furnish considerable shelter to the men. Lt. Joseph Dyer asked the officer he relieved why he could not occupy them. He was told not to do so, for the enemy always subjected these huts to a rain of shells the first night after a relief on our position. Sure enough these shacks received a thorough drubbing by artillery on the next night and were pretty well wrecked the next morning. How did the Germans know that we had effected a relief? They thought we might not be warned and would fill the place with men and they would kill the lot of them. Having the range perfectly, they could shower the position with shells during the night when such accurate fire would not be expected. We had heard much of the excellence of the French artillery. Our experience on the front taught us that the German artillery was also very fine. Quite as good as any army will ever want to endure, in fact much too accurate and skillful.

On one of my tours of inspection of my sector, I came upon a large and complete trench mortar battery, beautifully concealed and well situated in new trenches. There were at least six large trench-mortars, all brand new, and concealed in small dugouts were a large number of bombs for their use. All the necessary equipment and tools were neatly placed and the battery seemed ready for immediate action. But not one man, not even a single guard or sentry was in evidence. I could not understand it. This unit was part of the defense of our position, but useless with its personnel gone. Apparently some company had installed and prepared this battery and then gone off and left it. Thinking that it had been left by the division we had relieved and never manned by our own division, I reported its condition to regimental headquarters and suggested that Divisional Headquarters be asked for a company to man the mortars.

Some days later while riding through the woods in rear of this battery, I came upon some strange American officers and men and stopped to ask them who they were. The Captain told me they were trench mortar troops and their mortars were in position about a quarter of a mile out front. So the mystery was explained. He said they lived in the woods where they had protection and better quarters. I suggested that he ought to keep at least a sentry or two in his trenches to protect his equipment, but he did not consider this necessary, and as my authority over him was merely nominal as commander of the sector, I could not insist upon it. I told him I had reported his battery as without guard or gunners, but he said Divisional Headquarters knew all about him and nothing would come of my report. He said also that in case of need I could get his assistance by telephone.

Near the top of the slope, in rear of my P.C., were a number of large wooden shacks which had been built by the Germans. We did not occupy them, as they were not near the positions of any of our companies. We had decided to tear one of them down to use the lumber for some construction we had planned. There was a large room at each end, and we had thought the building contained only two rooms, but upon measuring it off I became convinced that there must be another room in the center of the building. Sure enough, upon examining the walls carefully, we discovered a door which we had overlooked. Upon entering we found a good-sized room, the walls of which were covered with shelves piled high with pyrotechnics, all kinds of rockets, starlight, flares, signal lights in large quantities, and neatly arranged and marked in German. This was an interesting find but not a very useful one, as we did not understand the stuff, and also had plenty of our own at hand. A shell hitting this building at night might have set off a fine display.

Our horses were suffering very greatly from the wet weather as we had no cover for most of them, and they lacked regular feeding. Divisional Headquarters issued a very stringent order that all horses be put under cover. There were some wooden huts below my shack unoccupied, so I had the few horses now with my battalion brought down the hill and put in them. A German raid could have easily captured them, but we did not fear much that they would. Our horses were such a poor lot, so thin and worn out, that I doubt if the Germans would have troubled to drive them off to their lines. But one could not help feeling sorry for them standing out in the rain, and I was glad they were under cover.

12

Holding the Line

While on the St. Mihiel Front the Germans never raided my position, but that did not prevent us from stirring up what was supposed to be a quiet sector by making frequent raids upon them.[1] This was new work for us, and we were not experienced and had no instructors to teach us. Lt. Gabriel joined me here, as battalion scout officer, and a braver, more self-confident and yet unassuming young officer I have never known. He not only made a number of raids on my own immediate front, but he and some of my best men went raiding on Capt. Paul Strong's front. All of this raiding was instigated by regimental headquarters. We on the front would have been satisfied to let well enough alone, since we were not annoyed but were content not to annoy the enemy. Also we stood a good chance of retribution on the part of the enemy, and no one enjoys close quarter night fighting. But regimental headquarters, being a mile in the rear, had no need to fear this, and they annoyed both us and the Germans with their plans for raids, most of which produced no worthwhile results. Some information as to enemy trenches and presence of their troops was brought in, and prisoners were taken several times.

I was at regimental headquarters one morning and saw a small group of these prisoners. Of course the idea in capturing them was to get information of the enemy. These men were Prussians, a little older on the average than our men, and they were well fed and well clothed. I remember one rather short, stout fellow, a sergeant, who stood looking curiously at us with a smile on his face. He did not seem in the least crest-fallen. In fact, the German soldiers were almost without exception very glad to be captured, as they were long ago sick of the war.[2]

---

1. In addition to being a useful way to gather intelligence, trench raids were thought to keep men active and to instill in them an aggressive spirit towards the enemy.

2. Morale had been steadily declining in the German Army overall since the Spring Offensives in 1918 failed to bring an end to the war. War weariness and exhaustion took

But it was not so with their officers. At least they did not act in a way that would make one think so. We captured very few German officers.

Not infrequently the enemy came over in small groups, generally in the very early morning, and surrendered. Near the ruined town of Herbeuville, below us, was stationed a battery of artillery. Why it was down there exposed to enemy raids instead of on top of the ridge back of us I never could reason out. But as I had nothing to say as to their position, I never inquired why they were there. I had enough to worry about without bothering about them. Well, one early morning the cook of this battery was walking in the village street, armed only with a butcher knife, when to his amazement he met a group of Germans. No doubt he had visions of a German prison camp and thought it was a raid long expected. To his surprise the Germans all threw up their hands and cried Kamarad. He marched them proudly off to the battery and was greeted with cheers and much laughter. Most of those who gave themselves up thus were Austrians, who were heartily sick of the war and had lost their spirit for fighting, and after four years of it one cannot wonder much.

The enemy artillery made up in activity for the lack of action on the part of their infantry, and they spoiled many a good night's rest for us with their shells. Most of these were high explosive, and we did not receive much shrapnel nor gas shells. Shrapnel shell, which bursts about twenty feet in the air above the ground and scatters thousands of lead balls around, is very effective against infantry in the open, but not when they are in the trenches. Hence the enemy used very little of it.

Gas shells are more effective against stationary than moving troops. They do not burst like other shells when they strike. For this reason they are sometimes mistaken for "duds" or shells which fail to explode. After a gas shell drops you will hear a light popping sound. This is caused by the heads of valves blowing off, and then the gas pours out and saturates the neighborhood, and it is time to move or put on the gas mask.[3] Sometimes a sector is simply deluged with gas shells, and

their toll and mass surrender was common. For more on the subject of German morale in 1918, see Alexander Watson's *Enduring the Great War* (Cambridge, 2009) and Jonathan Boff's *Winning and Losing on the Western Front* (Cambridge, 2012).

3. Americans wore British small box respirators, which had a mask and a tube that

as the trench must be held, the men remain for hours in their masks, which are warm and uncomfortable and give one a feeling of being shut off by himself from his comrades. Also the lower part of the mask gets filled up with saliva, which is most unpleasant, and the goggles get covered with mist. It is an abominable thing to wear, especially if you are moving forward and under exertion.

Every battalion has an officer called the gas officer and a sergeant, especially trained in gas defense. Lt. Fouraker was so designated in my unit. I remember one night we were awakened by a fairly intense artillery fire. Going out on the porch we soon realized that the Germans were showering the left of our sector, held by Company A, with gas shells. The gas shells passed over us and struck all along Company A's trench. Lt. Fouraker and his sergeant took their masks and pistols and hurried away in the dark to give Company A any help they could. I thought for a while that the enemy intended to raid that part of my position that night and sent out word to all my units to be prepared. We all stayed awake some time to make good our retreat up the hill to our trenches. However, the Germans were content to gas Company A thoroughly and let it go at that.

A curious physical phenomenon about shells is the difference of the speed of travel of sight and sound. Sight, of course, travels much faster than sound. This is generally understood, but it brings about some unusual combinations. One afternoon several of us were on our way to the outpost line. The enemy were firing some fairly large shells at the left of my sector. We stopped to watch them for a few minutes. Away off there on the hillside, perhaps three quarters of a mile distant, we would see the white puff of smoke of the bursting shell. Immediately afterwards we would hear the scream of that same shell, which it made when it passed over us, and following that would come the sound of the detonation of the missile. Curious to see the shell burst before we heard it pass over our heads, but such was the case, and it was hard to realize it at first.

There was much evidence on this front of the wastage of war. In the side of the hill near our shack there was a large dugout built by

led to a tin filter that was held in a bag that fitted around the wearer's chest. Though uncomfortable, the mask was largely effective, and deaths from gas exposure were comparatively low.

the industrious Germans. It had three or four good-sized rooms. A long passage-way connected these. There were two entrances, as there should be to every dugout, for you never know when one will be crushed in by a shell. In and all around one of the entrances of this dugout lay piles of German hand grenades of the large potato-masher variety. Hundreds of them. We did not understand them very well, so let them lie where they were, rusting there in the rain and mud. I did not want them gathered up for fear some might explode. We had our own grenades and did not need them. We considered them a menace and kept away from them.

At different places in our trenches there were piles of rifle cartridges and many belts of machine gun ammunition, all being ruined by the rain and mud. It was of no use to us, not being the correct size, and we had trouble finding places to store our own cartridges. So it was left there and tramped with the mud. Whether it was French or German I do not remember, probably both.

German steel helmets littered the position, and uniforms, boots, bayonets, and rifles all rusted or mouldy lay all over the place. I even found some American Springfield rifles in the field on the way to the outposts, so rusted that they were not worth picking up. In the town of Hannonville, which lay out in the plain three quarters of a mile in front of my right, there was a great quantity of German material. I saw piles of good German uniforms rotting and moulding in the streets, out in all the rain and mud, and no one bothered to put them under cover for of what use were they to us?

This town of Hannonville was really more than a mere village, being of good size with paved streets, fine large school buildings, and a large church. It seemed more modern than many villages we had been in. Being right on the railroad, it kept more in touch with the rest of the world. I was in this town several times and was much interested in its condition. Not a single native of any age or condition was living there, although the town seemed to have been spared by the artillery and was not much hurt by shell-fire. Of course many of the buildings had been struck by shells, but it could by no means be called a ruined town. We went into the large, high-ceilinged church, and there in the roof was a very large hole. This shell had burst inside, smashing the chairs and benches, and pitting the walls and pillars, but doing no great harm to the building. Apparently this was the only shell that hit the church, which was really a very imposing edifice.

All the natives must have fled when the Germans approached and very hastily at that, having no time to take much with them. This was evidenced by the condition of the homes of the people, into many of which we went out of curiosity. It was indeed strange to see all of these houses left just as if the inhabitants had gone off for a few hours, and it was also a pitiful sight, for many of these homes had been ruthlessly wrecked by the German soldiers. They had emptied the drawers and closets into heaps on the floor, in their search for plunder. Bedclothes, books, pots, pans, clothing, women's hats, shoes, linen, ornaments, everything belonging to a home was mixed up on the floor knee deep, all trampled and muddy and moldy. Utterly ruined, all of it.

Some of the houses had been very little disturbed, and we felt like intruders in the privacy of these homes. Of course, everything was damp and moldy and rusty. In the closets we saw linen, neatly piled, and clothing hanging on the hooks. In the kitchens the cooking utensils hung in neat rows on the walls, and children's playthings were on the floor. The mantle ornaments of brass and china were there, as well as the clock. I took down one little brass statue of the Virgin as a memento, but felt guilty about it and went back and set it in its place, where I hope the returning owner found it.

In this same town of Hannonville one of Capt. Paul Strong's companies suffered severely. I think it was about the middle of October. One night, without any warning of course, a drenching shower of mustard gas shells fell upon the town. Against mustard gas, clothing is no protection, for it burns right through to the skin, and on into the flesh, until a special salve we were provided with in large tubes is applied.[4] Those assisting others who are burned also get burned. It is a terrible and barbaric weapon. Eighty-five men of this company were put out of action this night, and the rest were driven back out of the town. The first aid station had a hard night's work attending to so many victims of this awful gas. Most of them had to go on to the rear to a hospital.

4. Mustard gas—sulfur mustard—is a contact agent that causes irritation and blistering to the areas of the body exposed to it. As Parkin indicates, it can linger in areas saturated by it and cause exposure well after the gas shells containing it have exploded.

I was in Hannonville the next day after this unfortunate event, and I was surprised to see no American soldiers there as I knew the town was occupied by our second battalion. The smell of mustard gas was very strong in the streets; it smells like horseradish, a very sweetish, unpleasant odor. We were careful not to touch anything, knowing we might get burned. Against the walls of the houses on the main street I saw many American rifles leaning. Most evidently there had been serious trouble here. I wondered if we might find the enemy in the town, and we opened our pistol holsters and took to the side streets.

Carefully making our way through the streets, we came upon no living thing until we came out upon the main street again at the other end of the town. Here we were surprised to see two American soldiers in the entrance of a cellar. I asked them what they were doing there and what had happened in the town.

"The Company holding this town was driven out last night by mustard gas and had a lot of men badly burned. We belong to a telegraph unit, with our station here in the cellar. We thought the Germans if they came in would not find us and we knew our troops would soon come back, so we just hung on to keep up telegraph communications."

I complimented them upon their courage and asked them if they were not afraid to remain there alone. They laughed in an embarrassed way and said the Heinies would not have found them.

On our way back to my P.C. we passed a garden well stocked with fine cabbages. Some of these we took back to our cook and they added considerably to our fare, which was mostly beef, bread, coffee and potatoes. All the German soldiers I ever saw, both on the front and in Germany, looked stout, too stout for our ideas of a soldier, and well fed.

Judge Kimbrough got us a lot of welcome supplies. We enjoyed the weekly and monthly illustrated papers and ate a lot of good candy and chocolate. We also consumed several boxes of good cigars. Take all you can when you can on the front, for it is often that you can get nothing at all. In a few days we were on the road again, deprived of all luxuries and often of food itself.

Not far from my shack was an old French graveyard. No dead of this war had been buried in it, but there were several graves of French officers therein, and their headstones were carved with the cross of the

Legion of Honor. German shells had split and broken a number of these monuments.

Our own dead were gathered into a small cemetery set aside by the French for us. Every night a wagon took out supplies to the outpost company and frequently brought back dead and wounded soldiers. This was a job the drivers did not much like, but it had to be done. When we first came into this sector we had some trouble in burying our dead, as the official cemetery had been changed or not yet definitively fixed. Chaplain McNary was very busy for several days over this matter and meantime several dead soldiers lay on stretchers in the old French cemetery, waiting for their final resting places, left alone there under their blankets.

Among those dead soldiers there awaiting a grave was a little Jew from Company A. Had his wishes and my efforts met with success he never would have been there cold and stiff. This thought came to me when I lifted the blanket and looked upon his dead face. His name I have forgotten, but not his almost frantic efforts to get transferred into the quartermaster corps. He came to me at Camp Meade shortly after he came to the regiment and requested a transfer, stating that he was an expert office man and also that he had heard the quartermaster corps wanted such men. I was too busy to give the matter any attention, having some two hundred raw recruits on my hands at that time. But he persisted and became a source of annoyance to me. One day when at the quartermaster's office, I thought of him and took up his case with the officer in charge. I filed an application for his transfer and spoke in his behalf several times, but he never got his transfer. I was willing to help him out of my company because I thought that he had not the stuff in him to make a soldier.

But I was wrong and had misjudged him greatly. He fought through our terrible five days in the Argonne Forest bravely and did his duty as a good soldier. Never after we got near the front did he bother me about his transfer. He had been killed by a rifle bullet on the outpost line near the town of Saulx while doing his duty manfully and bravely. I saw him after the Argonne fight and spoke to him. He had cleared himself in my estimation.

As I looked upon his dead face I was glad to know that he had made good and that he had known that his conduct in battle had squared him with his commander. And let me say here that courage and devotion to duty in times of terrible danger are not characteristics peculiar to any race or nation. We had Jews, Greeks, Italians, Germans, Russians, that is men of such parentage in our battalion, as well as our native-born Americans of American parentage. All of these men were equally brave and devoted. One of the bravest and most daring soldiers I had, in fact a man exceptionally so, was Sergeant Sheckart, a man of German parentage and a winner of the Distinguished Service Cross. I know but few soldiers of equal courage and devotion.

We heard many stories of the Drive that drove the Germans out of the towns we were occupying. Many captures were made and much equipment was taken from the enemy. It seems that the Germans expected our attack, but not quite so soon as it happened. At some of the towns where resistance was encountered, the Americans rushed on past the place on both sides and met beyond, thus cutting off all the Germans within and making them prisoners. In the streets were captured entire columns ready to move out. In one town a large headquarters military band just ready to leave was captured. So rapid and easy was the advance at times that one American infantry regiment assembled in columns of fours and marched for a long distance at night I believe. Such were the tales we heard. The St. Mihiel Drive was by far the easiest job the American Army had in France.[5] It was however the first time that the American Army had attacked the enemy as a separate army. What we had done before had always been as units of the French or British Army. Our commanders and their staffs gained much valuable experience from this Drive. It was only General Pershing's firm and unyielding insistence against all the pleas and arguments of the French and British military authorities that gained for us the right to act as a separate army. Our Allies wanted our troops to be used only a reinforcements for their own armies.[6]

5. The battle of St. Mihiel (September 12–16) was the first major battle planned and executed by the AEF. The Germans were withdrawing from their position when the American Army attacked, which is why Parkin describes the battle as an easy one, as the opposition was not as strident as it was at the Meuse-Argonne.

6. Parkin is correct here. Pershing defied relentless pressure from Allied military and political leaders—especially Marshal Ferdinand Foch, appointed Generalissimo of the Allied armies in 1918—to hand his soldiers over to French or British military command. Realizing that amalgamation would be a political nonstarter with the American pub-

One evening during the first day or two of our occupation of the Troyon Sector, St. Mihiel Front, I was walking down the steep road, returning from a tour of inspection of my trenches on top of the ridge. Off to my left against the base of the hill was an old, half-ruined hut and from its open door came pleasant glow of a good fire. None of my men had been placed there, to my knowledge, so I crossed over and entered the place. Therein I found two soldiers sitting by the fire, strangers to me I thought, although I did not know the faces of all the men in my battalion.

Upon my entrance the two soldiers sprang up to attention. The look upon their faces showed me that they were uneasy in my presence.

"What are you men doing here and what outfit do you belong to?" I asked.

"101st Infantry, 26th Division, sir," one replied. "We got left when our outfit pulled out."

They were stragglers either intentional or innocent, a thing hard to determine. In spite of the greatest efforts on the part of the officers and the military police, there were thousands of these offenders in France, and they caused a great deal of trouble and annoyance. Consequently my attitude to these men was somewhat hostile. Orders had been issued to arrest all such when found. They were decent looking fellows, and their story of being overlooked and left on outpost might well be true. I told them that I ought to arrest them and give them over to the military police. The American private soldier of the proper sort, and these men seemed to be of that class, had enough and to spare of trouble and hardship in France, so I told them that if they moved out early in the morning and tried to overtake their outfits, which were on the road to the Argonne Forest, I would let them off. They seemed relieved and grateful. Strictly speaking I had not done my proper duty in this matter, but orders should be considered with a view to the circumstances and the best results.

I often thought that I did not have enough men to hold my front properly, as they seemed so terribly scattered. Several times, at night, large detachments were taken away from me to work on the lines of

lic, President Woodrow Wilson and Secretary of War Newton Baker both supported the AEF's commander on this issue. The President also viewed the American Army's contribution to the war effort as an important component of leverage at the peace table.

our other battalion or join them in raids, thus leaving me with still less force. I complained to regimental headquarters on such occasions and said I would not be responsible for the safety of my lines if they took away so many men. As a matter of fact, I believe the machine gunners and the artillery could have defended the place without any infantry at all, so strong was our position. That is looking back on the situation I believe so now, but I did not at the time. Responsibility and anxiety when laid upon a man make things look very different to what they do when these cares are removed. I was not so sure then that our high command was all seeing and all powerful. I could only think of the few men I had to hold those long trenches and of what General Kuhn would say to me if I survived after being driven out of my lines. Death is not the only thing an officer fears in battle. Failure and consequent disgrace have an equally large place in his mind.

Being on the extreme right flank of my sector one afternoon, I went down the steep slope and visited my good friend and comrade, Capt. Paul Strong, commanding our Second Battalion and holding the line on our right. At the lower part of the slope I passed through the neatest and prettiest village of rustic huts built right on the hillside, by the Germans of course, that I had yet seen in France. They were all one story, some of them quite large, built of small logs with green shingle roofs, and all had large verandas with artistic rustic railings and steps, decidedly well and neatly built and looking very pretty amongst the trees. Lawns had been graded and planted, and flower beds added to the appearance of the whole. Of course these latter not so well kept as when the Germans tended them. Officers' quarters these, probably a headquarters staff, to judge from the number of the cottages. Other larger simpler buildings for the men stood off some way. Strange to say, the German shells, which fell in great numbers on our lines, had done very little harm to this artistic woodland village. They were not occupied by our men, who were in trenches. They might be shelled any hour of the day or night.

In the village I met one of our soldiers wearing a pair of German army boots. It was not my place to correct him for so doing, as he was not of my battalion. So, out of curiosity I asked him where he got them.

"Took them off a dead Jerry, Sir," he answered.

"Jerry" and "Heinie" were the soldiers' names for the Germans. He said they were comfortable and that he liked them better than his own shoes and wrapped leggings.

I found good Capt. Strong ensconced in a fine concrete house at the foot of the slope. It was very strongly built, with heavy walls and roof and had close in front of it a very stout concrete wall to stop shells. It was, I think, proof against everything but the very heavy shells, of which not many were sent against us, and yet he had later to give it up and go up on the ridge, the Colonel fearing he might be captured by a German raid. He did move, having a place to go to, but as I have explained, I never did do so.

He stoked up his smoky iron stove, and we sat by it for a while, compared notes, and talked over many things. It was a pleasure to be with this good comrade, whom I had seen rarely since we came to France. We had trained in separate villages, some distance apart, and I saw very little of him on the march and in battle.

We were interrupted by a lieutenant who came in to report, Lt. Ira Lady. I jumped to my feet and shook him warmly by the hand. I had heard that he was with Capt. Strong's battalion, having only recently joined from the Officers' Training Camp at Langres, where he had recently earned his commission. This officer had been a drafted man, a private in my own company at Camp Meade, Maryland. One cold blizzardly day during the previous winter, I had been ordered to select twelve men to go to France at once in a regular infantry regiment. We were out on the drill ground in a driving snow storm—bad weather never stopped our training—when the order reached me. I read out the order to the company and asked for volunteers, as I always did, and I never failed to get them. I did not like to pick such men arbitrarily. Ira Lady was one of the volunteers that day, and he left us the next to go overseas. At that time I realized his worth and had him in mind for promotion and was sorry to lose such a good man. This was the first time I had seen him since that day, and now he was an officer.

I had judged him rightly. We had a good talk, and he told me of his experiences, and I said I regretted that he had not been sent to my battalion. He was very glad to be assigned to his old regiment and would have liked much to come to me but was very happy with Capt. Strong.

He made a brilliant, courageous, and fine officer, but was not to wear his well-earned shoulder straps long, for, poor fellow, he was killed within a month, leading an attack against Hill 378. Little did we guess that this day, we were so glad to see each other. Many young officers had an equally brief career in their new positions, going as they did from the training schools in France direct to the front line regiments, where they were badly needed, as officers did not live long in most cases on the front. At this time I had with my battalion only five officers, and should have had twenty-seven. Twenty-four line officers with the companies and three staff officers, an adjutant, a scout officer, and a gas officer. Why they did not send me more I never knew. I applied for them right after the Argonne battle nearly a month since. There were plenty of officers in France to fill my vacancies, and they knew full well we needed these officers desperately. The staff actually sent us private soldiers. I received three hundred and fifty men for my battalion on the march up to Verdun, but no officers, and not even a corporal or sergeant. Can one wonder at the intense antagonism which often exists between the line and the staff officers? We were called upon to do the bloody and dirty work of the army, and they would not give us the means to do it.

Towards evening I started back towards home and took a path leading through the trees and undergrowth, which ran along about half way up the front of the ridge, and I had another adventure with enemy shells. The path led through open spaces as well as woodland, and it may be that German artillery observers saw me and determined to get me. At least so it seemed to me then. As I walked along, deep in thought, I was startled by the burst of a shell near the path not far ahead. This was closely followed by another explosion fifty yards behind me and at about my level. Bracketing a target, they call this in the artillery, and I realized that I was bracketed and very neatly at that. To stand still would be to be very near the next shell, so I hurried on, and the third shell crashed behind me. It was best to get as near home as possible if I was going to be hit, and I made good time, crossing the few open places at a dead run. They must have had the range of that route down pat, for they kept me moving briskly all the way home and fired at least a dozen shells, most of them bursting behind me but some striking ahead of me. It may have been only part of their evening bombardment, which happened to fall along my route, but it followed me so persistently that I thought they were after me. At any rate I got home in good time for dinner, and otherwise I am sure I should have been very late.

Another evening Judge Kimbrough and I were nearing home after a tour of the right of our lines when a deluge of shells, both large and small, began to fall between us and the path leading down the hill to our shack. Everybody in sight ran for cover. The shelling was confined to a space on the top of the ridge some hundred yards or less in front of us. It did not spread, so we were in no great danger, but one piece of a heavy shell hurtled along the ground and came to rest close to us.

"That will make a fine souvenir," said the good Judge, and he picked it up, but dropped it quickly with a cry of pain.

It was so hot that it burned his fingers.

We lived nearly a month in our shack, in full view of the Germans, and why none of their many shells ever struck it will always be a mystery to me. They could see by their glasses that it was occupied, and the number of people about must have shown them that it was a headquarters. Being at the base of the hill it was probably in uncertain light and hence a poor artillery target. It was not a safe, but it was a most comfortable place to live in, and such places on the front were very few. For comfort we risked our lives, which shows how much we valued our ease and what it must have meant to us, who were always tired and sleepy from physical exertion and continually interrupted rest at night.

Lt. Col. Robert Meador and Capt. William S. Manning with orderlies came down the hill to visit me one day. Brigade headquarters was and had been harassing these poor fellows for continual and seemingly endless and often foolish reports. So they were not in good temper and a little inclined to take it out on us front line commanders, from whom all this stuff must originate. So I came in for some criticism in this matter. In defense I stated that my adjutant, as they well knew, had been killed in battle and had not been replaced. This had been his work. I had very little time to devote to it, as other duties kept me busy. My job was to look after my front and my men and not be a clerk. My sergeant-major, Robert S. MacCormack, was doing his level best and working hard to do both his and the adjutant's work, but the company headquarters were widely scattered and the information wanted very hard to get. I was a little peeved and ended up by saying that I supposed I would be relieved of my command on account of a lot of d— fool reports, which did no good anyway as apparently no attention was paid to them and our proper demands for men and equipment.

They then told me how they were being harassed by Brigade and Division Headquarters and that they were obliged to pass a part of the work on to me. We all agreed to work together and do the best we could. Manning was the sort of man, if you knew him well as I did, that you could not help admiring and wanting to work hard for. As a matter of fact, he was really the head of the regiment at this time, as Col. Meador took no real interest in affairs and merely signed orders and plans that Capt. Manning, assisted by Capt. Carl E. Glock, regimental intelligence officer, made up between them. They were the brains of regimental headquarters, together with Capt. M. E. Goetz, regimental scout officer, and Capt. James P. Montgomery, personnel officer. In these officers we had four fine intelligent staff officers at our headquarters, but Manning was the natural leader as well as the ranking officer among them.

Col. Meador and Capt. Manning desired to visit my outpost company. As I had been out there all morning and was tired I sent Lt. Fouraker, my gas officer, out with them and begged to be excused.

Just before they started they took out their pistols and looked to see if they were ready for service. One never knows what will happen when on the extreme front. Manning shoved his pistol back with a laugh and said to me, "This reminds me of when I played Indian as a boy." And I never saw him show any more fear nor anxiety of the close proximity of the enemy than that. Col. Meador was rather bored with the whole thing than anything else. I would not disparage their courage for anything, but it was a bright sunny day when one could see all things. It might have seemed just a little more dangerous had it been a dark, wet night, as it often was for us, but even so these two gentlemen even in the face of greater danger would, I am sure, have shown no more concern over it. They got back about dusk and hurried on their way to Regimental Headquarters, refusing my pressing invitation to dine with us, saying they must get back at once and get in touch with things again. It would not take them long in their sturdy little Dodge car, which was awaiting them at the top of the ridge.

When the Germans occupied our shack they had electric lights, as they did on practically all of the fronts they had held so long, two or three years or longer. For some reason we were never able to operate the engines and dynamos, which were left apparently in good condition. If these machines were out of order they certainly did not have that appearance. At any rate we did not use them and were reduced to old-fashioned candles, which do not give much light. Five or six of them burning at once on our table gave enough light to work with and read, if you sat up close, but they affected the air, especially in a dugout.

Since Lt. Dan Keller had met his death in the Argonne Forest I had had no adjutant, and I greatly missed the services and assistance of such an officer.[7] Many reports were asked for and demanded in haste by Regimental Headquarters, and Sergeant-Major MacCormack and I had this work to do in addition to many other duties. I had applied to Regimental Headquarters for an adjutant, requesting Lt. Joseph Horne, an old Pittsburgh friend who was willing to accept the position.[8] Much to my delight he was assigned to the place and reported to me while we were on the St. Mihiel Front. A major and his adjutant live together on very intimate terms, eating and sleeping together, as their work requires that they be with each other practically all the time. It is therefore very pleasant when they are old intimate friends, and we were. Mrs. Horne, his mother, and my wife had become great friends at Fort Niagara, New York, where Lt. Horne and I had trained at the First Officers Training Camp. For all these reasons our new relations to each other pleased us both very much. Lt. Horne was not only a good old friend, but he was a good, reliable officer, who would attend to his duties well and carefully.

The first night Jos. Horne was with me we were aroused very late by the bursting of large shells very near our shack. They struck both above and below us on the slope and at just about the correct range to get us. We sat up several times and debated whether we would go out in the

7. An adjutant is a staff officer who is responsible for the clerical aspects of a battalion's management. Often, this person serves as the right-hand officer for a battalion commander.

8. Lt. Joseph Horne came from the family that owned the Joseph Horne Company, a regional department store chain in Pittsburgh founded in 1849. He was a graduate of Yale.

rain and mud to reach the safety of our nearby dugout. Just when we would agree that it was time to flee to safety, the shell fire would let up and we would sink back under the blankets. Aroused this way a number of times, we finally got disgusted and agreed to stick to our bunks and take a chance on it. Such is the indifference or fatalism developed by frequent exposure to great danger. One shell directed just a little bit more to the right or left would have brought an awful mangling death to us, and we chanced that just to enjoy our warm beds and not have to spend the night in a cold and damp concrete dugout where safety was assured.

I did not enjoy Lt. Jos. Horne's company and services for long. Two or three days after he reported to me, to his intense disgust and my great disappointment, an order came down from Regimental Headquarters directing him to proceed to the town of Gondrecourt to attend one of the army schools, a number of which were being run by our army in France for the special training of our officers. His captain had put his name in for this course many weeks before, and he had forgotten all about it.

So I was again left without an adjutant. I had a gas officer, Lt. Fouraker, whose duties did not take much of his time. He could have done most of the work and was perfectly willing to do so, but was prevented by a divisional order which forbade gas officers to assume any other duties than their own, so important was their work considered. However, he did help us out some with the compilation and writing of the endless reports.

Some of our men who had got lost from their companies in the dense woods of the Argonne rejoined us on the St. Mihiel Front. Not all such men are willing stragglers by any means. Mechanic Eby, one of my good and trusted soldiers of Company A, rejoined us here. I met him by chance when he arrived and was very glad to have him back. We did not know whether he was dead or wounded or what had happened to him. Having got lost from his company he had been with another unit and had been hunting us for many days. Needless to say Eby was very glad to get back to his old friends and comrades, for a soldier's only home in France was his own regiment, and he felt lonely and unhappy among strangers.

13
To Verdun

Toward the end of October, rumors that we were going to move and go back into the "Drive," which had been furiously going on all this time, became prevalent. Although generally incorrect, these rumors are often astonishingly accurate and reached us days before the official orders. It is impossible in most cases to trace them to their source. Enlisted men, working at the different headquarters, often hear discussions or telephone conversations, and learning something of interest they pass it on to their buddies, and so it gets around. Officers, as a rule, keep things more to themselves. Consequently, we officers often knew less about what was going to happen than did many of the men.

As I had been told officially that we would stay on the front line for a time and then be relieved by one of our other regiments and have a spell in the rear to refit, reorganize, and rest up, as two of our regiments had been doing all through October, I did not of course give any credence to this rumor. Also I did not believe that they would send us back into battle in our present condition. The men had had no rest and had been continually wet and cold. We had very few officers left. I still had just five in my battalion and should have had twenty-six. All the rest were killed, wounded, or sick, except three or four who were at school.

Furthermore we had been on the front line ever since our terrible experience in the Argonne Forest, our first battle, and we had no real chance to recover our morale and our proper spirits. Knowing the condition of my battalion and realizing that it was poor, both physically and mentally, and convinced that the very few officers I had left would not last long in battle, leaving the men without leaders, I was terribly depressed at the prospect of going back into the Drive, as I felt absolutely convinced that we did not have half a chance to "make good." We had done well in our first fight and now we were in danger of ruining our reputation.

These rumors persisted, and in consequence I put in some of the bluest and most down-hearted days of my life. It was extremely hard to keep a cheerful countenance and not let my depression spread to my officers and men, who as I have said were already low-spirited enough. If the leader of a unit loses his nerve and his men get to know it, there is small chance for it to do its duty in battle.

Confirmation of these disturbing rumors came to me on one of my visits back to Regimental Headquarters. Major Cornwell, our regimental surgeon, took me aside and very gravely told me that the regiment would soon be moved and would go back into the "Drive." Convinced as I was that we were not fit for battle, I even doubted the good major's information, but he assured me that it was no mere rumor and that he had already received orders to make his preparations and get his supplies to handle our wounded. Part of his supplies he had already received, and as he did not have wagon room to move it all, he intended to entrust a part of it to each battalion. He said that he would turn over to me in a day or two a small box containing anti-tetanus serum and begged me to give it very great care and be absolutely sure that it reached the Front with us, as once there we could get no more, and it might be the means of saving many lives, for wounded men lying on the ground with open wounds were in serious danger of lock-jaw if they did not get an injection of this serum. And so I became convinced that the rumors were true and that we would soon be on our way to battle again.

I might as well here finish the story of the precious box of anti-tetanus serum. When we moved off the St. Mihiel Front, I put my gas officer, who would have nothing in his own line to do on the march, in charge of my battalion wagon train. It had already been lost a number of times and had been a great care to me. I told Lieut. Fouraker, the gas officer, to take command of it, and I gave him our route and halts and instructed him to keep up and not get lost. I gave the box of serum into his personal care and told him about its great importance to us. Upon our arrival at the famous city of Verdun several days later, I inquired for the box and learned to my dismay that it had been left behind at the town of Genicourt, where we had rested two days. The wagon carrying this box was overloaded and some of its contents had to be left behind, and in spite of all my orders, the box had been abandoned. I don't think anything happened in France that provoked me more than this. A detail was immediately sent back to recover the box of serum, and to my great relief they found it and brought it back to us, making the journey back and forth on passing army trucks. Thereafter I personally saw that it continued the journey with us.

The same day that Col. Meador left us, going away in the regimental car and, strange to relate, taking with him a favorite chair he had picked up, there came to us a new colonel, a real honest to G— soldier, and a kindly, helpful gentleman as well, Colonel George Williams of the regular cavalry. He had brought over a pioneer regiment, but had applied for a combat unit and had been sent to us. We were in great luck, at last, and now had a commander whom we could both love and respect and for whom I knew that we would all go the limit and a little more.

I was summoned back to regimental headquarters to meet the new Colonel, and at first glance I felt a great relief come over me. My good old friend, Col. Alden C. Knowles, in command of our brigade, General Noble having also been relieved after our first battle, introduced Col. Williams to us battalion commanders. Capt. Paul M. Strong and Capt. John Somers commanded the other two battalions, replacing Major John Baird Atwood, killed in the Argonne Forest, and Major Albert Dodge, relieved of his command before we went to the Front.

Col. Williams shook hands with us very cordially, and as I have said, immediately made a very fine impression upon us. His talk with us on the condition of the regiment and the work ahead of us only improved this impression. He asked us to draw up chairs close, and he questioned us closely about our commands. Our report upon the tired and worn-out condition of our men and our general unfitness to go into battle would have discouraged most colonels new to a regiment, but not so with Col. Williams. He gave us encouragement and advice and real help. One of the things he said and repeated forcefully, I have never forgotten.

Speaking of the condition of our men, he said, "On the Front you can feel a real sympathy for your men, but you must not express it or show it, as encouragement and help are what they need, not sympathy, and by being sorry for them you only make matters worse and do not help them to buck up and be men."

And he was right. Encouraged and heartened up, "with our tails up" as the British so aptly put it, we went back to our commands, determined to make good and put the pep back into our units.

The prospect of going back into battle did not look quite so bad now that we had such a commander to lead us. Capt. Paul Strong and I journeyed back to the front lines together, and as we went we talked over our new commander, who we both agreed was a real God-send to us in time of trouble and discouragement.

On the night of October 17 our reserve battalion, the Third, under Capt. John Somers, was also put into the front line, relieving a French regiment and leaving our front, now about seven kilometers long, without any reserves of any kind at all. Very apparently Divisional Headquarters anticipated no attack in any force on the part of the enemy. But, as I have explained, our position on the high ridge was very strong, and we had ample support of artillery and machine guns.

While I was in close touch with our Second Battalion on our right, my left flank was "in the air," as they put it in the army, since I had no touch on that side with the 313th Infantry. There was a wide gap here in our line, and it was only covered by patrols from my battalion and from the 313th Infantry. However, the outpost line was practically continuous, and we hoped, after having warning from it, to reach the attacked point before the enemy did. I presume this part of the line of defense, which was practically unprotected by the infantry, was protected by artillery and machine guns, but I do not know for sure as to that. Our division had two regiments of infantry in the rear and could easily have filled in this open gap in the line. The fact that it was left open indicates that headquarters was not worried over it, as they knew of its existence. I reported it myself, and I presume the 313th Infantry did likewise. The fact is that the Germans were kept too busy elsewhere, resisting drives being made by the French, British and Americans, to start any attacks on fronts where they were being given some relief from actual attack in force.

Good Major Cornwell, our regimental surgeon, came down to my P.C. one day, bearing an order from the Divisional Surgeon directing that the men be given regular baths.

Apparently the Divisional Surgeon had not been up on the front, or he would never have issued such a fool order. I could tell from

Cornwell's face that he was amused at the order, and I laughed outright when he showed it to me. It was a joke and was treated as such. No attempt was made to carry it out, simply because under the existing circumstances obedience to the order was utterly impossible. Water was not plentiful with us in the first place; in fact it was scarce. And then we had no means to heat the water and no place for the men to bathe, even if they used cold water, which they certainly would not do as the weather was quite cool and often wet.

On the open slope, below my shack and in full view of the enemy artillery, which would always fire at small groups of our men, was a large concrete trough with running water. Cornwell suggested that some of the men might bathe there. He would have liked to report that the order was being complied with. To give him this small satisfaction I told him they might, but I did not tell him they certainly would not do so, and they never did.

Trench digging and preparations for defense against an attack in force, which we officers on the front felt convinced would never develop, continued during all of our stay in this sector, but being convinced of its uselessness, the officers did not push the work, and the men were always tired and lacking pep due to their miserable living conditions. No inspector ever came up from the rear to look over our work, and no engineer officers ever showed up to direct us. We kept the digging in the woods, to protect the men from the active enemy artillery. Some of my trenches were dug in certain places not because they were effectively located there, but because the woods were there. I considered the whole thing a waste of energy, and the men certainly loafed shamefully on the job. It used to amuse me to hear the sounds of the picks and shovels cease after I had passed out of sight, when on one of my frequent tours in inspection. It would have been very different had there been any real need to do all of this trench work.

Our time on the Troyon Sector, St. Mihiel Front, was now up. We had been here since October 8, and on October 24 we were relieved by the 132nd Infantry of the 33rd Division, a National Guard outfit, whose ideas of discipline were not such as prevailed in our division.[1] Na-

---

1. The 132nd Infantry hailed from Illinois and had been fighting at the Meuse-Argonne.

tional Guard officers are elected by the men. Such a system is wrong and is not conducive to proper military discipline. However, the fighting record of the National Guard is so good that there can never be any question of their courage.

It was always customary, in our division, to send ahead parties of officers to look over the new sector to be occupied and get familiar with its positions and trenches. No such advance party came to us from the 132nd Regiment. I was informed that we would be relieved on the evening of the 24th and directed to send out qualified guides under an officer to meet the incoming regiment and guide its companies, which were to relieve my battalion, to their proper positions. This I did, and the relief was effected without any trouble or confusion.

Lt. Dyer, commanding Company A, which was on the outpost line, told me that when the relieving company reached his position the men complained loudly at being placed so near the enemy, saying they had been promised a rest. When their officers tried to quiet them, the men were impudent and talked back to them. Also unauthorized rifle firing started, and bullets flew in all directions. Never did men act so in our regiment.

Early in the evening there appeared at my P.C. a young captain, who informed me that he commanded the relieving battalion. They had lost their major in the Argonne Forest drive, from which they had just come. This officer was so utterly tired out from the battle and the night marches that he could keep awake only with the greatest effort. He sat in a chair beside me at the table, on which I had spread out the maps of our sector and was attempting to give him all the detailed information I had as to our positions and our information of the enemy. He looked at the maps with eyes glazed with weariness and kept falling forward on top of them. I felt sorry for him, as I had been in the same condition, but it was necessary that I inform him as to his new sector, so I kept at it until I covered everything, and he said that he understood. I knew that he did not and next day those maps must have looked strange to him.

I waited there by the telephone until I got word over it from each of the company commanders that they had been properly relieved by the new companies. It took over an hour longer to replace the outpost company out at Saulx in front than it did the companies on the main line of defense. My orders were to remain just behind the main line of defense for the rest of the night to support the new defenders of the line, and to march out in the early morning, and it was then that my battalion assembled. All reports being in and satisfactory, and as it was some hours yet until day-break, I rolled up in my trench coat and lay down on my bunk to get some sleep. My bedding roll had already gone, so I had no mattress, but slept on the wires which took the place of springs in the bed. In spite of this discomfort, I got several hours of sound sleep.

My faithful orderly, Corporal Euwart, awakened me early in the morning just about day-break and told me my horse was saddled and waiting outside. The Captain still slept the sleep of exhaustion in his chair. My cook gave me a hasty breakfast, which I ate standing by the warm stove. All of my staff had already departed except Chaplain McNary. I looked into his room and told him it was time to go. He complained that he was very tired and asked to be allowed to sleep longer, promising to overtake us on the road. Making sure that he knew our route, I left him, and mounting my great black French horse, rode up the hill to the place of assembly.

Shortly before my arrival the companies had been scattered by a burst of shelling by the German artillery. A farewell touch from our friends, the enemy. Doubtless they knew that a relief had been effected during the night and guessed rightly that we would assemble on top of the ridge before marching out. Fortunately there were no casualties. The men came hurrying out of the woods and trenches and dugouts and soon the column was formed on the road among the trees. Corporal Euwart came up to me carrying the battalion flag, which had been in my shack and had been forgotten purposely I feel sure, by good Captain Knack, whose company carried it, because he rightly felt that it was a useless impediment on the front. Riding down the column flag in hand, somewhat to the suppressed amusement of the men, I came to Capt. Knack and gravely handed it over to him. He took it without enthusiasm, to say the least. I never saw it again and made no inquiries about it. It was well and properly lost the next time and bothered Capt. Knack no more.

We marched on down the rear of the ridge we had been holding so long and were now out of sight of the German artillery observers and free to walk along in the open without fear of hearing the shriek of an approaching shell. This meant more to us than can easily be imagined.

For nearly a month we had not been able to appear in the open without being shelled, and the situation had got on our nerves.

The men did not look overly well. Their faces were thin and drawn. They did not look stout and hearty as they had at Percey-le-Grande in August, when they were training hard but were well and regularly fed. What they needed badly was a real rest and some good, regular food to put them into first class fighting condition, but more fighting and no rest was what was in store for them in the immediate future. It made me downright blue and miserable to think of taking them back into battle in their run-down condition.

We crossed a small valley and climbed a long, steep hill; the heavily loaded and tired men made slow progress. We halted frequently to rest. Here the road climbed through a fairly deep cut, and under the banks on both sides, well concealed, the French had built almost continuous lines of huts of wood and stone, capable of sheltering hundreds of soldiers. Many of these were occupied by French and American soldiers, and it was like passing through a long village.

The country we now passed through was dismal and desolate and had a depressing effect upon all of us. It had all been fiercely fought over and was simply wrecked by shell-fire. The forests were nothing but groups of shattered masts, for the leaves and limbs and branches had all been blown off the trees. It was a wasteland of shattered homes and villages and empty weed-grown fields. There was no one in all the country-side, no signs of life, nor cultivation, for miles, and we met only soldiers on the road.

Many graveyards along the way did not tend to raise our spirits. Some of the graveyards were very extensive seeming to hold thousands of graves, and there were also many small ones, and frequently we came upon single graves. Over the entrance to all of the larger French cemeteries there was always an inscription. Capt. Manning, our regimental adjutant, wrote it down and translated it for me. He promised me a copy, but he was killed, and I never got it.

The Germans had set up many massive monuments cut out of heavy stone, and most of them were beautifully carved and, except for their size, in very good taste. They certainly were permanent. On all of them was cut the iron cross, and on many were regimental crests. They were mostly erected over some officer's grave, but many were to the dead of some regiment. Here and there we saw a single monument, all by itself, on the roadside or out in a field. These scattered monuments will interfere with the cultivation of the land, and I wondered as I rode along whether the French would permit them to remain after the war, or would gather all these bodies of the devastators of their country into large cemeteries. Surely France will not want her countryside ornamented so with monuments to her ancient enemy.

Filled with such sad thoughts, I rode along through this stricken wasted countryside. My men marched silently behind me. They raised no song, they talked in low tones, and there was but little laughter. Their thoughts were as mine, inspired by all the wreck and ruin and evidence of death we saw.

We passed a National Guard infantry battalion on its way into the front we had left. I looked these men over with great interest. I was surprised at the youth of many of them, mere boys of seventeen and eighteen. They could not have got into the National Army and should never have been accepted for the Guard. Doubtless they lied willingly enough about their age. The armies of all wars have been full of such adventurous youths. Nevertheless it struck me as a great shame.

At the head of this column rode a young captain. He was not more than twenty-five, if that old. Evidently he was senior captain and in command. I envied him his fine bay horse, compared with which my awkward, hairy, old plug made a very poor show. Evidently they had suffered heavy losses, for their companies were not much over half strength, and there were but two or at most three officers to a company, and there should have been six. All of their officers averaged younger than mine. In truth, it was a boy battalion.

Their appearance was not what it should have been, even at the front in war time. Troops may be dirty and muddy and unshaven, as my men were, but at least they can be dressed and equipped in a uniform manner and most certainly should be. These National Guardsmen wore a great variety of head-dress. Some had steel helmets, some overseas caps, some campaign hats, and others even wore black felt hats. These last had no doubt been found in the French villages. As to clothing, the men wore raincoats, or overcoats, or blouses, just as the individual pleased. My own men, without exception, were all wearing steel helmets and overcoats. Their uniform appearance certainly made the other column look very poor in comparison.

There was very little exchange of friendly greeting between the troops as we passed. The National Guard, being practically all volunteers, in fact all I believe, did not think much of the drafted men of the National Army, and on account of their poor appearance and well-known lack of discipline, our men had no admiration for them.

Their column was not followed by American Army wagons, as was ours, but by small two-wheeled French carts in which they carried their baggage. The drivers of these wore ragged overalls and any kind of a hat and looked like poverty-stricken farmers going to market. Their get-up, no doubt, amused the French and British even more than it did us. These carts were drawn by two horses, which looked as if food had been a stranger to them for many days.

About noon we reached the camp in the woods near the town of Rupt-en-Woevre, in which we had rested for a few days before moving into the Troyon Sector, St. Mihiel Front. All the country we had marched through all morning was strange to us, for on our way in we had passed in the darkness of night. Hence, this old stopping place of ours was the first familiar place we came upon. Here the men were given a hot meal from the traveling kitchens. We found our old camp occupied by a regiment of our engineers. The lieutenant colonel in command very hospitably invited me to his hut to rest and took me to his table for lunch. He expressed his regret that a shortage of food did not permit him to invite my officers. He was a temporary officer, recently promoted from major. He told me that they had but recently come from the Argonne Forest, where they had been occupied in constructing trenches and positions of defense in rear of the advancing infantry. These were no doubt intended for use in case the Germans drove our army back. Needless to say these trenches were never used. The lieutenant colonel seemed rather proud of his part in that battle and said he had won his spurs there as was evidenced by his promotion. When I thought of the hundreds of fine officers and men we had left there unburied, I could not bring myself to much praise of what his regiment had done. Of course, this is hardly fair. Engineers are supposed to do just such work as this regiment had been doing. And on a number of occasions the engineers did join in the battle, and they did a great deal of their work under shell fire.

The medical major of this engineer regiment made a great fuss because my men were making the camp unsanitary in attending to the duties of nature. He blustered a great deal and threatened to report me to his Divisional Headquarters. The major was quite in the right to object to such actions on the part of my men, and I issued orders at once, stopping the practice. But even after my men had quit and were busy cleaning up, he continued to complain, and then the Lieutenant Colonel and I both jumped him and finally quieted him. It must have been a great bore to have him around all the time.

We took the road again after lunch and just as dusk fell we came to the town of Genicourt, near the Meuse River. This fairly large town showed very little evidence of shell fire, but it was practically deserted by its people. As I rode into this place I was much surprised to see Lt. Hurley, who had been wounded during our first battle in the Argonne. He had with him a lot of strange and very clean looking soldiers. He reported, after we had exchanged greetings, that he had recovered from his wound, a slight one in the ankle, and that he had brought me one hundred and eighty men as replacements to fill up my battalion, at least partially. I was glad to have these men. A good looking, sturdy, clean crowd they were. They came from an Iowa regiment of the National Army. I was greatly disappointed to learn that not a single officer, in fact not even a corporal had been sent to me. I had, as I have explained, repeatedly asked for officers, and I needed officers more than I did men, of whom I already had more than my very few officers could properly handle and lead in battle.

I got off my horse and went to have a closer look at my new men. They seemed so new and fresh compared to my old men. As the column passed these replacements closely inspected the veterans, dirty, muddy, and unshaven but lean and hardened as they were. They, the new men, were evidently much impressed at the thought of joining with these soldiers, who had been in battle and on the front.

I spoke to one of the new arrivals, a tall, red-headed young fellow with an intelligent face, and asked him some questions about himself and his comrades. He stood in front of me in a sloppy, indifferent attitude, answering my questions in an easy and not overly respectful manner. I asked him if he had ever been trained in the proper manner to stand when spoken to by an officer. He blushed furiously and came smartly to attention, putting a "sir" on all of his answers. He had been trained properly and just needed a little jacking up. His comrades noticed the incident, and it no doubt braced them all some. In battle or front line trenches military formality is not expected nor required, but it was always brought back sharply when we were back of the front.

The new soldiers were divided equally among my four companies, and they went off with the veterans down the streets, seeking their billets. Many a startling tale these new men heard that night from their more experienced comrades, no doubt. They were accepted by my men without friction and were quickly absorbed into the battalion. A few night marches in the rain and mud made them look as rough and dirty as the rest of us.

My billet in Genicourt was large well-built house of the better class. The rooms were large and had high ceilings. There was sufficient furniture for our needs, consisting of chairs, tables, and beds. The floors were bare and not clean, so many people tramping in and out in their muddy shoes kept the floors dirty all the time. As to warmth and comfort, there was very little of either. In fact the house was as cheerless and as cold as a tomb. All of my five officers lived here with me, as well as Judge Kimbrough and Chaplain McNary. There were so few of us left now that we liked to keep together for company.

My cook and orderly soon had a fire going in the roomy kitchen, and we all went in there frequently to get warmed up. Capt. Knack and I hunted for some wood to build a fire in the dining room. All we could find were some new pieces of timber about 3″ x 4″. As no one claimed it, he and I sawed a lot of it into short lengths and soon had a roaring fire, about which we all sat talking and waiting for dinner. Lt. Hurley's gold wound chevron, on the right sleeve of his coat, attracted much attention and comment. It was the first of these decorations we had seen.

Our supply of fire wood was small, and as I thought we would be given a few days' rest here, at least, I made out a requisition to the town major for a wagon-load to be brought in for us from the country and sent it to that official. A half hour later Lieutenant Rochat, one of the French officers attached to our division, came in and, taking me aside, said there was no use in getting the wood as the division was going to move on to Verdun the next evening. He assured me that this was true and that we were not going to have but one day's rest tomorrow before going on up to Verdun. This information angered me, and I told him what I thought about it. He smiled grimly and replied, "Tough luck, Major, but c'est la guerre." Not much comfort from him.

We had a good dinner that night, and the cook did himself proud. There was a roaring fire and plenty of candles on the table. The room was warm and cheerful, and we had plenty of good wine. It was a long time since we had been together around the festive board, and we forgot our troubles and our weariness and spent a jolly evening together. Few of such parties we had in France, and this was the last one. In a few days we were separated far apart never to come together again in this life. One of those officers, Captain Knack, was soon to die in battle; three, Lt. Symington, Lt. Dreher, and I were to be wounded; and three of us, Lt. Hurley, Lt. Fouraker, and I were to be captured in close-fought battle by the Germans.

The next day was spent in what few preparations there were to make to go into the front trenches again. Orders were issued to leave in Genicourt all officers' baggage and bedding rolls. I had the officers' suit cases and bedding rolls gathered in a small room on the second floor of the house we were occupying, and I placed a corporal, whose foot was so sore that he could march no more, and a private who was ill, in charge, with strict orders to allow no one to touch our things unless they knew him as one of our officers, or unless a written order was delivered to him. My best whip-cord uniform and other things I valued and could not replace were in my own suitcase. If my memory is correct, the regimental and company records were carried on and left in Verdun in charge of the clerks. I gave the corporal a written request to all mess sergeants to supply him and his comrade with food. He did his work well, as I afterwards recovered my suitcases and bedding roll with contents practically untouched.

The battalion fell in for our night march to Verdun just as the shades of evening began to fall. I mounted my poor old French horse and was riding through the streets on my way to the place of assembly when I met Col. Williams. He spoke to me and, as military courtesy demanded, I halted and dismounted. After I received his orders, I started to mount again. What with my heavy personal equipment hanging all over me and the unusual height of the horse, I had considerable difficulty in getting into the saddle and was only able to do so with the help of the Colonel and a passing soldier. I met the Colonel again later, and as he spoke to me I started to dismount again.

"For God's sake, stay on the horse, Major," cried the Colonel, remembering the trouble he had getting me mounted the last time. At this we both laughed.

As dusk fell we marched out of the town on our way to the famous city of Verdun, and to the front-line trenches beyond. I was riding along later in the evening, busy with my thoughts, when an automobile came up in the dark and a voice called my name. I answered, and Capt. Manning got out and saluting me, informed me that I was in command of the regiment, Col. Williams having taken over command of our brigade. I had not expected this responsibility and was not pleased to receive it, as I felt a battalion was enough for me to handle on the Front. However, I was now the senior officer of the regiment, and I did not have a choice in the matter. Calling up my trusted friend, Captain Knack, I turned over the command of my battalion to him, repeating my orders, and I also let him take my horse, which he did not want. I then joined Capt. Manning and Capt. Carl Glock in the regimental car, a Dodge, and we set out for Verdun to arrange billets for our troops.

It was a very dark night, and as no lights were allowed at or near the Front, I wondered how the soldiers' chauffeur could see. Personally, I could not see the front of our car from my place in the rear seat. Experience in this, as in all other matters, had given him proficiency, and we rode along at a rate of speed that made me nervous. This great highway along the Meuse River to Verdun was crowded. Huge trucks, ambulances and other cars sped past us, many of them much too close for my peace of mind. Strange and most unusual to be on a teeming, roaring main road, in the pitch blackness of night, and not a single light greater than the glowing end of a cigar or cigarette to illuminate the whole mass of rapidly moving traffic. Yet not a single accident occurred.

At one time we slowed down very suddenly and found ourselves in the midst of a mass of marching troops. French infantry they were. We could hear them talking and laughing all around us. Some of them seemed provoked at our narrow escape from running them down, and very naturally I thought. The chauffeur explained that he had rounded a curve and come upon them unexpectedly, but was used to such close calls.

We came upon a number of cross-roads at which there were neither military policemen nor signs, but our direction was northeast, and we always took the road in that general direction, and finally, after what was to me an exciting and most interesting ride but was ordinary travel to the others in the car, we came to the outskirts of Verdun, a city of which I had read and heard a great deal and was now to enter.

The streets were very narrow, and at all the intersections we found military police, who directed us on our way to the town major, whom we must see in order to reserve billets for our regiment. We passed many ruined houses and buildings, evidence of how the city had suffered. However, the streets were kept open and clean, all of the debris being removed from them. My recollection now is that we were permitted to put on our headlights, but I cannot really believe it for I remember how strict the police were about even the light of a candle showing in our billets.

We found the town major, a French officer, established in a comfortable office. The rugs and easy chairs and warm fire seemed quite strange to us. Manning and Glock had a long talk with him, in French of course, none of which I understood. I did not concern myself with the billeting arrangements, as I knew these capable young men needed no assistance from me. The arrangements being satisfactorily completed, we set out to find our marching battalions and direct them to their billets. Having accomplished this—we met the troops on the road not far south of Verdun—we returned to the city and went to our own quarters, which were in the historical citadel of Verdun, and of this wonderful place I want to attempt some description.

This great fortress is cut out of the solid mass of rock which forms a large hill in the city. According to an inscription cut in the wall of the Salon of Honour, a large room devoted to the display of the military decorations which have been conferred upon the city by a number of nations on account of its stubborn and wonderful defense, the work of cutting this great place out of the living rock commenced in 1743. One is impressed with the fact that a tremendous amount of work has been done since that date. It would almost seem that the entire hill has been hollowed out. You enter through great massive doors on the street level, or you can ascend the hill by a roadway in your car and enter at different levels. These levels or floors, of which there were at least three or four, are all connected by spiral steel stairways. The many rooms or halls are mostly very large with high arched ceilings. In some of them whole battalions were quartered. In another I saw a large theatre with stage and scenery and many rows of seats. Complete bathing establishments with all modern facilities, toilet rooms, restaurants, canteens, reading rooms, and offices with plate glass and mahogany furniture occupied the large rooms. Electric light flooded the whole place, and steam heat radiators were numerous. There was none of the dampness usually found underground. The air was good, so there must have been a scheme of ventilation.

I was told that they could quarter 20,000 men in the fortress and that it was always kept provisioned for a siege of five years. A plentiful water supply was assured by wells sunk inside the citadel. On the slopes of the hill outside I saw gun emplacements from which many guns, some of them large, protruded their long, wicked-looking snouts.

This vast mass of solid rock was absolutely impervious to the shell fire of artillery. Many shells of heavy calibre struck upon it during our stay, and it was an utterly useless waste of effort and money, for we were totally unaware of them and felt no shock nor vibration. I do not believe that artillery could ever reduce this stronghold nor even damage it to any extent. On the top of the hill was situated a group of fine large college buildings. Shell fire had reduced these to a broken mass of ruins.

Our quarters and regimental post of command were in Casemate D, Gallery C. It was a large room with high vaulted ceiling. Bedrooms built of rough lumber with partitions about seven feet high and no ceilings were assigned to us. In each there was a bed with a mattress and tables and chairs. The furniture was rough and unpainted but served its purpose very well. I regarded the mattress with considerable suspicion. It did not look very clean, and it smelled musty. However, it was so much cleaner than all of the others I had seen on the Front that I had my bedding roll spread out on it. But I would not have slept upon the mattress itself and would have preferred bare boards. I was convinced that these old mattresses were the breeding places of the cooties which harassed the army so much. I never did use one of these mattresses, and I never had any cooties upon my person, and I was one of the very few who were not annoyed by them.

After I got comfortably settled in my bed and was congratulating myself upon being so well fixed, so warm and dry, so safe from shells, I heard a certain crusty old brigadier general, an old regular, complaining bitterly of the quarters assigned to him. He was just as well fixed as the rest of us, and we were all greatly pleased. I thought him very hard to satisfy and should very much have liked to call to him to shut up and go to sleep and be damn glad he was so well fixed, but majors do not talk to brigadiers in that manner in the army, and he continued his complaints keeping everybody awake for a while.

14
Near Hill 378

The next morning, October 27, afforded us an opportunity to walk about Verdun and see this famous city.[1] At least half of the houses were in utter ruin, perhaps more. The streets were kept clear of the debris of the wrecked houses. I had expected to find the city an utter ruin, but while badly wrecked it was far from a ruin. There were many civilians and soldiers about. Shells fell continually, but not in any great number, and the people in the streets paid very little attention to them, an illustration of the fact that you can get used to anything.

In the afternoon Captain Manning and Captain Glock and I went up the west bank of the Meuse River, a very small river it was, to the Bois de Forges, which was to be our next stopping place. We passed through a most desolate war-wrecked section. The forests were reduced to large groups of shattered poles, the trees seemingly blasted by shell fire, and all the life seared out of them. Villages utterly wrecked and smashed beyond recognition as such. At some of them signs were erected carrying the names of the villages which had existed there. The roads had not yet been properly repaired, and the going was often rough and difficult. We noted the route and the distance carefully, so as to direct the marching battalions, and selected our halting place in the forest. There was no choice, as it was all equally bad and muddy, but a destination had to be chosen. From these sad and melancholy woods the Americans had driven the enemy some weeks before.

We returned to Verdun and the citadel and there received orders from Colonel Williams, our brigade commander, to march out that night to the Bois de Forges. We had expected a rest of a few days here and were greatly disappointed at these orders. To make matters worse

1. Verdun is a French city along the Meuse River. Heavily fortified before the First World War, the city was subject to a ten-month attritional battle in 1916. The city became a symbol of French resistance and endurance.

it was raining hard, and we would find no shelter in the forest at the end of the trying march. While we were at dinner in the officers' mess the brigade adjutant came in and cheered us all up by announcing that orders had been changed and we would not move that night. This was good news and assured us of another comfortable and dry night. After dinner Judge Kimbrough and I went to his quarters; for some reason he was not quartered the citadel. We were congratulating ourselves on the way back upon another night in Verdun, but were disgusted upon reaching the citadel to learn that our orders had been changed a second time and that we must move out and spend the night on the road in the mud and rain.

I sent runners with marching orders to the three battalions, and soon the entire regiment was on the road, plodding along through the mud and rain. I stood in the street and watched them move out. After all the troops had gone we, the regimental staff officers and I, returned to the citadel to pack up and follow them in our car, the Colonel's Dodge touring car. We could cover the night's march in two hours or less, so we were not in any hurry to get started. Capt. Manning, Capt. Carl Glock, and Major Cornwell, Regimental Surgeon, rode with me.

At one place we were held up by a stalled French truck train. Our chauffeur got down and examined the ground along the right side of the road. I could see but little, and I could make out only a mass of mud there. He said that he thought the Dodge could get through to the right of the trucks. I felt sure that we would only get hopelessly mired, but upon his insistence allowed him to try it. We pulled off the hard road and immediately sank into our hubs. But that stout little car pulled us right through a hundred yards or more of that soft, wet ground to the surprise of all but the driver, who knew his car.

We found all of our battalions on the road, and I spoke to the commanders. They were getting along well and understood their routes and destinations. I came across Major Lloyd of the 315th, marching along on foot at the head of his men. I wondered why he did not have a horse as I did, but many majors were on foot by this time, their horses being needed to pull the wagons.

I was now the only major left in our regiment. Atwood was dead, Dodge had been sent to other duty, and Manning had not yet been promoted. Capt. Paul Strong and Capt. John Somers, the other two battalion commanders, were both on foot. They had tried to take my old black French horse away from me, claiming they needed it for the wagon train, but an energetic protest on my part had prevented this. Both Col. Charles and Major Cornwell had given up their horses, but as they road in the Colonel's car, they did not need them. I was entitled to a horse and intended to keep mine as long as possible. To handle four companies and a wagon train on the march in the darkness and confusion would have been a very hard task to accomplish on foot. It was hard enough to do on horseback.

We finally reached the Bois de Forges, our destination, a shattered woods near the Meuse River and not far from the lines we were to take over the next night. We got out of the car, and Capt. Carl Glock found a Nissen steel hut, or elephant hut as we called them. These are built of steel plates and are half circular in form. They are water tight and dry and warm. We lit candles, and by their light saw that the place was in very filthy condition. Glock produced a can of jam and some hardtack, which we ate. We preferred to sleep in our car by the road side, rather than endure the filth and rats. We awoke very early and found ourselves stiff and sore, but dry and clean. The regiment passed what was left of the night, after their arrival, in the wet and muddy woods without fires or protection from the rain.

I was sitting in the car in the early morning, all the others sound asleep in various attitudes, and looking about in the dreary, soaked, and shell-wrecked woods, a truly dismal scene, when I noticed, some way down the road, piled on the wet grass near the gutter a heap of food. It consisted of loaves of bread and boxes of canned stuff. A food dump left there by some American truck for some unit nearby. Probably some engineer unit, as there was evidence of such work going on in the forest.

I heard voices and saw some French soldiers coming along the road. They stopped at the dump and laughing among themselves picked up two of the large brown American loaves and turned off into the woods. I would have called to them to put the bread back, but I did not want to awake my weary comrades. The Frenchmen did not see me nor our car. Such mean stealing angered me. Bread has a very high value on the Front.

We made our breakfast this morning on bread and chocolate bars and water. No hot coffee to cheer us and pep up the inner man. Our lunch and dinner consisted of the same tempting menu. Army bread is very good. I don't think I ever ate better, but one can get tired even of it. Our chauffeur had some trouble getting the Dodge started, but we were soon on our way to the sector of trenches we were to relieve.

Near the ruined town of Brabant we found Col. Williams, our own colonel, but temporarily in command of the brigade, and Col. Tenny Ross, Chief of Staff of our division, together with a number of other staff officers of the Divisional Headquarters. They were all crowded into a small place of several rooms, buried deep in the hillside, and there was scarcely room for us to get in. A large map of the sector engaged their attention. Manning and I had a short talk with Col. Williams and learned something of the situation of our trenches from him. We then climbed the long, steep hill through Brabant, and at the top were stopped by the military police, who said that we could not take the car any farther. Autos were too valuable to risk under the shell fire. Officers and soldiers had to go on and take their chances.

We found the brigade P.C., another dugout, deep in the hillside. Here were more staff officers, both of our own division and of the one we were to relieve. We checked up our maps here and received finite and final information and instruction for the relief to be effected that night. On leaving this place to go on farther up to the regimental P.C. some half a mile nearer the enemy, we met General Kuhn and several staff officers. We saluted him, and he stopped us. He spoke to me in a very complimentary manner upon my capturing of the Bois de Cunel in the Argonne Forest, in doing which I had penetrated further in amongst the Germans than had any other officer of the division. He was very nice and friendly to me, and I was greatly pleased if somewhat embarrassed by his praise.

General Kuhn asked me if I could hold my front against the Germans. I had not yet examined my position and did not know whether I could hold it or not, but I did know the answer the General wanted, so I replied, "Yes, Sir."

"That's right, Major," he said, "don't you give the Germans a damn inch of it."

I never did give them an inch of it, perhaps because they never tried to take any of it away from me.

Captain Manning and I went on towards the front lines, after leaving General Kuhn. Our way took us along a narrow road through the forest. Many enemy shells were bursting ahead of us and on both sides of our road. They were close and became thicker as we went forward. It was our duty, however, to go to the regimental P.C. of the regiment we were to relieve that night, and so we must chance the shells and go on.

As we approached the locality of the dugout we sought, we saw but few soldiers. They were all underground except the few runners we met. One of these pointed out for us the position of the dugout, and we were soon deep underground and there met Colonel Rickard, a Baltimore man and a very fine gentleman and good soldier. He commanded the 115th Infantry of the 29th Division. He and his staff officers all were gaunt and haggard from hard work and little sleep. Evidently we were taking over a tough sector and trouble and grief lay before us, which proved to be the case.

This dugout was twenty-five feet underground and consisted of four good-sized rooms. It gave perfect protection from the shells of the enemy, but it was many times badly shaken by the large shells bursting on the ground above it. The whole place would tremble, and the earth would come sifting down through the cracks between the boards of the wooden ceiling, for it was not lined with concrete. At such times we would sit silent and terrified, thinking the end had come.

Colonel Rickard got out his maps of the sector and we studied them carefully, being of course greatly interested in the lines we were to take over. The information on the enemy was not as complete as we had received in the Troyon Sector, but it was an active fighting front, and information was harder to get. Having found out all we could and after asking many questions, Capt. Manning and I took our leave, assuring the Colonel that we would return that night to relieve him.

We found our car, after a long walk, during which we saw a most unusual sight. We passed an army cart standing in the road. The team had consisted of a black and a white horse. A shell had struck the black horse fairly and blown him into small pieces, but the white horse, standing right beside him, was apparently unhurt, at least as far as we could see, and it was covered with the blood of its mate and looked an awful sight with the red blood dripping off its white body. The poor beast stood there all trembling and terrified. The driver was also unhurt. A motorcycle messenger was passing at the time and he was also unhurt, but his person and his machine were soaked with and dripping with blood. In the ditch at the side of the road was a soldier on his knees, stone dead, killed by this same shell. The quantity of blood was astonishing. It was remarkable that all of these men and both of the horses were not blown to pieces. All this had happened just a few minutes before we reached the spot. The driver was still stunned, but the motorcycle rider had recovered sufficiently to curse vigorously as he stood looking at his messed up machine. Since the only man hit was beyond any help, we did not tarry long and left the survivors to their own resources.

We got into our faithful Dodge and ran down a long hill road to Consenvoye, a half-ruined village on the east bank of the River Meuse. Here a long, narrow bridge crossed the two narrow channels of the river and an island between them. We were stopped by a sergeant, who advised me not to cross the bridge as it was under observation by the Germans, who shelled all cars going over. I looked out on the bridge and saw many places in it recently repaired with new planks. Evidently the German artillery had been making good practice with their shells. I asked the sergeant if the fire on a single car amounted to much. He replied that six shells per car was the usual allowance. Our troops were on the other side. We must choose either a short and fairly dangerous ride or a long, safe one down the east side of the river to Verdun and back up the west side to the regiment. As I have said before on the Front, one gets fatalistic about shells. Manning and I decided to take the chance and cross the bridge.

We started across and had just got away from the protection of the ridge behind us when the German artillery observers spotted us, and the race between our car and the shells began. It was in reality a race with death. We were half across the first channel when we heard the first shell coming after us. By the sound of it we knew it was going to be very close, if not a direct hit. But we were committed to the test, and there could be no turning back now. The shell passed close on our right with a terrifying roar and struck the water just ahead of us near the bridge. We sped past before the water thrown up by it had fallen back. "One," counted Manning with a laugh. A weak smile was all I could give him. Our chauffeur put the car up to high speed. Again we heard a shell coming. It also passed close on the right and struck the railing of the bridge ahead of us. We tore through the smoke of it. "Two," counted the smiling Manning. The third shell passed very close over our car, seemingly only a foot above us and burst in the middle of the road on the island ahead. We rocked through the shell hole with an awful jolt a few seconds later. "Three," said Manning as he lurched against me.

The fourth shell was high and struck the trees on the island beside the road. I heard Manning count, "Four." Two more of our allowances were yet to come. We were going at terrific speed now. I was convinced that either the shells or an accident to the car would finish the lot of us. I realized that we were fools to take such chances with death to save a few miles of travel. The roar of the car lessened the noise of the fifth shell, which was close and burst in the water of the second channel at the side of the bridge. I don't know where the water thrown up by this shell was when we passed. I did not care at the time. The car was simply flying now. But the good Manning counted, "Five." He was a man of wonderful nerves and self-control. And now we heard the sixth shell coming, heard it above the roar of the car. By the sound it was coming directly at us. There is no mistaking the noise or scream of a shell which is headed directly for you. Utter conviction that our time had come possessed me and Manning too. We crouched low behind the back of our seat, as if the thin steel body of the car could afford us any protection. The shell came upon us with a hissing scream and passed so close over our car as to leave us breathless with fear and emotion. I thought it had passed through the top of the car it was so near to us.

A short way ahead I saw a stone wall, the road on the other side of the river running close to the bank, and we must turn sharp to the left. We could never make it at our terrific speed. I shouted to the chauffeur to put on the brakes. He saw the wall and did his best to lessen our speed. We rounded the corner at a great pace and on two wheels only, just grazing the wall. With the exception of the sixth shell, this was our closest call with the end of all things.

When we settled down upon four wheels again and recovered our breath and some of our composure we looked at each other with grim smiles and agreed that that was about as close a call as we had ever been through together. We decided also that no more should that bridge be burdened with us by the light of day. And I could not help chaffing my good friend Manning, and I said to him, "You forgot to count the sixth shell." He admitted it with a shrug of his shoulders.

We stopped in the Bois de Forges where the regiment was passing the day in the damp and muddy woods, without fires to warm their bodies and dry out their clothes. However, the traveling kitchens had joined them, and the men enjoyed a good hot meal, the last of its kind they were to have for a long time. I had the bugler sound officers' call, and when they had assembled from all parts of the woods and stood around me, all giving me their close attention, for I was their only source of news and information, I described our new sector to them and told them what was expected of us. My description of the difficult and dangerous lines we were to take over was not and could not be very cheerful, as I could see by their faces, but I knew these officers. They had all stood well the test of battle, and I could rely upon them fully to do their duty. Nor had I any concern about the men, who would follow their officers willingly. General Kuhn had told me when I met him up in our new sector that we were not going to attack the enemy, but were only going to hold our new front against them.

I told the officers that we were not going to attack the enemy or "go into a drive," as we expressed it, but were only going to hold the new sector. This news had been a relief to me, and it was to them also. None of us felt that our regiment, which had had no rest since reaching the Front, was in proper condition for battle. We were all tired out, and our spirits were not high by any means. Also we had been in battle, and no man enjoys the prospect of going into another one.

I gave the battalion commanders detailed orders and directions for moving into the lines and relieving the troops there. I also told each where he would find the guides, which would be sent to certain places to lead him in. It would be pitch dark, and once they had started I could be of little if any help to them. I told them I would be on the roads to help all I could and that they could reach me by phone at regimental Post of Command, where they would report to me by phone when they had completed their relief. All being understood and all questions answered, I wished them good luck, and getting in my car with Manning, went down the river to Verdun, for what purpose I do not now remember. At Verdun we got caught on the bridge in a jam of loaded artillery caissons and had to remain on it some time while the Germans dropped shells in the river on both sides of the bridge and very close to us. Had one of these shells hit one of these loaded artillery wagons there would have been a disaster which would have destroyed the bridge and a great many of those crowded on it. We were greatly relieved when the jam was straightened out and we got off the bridge safely.

Our mission in Verdun accomplished, we returned to the Bois de Forges in time to see the battalions started on their journey to the trenches they were to take over. They had had a hot meal from the traveling kitchens, but Manning and I had not, and there was nothing left for us. We munched army bread and chocolate bars for our dinner as we rode along and washed it down with water from our canteens. When a regimental commander, as I was temporarily, has started his three battalions and his extra companies, the machine gun and headquarters companies, for the front lines, there is not much more for him to do but get to the new regimental P.C., where he can be found or reached by telephone. He must trust his battalion commanders to carry out his orders and find their trenches in the blank darkness.

We of the regimental staff, in our car, crossed again the river bridge at Consenvoye, on which Manning and I had been shelled in the afternoon, but no shells fell now. Evidently the Germans were not aware that a relief was being effected; otherwise the shells would have been falling heavily. We got into a bad traffic block in the town of Brabant and were held up for a long time again in an artillery ammunition train, and I was thankful that the German artillery was silent. We finally got through and reached a point beyond which the military police would not permit an auto to go. From here we walked on up the long hill well loaded down by our equipment and blankets.

Colonel Rickard, the commander of the regiment we were to relieve, had attended to his part of the relief in good style, and we were met on the road by guides, who helped us carry our equipment and let us to the dugout we had already been in, but which we would have found very difficult to locate in the darkness.

Down in this deep and large dugout we were cordially welcomed by Colonel Rickard. We found it warm and dry, a stove in the corner being fired up, and well lighted by candles. The air in this dugout was always good and never smelled musty and damp. Sleeping accommodations were very limited and consisted only of a narrow wooden bed, which the good Colonel occupied; his adjutant slept on the board floor under the Colonel's bed. There were several chairs, and in one of these I passed a rather uncomfortable night, but got some sleep nevertheless. Before going to sleep we sat talking together, waiting for the reports of the battalion commanders to come in over the telephone, telling us that the reliefs had been accomplished. In a couple of hours the last of these came in, and we settled ourselves to get what sleep we could.

We were all awake early next morning. Our sleep, as is usual on the Front, had been frequently interrupted by telephone calls and the arrival of messengers throughout the night. We could hear the racket made by the bursting enemy shells above on the surface. About seven o'clock Col. Rickard looked at his wrist watch and said, "Gentleman, we can go up now and have breakfast."

I was considerably surprised at this, for I could still hear the bursting shells above and was perfectly willing to eat a cold snack in the dugout, rather than a warm breakfast up there among the shells. The Colonel started unconcernedly up the long flight of steps, and of course I followed, but not with any zest for this dangerous breakfast. When we got about half way up the steps the shell fire ceased abruptly, and all was quiet and peaceful when we emerged on the surface among the trees.

In a partially shell-ruined wooden shack, and at a table punctured by pieces of shells, we were served with a very good breakfast by the Colonel's orderly, consisting of hot corned beef, bread, jam, butter, and coffee. We sat at the table smoking and talking for about a half hour after the meal, and then the Colonel looked again at his watch and said that it was time to go below. We had not got settled into our chairs down below before the sound of bursting shells up on top came to our ears again. I must have looked at the good Colonel in a quizzical manner, for he and his officers burst out laughing at me. He then explained that the German artillery on this front had got settled into a regular firing schedule, from which they very seldom departed. Our new friends had learned this schedule and knew at what hours of the day the enemy laid off to eat and rest, at which periods it was perfectly safe to be above ground. We made a careful copy of this schedule for our own use.

At ten o'clock, during another period of quiet, Colonel Rickard and his officers bade us goodbye, wished us good luck, and went off to the rear to overtake their marching regiment, and the full responsibility of holding the line and managing a regiment on the Front descended upon my unaccustomed shoulders. With the good help of Captains Glock and Manning, I managed to get by for a few days with a job which I felt was too big for me.

We had effected our relief on the night of October 28 and taken over the lines of the 115th and 116th Infantry of the 29th Division, a National Guard outfit I believe.[2] On our left we found a regiment of White French Colonial Infantry, and on our right was our sister regiment, the 315th Infantry, under our former lieutenant colonel, good Colonel Alden C. Knowles, a fine and efficient officer, who knew his job from the ground up.

Our battalion in marching into this position had been subjected by the Germans to a heavy shell fire in which a good many gas shells were mixed. In some way the enemy knew a relief was being effected, and they poured over the shells to make it as difficult and dangerous as possible. The men had to march through the utter darkness wearing their gas masks. There is no more unpleasant task for a soldier than this.

During the early part of our first evening in this deep and large dugout, the German gunners had a piece of good luck, and it was only luck of course. They dropped a large gas shell exactly into the entrance of our dugout. It burst—a gas shell does not have a real burst like an explosive shell; some caps are blown off permitting the gas to escape. The cry of "gas" was heard at once, and we all hastily put on our masks, which we always wore in the alert position, that is they hung on our breasts just below the chin. We had to wear these uncomfortable masks for two hours or more. The orderlies under the direction of the gas officer, Lt. Fouraker, fanned the gas out and up the stairs with gas brooms, handles with pieces of carpet or bagging attached to them. The gas is very thick and heavy and can be moved in this way.

After working in this manner with the gas for a long time, the gas officer, who could see the gas when it was heavy enough, being

2. The 115th Infantry consisted of Maryland National Guard and the 116th Infantry of Virginia National Guard. Both were part of the 29th "Blue and Gray" Division, so called because it was comprised of soldiers from both sides of the Mason-Dixon Line.

convinced that it had mostly been swept out, would test the amount of gas remaining in the dugout in the following manner. Being heavier than air, the gas was densest on the floor. He would get down on his knees, and with his face close to the floor, he would open his mask just a very little by pulling the rubber face covering away from his face with his hand, and then he would sniff the air to tell by the smell how much gas remained. After several such tests, finding the air pure enough to breathe without harm to us, he would take off his own mask and give the order to "Off masks," and we would take them off with a great sigh of relief. Our faces would be covered with sweat, and the lower part of our chins would be wet with saliva. No one dared to remove his mask until the gas officer gave the order. Death by gas is the most terrible form in which the soldier meets it.

During all the time that the dugout was filled with gas, the business of the regimental Post of Command must go on as well as possible, and we were very busy all of the time. Messengers arrived with orders and instructions. These must be read through the misty and breath-befogged glasses of a gas mask. Orders must be written and sent off. Instructions had to be shouted through the masks with your head close to the individual to whom you were speaking, and even the telephone must be answered. All this was difficult and exhausting. The more you talked the worse your mask got until you really got disgusted and tired out. Hence the supreme relief of finally removing the wet and sloppy mask can be appreciated only by those who have tried to carry on their work for several hours while wearing this necessary but most aggravating protection.

A colonel of the Inspector General's staff found his way down into my dugout. We did not see many of these gentlemen so close to the Front, and it was relief to be free of them, for they made us much useless trouble when we already had our hands for than full. This neatly dressed and highly polished gentleman, just out of his limousine car, was greatly horrified at the number of dead and rotting horses lying about our sector. I explained to him carefully that we had just taken over the sector and that the dead horses had been left by the division we had relieved. That made not the slightest difference in his gilded life. The horses must be buried and at once.

On behalf of my wearied men I made as much protest as a major can make to a peppery old colonel, and believe me that is not much. He took my name, rank, and regiment in order to report me to his head-quarters. I did not give a damn about such rot and showed him so as much as I could. Now it takes a hole in the ground as large as a small cellar to bury a horse, and it is very hard work to do with entrenching tools, which are short and small. I had some of the men of the company I was holding in reserve in the rear of my sector put on this work, and we made a bluff at it, but we did not bury many horses. Major Cornwell had quick lime thrown over those that remained above ground, which purified the air considerably.

In this sector, called the Grande Montagne, a part of the Verdun Front, for no other troops than those of our brigade stood between the Germans and Verdun some fifteen miles south of us, our line ran through dense forests, and we had no regular trenches, no continu-ous lines of defense. Groups of our men, in touch with each other and generally in sight of each other, situated in shell holes or holes they had themselves dug, and always behind the undergrowth of the for-est, held our front. It was extremely difficult to visit and inspect such a front. If you did it in the daytime you were very likely to give away to the observing enemy the positions of your men and so bring upon them rifle and machine gun fire and cause useless loss of life. And in the dark of night it was utterly impossible to find the men. Hence I had a good general idea of the position of my line of defense, but not an accurate one, and I could only place it on my map in an approximate position. Of course this did not satisfy Brigade Headquarters, who wanted the line of defense exactly to an inch on their map, but we fixed a line for them, and they did not know the difference.

While crawling along our front line one day to visit the men there, I came upon a group of six behind a good-sized bush, and getting into their shallow depression on the ground, I questioned them about the enemy and the line of defense. While talking with them I happened to look towards the enemy line, which lay above ours, we being at the base of the hill, and saw a number of Germans walking about unconcern-edly and with not the least effort at concealment. I asked the sergeant why he allowed that. He replied that the men they had relieved had told them that they did not fire on the Germans nor did the enemy fire on them. Sort of a mutual agreement to let each other alone. Doubtless my own men had been out in the open also, and only took proper cover at my approach. I did not criticize the sergeant for his attitude toward the enemy, nor did I order him to open fire upon them. I simply left the situation as I found it. Piecemeal killing in the front lines leads to no real result or advantage to either side and only makes the lot of the men there more miserable.

The other sections of my line did not seem to have such an understanding with the enemy, at least I did not see any more Germans walking up and down in the open. In fact I had to be very careful to keep under cover, and when I had to cross a road or a path I was advised to jump over with all possible speed, as machine guns of the enemy fired along these places.

Col. Williams telephoned me from Brigade Headquarters one morning and told me that the French regiment on our left had complained that a German patrol had gotten through the left of my line and had then invaded the right of theirs and taken a French corporal away as a prisoner. They had their nerve to assert this. If it was true why had not the Germans taken an American prisoner? Furthermore, I had been along the left of my line that morning, and the men had stated that all had been quiet the night before and the Germans had not bothered them at all. This I told Col. Williams and made a denial of the whole thing. He was glad to report my opinion and observations to headquarters.

During one of our first days upon this front and before we were located in our deep dugout, or at least before he moved in with us, Capt. Glock and his staff were established in a heavy concrete hut, which was only partly below the level of the ground. There were quite a number of shelters of this type scattered through the woods (they were still there in 1926 when I revisited this front and in perfect condition). These huts were built by the Germans and were of very heavy concrete, at least two feet thick or more, and each had two or more rooms. There were doors at each end and windows on the sides. From everything except the very large shells they afforded ample protection, unless a shell should happen to enter a door or window. And this is exactly what happened. While Captain Glock and his men were busily working away on the regimental papers, a shell entered the window of the room next to the one they were occupying and burst with a tremendous crash.

Had it exploded in their room all present would have been annihilated. They were stunned by the concussion and blinded by the dust. Fortunately the heavy walls held. For a few minutes they did not know whether they were alive or dead. Concluding that they were still alive they all rushed for the windows and scrambled out through the smoke and dust. I was passing at the time and could not help laughing at their frantic efforts to escape. However, the affair did not strike them as humorous. They were glad to be alive.

On November 1, I was up front in the dugout of the first battalion, now under Captain Knack, on one of my frequent tours of inspection of the Sector. The telephone rang, and the orderly told me I was wanted on the line. I heard good Colonel Williams' voice over the wire, and he gave me the good news that Brigadier General Even M. Johnson had arrived to take command of the brigade, so Col. Williams was back in command of our regiment, and I would return to my own battalion. I told him how glad I was to have him back and how relieved I was to turn over the command of the regiment to him, as it was too much responsibility for me. He laughed in his pleasant way and said I had done well, and he had not been worried about the regiment.

And so I remained in my own dugout about a half mile nearer our front lines than the Colonel's dugout. I went back to see him and make a report of the condition of the regiment and the sector, and my orderly brought my two blankets and rain cape up to my own Post Command. Our bedding rolls had been left behind at Gondrecourt. The dugout I now occupied deserves some description. It was fairly large and had two rooms, each about ten or twelve feet square. It was built of large logs about a foot and a half in diameter. A layer of these stout logs composed the roof. On top of these were two layers of railroad rails laid at right angles to each other. On top of the rails was a layer of large stones, and to top the whole thing was a thick mass of earth in cone shape. I thought no shell could ever crush in so stout a protection and took much comfort out of it, until one day in the woods I saw another dugout of exactly the same sturdy construction, and it was all smashed in by a great shell. This sight spoiled some nights' sleep for me afterwards when the large shells were falling about us. The floor of this dugout was five or six feet below the level of the ground, so that the whole thing did not stand very high on the outside. It was completely lined throughout with wood and had a wooden floor. It was absolutely dry and comfortable, and the air was good. The room I used had two wooden beds with chicken wire springs and a good-sized round table and four or five chairs. There were also a desk and an iron stove, which kept us very comfortable. The other room had a cooking stove, two tables, and a large tier of double bunks. Each room had an entrance with steps and a gas curtain.

Lt. Fouraker and I slept in the two beds in my room, and Judge Kimbrough, Chaplain McNary, Sergeant Major MacCormack, and Cook Gray slept in the tier of bunks in the other room. My orderly, Corp. Euwart, and my mess orderly slept on the floor. We were all dry and warm and very lucky to find such excellent quarters. Below the floor and at one side about ten feet lower down was another chamber dug out of the earth, to which we could retire if the shelling got too heavy. This room was thus about fifteen feet below the surface of the ground. A door from my room and steps led down into it. I never went down into this place, as it seemed damp and dark, but here the battalion runners and wire men lived, glad to be out of the rain.

Just outside the dugout was a large, high tree, in the top of which was built a flimsy observation platform. On the trunk were nailed cleats, most of which were loose. Shells flew frequently near this tree, and occasionally it was hit. I climbed part way up one day and decided it was too dangerous a place for me. But Lieutenant Gould, I think it was Kingdon Gould the tennis player, who was observation officer of our Divisional Headquarters, spent a great deal of time in this tree attended by a sergeant, observing the enemy lines.[3] He sometimes stayed up there all day in the rain, with the shells flying around him. I thought him a very brave man and admired him considerably. He was very modest about it all, and when he occasionally stopped in my dugout to see me he was very particular as to military courtesy. I invited him to dinner one night, and we had soup, roast beef, some vegetables, and a pie made of dried peaches. Cook Gray did himself proud, and everything was very good, especially the peach pie. Lt. Gould said that I had better meals than the people at Divisional Headquarters, and I told

3. Kingdon Gould (1887–1945) came from a wealthy New York family that made its money through railroads, finance, and real estate. He was a staff officer in the 79th Division. It was Gould's brother, Jay Gould II, that was the champion tennis player.

him not to tell them so as they might take my cook away. A few days later, unfortunately, Cook Gray got caught out in the woods without his gas mask by some exploding gas shells. He was gassed and had to go to the hospital. We did not miss him for long, for a battle broke up and scattered the headquarters of my battalion within a day or two after he left us. Fate had death, wounds, and captivity amongst the enemy in store for most of us, but the tale of all that shall come in its proper place.

One dismal afternoon I was walking along the muddy path towards my own dugout when I met and passed a military policeman escorting four young red-cheeked German prisoners to our rear. All saluted smartly, and they were smiling and seemed happy to be prisoners and out of the fighting. So they always seemed to us. It may just have been their manner to conciliate their captors. But I think four years of war had sickened and wearied the Germans of the whole thing, which is not to be much wondered at. These four were nice-looking young fellows, and I really felt glad that they were on their way to the rear and safety. Their parents would see them again. I had gone on not fifty yards when I was shocked by a tremendous explosion behind me. I turned and saw a horrible sight, and one which filled me with pity. A shell had struck squarely upon the group I had just passed and had annihilated all five of the soldiers composing it. Blood and raw flesh and entrails covered the ground. All of the bodies were horribly torn and mutilated. All were instantly killed and without the slightest warning.

While in command of the regiment and living at the regimental P.C. my food had been prepared and served by the Colonel's cook and orderly. Meals were not banquets by any means on this front, but we got enough to satisfy our wants. When I returned to my own battalion I found that my own people had been living on crackers and chocolate, and what food they could occasionally get from a company kitchen. Two of my four rolling kitchens had been hit by shells and destroyed, since we arrived in this sector. Hence the four companies had to be fed from the two remaining kitchens, and there was not much if any food left for battalion headquarters. The trouble at my dugout was caused by the non-appearance of my own cook and orderly waiter, neither of whom we had seen since we left the town of Gondrecourt south of Verdun.

It provoked me considerably to have these men leave us in the lurch in this manner. They had always been faithful and had never shown any fear of the Front, and I could not understand their absence. I sent out a runner to hunt for them with orders for them to report to me at once. He found them with our wagon train back in the rear at Brabant. They reported to me in a shame-faced manner, and I gave them a sound rating for neglecting me and not hunting me up. Their excuses were very lame, being that they had no orders and had got lost. These men were not cowards and never showed any fear of the many exploding shells. They simply had a soft place with the wagon train with no work to do, and they were loafing while they could. I told them that if they ever pulled that stunt on me again I would put a rifle on their shoulders and put them out in an outpost close to the Germans, but my wrath worried them a great deal more than a prospect of getting up against the enemy at close quarters. With their return we again had good hot meals.

Lt. MacKenzie, the medical officer attached to my battalion, established his first aid station in a dugout about half way between my P.C. and that of Col. Williams. MacKenzie was a fearless, capable, and faithful man, who stuck to his post and his duty in spite of very heavy shelling and great danger. Many a time, when on the way between my place and the Colonel's, I was driven to take hasty refuge in his dugout by the close falling shells. I always found him cheerful and ready for any emergency. He was often amused at my precipitate arrival.

One rainy evening on returning to my dugout I found a strange officer there, a machine gun captain from the brigade machine gun battalion. He had been sent to me to strengthen my front with his guns. He said that he was also to live in my quarters. I was tired and cross and we were much overcrowded, so I did not receive him as cordially as I might have, but we crowded him in and he proved to be a fine fellow. He came from Pittsburgh, and I had done business with his father in what seems the long ago days. The field of fire for machine guns on our front was greatly limited by the thick forest and the many large trees. Nevertheless their presence was a great addition to the strength of my position, and they could be trained upon all the paths and roads, and by these avenues only could a body of the enemy attack us, and hence these approaches could be absolutely denied to the Germans.

So secure did we feel that we made no attempt to improve the defenses which we took over from the regiment we relieved. The defenses consisted of an outpost line in shell holes and small prepared positions held by one company. They were scattered along our front and while close to each other did not form a continuous line. At the top of a steep, heavily wooded slope some two or three hundred yards in rear were placed two more companies in large dugouts, in immediate rear of these was my dugout, and a quarter of a mile still farther behind my post was my fourth company in reserve. We had no trenches at the top of the slope where the two companies were placed and which was my main line of defense. However, there were but three ways of approach leading to my main line of defense, and the officers with the companies in the dugouts there understood the scheme of defense and could quickly cover these avenues of approach with sufficient forces of riflemen to support the machine guns constantly there and make these places secure against attack. Such being the situation, we did not trouble to dig trenches which we felt were not necessary. The French, on my left, were more cautious and had regular continuous trenches along the crest they held. We were never attacked and never needed such trenches. In fact, to the best of my knowledge we never dug any trenches in France. We always found them ready for us or did without them or went over the top and took them from the Germans. I believe the Germans dug nearly all of the dugouts and trenches we used on the Front. They certainly did a lot of hard work, of which we got at least a part of the benefit.

We had not been settled in our new position more than a few days when rumors of an attack by our regiment upon the positions of the enemy began to circulate amongst us. The greater part of such rumors were entirely false, but as I remember it, those concerning an approaching battle were generally correct. They proved to be in this case.

On our left was a regiment of French Colonial infantry, not native troops, but white men from the French Colonies.[4] Acting upon a direct hint from Colonel Williams regarding the probability of our attacking the enemy in the very near future and understanding also that this French regiment on our left would also participate in the action, I

4. The French 15th Colonial Division.

went over one afternoon to get acquainted with the French officers in command and work out a preliminary plan of cooperation with them. After a long walk through the dense woods we came to the dugout serving as P.C. for the French regiment. It was very deep and large. Smoke poured from the entrance, from a stove pipe which was not long enough to reach the surface of the ground. Apparently the cook was preparing dinner. Down through this thick smoke we went, half choked and stifled, and found ourselves in a clean and dry dugout. I had with me Lieutenant Henri Castel of the Alpine Chassuers, who had been loaned to our regiment by the French Army. He was a young and handsome man, who had been in the war four years, and he spoke English perfectly. He was a liaison officer to keep us in proper contact with French units near us, and his advice as an experienced veteran on war matters was of great help to all of us. He and Captain Feuardent, also of the French Army, were with our regiment constantly while we were on the Front.

Arriving at the foot of the long stair-way leading down into the dugout, we were met and pleasantly greeted by a French officer, who led us along what seemed a long corridor to a small room lighted by a candle. Against the walls were two wooden bunks, with blankets hanging in front of them. A rough wooden table and two chairs completed the furniture. On the wall hung faded gray overcoats and officers' equipment, belts, pistols, field glasses, canteens, all worn but clean and ready for service. The air was bad here, and the place seemed small and confined, really a mere hole deep underground.

Apparently the room was uninhabited, but our escorting officer spoke and the blankets in front of the bunks were thrust aside and two middle-aged officers emerged from behind them into the room. Lieutenant Castel made the introductions all around, and we were courteously welcomed. The commanding officer of the regiment, a major, or commandant as the French entitle him, apologized for being in bed at that hour of the day, but protested smilingly that he had not had much sleep at night of late, and the daytime was the safest time to sleep on the Front anyway, which of course was quite correct. These two officers were both ten years older than I, and yet one was a major and the other a captain. I studied them with great interest. They were large, sturdy men with good honest faces, which years of war had prematurely aged, and their thick black hair was well streaked with gray. War had become their business, and life on the front with its constant risks and responsibilities had become their normal existence. We Americans had yet to acquire their professional attitude toward the war.

Lieutenant Castel explained that we had come to plan cooperation with their regiment in the attack soon to be made upon Hill 378. They knew of it, and we discussed the details and arranged for mutual support and for communication between our regiments during the fight. However, our careful arrangements came to nothing when the attack came off.

On our way back to my dugout I asked Lieutenant Castel why the commander of the French regiment had only the rank of major. He replied that it was often the case in the French army during the war. Majors commanded regiments, captains commanded battalions, and lieutenants commanded companies, not temporarily but permanently. He said that they did not give them their promotion to the proper grade for their command because France was under such a terrible financial burden to keep up her great war army that she effected a great saving by having these officers of lower grade fill higher grades. They had the responsibility and the authority, but they did not have the rank and pay proper to their commands.

By the time we reached my dugout I had recovered from a drink of the most potent and fiery brandy that it has ever been my task to swallow. The good French major, just as we were about to take our leave of him, had taken down a canteen from the wall and poured out in tin cups large drinks for the four of us. We all stood and drank a health to our success in the coming attack. With an effort I got my drink down, but it burned me all the way down, filled my eyes with tears, and finally choked me. The French officers seemed to enjoy the drink, and could not help smiling at my discomfiture.

Some spools of barbed wire were sent up to my dugout one day, and I received orders to erect it on my front at certain specified points. We had not much heart for this sort of work, for our position was naturally strong, and it was well manned with infantry and machine guns. Also, as I have said the avenues of possible approach to it were very few, due to the think woods. But orders were orders and must be obeyed, at least there must be an appearance of obedience. Hence, I set out one afternoon with a party of men carrying the barbed wire and some tools. The woods were so thick that the wire could as well be put up in the day-time as at night. Well, we got lost and wandered vainly through the woods, unable to find the positions on our front that we were in search of. We finally came upon the French trenches on our left, to the astonishment of the defenders, approaching them from the direction of the enemy. Fortunately, it was daylight and they recognized us. The movement of our party through the woods brought down some German shells upon us just as we reached the French trenches, doubtless to the great disgust of the French, who hastily took to their trenches. We remained out in the forest. The shelling was not heavy. We finally found our way back to our main line of defense, tired out by our long walk. It may seem strange that we should get lost, but at the time we had not been in the sector long, and the thick woods and winding paths were very confusing.

Captain Knack of Company B had got hold of a German machine gun and a quantity of ammunition for it. Whether they captured it from the enemy or found it abandoned in the forest I do not remember; probably they found it. It was mounted on the top of a mound of earth, and they used it to fire at German aviators who ventured to fly low. They made a great deal of noise with it, but never brought down a plane. When we moved forward it was left there on the mound.

My dugout was only about half below the surface of the ground. On the side towards the Germans there was a good-sized window which had no protection whatever from the shells, which fell very thickly at times and very close. It was nice to have the light from the window, but I became convinced that it was too dangerous to enjoy this privilege, and so I had Lt. Fouraker take a few men and build a protection of heavy logs outside the window. We felt somewhat safer after taking this precaution.

One miserable wet night an officer, whom none of us recognized at first, entered our dugout. To our great surprise and pleasure it proved to be Lieutenant Maxwell McKean of my own battalion.[5] He had been taken seriously ill with pneumonia during the battle of the Argonne

5. Maxwell McKeen (not McKean) was from Easton, Pennsylvania, and educated at Lafayette College.

Forest, and to his great disgust had to be carried to the rear upon a stretcher. He was of a type of officer to whom this manner of leaving his men in battle was a great humiliation. But it could not be helped, he was too weak and too sick to go on farther and had already kept up bravely for several days in spite of his serious condition. Now here he was back with us again and most welcome, but he looked very thin and very pale.

I told him that I did not think that he was fit for front line service and that I thought he had come back too soon. I asked him why he had not been given a month on the Riviera in the south of France to regain his health.

"I was ordered there for a month, Major, but I heard the Division was going into action again, and I did not want to miss any more service on the Front, as I had already missed so much. I am all right and can do my duty. So I refused the sick leave and asked to be returned to the regiment."

Such was his reply. Had it not been for his splendid spirit and my great need of officers, I would have ordered him back to the hospital as unfit for duty. He went into the battle for Hill 378 a few days later, and while bravely leading his men in the attack upon the enemy, he was mortally wounded. He refused to allow any of his men to remain with him and assist him, but directed them to go on up the hill and leave him, and there all alone in the mud and rain he died. After the war I recommended Lt. McKean for the Distinguished Service Cross. The Board of Decorations at Washington refused to make a posthumous award to him, but did give his memory a War Department citation and awarded a Silver Star. This was recognition in a small way of his heroic service, but not a sufficient nor satisfying award.

As I have already stated, we had been assured on coming into this sector that we were only going to hold our lines against the Germans and were not going to make a drive. We had been informed that the Sector was an extremely active one and that holding our lines might be no easy task. Except for fairly heavy and almost continuous artillery fire, and an occasional night raid on our outpost line, we had not found the enemy aggressive. But rumors of an attack upon the Germans began to circulate, and they became so persistent that I came to accept them as facts, which they soon proved to be.

Captain William Sinkler Manning, regimental adjutant, one of the very best and brightest officers in the 79th Division, a son of Governor Manning of South Carolina and a very close friend and comrade to me, received his long-delayed promotion to major on October 29, 1918.[6] We had had a vacancy in this rank in our regiment for over three months due to Major Dodge's transfer out of the regiment, and Major Atwood's death on September 28 had made another vacancy, but it took a long time apparently for promotions to get through headquarters of the army and back to the regiments.

On the evening of October 29, Manning came into our dugout, and saluting me said, "Sir, Major Manning reports as adjutant of the regiment."

This was his way of telling me that he had received his promotion at last. I jumped to my feet and grasping his hand congratulated him heartily. I then asked him if he had any major's insignia, gold oak leaves, to wear on his shoulder straps. He replied that he had none and could get along without them. To do so would take away a great deal of the pleasure of his well-earned and well-merited promotion. I had an extra pair of gold oak leaves in my pocket, which I had taken off the shoulder straps of my overcoat. On the front the less insignia that an officer shows, the better are his chances of not being killed by a sniper. I produced the oak leaves and told Manning it would be a pleasure to me to give them to him and that I wanted to pin them on his shoulders. So I made him sit in my chair, and I took off his captain's silver bars and pinned on the oak leaves.

Dear old Manning, he had but seven days of life left in which to wear his gold leaves, for he was killed on November 5 while gallantly leading his men in an attack on Hill 378. A lieutenant who was close to him in this attack told me the story of his death in a hospital in Paris. He said that Manning's battalion was subjected to a very heavy artillery fire as it formed for the attack, and the survivors wavered in the advance. To encourage them, Major Manning, dressed in a black waterproof and carrying a cane, strode in front of the men and by his words

6. Parkin clearly mourned Manning dearly and valued his friendship. Manning's body was eventually returned to the United States and buried in Arlington National Cemetery. As the son of a governor, his funeral was well attended with many notable dignitaries including General John Pershing. See http://arlingtoncemetery.net/wsmanning.htm.

of encouragement and brave example drew the men after him up the slope. They reached the crest and drove off the enemy, and then at the moment of success a bullet struck him in his open mouth as he was giving orders and killed him instantly. His heroic conduct was rewarded posthumously by the award of the Distinguished Service Cross.

After I got home from the war I wrote Governor Manning a long letter telling him all I could remember of Sinkler's last days of life and of our close friendship. I gave him in detail the incident of my pinning my extra gold leaves on Sinkler's shoulders. I received a very fine letter in reply from the Governor and an invitation to be their honored guest, as he put it, when I came to South Carolina. The Governor said that Sinkler's gold oak leaves were among the very few effects that had been sent home to his wife.

And so ends the life story of one of life's really fine and heroic young men. And are we that survived to become old men in time and be set aside and disregarded, our war stories of such men as Sinkler Manning wearied of, are we the fortunate ones or are those who died in the full flush of youth and in the great moment of their lives, doing something wonderfully fine and heroic, something worthwhile, something utterly unselfish, are they the fortunate ones? Sometimes I wonder.

15
Wounded and Captured

Editors' Note: *Parkin's account of the final German counterattack on Hill 378 on November 4, 1918, opens in medias res, perhaps an hour or so after machine gun bullets struck the major in both legs. Why he chose to narrate this portion of his story in this manner is unknown. Perhaps he could not bring himself to relive a moment of traumatic injury. However, modesty seems a more likely explanation. Despite his wounds, Parkin remained in command and continued to fight, conduct that earned him the Distinguished Service Cross. He may have felt uncomfortable including his personal heroics in an account that so often celebrates the courage and dedication of lost comrades. For more on this section of the memoir, see the introduction to this edition. For an account of the events missing from the narrative, see Appendixes A and B.*

Sergeant-Major MacCormack suddenly cried, "Here they come, Major!"

"Who?" I asked in dread, well knowing his answer.

"The Germans," he replied.

My heart almost stopped. I was lying in a battered trench on the summit of Hill 378, the Borne de Cornouiller, a part of the Verdun front, rendered helpless by four machine gun bullets through my thighs.

Early that morning of November 4, 1918, we, Company C and Company B of the 316th Infantry, together with the staff of the First Battalion, had captured the hill from the enemy, had later driven off their counterattack by a bayonet charge, had then endured a heavy and concentrated artillery fire, and now, with three-fourths of our men dead or wounded, the Germans were again upon us.

The Sergeant-Major began to fire my pistol. He emptied it twice, then said, "They are very close. All our men in the trench in front of us are either killed, wounded, or captured. I can see none of our officers. What shall I do?"

I told him we could do no more and directed him to stop firing, as further resistance would simply be a useless waste of our lives. I ordered MacCormack to get out of the trench and surrender and I pulled myself from under cover. Almost at once, a great savage-looking German, with a large hand grenade in each hand, stood above me. Seeing my bloody clothes, he lowered his hands and said, "*Heraus.*"[1] I told him I could not get out of the trench. A passing German officer spoke to him gruffly, and ordered MacCormack and another soldier to help me out and directed us down the hill to the German rear. I saw that the attacking party was large and that they had captured about twenty of my men, the only unwounded survivors on that end of the position. Many dead and wounded Americans were lying around. Passing close to poor Captain Knack's body, I noticed that his face had already taken on the yellowish tinge the dead soon have. Even in death there was a smile on his face as there almost always had been in life. Never have I felt more humiliated and miserable than at this time. I was filled with bitterness at our failure.

Several hours earlier, on our way up the hill, I had met the Captain of the Machine Gun Company and had ordered him to have two guns follow me at once. These guns arrived, but went to the right of my position where Lieutenant Dreher made good use of them in stopping the enemy and holding his line. Had these guns been with me on the left, it is probable that we would have beaten off the attack.

In this attack, the cooperation between the German infantry and artillery was perfect. They continued to shell our position heavily while their infantry climbed the slope; and they timed it all so accurately that the dust thrown up by their last shells had hardly settled when they poured over our trenches. Our surviving men (and there were but few of them), demoralized and shaken by the awful shell fire, were suddenly overwhelmed by greatly superior forces and had no chance whatsoever to resist, being immediately surrounded and covered.[2]

When I passed through the Germans on my way to the rear, I looked

1. Trans. "Get out."
2. Parkin was with Company B of the 316th when it was counter-attacked by German infantry after taking significant casualties in their attack on Hill 378 on November 4, 1918. After Parkin was wounded, Captain Knack took command of 1st Battalion only to then be killed. Outnumbered and surrounded, three officers and twenty-one men surrendered.

at them with great interest. The faces of the enemy were set and white. They had the appearance of men doing a desperate deed, and their attempt to capture the hill soon proved to be exactly that. They were led by a short, stout Lieutenant and a number of non-commissioned officers, all older men than the rank and file. These leaders were armed with pistols and hand grenades. Their warlike helmets and bristling moustaches and drawn faces gave them a very fierce appearance. That long line of helmets coming into view was the most terrifying sight I have ever beheld, as I saw it as I sat there in the trench helpless and with nearly all my men lying around me dead or wounded.

We walked slowly down the slope. I leaned heavily on the shoulders of the two men who were helping me. As my wounded legs served me but poorly, frequent stops were necessary. We passed more German soldiers coming up and all were kind. One gave me a drink of cold coffee, another, a drink of brandy. At the foot of the long, steep hill, we met a group of Germans coming up. They approached and looked us over curiously, but not in an unfriendly manner. No doubt we were the first Americans they had seen, at least at close quarters. I no longer felt much interest in them, but I remember one of them very well for I thought for a moment that we would have trouble with him. He was an officer, a Captain, short, fairly stout, and dressed in a long, very clean, dark gray overcoat and a steel helmet. He wore glasses and a Van Dyke beard. I would guess his age as thirty-five. The only equipment on his person was a pistol and a pair of field glasses. His orderly carried the rest of it. He spoke to me in German and seemed sympathetic in a dignified way. I did not understand him. MacCormack asked him in English the way to the nearest First Aid Station. He did not answer and moved on. MacCormack took hold of his arm and asked the question again. At this, the officer bristled up and jerked his arm away.

The angry, haughty manner in which he looked at MacCormack made me alarmed for the Sergeant-Major's safety. It is not permitted for German soldiers to lay their hands upon the high-born officers. They are very apt to get shot if they do so, and this is what I feared would happen to MacCormack. We had a very tense moment in which I forgot my leg entirely. Then, the Captain relented and motioned the direction in a general way with his hand and went on up the hill, no doubt thinking us some of those undisciplined Americans. It was very apparent that he had sent his Lieutenant to capture the hill and was coming up after the job was finished.

A little further on, we met a soldier of the German hospital corps. He stopped and examined my bandages. On leaving us he remarked, "Don't worry, the War will soon be over; we are going to kick out the damned Kaiser."

I was much surprised to hear such a disrespectful remark and one so disloyal from a member of the supposedly strictly disciplined German Army, but I was to hear a great deal more of it.

The hospital corps man had pointed out to us a white house at the foot of the slope, and had said that I could receive medical attention there. It seemed a long way off and I did not think I could reach it. American shells began to burst very close to us. They were soon so numerous that our chances to get through seemed small indeed. But this new danger helped me to keep up and drove us on to a place where we had some protection from them. On the way we passed the machine gun battery that had caused us such losses. I felt very bitter towards the men in it who looked at us and grinned. We finally reached the white house amid a shower of shells and hurried, as much as we could, around the corner to get away from them. I dropped on some steps and nearly fainted. The shells kept hitting the house and the barn close by. I thought they would knock down the whole place, but the house was strong, being built of stone. Rows of dead Germans, all bandaged up, lay in an open shed before us.

The Red Cross man said we could not get attention here but must go on to another place on the hill, 1,000 yards away, and there an ambulance would pick me up. I was sure I could not make it and was for giving up, but MacCormack, bless that little man, would not leave me and urged and coaxed me into going on. We went on, but had to halt frequently. The heavy shell fire from the American guns never ceased.

A kindly German officer came up and expressed his sympathy and regretted that he could not help me. He spoke English perfectly and his small, neat moustache gave him a very English appearance. I remember he said, "I am sorry to see you so knocked out, Sir. You will soon reach the First Aid Station." He looked about for stretcher-bearers, but all he could see were already carrying wounded men to the rear. Promising to send us any help he could, he went on up the slope towards the top, now occupied by his own troops. I was impressed by the extreme neatness and cleanliness of his appearance. Also, by the fact that although the shells were falling all about us, and thickly at that, he did not wear a steel helmet, but just a cloth cap. No doubt he was a staff officer out for information. He could not have been more considerate of a brother-officer of his own regiment.

We struggled up the hill and larger American shells began to fall very close, tearing great holes in the earth all about us. I did not see how we could get through. Twice I collapsed in the midst of the shells and was obliged to lie on the ground for at least five minutes each time.[3] As I did not consider it fair to those two brave men to keep them exposed to such great danger when they could have gone on and soon been beyond the peril, I first asked them to leave me; then I ordered them to do so, but MacCormack only laughed and the other man stood fast.

Several times the earth and stones were thrown upon us by the explosions as we stood huddled together, wondering that we were still alive. Finally, after great efforts, we reached the top of the hill, beyond the shells and near the second house. Resting there behind a railroad bank, I remembered that I had the secret message code of the army and other important army orders in my pocket.[4] I gave them to MacCormack, who carefully buried them in a ditch. A German Red Cross man came up and told us we must go half a mile farther as the hospital had been moved. At this I finally gave up and refused to make any further effort as I was exhausted and my wounds were painful. MacCormack could not get me up, so he told the Red Cross man that I was an American major and asked for help. He proved a good fellow and, taking the American private, went off to hunt for a stretcher.

The sun had gone down and I began to feel cold, and my leg became very stiff. The German returned, but he was unable to find a litter for

3. Parkin indicates that he took four machine gun bullets to his thighs. It is striking that with such injuries he does not record significant bone and/or tissue damage. It is possible he was shot with bullets through both legs, giving the impression he took four rounds judged by entry and exit wounds. This would still make his being able to be moved very difficult even if he was aided by soldiers.

4. As a field officer, it is surprising that he was not immediately searched after his capture by a German officer.

me. He had a shelter-tent half and a long pole. I got on the canvas and they tied the corners in knots over me. Through these they put the pole and so lifted me up. I held on to the pole so that if the knots became untied I should not be dropped. I had to be carried a long way, at least a mile, and as I was no light weight, it was a hard task, and the men had to rest frequently. Finally, after passing close in rear of a German Battery which was hammering at our lines, we arrived at a sort of dugout and there a very friendly young German doctor examined my wounds and put on fresh bandages. He cut off the tourniquets, which was a great relief to me, as they were cutting my leg cruelly. He also gave me an injection of Anti-Tetanus Serum, which I was glad to get, having heard much about this dreaded disease.

I asked the surgeon if I could take Sergeant-Major MacCormack along with me as my orderly. He replied that officer-prisoners were not allowed orderlies and that we could stay together only until we reached the ambulance. Then the Sergeant-Major would have to go to a military prison while I would be sent to a hospital. This was a keen disappointment to us.

When the surgeon had finished with me, he tied a wound-tag to the front of my coat. It was a long piece of heavy paper, about four and one-half inches long and two inches wide. He did not seem to be able to understand my name, so Sergeant-Major MacCormack wrote my name and rank on the tag. The Doctor filled out all the medical details in German. There were strips on the sides of the tag, one of which the Doctor tore off. According to the printed directions, if a wounded man was in too serious condition to be transported, both strips were left on; if he could be moved, one strip only was left on; and if he was able to walk, both red strips were torn off. Thus at a glance, the Medical Corps would tell the condition of a man as he passed through their hands. I thought it a very good system. I presume we have something like it in our own service.

After having tagged me, they brought a stretcher. One of the bearers was a pleasant-faced man who looked like Conrad Peterline, a gardener we used to have at home. I told him so and it seemed to please him. Although I already had a blanket over me, he got his overcoat and tucked it around me. The doctor and I exchanged salutes, and I extended my hand, which he shook very cordially. Before we started, the stretcher-bearer who looked like our old gardener, Conrad, for that is the name I now gave him, said something to the Doctor and received from him a very sharp reprimand. I saw that after the doctor turned away, Conrad repeated part of what the officer had said to another soldier, in imitation of the doctor, and in a very bitter and insubordinate manner. This was more evidence that discipline in the strict German Army was not all that it should be.

The two American soldiers who had helped me to the rear and two Germans lifted the stretcher and carried me up a long, steep hill. It was a hard task and they stopped several times to rest. They carried me shoulder high and I felt uneasy for fear I might roll off the stretcher. Every time we stopped to rest the bearers, Conrad came to me to see that I was alright, and he kept tucking in my blankets and fussing over me, smiling all the while, treating me as if my comfort was his sole thought.

After a considerable journey we stopped and I saw quite a group of Germans around a rolling kitchen. Conrad gave me hot coffee and a plate of good thick soup, both of which I enjoyed. It was at this place that I was obliged to part from Sergeant-Major MacCormack and his comrade. To separate from them there, in the dusk, and to be left alone amongst the enemy, helpless, was the hardest thing I had to do on this day of great trials. I know the Sergeant-Major felt it as keenly as I did. We said "Good-bye," gripped hands hard, wished each other good luck, and they were marched off on their way to prison. Then I was helped to the driver's seat of a rolling kitchen, the auto ambulance having left some time before. A group of soldiers gathered round and offered brandy, cigars and cigarettes and were very sympathetic and friendly. Some had the Iron Cross and were pleased when I noticed their decorations.

One of these soldiers asked me if I had any children, and I said, "Yes, one son."

He brought up a small man and said, "Herr Major, this little fellow has eleven, and the big Herr Major has but one."

At this, the whole crowd roared with laughter, and I joined in heartily, even if the joke was on me. The little soldier was somewhat embarrassed, but also rather proud of himself.

A battery near us fired constantly and the noise bothered me greatly. They wrapped a blanket around me and put another over my shoulders.

After I had been placed on the rolling kitchen by Conrad and his helper and just as we were about to move off, being anxious to show my appreciation of his attitude to me, I called out in the dusk, for I could not see him, "*Hier*, 'Conrad.'" Understanding that I meant him, the faithful fellow came running and stood beside the vehicle at salute. I had been touched by his friendliness to me and leaning over, I gave him a hearty handshake and said, in German, "Thanks, 'Conrad.' You are a good man." He seemed greatly pleased, gripped my hand hard and thanked me, saluted again, and went away in the dusk.

The other German soldier who had helped to carry me, not to be outdone by the good Conrad, came up to me, saluted, and held out his hand. He had shown me no attention at all, and I was somewhat amused. However, I shook his hand and thanked him, but not in the manner I had his attentive comrade. This gruff fellow had complained that my two American soldiers had asked for too many rests when they were carrying me up the long, steep hill. He said the Americans were not strong soldiers and he had stamped around the stretcher to show me he was not tired.

The rolling kitchen now started off down the road; as it was rough in many places, every bump caused me pain. I clenched my teeth and said nothing, but the driver noticed my facial contortions and was as careful as possible, and at every jolt he cried out in sympathy for me. We talked as well as we could and he said I would not be a prisoner long as they would soon have a Republic and throw out the Kaiser.[5] Some American shells burst near us and I thought I would never get away from them. We passed large wagons loaded with shells going up to the German guns.

After a long ride, we reached the partially ruined town of Brandeville. At the hospital, formerly the town hall, we stopped, and, after some loud calling on the part of the driver, attendants came out. A big man took me on his back, and carried me into the building. He took me into a ward where many wounded were in bed—German, French, and one lone American private. They cut off my right boot and cut away the remnant of the right leg of my breeches and my underwear. My

5. The Kaiser abdicated his throne five days later on November 9, 1918, and went into exile in the Netherlands.

bandages were examined and they gave me coffee and bread and butter, and put blankets over me, but made no attempt to undress me. I took off only my overcoat and helmet.

It was evidently only an overnight hospital. The American private was shot in the arm and side and suffered quite a little, but was not in serious condition. Next to him a poor French soldier who had been badly gassed, suffered horribly. To get his breath he assumed all sorts of positions, even getting out of bed and kneeling on the floor. The Germans seemed to have great sympathy for the poor fellow and helped him all they could, but were able to do very little.

Suddenly we heard airplanes overhead and the Germans seemed uneasy. Heavy explosions followed, and I realized the town was being bombed by airmen— "Those damned Americans," the Germans said. The explosions came nearer and the attendants all fled to the cellar, leaving us wounded to our fate. One tremendous explosion, seemingly just outside in the street, shook the hospital and I thought the end had come. Was I never to get away from American shells and bombs? Soon the noise ceased, the attendants came back, and I went off to sleep and slept well.

In the morning I was awakened about seven o'clock by voices. They had just brought in a very handsome, young German officer and the surgeons made a great fuss over him. He lay on a stretcher and smoked a cigarette and did not seem to suffer much. He was wounded in the leg. We had coffee and some German war-bread with honey on it. I did not find it bad eating, but I was to get very tired of it later. After breakfast they began to take out of the ward those of the wounded who would walk. I was told to get up as I was to go to the train. One of them, not a big man at all, got me on his back, a most uncomfortable thing for my wound, and carried me out of the hospital. They seemed to have no litters there.

I was put into an ambulance already nearly filled with wounded who could sit up. My helmet and right boot, which had been taken off, and gas mask were handed in to me. I noticed that the rubber bands which hold the mask in place had been cut off. The attendant said I would need it no more anyway, so I threw it under the seat. As we rode out through the town, I saw that many of the houses were in ruins, showing that the Germans had been heavily shelled here by the Allies. Several newly killed horses showed that the bombing of the night before had caught at least these poor brutes. We rode out of the town and along a fine well-kept road. One young German private with his arm in a sling made some jesting remarks about Americans in a laughing way, but as they did not amuse his comrades he fell silent.

It was during this ride in the German ambulance that my comrades of the American Artillery made their last attempt to kill me. Of course, this statement must be taken as a jest, because they did not know anything about me and had to continue shelling the enemy in spite of the danger to American prisoners. At any rate, they turned some extra long range guns on the road we were travelling over and burst a dozen large shells very close to it. I can testify, from personal experience, that the American Artillery was very good and most persistent and that they fired no "duds," as all of their shells exploded. Much as I admired their efficiency, I was, nevertheless, very glad when I finally got beyond the range of their guns.

After a half-hour ride, we reached a narrow-gauge railway and boarded a third class Carmen with plain hard seats. I was the only officer there and there was no special place for officers, but the soldiers helped me on and made me as comfortable as possible and gave me cigarettes. I sat down next to the car window and looked out.

Along the road, parallel to the railway, came a strange group of soldiers. In front, striding along at good speed, was Sergeant-Major Mac-Cormack and the private soldier from whom I had parted the night before. Immediately behind them trotted two German cavalrymen armed with long lances. I waved to them, leaning far out of the window, but they did not see me, to my great disappointment, and passed on down the road out of sight.

It was in this train that I got acquainted with a good-hearted German who helped me greatly. I had noticed one of the soldiers, seated across the car, studying me. Finally, he came across, saluted, and asked in English, "Are you an English officer, Sir?"

"No, I am an American officer," I replied.

"*Mein Gott*! You are an American!" he exclaimed, and asked me from what city I came. I told him Pittsburgh. He said that he knew Pittsburgh, Chicago, Cincinnati, St. Louis, Buffalo, and most of the cities in America. He spoke good English and had traveled for years with

Barnum's Circus in America and had also performed in vaudeville. His was a strong man's act, swinging things and people with his teeth. He showed me many pictures of himself and three young German ladies in tights who were in his troupe. He had traveled all over the world and was a very interesting, if a rather ordinary fellow. He had the Iron Cross and another medal. He said he had been in many battles but had also spent a great part of his time with a group of entertainers traveling around the German rest camps. When the war broke out, he was in Italy with a circus. Being a reservist, he had hurried home to his regiment. He thought now that he had been a damned fool for doing so and would never do it again. He was now sick with appendicitis and was going to the rear. The war would be over in a few days anyway and the Kaiser would be kicked out. When I look back over it now, I am surprised that so many German soldiers knew that the Armistice was coming and guessed its date so closely. It was evident that trouble had been brewing in the German Army for some time, but no one in our army seemed to have any idea of it.

We traveled for several hours, during which I observed conditions in the German rear with much interest. The rolling stock was much run down and in bad repair. At one station I saw some Germans building brick buildings. This did not look much as if they thought of retreating. There were many soldiers and officers at all stations along the line, and I was the object of much respectful curiosity at every stop.

We reached the main line and were transferred to a standard size train and put into another third-class coach, furnished with wooden bunks across the car. When we entered the car, it was already almost full, but my new friends helped me on, hustled a young German, wounded in the hand, out of a bunk, put me in, and covered me with a blanket. I thanked the young soldier whose bunk I had, and he smiled and nodded and sat on the floor near me, without any apparent resentment.

I was now very comfortable for the first time since leaving my bed in the hospital, but the car was hot, the stove in full blast, and all the windows shut. They always are in Europe. After a while, a Red Cross man came and put a new bandage on my leg. It was of fine, soft paper with only a little linen on the outside, which showed to what state

Germany was reduced. I was amused at my circus friend. As soon as he saw the Red Cross man, he began to give every evidence of suffering and groaned and writhed and held his side, actually getting pale in the face. The Red Cross man was quite concerned over him; but as soon as he had left, my friend laughed and lit up his pipe again, and the whole car roared. He certainly was a clever actor.

Towards evening we reached the large town of Montmedy and I was taken off the train and laid on the ground between the tracks, my friend hurrying off to get me a stretcher. My position on the crushed rock between the railroad tracks was neither comfortable nor very safe, especially for a wounded man unable to walk. My train remained on the track very close to me and other trains passed slowly on the track on the other side. There is not much room between railroad tracks and I was really partially under those trains. As long as I lay still and the cars kept on the rails, there was no real danger, but it was not a pleasant resting place, to say the least. Some of these passing trains were full of German soldiers. Hundreds of them looked down on me from the car windows.

One of the trains stopped beside me, and from it a young, very neatly-dressed Sergeant-Major dropped to my side. He wore dark gray wrapped leggings, the first I had ever seen on a German, as they usually wear boots. He asked me very solicitously how I came to be there and I explained.

"You must be taken away at once. I will get a stretcher for you," he replied, in the good English I was to hear so much of among the Germans. He hurried away between the trains. Before he returned, his own train began to move and I feared the good fellow would be left. I soon saw him hanging low on one of the slowly moving cars, and as he passed he shouted, "It's alright, Sir. They are coming for you at once."

I nodded and smiled my thanks and waved my hand as he went by. Could an American comrade have done more for me?

Two Medical Corps men came presently and carried me away to the station platform where the stretcher was hung in a frame on wheels, bearing on springs, a most comfortable way to move the wounded. One of my bearers knew that I was an American. He had been a butcher in Buffalo for five years and, of course, spoke English well. Then the War came, it caught him visiting his relatives in Germany; and, as he had not taken out his papers in the United States, he was obliged to go into the Army.

He said to me, "Now that all this hatred of the Hun has started, I will not be able to go back to Buffalo after the war."

I told him that if he put on his American clothes and talked English as he did to me, I thought he would not have any trouble getting back. But he did not agree with me and said he would go to South America.

I saw the circus man on the platform. He began to tell me that all the time I was lying between the tracks he had been doing his best to get a stretcher for me. An officer came up and ordered him away and that was the last I saw of my friend.

I was wheeled through a large crowd of wounded Germans, most of whom could walk and who regarded me with curiosity. A wounded American officer was apparently a rare thing in those parts. We stopped in the rear of the station and some good-looking German nurses came and leaned over me and smiled. They were fine, big, buxom girls in clean white clothes. A doctor came next. He opened my overcoat, looked at my leg and said something about the officers' car. Then the nurses wrapped me in warm blankets and I was wheeled off up the platform and stopped at a first-class car into which wounded and sick German and Austrian officers were being helped. I was not pleased at being put into the officers' car as I did not like to leave my soldier friends who had been so good to me, and I thought the officers would be unfriendly. They put me in and placed me on an upper berth. Half of the car was filled with berths supported by iron pipe frames, the other half, with big, easy, cushioned benches. I lay there quietly for an hour, determined to let the officers make any advances that were made. They kept looking at me and talking together but no one came near.

After a while I got out a cigarette and started to search for my matches. An old German Colonel, lying in the bunk across the aisle, grunted at me and handed me his cigarette for a light. I thanked him, took it, and handed it back to him. He took hold of it in such a way that he burned his fingers and he dropped it with a curse. This was rather a poor beginning for me, but I offered him a fresh cigarette, which he took, demanding a light from me with a laugh. He knew some English and I a little German, so we began to talk. Soon he got up, got out some cooked meat and bread and butter, made a most tempting sandwich and, to my surprise, came over and handed it to me. It was very good. Next he gave me a drink of brandy, so strong that it nearly choked me, and then another sandwich; a fine and friendly old gentleman, gruff, but generous.

The Colonel was either smoking, eating, or drinking all the time and he always tried to include me in these pleasant habits, but I could not keep pace with him. The other officers followed his lead and became friendly and attentive. I can truthfully say that during all the time I was a prisoner, I was never the object of an unfriendly look, nor an ungracious word from my captors. My person was respected and I was not even searched for papers. I was rather surprised not to be gone over for purposes of information. Furthermore, I was never questioned by their intelligence officers, as I had fully expected to be. Nothing was ever taken from me except the rubber bands on my gas mask. One of the officers traveling in the car with me, a young Staff Captain, a small, slight man, who was ill, once asked me for one of the gold leaves on my shoulder straps, saying he would like very much to have it as a souvenir. I did not refuse him, but explained that they were the only insignia of rank on my uniform and that if I lost them I might not be treated as an officer in the hospital. He readily agreed that I was right and did not take the oak leaf, as he could so easily have done.

The officers and I managed to talk together and exchange views and ideas on the War. Most of them were young and good-looking men. These officers overfed me and kept me smoking all of the time. One Austrian chaplain who spoke a little English was particularly kind and attentive. His home was in Budapest, so he really was a Hungarian. He was a man of great refinement and intelligence, but was not above performing some personal service for me, scarcely to be expected of a man of his class, during the absence of the orderly. Austria had made peace and he had not been well, so he was going back to beautiful Budapest for a rest.

There was, of course, no talking among the officers of throwing out the Kaiser. They agreed that the coming of America into the War was too much for them, and they did not think they could hold out much longer. They said they could not fight the whole world indefinitely and did not consider defeat, under such circumstances, as disgraceful in the least. When I told them that we had registered 23,000,000 men of military age, they were astonished and said it was of no use for them to go on with the War. They thought we had done wonderfully well to raise so large an army in so short a time. I was asked what I thought of their artillery and I said it was too damn good to suit me, at which they laughed heartily.

Soon we began to think of rest, as it was getting late. With many a "goodnight," they went to their bunks. The stove was right at the head of my bed and it was kept fired up all of the time. Some of the officers had made toast on it and this, with the tobacco smoke, had made the air very bad, but that did not bother the Germans. No one made any attempt at ventilation. After all were settled I quietly lowered the window a little. It was not very cold outside and the fresh air felt good and I was almost sick for want of it. To my great surprise a hand was raised from the bunk below and a voice said, "It is too hot." Here was a German who liked fresh air and he opened the window still more. The old Colonel opposite, feeling the draft, looked over in surprise, pulled his blanket over his head and went off to sleep. No doubt he thought it an imposition, but was too decent to interfere. I slept well all night and my leg did not bother me.

All next day we traveled at rather slow speed, making long stops at the stations. We passed many freight and some troop trains going up to the front. Most of this day we traveled through the Duchy of Luxemburg, a beautiful, smiling country, entirely untouched by war and apparently very prosperous. When we stopped at the stations, my traveling companions would often invite the officers there to come in and see the American Major. Most of these officers spoke English. They expressed their sympathy and their hopes that I would be well treated and not be kept a prisoner long. Several of them gave me packages of cigarettes. I also received some cigars which I did not enjoy much, their idea of good tobacco being quite different from ours.[6]

The city of Luxemburg with its many imposing buildings looked very fine from my car window. Many healthy, nice-looking school children, with little knapsacks on their backs, I saw along the way. Some of the

6. These could have been European style dry-cured cigars, which differ in composition from those made in the Americas. They are typically spicy and can be bitterer in taste.

boys were about the size of my son and the sight of them made me long for that little rascal. At all the bridges and stations there were German sentries, but we saw no German camps nor any bodies of German troops. They were apparently holding the railroads only. Cattle, the finest cattle I have ever seen, were plentiful and the country looked fertile and rich. We stopped twice during the day for meals, and hot coffee and bread and good thick soup were brought to us. At one stop I bought thirty cigarettes for ten francs, a simply awful robbery. Towards evening my wounds asserted themselves and I was glad, when about eleven o'clock, the train stopped at its destination.

The town was Trier, in Germany, or Treves, as it is better known. I had no idea what was to become of me. The officers thought I would be sent on to the officers' prison camp at Magdeburg, a day's ride farther on.[7] The question of what would be done with me worried me considerably. I did not want to be sent into the interior of Germany, where I might starve to death or have great difficulty in getting out of the country even if the War was over. I wanted to be put in a hospital near the German frontier. I called on my good friend, the Hungarian Chaplain, for help and asked him if he would not see the medical authorities at our destination, which I understood was near the border line, and request that I be placed in a hospital at that place. He readily agreed to try and thought he could arrange it.

When we reached Trier, he had me left in the car, while he went to the station to endeavor to carry out my wishes. All of the officers who had traveled with me crowded around and shook hands heartily, wishing me good luck and a safe return home. The lights were all put out and I waited alone there in the dark until I thought I had been forgotten. Then, just as I was beginning to get nervous about it, I heard the Chaplain's voice calling to me and he came down along the train, carrying a lantern, accompanied by two stretcher bearers. To my great relief he told me he had arranged everything and I was to remain in Trier. I thanked him most fervently for his efforts on my behalf. I was carried off the train into a large shed, well-heated and lighted. Here I was laid on the floor on my stretcher amongst a great many German wounded,

7. There were four officer's prison camps (or Offizierlagers) in Magdeburg. Parkin's fear of being shipped into central Germany was unfounded as American officers were typically held in camps near the western or southern borders.

all as helpless as I. It was here that I parted with great regret from my good friend the Hungarian Chaplain.

Standing in line, waiting for food, not far from where I lay on the floor, were two American private soldiers. I was considerably amused by their "very much at home" attitude. They were greatly surprised to see me. They came over and expressed their regret at my condition. I assured them I was alright and well cared for. They told me they had been slightly wounded and captured seven days ago. Both were of German parentage and spoke German well. Traveling with the German wounded, without guards, they had received good treatment and were not much concerned about the future. In fact, they were very light-hearted. I had quite a talk with them and it cheered me up not a little. Their particular group of wounded Germans began to move out of the shed and, with many expressions of good wishes and after gripping my extended hand, they hurried off to join their friends.

16

In Germany

I lay there in the station for two hours. Then, the attendants placed my stretcher on a light carriage and started off with me through the dark streets of the town. We finally stopped in front of a large gate, which, after some parley and argument, was opened and we entered a large courtyard. I was carried into a hallway and in spite of the lateness of the hour, it being near two o'clock in the morning, found there a long line of German wounded waiting to be admitted to the hospital. My rank gave me preference, my wound-tag showing the hospital attendants my standing in the American Army. Here the police asked me a few questions of a personal nature and filled in some cards. I was not searched nor asked questions on military matters.

After the examination, the hospital people took charge of me and I was carried up a stairs so steep that I had to hold on to the stretcher with both hands to keep from sliding off backwards. I was taken to a bathroom where two elderly nurses took off my muddy and bloody clothes, placed me in a tub and thoroughly scrubbed me. A much needed attention. Not since early childhood had I received such intimate services from the gentler sex. The word "embarrassed" does not fully describe my emotions. I was inclined to hasten and skimp the job, but the nurses kept stolidly at the work which was well and thoroughly done.

They then put clean night clothes on me and fresh bandages on my wounds. They carried me into another room, put me into bed, turned out the lights, and left me. The clean clothes and the soft, fresh bed felt wonderfully good to me; I lay in comfort and ease at last now, two and a half days after I had been wounded. My mind also was at ease as I no longer felt any concern as to how the Germans would treat me.

When the door shut, a voice said out of the darkness, "Are you an American?"

I answered, "Yes. Are you?"

"Yes, and there are four of us here, all lieutenants."

He asked my rank and regiment and I told him. He said he would introduce me to the others in the morning. We talked a little, then went off to sleep. We were awakened at seven in the morning by the orderly, a French soldier-prisoner. We called him Pronto; a faithful, willing fellow, but rather stupid. He was a Paris shoemaker before the War.

My questioner of the night before introduced me to my roommates; Lieutenant Walker of North Carolina, Lieutenant Kendall of Santa Ana, California; Lieutenant Nelson of Chicago; and lastly, a young French Lieutenant named Deldon. The master of ceremonies was Lieutenant Apgar of Plainfield, New Jersey. All were infantry officers except Kendall, who was an aviator. All had bad leg or arm wounds. I was very glad to be among Americans again and was to become good friends with all of them, especially Lieutenant Walker, who was a very fine chap and appealed to me greatly. He and I became close comrades and stuck together afterwards in our journey out of Germany.

Attached to the head of each bed was a small blackboard on which, painted in white, was a complete description of the patient. The full name, nationality and regiment were written at the top, and below were given the medical details and the history of the case. My name seemed to give them a great deal of trouble and the board had to be corrected twice before it was right. The methodical German would have it exact.

Each day began by Pronto bringing us basins of water and towels. There was no soap, but we kept clean. Breakfast at eight consisted of coffee made of roasted acorns. Not at all bad to the taste, although somewhat bitter, served without cream or sugar—and German warbread with a sort of honey. The war-bread was dark brown in color and rather damp and gummy. It never seemed well baked. The others were sick of it. We made a joke of it, but we had to eat it nevertheless.

The Germans were generous with the stuff and what we did not eat we piled up on the windowsill, saving it for a Senegalese soldier who visited Lieutenant Deldon.[1] He was a great, jet-black native of fero-

---

1. Like the Vietnamese truck drivers featured earlier in the narrative, this soldier from Senegal is a reminder of military manpower drawn from French colonies. As signaled by Parkin's use of the adjective "ferocious," Senegalese troops were seen as notorious

cious appearance and had been wounded in the elbow; his forearm and hand had, in consequence, shriveled into a long claw, perfectly useless to him. He seemed glad to get these stone-like pieces of bread. He had wonderful, large, white teeth and he would need them. Once Lieutenant Deldon asked me if our colored men were as "beautiful" as this black man. Deldon's use of our language gave us many hearty laughs, but he never became offended. Fortunately the French officer-prisoners in Trier received, through the French Red Cross, more white war-biscuits than they could eat and they sent some to us. The biscuits are very thick and extremely hard. To prepare them for eating, you first bore a hole about the middle, pour water into it and then place them on a heated stove for a short time. They expand and soften and nearly double in size and the result is excellent white bread, which, with our jam, later received from the Red Cross, made very good eating.

About ten o'clock, the German doctor, an efficient and courteous gentleman, accompanied by a nurse, made his rounds to examine us. We all liked him very much and he was most friendly and considerate. I forget his name. He impressed me, as did all the German military doctors by whom I was treated, as knowing his business thoroughly. He knew a little English and spoke French well, and was apparently very well-liked and respected by all the patients and the military staff. He was a tall, slender, dark-haired man, an unusual type among the Germans. He designated those who were to be taken to the operating room each morning and the attendant made a list of their names. Later on these patients were taken out on wheeled stretchers by two big French orderlies who were very gentle and did their utmost to make moving us as painless as possible, which was not easy to do.

After the doctor left, we put in the morning reading novels and talking. Where these few books came from no one knew. Some of them probably came from the French prisoner-officers, a fine lot of gentlemen, of whom there were three hundred and fifty in the prison camp at Trier, many having been there three years.

Captain Julien and Lieutenant Delegie were both in our hospital, having been sick, and Lieutenant Fourer-Selter visited us from the

---

for their prowess at hand-to-hand combat. European and American observers tended to exaggerate such qualities when portraying Senegalese soldiers in the press and in propaganda.

camp.[2] These three were my best friends among the French. We became acquainted with Lieutenant Fourer-Selter in a rather unusual way. One day I received a letter from him addressed to the American Major. It was written in perfect English and stated that the writer had had American friends in the hospital, but that they had been taken away; he would like to visit the American officers in the hospital and get acquainted, but was not permitted to do so unless we sent a written request to the C.O. of the prison camp. I sent the written request, also a note to the Lieutenant telling him I would be very glad to see him.

The next afternoon, a very handsome French officer entered the room and asked for Major Parkin. It was Lieutenant Fourer-Selter and we soon got well acquainted. He proved to be a very likeable gentleman and came every day. We enjoyed his visits. He brought us English novels, biscuits and sugar, all much needed and most welcome. Fourer-Selter had taught French in an English school before the War and his English was excellent. He had been a prisoner for two years.

Captain Julien was the most popular man in the hospital. With everybody he was the soul of good cheer and optimism, always cheerful, always laughing. We were glad to see him come in and everybody cheered up as soon as he entered. He suffered greatly from rheumatism in his legs, but never complained.

To return to the routine of our hospital life. At twelve we had dinner, boiled potatoes and cabbage, sometimes there was just a little meat in the dish. Occasionally, we got a fried egg and a little cheese. There was always a small glass of wine and some war-bread. My comrades spoke hopefully of the boxes of food the Red Cross at Berne, Switzerland, had promised to send. After dinner more reading and talking and almost always a lot of French officer visitors, very polite and friendly, but nearly all unable to speak English. Most of them really came to see Lieutenant Deldon. At four we had coffee and war-bread. Then, at six we had supper, more potatoes and cabbage, war-bread and wine. In the evening we read or talked. At nine-thirty the lights went out, but generally we talked until around eleven before going to sleep.[3]

2. In the manuscript, the Captain's name sometimes appears as "Julien," sometimes as "Jubien." For the sake of consistency, we have used "Julien," which may or may not be correct.

3. Parkin's account of being treated well and having ample food, despite shortages

Twice a week our room was thoroughly scrubbed. We had a fire in the stove which kept the room comfortable except on a few days when the coal gave out. On the fifth day a great event occurred. The Red Cross food boxes arrived from Berne. We each took two and several more apiece were locked in a storeroom of which I had the key. These boxes of heavy paste-board were of good size. The Germans were entirely honest with us in handling this food. The boxes were never opened. When we gave some of it to them to be cooked, they always very carefully accounted to us for what they had used and what they returned. There were quite a number of American enlisted men in the ward on the floor above me. Of course, we shared this food with them. Some of them visited us, and I made one of them custodian and distributor of supplies. In the packages we found tobacco in bags, cigarette papers, rice, beans, coffee, sugar, prunes, corned-beef, potted tongue, condensed milk, bacon, jam, and hard bread. To my friends these boxes were a wonderful treat. I had not been there long enough to really appreciate what they meant. We did not eat much German food after that.

Of candy and chocolate we had none. I had been used to a lot of chocolate in our army. I missed it terribly and my sweet tooth positively made me suffer. Lieutenant Deldon in the bed next to me, who spent the time industriously studying English and appealing to me continually for assistance, had heard me lamenting our entire lack of chocolate. One night after the light went out he surreptitiously slipped me a half bar of this much desired delicacy. I was much surprised and pleased. It was too small to think of dividing with the others, and anyway I was too greedy to do so, so I selfishly enjoyed it all by myself and was a more attentive instructor to him the next day.

On the third day after my arrival, another wounded American officer was brought into our ward. He was Second Lieutenant A. H. Treadwell of the American Air Service—a slight young man of about twenty-two or three. I could tell from the condition of his uniform, which was almost black with dried blood, that he was badly wounded and had lost

in Germany, is consistent with other POW accounts of the war that indicate German fair treatment of American, British, and French officers. This was not the case for enlisted men. See Heather Jones, *Violence Against Prisoners of War in the First World War* (Cambridge, 2011) for an alternative account of POW treatment.

most of his blood. He seemed very low at first and could hardly talk, but he was greatly pleased to be with us and insisted upon telling who he was and something of his adventures. Truly, he had had a terrible experience. Shot down by a German aviator, he fell in a forest. Landing upon a tree, in which his machine lodged, he fell on down to the ground. No one came to help him and he crawled half a mile to the edge of the forest and was found there the next day by the Germans, who treated him kindly and sent him on to our hospital. He was shot in the back by a machine gun bullet which had passed through his right lung and come out between his ribs.

For several days he seemed to improve, but I noticed he ate extremely little and, knowing he needed strength, deemed that a bad sign. The poor boy died the evening of November 16, passing away very quietly and without pain or suffering, being under the influence of drugs. He made no struggle at all but just seemed quietly to stop breathing. His face was as white as the sheet. The doctor and the nurse stood by him until the last, and we all lay or sat silently on our beds until it was over.

They dressed him in clean night clothes and carried him out at once. Then the bedclothes and mattresses were taken away, and the springs and bed frame carefully washed with hot water and soap. It was very quiet in the ward that evening, voices being low or silent.

The Germans were very short of X-Ray and all other medical equipment and took but few pictures. Lieutenant Deldon had been shot in the thigh and he had an X-Ray picture of his leg, which he showed to us. It very clearly showed the thigh bone with a bullet half embedded in it. The German surgeons wanted to operate on him and take out the bullet, but he preferred to wait until he returned to France and have the doctors do it. His wound was clean and healing nicely, so there was no danger in waiting. My wounds healed so quickly that both the doctor and myself were surprised. He said one morning, with his pleasant smile, "Herr Major, you are as healthy as a young bull."

On November 9, the Revolution had broken out in Trier and the nurses and the attendants were greatly alarmed over it. They told us that the officers had been locked up in their quarters, their shoulder straps cut off, their pay reduced to that of a private, they were saluted no more, and a soldiers' committee would handle the local government.

The military surgeon of our hospital, who did not sympathize with the Revolution, was removed and a younger surgeon who favored it, or said he did, was put in his place. He was a first-class doctor who soon showed that he knew his work thoroughly, and he became boss of that hospital very quickly, and there never was any doubt of that. When he spoke, they all jumped. He was tall, well-built, soldierly looking, and wore a small yellow Van Dyke. He was very fine and sympathetic with us and very strict with the hospital people.

One evening a group of three dirty soldiers from the soldiers' committee came to him in the operating room, where a few of us were waiting for bandages. Their demands angered him greatly and he gave them the best dressing down I ever heard soldiers receive. The rough German language is fine and effective for this purpose. He lost his temper and for several minutes he lashed and berated them, while they stood scared and completely humiliated before him. When they had gone, he turned and said to me in English, "I'll show these dirty beasts who is running this hospital!" No more committees appeared while he was there.

I still had my steel helmet but I knew I could not take it away with me as I had to walk with two canes and would have a box of food to carry. I had had a Russian tailor, a prisoner, make me an overseas cap from the material in an old pair of breeches. It was a curious looking affair, but I intended to wear it as my helmet felt much too heavy on my head. So I decided to give the helmet to my good friend the doctor, as a souvenir of the Americans. One morning during his visit I had it on my bed and he examined it with great interest. I handed it to him and said, "A souvenir of the War for the Herr Doctor."

He was much pleased, thanked me effusively and shook hands with me. American helmets were extremely rare in Germany. He carried it all over the hospital to show what the Herr American Major had given him. Then he came back with it and asked me to write my name, rank and regiment on the chin strap, which I did and said to him laughingly, "Doctor, you must not tell your folks that you killed in battle the American Major who wore this helmet."

"Oh, that is a fine idea! I must make up a story of my terrible struggle to kill you in a dugout," he replied, and we all laughed.

The Revolution continued in power and the soldiers released their officers in a few days but gave them no authority nor rendered them any military courtesy. I used to sit at the window and watch the soldiers loafing about the square, sloppy and indifferent, with overcoats unbuttoned, hands in pockets. They passed their officers without saluting or paying them any attention whatever. Such a curious, unusual sight in a Prussian drill-yard!

The first night of the Revolution, the soldiers had celebrated by firing off rockets and Very Pistol lights all over the square. We expected a fire to start. Some few hand-grenades were also exploded, but no damage seemed to result. Frequently during the day the mutineers would gather in several large groups in the square around some soldier on a box, who would read a paper or an announcement to them. Occasionally there would be cheers. All military drill had stopped.

We got the news of the Armistice on the eleventh of November; in fact, we knew several days before that it was coming. All the Germans knew it beforehand. They were extremely glad the long, hard war was over and took no shame upon themselves for their defeat, claiming that they could not fight the whole world and that their fool government had brought more enemies on their shoulders than they could carry. Nearly all were very bitter against the Kaiser and his advisers.

All but one of the old nurses agreed that a Republic would be much better for the people. This dear old lady, our head nurse, when asked if she was not happy over the Republic, shook her head, tears filled her eyes, and she left the room. Another nurse told me that the Kaiserin was head of her Order and had been very good and generous to her. Hence, we could not blame her for her loyalty.

The French officers read us the terms of the Armistice in the French and German papers, and we were told that the Fourth and Fifth German Armies would retire beyond the Rhine, through Trier. One evening we heard the music of a fine military band, and a German regiment marched into the square, broke ranks, and entered the barracks. I noticed that the band was the largest unit, losses having reduced the infantry companies from two hundred and fifty men to forty or fifty, and this was true of all the other regiments which followed. In this War, the bandsmen were not allowed to go into battle. Trained musicians were hard to replace. After the troops, came the wagon trains. For hours they poured into the immense square until it was packed almost full. Such a variety of vehicles I had never seen before. It looked like the migration of a nation. Army wagons, rolling kitchens, park traps, buggies, Russian droskies, carts, farm wagons, two-wheeled traps, almost every type of vehicle ever built. All were filled with bags of grain, bales of hay, calves, goats, sheep, boxes of food, and clothing; many of them had horses and cows tied on behind. All was orderly and disciplined. Mounted officers were in charge. I was told the soldiers had restored to the officers just sufficient authority to direct their retreat.

From three o'clock until nearly dark, the square filled in this way, every day for five days, which gave an idea of the immense transport the Germans had with them. Each morning, before daylight, we could hear them moving out; and by the time we were up, they were all gone. Each evening at five, their rolling kitchens were steaming and all this great crowd of men lined up and were served a hot meal of soup or stew and bread and coffee. It was very evident that although the Germans were defeated and had suffered heavy losses, they still had great numbers of men and much artillery, many guns being mixed in with all these convoys.

On the eleventh of November, the Germans told us that we were free, but they said they could not at that time offer us transportation. We heard later that the American Army was to occupy Trier and decided to remain there and wait for it, even if transportation should be offered us. We waited in vain until the twenty-first, when we were told that those of us who could walk, could leave at once by train. Lieutenant Walker and I decided to go and went down to the hospital office where we found a crowd of cripples of all sorts and nationalities, all very anxious to leave. Here we were informed that we would have to walk a mile across town to the railway station. As that was an impossible feat for our wounded legs, we were very regretfully obliged to give up hope of a start then. The next day, the Germans said there would be a train at two-thirty in the afternoon and that automobiles would take us to the station.

Though it was still rumored that the American Army would be in Trier soon, we had learned to distrust such rumors, and Walker and I decided to take the chance of getting back to France. We were obliged to leave behind our friends, Lieutenants Kendall, Apgar, and Nelson, and the French officer, Lieutenant Deldon, who on account of their wounds were unable to undertake the journey. We promised that we would report their whereabouts and condition to the proper authorities as soon as we possibly could. I took the names and addresses of their parents and offered to send cable messages to them at the first opportunity. I had a feeling of guilt at leaving these poor wounded young officers there, so far from their friends and their own country, but it could not be helped and they urged us to go. I am sure there was not a dry eye in the room at the moment of parting. It was one of those rare moments in life that one never forgets.

Walker and I had prepared a box of Red Cross food to take along. We went down to the office again to depart, but no automobiles came. Finally, it was arranged for us to go to the station in a street car. We walked two blocks from the hospital to the car track and waited there, quite a group of us, for the car. While standing here, a German Artillery Regiment, headed by the usual good band, passed before us. The horses were thin and bony and the equipment looked worn and shabby, but the guns were clean and serviceable, as I well knew from experience. As it was light artillery, most of the men marched; and as they marched, they sang in perfect time to the step. I have never heard better singing. The guns, caissons, and horses were all decorated with wreaths and flowers, streamers and banners. Seemingly, the return of a conquering army, but the decorations were, as explained to us, in celebration of the new German Republic.

At length our car came and we cripples hobbled and limped into it, and we slowly crossed the city to the station. Trier is a clean, modern city with fine buildings and streets. It looked like an American town. The store windows seemed well stocked. We passed the famous old Roman gate, built in the third century and wonderfully well preserved. The streets were filled with prosperous looking citizens, who dressed more like Americans than any people I had seen in Europe. At the station we had to wait on the platform for nearly two hours. I sat on a box, watching the great throngs swarming everywhere and mobbing the trains. There was absolutely no order and no one with any authority. I do not believe that anyone bothered to buy tickets. I know we never had any and were never asked for any. I saw Italians, Russians, Frenchmen, Americans, Britishers, and men of other nations. None of the Germans paid any attention whatsoever to these people. I felt discouraged at the thought of having to mix in with that mob, handicapped as I was by my crutches.

My thoughts were interrupted by a British soldier, very much the worse for liquor, who came up to me. He placed his hand on my shoulder and, leaning over, told me what he thought of the Germans. They would not have appreciated his opinion of them, to put it mildly. His voice was not low and I feared he would get us into trouble. Also, I did not like his familiarity and very soon put him in his proper place, standing at attention before me. He belonged to an Australian tunneling company and had been a prisoner a long time. They had put him out on a farm where, he said, he had been overworked and underfed and obliged to sleep in the stable. But he was drunk and disgusting and I told him to go away; nevertheless, he and another drunken Britisher attached themselves to my party which consisted of Lieutenant Walker and some twenty-one wounded American soldiers.

Finally our train arrived and I was disheartened to see every window full of soldiers, packed in and hanging out. There was no one to get us places; the few women officials, dressed in men's clothes and looking rather ridiculous, made no attempt to help us. I walked along the train, looking in vain for a place to get in, when Captain Julien, who, with Lieutenant Delegie, had joined us at the station, came running after me and said he had found room for Walker and me. We three struggled into a compartment already packed, but two German soldiers got out and made places for us. There were German civilians, German soldiers, Americans, and Frenchmen in that compartment. Thirteen in all where five should have been. Lieutenant Delegie managed to get into another compartment and we saw him from time to time during the day.

The train seemed to be a local one as it stopped at every station, of which there were many and very close together. Every time the train stopped there was a mad rush for it. German soldiers, without arms or equipment, except their knapsacks and belts, seemed to swarm at all the stations. All rushed for the first-class compartments and struggled and jammed to get in. If one or two people left at a station, several new passengers crowded in. Walker and I were nervous because of our wounded legs which were stumbled over many times that day. But when we would call attention by pointing to them and say, *"Verwundete,"* the passengers would apologize very sympathetically and be very careful. We fixed our crutches to protect our legs as much as possible. We had five or six German soldiers with us, two of them the worse for drink, but they were not offensive, just jolly and talkative. They were from Alsace and Lorraine and said that now they were Frenchmen.

One of these wine drinkers sat next to me and looked at my shoulder straps. Captain Julien told him I was an American Major. That apparently was too much rank for him, for he shrugged his shoulders, gave a loud grunt, got up, and moved over to sit beside Captain Julien. They had a loud laughing talk together as brother Frenchmen, with much slapping of each other on the back. Soon this man's wine got the best of him and he went to sleep with his head in his hands, much to the amusement of his friends. Another of the wine-drinkers, a red-headed, simple-looking fellow, the wag of the party, sat down beside me, and, becoming drowsy from many libations, his head sank on my shoulder and he slept heavily. Under such circumstances I permitted the familiarity and was going to let him sleep on, but some of the other German soldiers saw him and were apparently horrified at the idea of a private soldier sleeping with his head on a major's shoulder. I motioned them to let him alone, but they woke him at once and moved him away to a seat on the floor. Poor fellow, he was all in. Another of the soldiers was a tall, very handsome young man from Lorraine. He looked and acted like a man of refinement and I enjoyed talking to him in my rather poor German. He had been in the War over four years, being in at the very first, and had been shot through the bowels. He was heartily sick and tired of it all and glad he was not to be a German. Altogether, the German soldiers that we met this day were a decent, well-behaved lot of men, quiet and polite and making no attempt to annoy other people.

I asked one of them how he got leave at this time.

"Leave?" he answered. "My battalion are mostly from Alsace and Lorraine. We simply threw down our arms and disbanded when we heard that our country was to go back into France. And, I saw Prussian soldiers who did the same thing."

At one station two large German girls pushed in and stood between the seats, all of which were overcrowded, Lieutenant Walker and I being the only ones who had seats to ourselves. A German soldier pulled one of the girls down on his lap and Captain Julien took the other, and there was much talking and fun over it. Captain Julien was very small and slight and the big girl fairly covered him out of sight in his corner with her generous proportions. At first, he was very pleasant and smiling, but later I saw his face contorted with pain. Her weight was hurting his knees in which he had rheumatism, but he was too gallant to mention it. He looked over at me with grimaces, but I laughed at him and said, "It might be worse," and he smiled back.

At all of the stations there were great mobs of disbanded soldiers, many with their shoulder straps cut off, waiting for or struggling on to trains. Many officers also I saw, but they were ignored and jostled by the crowd. They neither attempted to exert nor appeared to have any authority whatsoever.

All the afternoon we traveled through this disordered and struggling mass of humanity. Each stop was almost a riot and the crowd, while offering us no violence nor disrespect, was rough and jostling with their own people. At the stations our two British prisoners leaned out of the car window and cursed the Germans and called them foul names. I was in continual fear they would start a fight and was much relieved when we left them behind at a station where they got off to hunt for more liquor.

All the roads along the railway were filled with columns of troops marching in good order in their retreat to the Rhine. They carried many flags and were decorated with flowers, wreaths and greens. A strange sight to see retreating, defeated soldiers wearing the symbols of victory. At some stations we saw many companies of troops in line and noticed that nearly all of these men were middle-aged and looked like fathers of families. There were many evidences that the great German Army was fast going to pieces, and I felt sure it would fight the Allies no more as its power and strength were gone. Germany would be obliged to sign the peace, not being able to resist any longer.

The German towns we passed through were clean and prosperous looking and the country was fertile and well cared for. There were no signs of war and devastation such as I had been used to in poor France. We passed through the largest vineyards I have ever seen, all in the most wonderful condition of cultivation, with long lines of women working up the hillsides.[4] Millions and millions of poles, all in exact and ordered rows, extending as far as one could see and running up the sides and clear over the tops of large hills, the slopes of which were carefully terraced.

But when I saw all this and remembered stricken France with her ruined, smashed towns, her forests cut down and destroyed by war and shell fire, and her fields idle and weed-grown, I felt that these people should suffer for it, and pay—and pay well—for all they, by the ambition of their conscienceless government, had inflicted upon their neighbors, Belgium and France. And I felt sure, as I rode along through their prosperous and fine country, that payment in full would be exacted of them.

The half-dozen soldiers in our compartment, in spite of their gray German uniforms, looked to me more like Frenchmen than Germans. All had dark hair and dark eyes and were of the French type physically. They were tall and slender, not stout and bulky and of light hair, eyes, and complexion. I could easily believe them when they said they were from Lorraine and not from Germany. They seemed proud and glad to claim that now they were Frenchmen.

Towards evening we entered the outskirts of a large town and one of the soldiers said it was Saarbrücken. We passed great blast furnaces, as large and modern as any I have seen in Pittsburgh.[5] They seemed to be running full, and I saw large numbers of big, husky German girls, good-looking for the most part, busily engaged in unloading coal and ore from cars and firing the boilers. They all had light yellow hair and light blue eyes, true German types. They seemed a cheerful, smiling lot and were dressed in blue linen jackets, knee breeches of same material, black stockings and heavy shoes.

We passed through enormous freight yards filled with thousands of cars. When we were still in the outskirts of the city, we ran beside a broad street and, while doing so, we were suddenly surprised to hear the clear silvery notes of French bugles—an unmistakable sound. The French officers and nearly all of the others sprang to their feet with a

4. He is moving through the Rhineland, known for its German white wines.

5. Saarbrücken is an industrial city in the Saar region, known for its coalmining. Its close proximity to France meant that it was within bombing range of the allies and was indeed bombed several times by allied aircraft.

shout of joy and crowded to the windows. My poor leg suffered in the confusion but I protected it as well as I could with my crutch.

Our train had overtaken a column of French Infantry, their helmets shining, their bayonets gleaming, and their blue-gray uniforms clean and neat. They were entering the town in full military pomp with their colors flying, the band and bugles in full blast, the rank and step in perfect military form. The column was preceded by French cavalry which left a guard at all street crossings to hold the line of march. There seemed to be a great many of them. What a splendid sight it was to us Americans to see those friendly troops so far from our own army, and how it did cheer us up. What a wonderful sight it must have been to our French officer friends, who had been prisoners for three years. They leaned far out of the car windows and shouted, "Vive la France!" at the top of their voices, and waved their caps frantically. Some of the officers in the columns returned their greetings by lifting their swords, but the men in the ranks marched steadily on and we could see the proud smiles on their faces. Here was France, for four years the underdog, now entering in triumph one of the largest towns in Lorraine, wrested away from them in 1871. Surely it was a proud and happy day for Frenchmen.

The German soldiers from Lorraine cheered as heartily as the French officers and shouted, "Vive la France!" It did look odd to see men in German uniforms cheering French troops, but they now considered themselves French and were glad of it. During the excitement there was much embracing and pounding on backs, and as Captain Julien turned to me with flashing eyes, I feared he meant to embrace me "a la Francaise."

In a few minutes the train drew away from the troops and we resumed our seats amid excited talk and comments. Then, it was that a German lady, well-dressed and of refined appearance, spoke to the soldiers in German uniforms and rebuked them sharply for cheering French troops. They listened to her respectfully enough, but when she had finished—and she was much worked up over the incident— several of them answered her in no mild manner. Captain Julien, who translated the conversation to me afterwards, said she had told them she was bitterly ashamed of their actions as German soldiers in German uniforms; that Germany was in terrible trouble and that all good

Germans should stand together. They had replied that they were no longer German soldiers and never had been willingly, but had been forced into the army, and were now again Frenchmen of Alsace and Lorraine, a French province. Somehow I could not but admire her stand nor could I help being in sympathy with the soldiers

The train presently reached the main station of Saarbrücken. That being our original destination, all of the Americans and French, with much difficulty, many groans and great clattering of canes and crutches, got down from the cars and stood in groups on the platform, uncertain where to go or what to do next. Then the gentlemen who had conducted the tour all day, Captain Julien and Lieutenant Delegie, again came to our rescue, asking me to keep the men together while they went off to seek information and the station master. We Americans would certainly have been helpless and utterly lost had it not been for these two very kind and helpful French officers, for no German official paid any attention to us nor offered us any help or advice.

In a short time they returned and reported that the French were not yet in control of the town. The German station master had said that we might sleep on the floor of the station, but he could not offer us blankets nor any food, nor could he permit us to leave the station. As to trains south to France, there might be one tomorrow or next day, he could not be sure. He told Captain Julien that the French troops were in control of Saargemünd, a town two hours farther along the line and to which our train was bound. After a short discussion we decided it would be best to go on to that town. So I ordered the party of cripples back into the car and we had just succeeded in getting back into our seats when the train started.

After two weary hours, mostly in the dark, for we had no lights, we reached Saargemünd. On the platform, as we entered the station, I saw groups of French soldiers; all was quiet and orderly, so different from all the other stations we had passed that day. I was filled with a sense of relief and satisfaction to reach the French and return to order and discipline.

17

Back in France

We left the train, and our French officers were greeted by the officers in charge of the guards. Captain Julien again requested me to keep the men together on the platform while he made arrangements for us. We sat there in the semi-darkness, for there were but few lights, and waited for what seemed a long time. Even in my heavy overcoat lined with wool, I was cold, and I wondered how the wounded American soldiers, most of whom had no overcoats, were standing it. Few people were allowed in the station; all trains were met by the guards, and passengers were hurried from the platforms.

After a long wait, a French officer came down the station calling my name. I answered, and, finding me, he told me that Captain Julien had gone to see the General in Command and had sent him to take Lieutenant Walker and me to the guard-room to wait for orders. I asked him about our men and told him they were all wounded and suffering from cold and hunger, and he assured me they would very shortly be cared for. As we walked away, my Sergeant came running after me, calling to me, distressed that I was leaving them there alone. I walked back to the men, who gathered around me in an anxious group, and told them not to worry, but to be patient a little longer and I would see to it that they were provided for. I said also that I would not leave the station until they had been taken away.

The French officer led us to a large room in the station, used as a guard-room. It was warm there and Lieutenant Walker and I were given chairs. I did wish that all of our party might be brought in at once, but the room was already overcrowded. I sat and watched the guard with much interest. They were mostly men of middle age and were eating their dinner at a large table in the middle of the room. The meal consisted of a most savory stew—to which all helped themselves from a large pot at the end of the table—white bread in huge loaves and rich, red wine poured from large canteens. I had not eaten for a long time and the sight of this food made me very hungry. Although we sat near the table, we were not invited to eat; but the French officer explained that we would eat later at the General's table. Now and then a group would come in off guard and help themselves with zest from the steaming pot and the wine canteens, both of which the cooks kept well replenished.

All around the walls stood lines of rifles, clean and bright, with the evil-looking French bayonets attached, and here and there an officer's sword leaned amongst them.[1] Under a light, a small group of officers talked in low tones. The men of this guard evidently belonged to some distinguished regiment, since they wore the shoulder cord of "four-rageres of the Croix de Guerre," which is of red and green and only awarded to a regiment cited for gallantry a number of times.[2]

We had to wait for an hour in the guard-room, and as I sat there watching these brave men with great interest, I wondered how they felt to be here as conquerors in a city out of which their fathers had been driven by the Germans in 1870.[3] It must have been a great joy to them to come back now; but if it was, they did not show it. Instead, they seemed very grave and serious at having taken over a city so long dominated by the Germans.

My thoughts were interrupted by a commotion at the door and the Sergeant that I had left with the men came in and reported that one of the wounded men had fainted from the cold. I explained to an officer who had the poor fellow brought in at once and placed in a chair near the fire. They gave him some wine and he soon felt better. The French guard were very kind and sympathetic.

About this time an officer entered and inquired for me. He was an

1. Nicknamed "Rosalie," the French Lebel rifle bayonet had a 20.5" cruciform blade designed to puncture, rather than cut, an adversary so that infection would be more likely to occur. It was indeed an "evil-looking" weapon and expressive of French hatred for Germany following France's humiliating defeat in 1871.

2. In some cases, American regiments who served with the French (before the establishment of the independent American Army) received the fourrageres. These included all of the infantry regiments in the AEF's 1st Division.

3. Saargemünd (now Sarreguemines) is a border town in Lorraine that passed from French to German control in the Treaty of Frankfurt (1871) at the conclusion of the Franco-Prussian War.

aid of the General in Command, who had sent him in a car to take Lieutenant Walker and me to Headquarters. Walker and I followed this man out into the chilly darkness through the ill-lighted station to where the car stood, with its military chauffeur behind the wheel. I explained to the officer that I had twenty-one wounded men in the station and could not leave until they were provided for.

"Our medical staff will take care of them, and ambulances now are on the way to take them to the hospital," he answered.

I replied that if it were not too much trouble to him, I would prefer to wait until I saw them started. He agreed, not over willingly, and we sat in the car a few minutes until the ambulances arrived and I saw them begin to load the men. I spoke to the Sergeant and then we started through the quaint, medieval-looking streets of this old city. I was happy to be in French hands and to know that the men were cared for. Just before we started, a number of girls surrounded the car and, on learning that we were Americans, they got excited and made quite a fuss over us. Walker and I laughed with them and tried to talk to them but did not have much success. They seemed greatly pleased at the presence of the French in their city. After a short, chilly ride, we drove into the entrance-way of a large building with sentries and French flags in evidence and were assisted out of the car and up some steps. We went along a hall and our officer-guide rapped on a door. We entered, finding ourselves in a large, well-lighted, warm room in the center of which was a long, wide table covered with green baize and littered with papers. At this table sat a dozen French officers, very clean and spruce in their handsome uniforms with their many decorations.

At our entrance, a big, fine-looking officer whose breasts was simply covered with medals and orders got to his feet and faced us, and we were introduced to the General in command of the division occupying the town, whom he proved to be. We saluted him as well as our crutches permitted and he shook hands and welcomed us very cordially. We talked with him for a few minutes; but as his English was not much better than our French, we soon ran out of conversation. He said he was very glad to see us and to be able to help us, that we would be given a good billet, and must be his guests while in town and eat at his table.

Here we again found our good friends and protectors, Captain

Julien and Lieutenant Delegie, who came over to us and told us that everything was arranged and that we would have the best the town afforded. We thanked them again for all they had so kindly done for us. They introduced us to a number of French officers and there was much saluting, bowing, and hand-shaking. The officers seemed much interested in us and were all very courteous and attentive. We were given chairs along the wall and told that we would soon go down to dinner, which was good news for we were, by this time, very hungry.

We sat there for a half-hour and watched this general staff function. Officers and messengers arrived constantly with verbal and written reports and each knew exactly which officer to report to. Several officers were constantly talking on the telephone. The General, who was studying a map with two of his officers, was but seldom interrupted. System and efficiency, the result of four years' experience in the war were very apparent in that room, and the machine ran smoothly. The room seemed so well adapted and furnished for a staff headquarters that I suspected it must have been used as such by the Germans.

One of the most interesting occurrences was the entrance and reception of a deputation of very German-looking citizens, three or four in number, to whom the General talked. They stood very respectfully before him, silk hats in hand, their black overcoats looking very plain compared to all the handsome uniforms of the staff. Their heads were close-cropped and most of them wore very thick-lensed spectacles. Their present situation must have been a decided humiliation to them. The General did not rise and was coldly courteous. After a few minutes' talk, they went out after much bowing on their part. I did not understand what the talk was about. After the door closed a smile went around the table and some remarks were made in French which broadened the smile.

Shortly after this, the General rose and put on his overcoat, and all the other officers, except two or three, followed his example. Captain Julien said dinner was now ready. We left the building and walked several blocks along the main street. Walker and I could not keep up and some of the officers stayed back with us. We went to the main hotel of the town, a good-sized place, with a high iron fence and garden in front, and, after washing our faces and hands, which attention was much needed by Walker and myself, we entered a large dining-room across the end of the hotel, brightly lighted and with a long, well-set table in the center. Such luxury had been unknown to Walker and me for many months. The staff carried their own cooks, waiters, table napery, and silver, we were told.

I was placed at the General's right and he very pleasantly insisted that the orderly serve me first with each of the four or five courses of the most excellent dinner and the good wines. I saw my reflection in a large mirror opposite and was truly ashamed of my appearance. Two days' beard, a soiled and stained uniform and my long hair certainly ruined my chances to look even respectable. The only redeeming feature was the gold oak leaves on my shoulders and I was glad to note that they still had some gleam left in them.

Many wound stripes were on the arms of the men around that table. The General had two, and I asked him if many French generals had been wounded.

He replied, "Oh, yes. Many were wounded and quite a few killed. But I got these two, early in the War when I was a Colonel."

The Chief of Staff created quite a laugh by courteously leaning over and filling my glass, by mistake, from a water bottle instead of a wine bottle. They thought this a great joke and had the water taken away. Our glasses were kept constantly full, even the General helping me occasionally.

After a most excellent dinner, we lighted our cigarettes and the talk became free and noisy. The General joined in all the jokes and laughed heartily. His officers seemed very fond of him, and they all appeared to be the best of friends. Of course, Walker and I missed much of the fun, though many of the jokes were explained to us. One of the officers played the piano well and several sang. There was much laughter over a small toothpick machine which the Chief of Staff took apart and could not get together again. He insisted it was an infernal machine placed there by the Germans.

I much regretted my very small knowledge of French as I should have enjoyed talking more with the General. A rather reserved but affable man who did not stand too much on his dignity. Strange to say, he had a German name, but I have forgotten it. He came from Lorraine and was now back home again at the head of victorious troops. He wore the blue-gray French uniform, with Sam Brown belt, riding breeches with double black stripes, and black boots.

At ten o'clock Walker and I made our adieus and were escorted to our billet, another hotel a few doors away. A small, but very good and clean hotel it proved to be, and the proprietor and his wife became our friends and made much of us. This hotel proprietor, Albert Uhl by name, spoke perfect English, as did his wife. He explained that he had been fifteen years in the United States postal service and had traveled all over the States. He had spent some years in Cuba and knew General Wood and General Bliss when both were majors.[4] To prove this, he showed me letters to himself from both of these officers. Before going up to our rooms we sat in the restaurant for a half hour and talked with Herr Uhl and his wife. At first they were very cautious and said they had very little food to offer, but after talking with us they became more frank and Frau Uhl said that she would give us a regular American breakfast in the morning. They served us that evening with some excellent cheese and bread and beer.

We found our rooms clean and comfortable, but the beds, typically German, were too soft and deep for me. I could not get my wounded leg into a comfortable position and for that reason did not sleep well. In the morning we made our scanty toilet, having nothing but combs and toothbrushes with us, and went down to our American breakfast, and it was indeed a good one—eggs and bacon, toast and coffee, cooked by the good Frau Uhl herself. We enjoyed it immensely and she was much pleased with our appreciation.

After breakfast we had a long talk with Herr Uhl. He was a real Prussian in all his sympathies and the defeat of Germany had left him stunned. He simply could not grasp it. Uhl was born on the Rhine and had come to Saargemünd after Germany took Lorraine in 1871. He had prospered and now owned his hotel, "The Hofbrau House," and also other property; and he told me he had made lots of money during the War. His hotel was the meeting place of the German officers of the

4. General Leonard Wood commanded Theodore Roosevelt's brigade in the Spanish-American War. Later he was Chief of Staff of the Army before then being passed over for command of the AEF in 1917. Tasker Bliss was Chief of Staff of the Army in 1917–1918. He was part of the American delegation to the Paris Peace Conference in 1919.

garrison and of those passing through the town. They had money and would pay well for food and drink. Uhl said the street in front used to be full of the chargers of the officers who filled his rooms and spent their money freely, and he regretted those days, not only for the money, but also because he missed the German officers.

Uhl could not persuade himself that the mighty German Army was defeated and driven clear back to the Rhine. He could not understand why America, which used to be so friendly, had come into the War against Germany.

I said, "You Germans kicked us into the War. Do you think we could stand for your sinking our ships and murdering our citizens? We had to come in or stand ashamed before the World."

But he could not see it that way. Like all Germans, he blamed England for the War. Uhl was a kindly, good-hearted man, not in the least the type of boorish German about whom we read. He felt the defeat of Germany so keenly that one could almost feel sorry for him.

Walker and I hobbled out to a barber shop, typical of those in a small American town and for four cents got a much needed shave. After lunch we returned to our hotel and sat in the main barroom, drinking beer and watching the new French citizens, all very German in appearance and actions. About four o'clock the room filled with stout burgers who sat in groups about the tables, smoking and drinking large steins and glasses of beer. Their capacity was a source of wonder and amusement to me. One fellow, in particular, drank ten or twelve large steins without any particular effort and then went home to dinner. They looked us over and did not seem to make us out. One of the bar-maids, a pretty, pleasant girl, spoke French to some of the French soldiers who came in and I could see the Germans nudging each other and making low-voiced comments. Herr Uhl told me he would remain in town and build a large moving picture palace which he had planned before the War. However, he had been so identified with the German officers that he may be expelled.

That night after we had dined with the French Staff, there was a fine torch-light parade; the French bands, very fine, and the local fire brigade band furnished the music. The town firemen in brass helmets and blue uniforms, all carrying large, bright axes, marched, as did thousands of French soldiers and citizens of the town. Many carried torches. The people and soldiers marched arm-in-arm, eight abreast, in a long, noisy, cheering, dancing column. The whole town was out. The enthusiasm was great and all seemed happy over the arrival of the French. It kept up until a late hour and we saw it pass several times.

After the parade there was a reception at a hotel near ours, but we avoided the crush and went home to bed. Long after we were in bed, we could hear the music of the orchestra, and I have seldom heard better or sweeter music. My bed was too uncomfortable for my leg, so I took some covers and moved over to the rather hard sofa and slept there.

In the morning our two French officer friends called on us, and I told Captain Julien that I must get some money as I was nearly penniless. He said he had a little and would share it with me. I replied that I expected to get it from the French Staff and would repay it as soon as I reached Paris. I told him I wanted eight hundred francs for myself and Walker needed five hundred. Julien was much in doubt about our getting it, but I felt sure the French Staff would lend it to American wounded officers and asked him please to see about it. He returned after a while and reported that the Chief of Staff had said that, if the American officers were out of money, we would please move to the hospital, where we would be cared for and returned to France along with the American private soldiers there. I determined to refuse to be treated like a private soldier and felt that the money should be lent to us, so asked Julien to carry my message to the General himself. Much doubting, Julien went away to see the General. He returned in an hour, greatly pleased with himself, and counted out the money to us in clean French notes. We signed receipts to "the Corporation of the 18th French Infantry Division." (The first thing we did on reaching Paris was to draw our back pay and send checks, on the Bank of France, to repay this loan, together with letters expressing our grateful thanks.)

Being now in funds again, I invited Captain Julien and Lieutenant Delegie to dinner that night. I told Herr Uhl to give us the very best dinner he could and also some champagne. We did have a fine meal. First came a good, thick soup in a large tureen, then steak and vegetables, bread and butter, champagne, and, finally, chocolate ice-cream and coffee. The very best meal any of us had had for months, and we ate and drank until we could do so no more.

The town of Saargemünd was profusely decorated with the French colors, blue, white, and red. Flags and banners and streamers hung everywhere and across the streets in lines. All, of course, in honor of the victorious French Army. One day Herr Uhl, in talking with us and his good wife, expressed his surprise that the town had been so suddenly decorated with the French colors, when so recently all the decorations had been German. She replied that the only difference between the two national colors was in one stripe. Germany had black with red and white, and France had blue with red and white. The women of the town had simply cut off the black stripe and replaced it with a blue one, as she herself had done.[5] Our host was visibly depressed over this necessary change in the colors.

The second morning of our stay in Saargemünd was the occasion of an impressive parade. Headed by one of their own fine bands and the local fireman's band, the French marched through the town to the cemetery to decorate the graves of their comrades who had fallen in 1871 and had been buried there, remaining in the hands of the Germans ever since. I thought it a very fine and thoughtful thing for them to do. First came the bands in full military blare, no funeral march; then a French General, with a large staff of officers; then, finally, several companies, under arms, followed by a number of soldiers bearing large and beautiful wreaths and decorations of flowers. These were followed by more French soldiers without arms and by quite a lot of citizens in frock coats and silk hats (which hat does not become the German countenance). Walker and I stood at the window and watched the parade pass. The French General saw us and returned our salute and smiled. We exchanged salutes with some of our messmates among the officers, with whom we saw Captain Julien and Lieutenant Delegie.

Later that morning as Lieutenant Walker and I were limping our way back from the very inexpensive barber shop, we were accosted by a man dressed in black frock coat and silk opera hat. His wife, a good-looking, red-cheeked Jewess, was hanging on his arm. He asked if we were English and was much surprised to learn that we were American officers. He proved to be quite a mixture. He was a Polish Jew by birth, a French citizen, had spent years in America, and had been doing

5. It should be noted that the Imperial German flag had horizontal stripes and the French Republic's flag has vertical stripes. If the women of the town did as Parkin indicates, it would still not resemble exactly the French tricolor.

business in Germany in furniture. They were very polite but asked us many questions. They inquired if we would honor them by coming to dinner the next day. We accepted with thanks. At the appointed hour, one o'clock, we found their flat, the three flights of stairs causing us both some misery. We were warmly welcomed in a combination living and dining room, the decorations, furniture, and hangings of which were in low German, to say the least—most glaring and awful reds and blues; but the dinner, from soup to nuts, was excellent and the wine very good. Unfortunately, we praised some small sweet cakes, which showed no lack of sugar, and the good Frau urged them upon us and filled our plates several times—and this, after six courses.

On our way back to the hotel, I saw in the show windows of a shoe store, piles of shoes made of black cloth in imitation of leather and with wooden heels and soles. Nearly all of the shoes displayed were so made, definite evidence of how hard put to it Germany was for leather. And yet, I cannot say that I noticed anyone wearing such shoes nor did their clothing indicate any unusual conditions. The people we saw in the streets showed no evidence of the lack of food; in fact, they looked well-fed. I presume the folks in the poorer part of the town would not look so well nourished.

Herr Uhl told us some things about the German food control which surprised us greatly as we had heard so much about the boasted German efficiency. He said that before food control became necessary, the government had gathered up all the able men of Germany; hence, the food control fell into less able hands and inefficiency was the result. Vast quantities of food were wasted. Trainloads of pork stood in the railway yards as Saargemünd until it spoiled and had to be burned. The same was true of cabbage and potatoes. The people did without or paid very high prices while hundreds of tons of food rotted on account of mismanagement. All this was hard to believe of the Germans, but one could not doubt that this earnest man was telling the truth.

While sitting at the window, after our return to the hotel, we became aware of a very pretty, well-dressed, young lady across the street, looking steadily at us. She came over and passed our window several times, then she stopped and looked up and down the street in a frightened manner. We saw that she wanted to speak to us and raised the window.

In broken English she said, "My father is a Swiss-American. You are Americans, are you not?"

We told her we were, and she gave us a note, saying she would stop for an answer. As it was written in German we got Herr Uhl to translate it for us. Her note set forth that the world was unjust to women, that their lot was hard, and that they had but small opportunity. It inquired how much it would cost her in German money to go to America, and if there was a good opportunity for women there. Herr Uhl was somewhat mystified by the note, and so were we, but we wrote an answer in English, telling her about what it would cost to go to America and, also, that American held many chances for young women. She stopped later for the answer, took it hurriedly and we never saw her again. Walker kept her note as a souvenir. I have since wondered if it could be possible that she was a secret service agent and her singular letter a message in code.

Many French officers and soldiers walked the streets with German girls and often brought them into the hotel for wine and beer. They seemed to get on very well together and to be good friends. These German girls were certainly the finest physical specimens of their sex that I have ever seen. They were sturdy, good-looking, and full of health—a little too buxom from our point of view. If the future of Germany depends upon the physical condition of its mothers, that future seems very secure. They were even finer specimens of humanity than were the men.

We went one day to call on our friends, Captain Julien and Lieutenant Delegie. They were at another hotel about two blocks away. These gentlemen seemed in no great hurry to leave the town, but Walker and I were most anxious to get away to Paris and our own countrymen. At their hotel we found them on most friendly terms with several fine-looking German girls, daughters of their host, which fact may explain their contentment in the town. We urged an immediate departure and Julien said we were to leave the next day.

On the front of this hotel they put up the Allied Flags in a group. Julien asked me which was mine and I replied that none of them was. He laughed and, pointing to a blue flag covered with stars, the "Union Jack" of our Navy, said, "They think that is the American Flag." We went into the hotel and the girls got out their encyclopedia, in which I showed them the American flag. The proprietor apologized and ordered the girls to make a copy at once and put it up.

We were much pleased one morning to receive a call from an American Lieutenant and also much surprised at his presence in the town. He was in charge of a Ford ambulance-train attached to the French Army and manned entirely by Americans. He had heard about us at the city hospital from the American soldiers we had brought to the town. He gave us cigarettes—a most welcome gift—and was very anxious to be of service.

This officer had served only with the French Army. It was generous of us to lend ambulances to France and let our own badly wounded be hauled out of the Argonne in rough trucks as some of my men and officers had been. It provoked me considerably to remember this.

We visited the hospital to see our soldiers there and found them very comfortable in a large, cheery ward with good beds and enough food. I have been in few finer hospitals. It was a large, brick building, modern in every respect, clean and cheerful, situated on a hill with extensive grounds overlooking the city. The nurses were German women but the medical staff all seemed to be French. The German medical officers doubtless left when their army retired from the city. We had our wounds dressed in an ultra-modern operating room, all white tile and enamel.

The American ambulance lieutenant invited us to lunch. His unit was quartered in a large room in the hospital but ate its own rations. We had "monkey-meat," or canned roast-beef, which I liked very little. It was a poor lunch, but much better than many we had eaten. His cars, all neat and complete little Ford ambulances, about twelve in number, stood in the yard. We examined them with interest. The Lieutenant had a Ford touring car for himself. He said that he expected to remain with the French and had no idea when he would go home. All of his men were college boys and they were a superior lot of fellows. The Lieutenant insisted upon giving us more cigarettes, saying he had plenty. His advice to Walker and me was to insist on being sent to Paris and to report to the Officers' Hospital at No. 3 Rue Chevreuse, telling us that it was the best of the lot.

The next day all the American wounded soldiers were sent on to

France and we never saw nor heard from them again, but we were assured by the French authorities that they would have the very best of care.

After three days in the interesting old town of Saargemünd, we started again on our way to France, leaving on November 25, 1918, at 6:50 p.m. It was raining hard, as usual, when we had to travel in Europe. The ambulance Lieutenant sent his Ford to take us to the train. We picked up Captain Julien and Lieutenant Delegie on the way. At the station we were given two second-class compartments, Walker and I having one and the French officers the other. The train-crew were young, sturdy German girls dressed in blue uniforms—jackets and knee skirts, heavy black stockings and shoes, and blue caps. They knew their jobs and managed that train in no uncertain manner. They were good-looking young women, but permitted no advances on the part of the passengers.

As our train traveled along, it gradually filled up and soon we had a motley crowd in our compartment. An interesting lot of men to study. In one corner sat a huge African soldier who had a badly wounded arm which caused him much suffering. He said nothing and sat back with closed eyes. Next to him sat an Italian, a soldier of the French Foreign Legion. He was in good spirits, having had considerable wine, and was the life of the party. He talked a little English, some French and, of course, Italian, and he was a very amusing and bright young fellow. He was very proud of his famous corps and he told us some tales of it, not neglecting his own heroic acts. Since he had several decorations, I was inclined to believe most of his talk. He got into an argument with a French soldier and the young woman conductor had to interfere, shoving him down into his seat with great energy. He looked at her club, then laughed and made no more trouble.

At eleven p.m. we reached Chateau-Selen, the end of the line. With our French Officers we searched the town for a bed, but could not even get a place to sleep on the floor, so Walker and I went back to the station, leaving the Frenchmen still hunting. Our wounded legs could endure no more. We were made welcome in the guard-room by the French soldiers there, all middle-aged men, friendly and hospitable, but smelling terribly of wine and onions. The room was very warm, the stove being red-hot, and there was absolutely no ventilation. These worthy soldiers had not bathed for ever so long, judging by odors; but the guard-room was our only shelter and we could not complain. Not only were we made welcome but we were given wine, and the men gave us some of their blankets, making beds for us on the floor, where we slept fairly well. Some of these men sat up all night that we wounded officers might have a bed.

In the morning, our French officers came along looking for us. They had been our good friends and comrades through this journey. We walked a half mile, which Walker and I did not enjoy, to a bare-looking, cold hotel where we had a poor, but needed, breakfast. Captain Julien told us that we were to go on from here across No Man's Land and the devastated area in a French camion, or truck train, to the town of Luneville.

When it arrived, Walker and I were put on the front seats of trucks beside the Tonkin Chinese drivers, gentleman of much sheepskin, much silence, and much smell.[6] Julien and Delegie rode in the rear seat of the camion-train officers' car, to their regret, I think, for it was raw and cold and they did not have the protection of a windshield as did we. I used to laugh at their red faces when they pulled off the road to let us pass. These French trucks are very large. Each had a crew of two Tonkinese. The regularity with which these truck-trains travel and the steadiness with which they keep their intervals of about twelve feet is astonishing. They run at a speed of about twenty miles an hour and at night have no lights on the front, and have only red tail-lights to keep their distance by. Of course, driving them is a matter of practice and experience.

We left Chateau-Selen at 8 a.m. A cold, raw day but no rain and no sunshine. This was a most interesting ride through a much war-torn and hard fought-over country. In the first part of the morning we passed fields, large fields, packed full of artillery of all kinds and sizes, nearly all painted in camouflage style. These guns had been left behind by the Germans in their retreat. I had never seen so much artillery. Also, we passed great ammunition dumps, both French and German. Wide fields stacked full of shells of every size, lying in great, ordered piles in endless rows.

6. "Tonkin" refers to the northern region of Vietnam.

Another item of war expense and waste we saw that day, in almost unbelievable quantity, was barbed wire. I did not know that there was so much of it in the world. It stretched across the country in endless lines, as far as the eye could see in all directions. Most of those lines were from twenty to fifty feet across and always many of them were in sight at the same time. During our ride of three hours we were never out of sight of rusted barbed wire.

Shell holes and mine craters, the former innumerable, fields for miles nothing but shell holes. Trenches, countless and endless. We were rarely out of sight of them. Devastated towns on all sides, the scenes of bitter and bloody bayonet fighting and terrible shell fire; the hiding places of the accursed machine guns—the serpents of war. In many places we saw soldiers working, digging up mines and shells, dangerous to anyone not knowing how to handle them.

In one of the villages we passed through, I saw a very unique gate, doubtless built to stop tanks. At each side of the road were great structural-steel posts. On the road between them lay a steel track and, to one side just off the road was a massive steel gate built entirely of railroad rails and mounted on heavy rollers. If anything could stop tanks, this gate would do so.

We arrived at Luneville at eleven a.m. Back in France again! This place was destroyed only in small part and was a large, old-fashioned French town, not modern like the German towns I had just left. In fact, France, after Germany, seemed a hundred years behind the times so far as appearance of the towns and cities counts. The French villages were all so terribly filthy and covered with manure, while the German villages were clean and sanitary. Why does an intelligent nation like France ignore so utterly all sanitary ideas in all except its larger towns and cities? The French country people have very clean houses, inside, but their village streets and yards are a shame and a disgrace to any civilized people.

Leaving the truck-train, after thanking the Commander, we went to the railroad station and with the assistance of an American Army interpreter—the first man I had seen of that corps (they wear the Sphinx on their collar)—we secured places on the train at 1:30 p.m. for Nancy. We paid the low military fare, which is one-fourth of the regular rate. Lunch was the next matter and we went to a restaurant not far from the station. It was not a very clean place and was full of French soldiers, but there we had a very excellent lunch and there seemed to be no lack of food and a considerable variety. On the way back to the station, we were stopped by a wagon loaded with hay, which completely blocked the narrow street. No driver was to be found, and as we could not get by, we poor cripples to whom walking was an effort, had to retrace our steps several blocks and go around another way. This provoked us considerably and caused us quite a little unnecessary effort. I mention it as typically French, as it could not happen in a German town, and it would cause a fuss in an American one, but the French simply submitted and went around by another street.

The large, fine railroad station and the luxurious first-class train, the first of its kind I had been in since coming to Europe, seemed to us like a return to old times, like the ease and comfort of pre-war days. Mud, rain, cold, lack of comfort, the slim shelter of ruined towns, had been our lot for many days previous to our capture. As we sank into the soft, gray plush seats and looked out through the polished plate glass, we hardly felt that we belonged there, so unused to it all had we become. After an hour's pleasant ride through interesting country, we came to Nancy, a large, hustling, crowded city, little changed by the war. Soldiers of many nations thronged the station platform.

Here was said farewell to our good friends and comrades, Captain Julien and Lieutenant Delegie. I greatly regretted to leave good little Julien. He had always been friendly, helpful, willing and cheerful, and he had done so very much for us. Our heartfelt thanks and a long, hard grasp of the hand were his only reward. I could have embraced the good, little man and thought, for a moment, he meant to embrace me. I believe he felt as I did about it but hesitated, knowing it was not our custom. We stood and watched them go out through the gate to the French hospital.

As I turned away, I saw standing before me a very neat and trim sergeant of American Military Police. He saluted and asked respectfully to see our papers. I was again under control of the great American military machine and was not sorry for it. I told the good sergeant that we had no papers and were returned prisoners from Germany.

"In that case," he said, "I must take you both to police headquarters."

We followed him outside and, at our request, he called a carriage. The driver wore a silk hat and a neat coat. Walker and I laughed— our first carriage ride in Europe. We went slowly through the crowded streets, our sergeant on the box beside the driver.

At police headquarters, a sergeant at a desk seemed inclined to take charge of our case, getting out some military forms for us to fill in— further evidence of being back in the army. He kept us standing in front of his desk. I knew this was the way he treated soldiers, but I knew it was not the way he should treat officers, so I stopped him and asked to be taken to the commanding officer. This gentleman, a kindly, Irish-American Lieutenant-Colonel, late of the 69th, New York, heard me and, coming to the door of his room, asked us in and had chairs brought for us.[7] He asked us many questions concerning our adventures and said that many returned American prisoners were passing through his office each day. We found that we were classed as Repatriated Americans. The Colonel told us that he was sending all such officers and men to the town of Tours. I was not pleased to hear this and told the Colonel that I wanted very much to go the officers' hospital in Paris, having been recommended to that place by American ambulance officers in Germany.

"Well," said the Colonel, "you are a good fellow, Major, and I will give you a travel order to Paris."

I persuaded him to include Lieutenant Walker, telling him we had been together through all our troubles and would not like to be separated now.

But a travel order was not sufficient to put us on our way to Paris. We found out at the station that we could get no accommodations for several days. We went to a hotel for dinner, very much discouraged. In the washroom I got into conversation with a very pleasant and much decorated French captain who had just returned from service with the Roumanian Army. When the Germans defeated and broke up that army, he had a very hard time getting out of the country and back to France.

7. The 69th New York Infantry Regiment was a unit with Irish American heritage in the New York National Guard. It was renumbered the 165th Regiment in World War I and served with the 42nd "Rainbow" Division.

When I told him of our failure to get away to Paris, he said, "I think I can help you. The officer in charge of the station is an old friend of mine."

With him we went again to the station and he left us in the waiting room, while he went to see his friend. He came back shortly and said it was all right. He had secured us two first-class seats, but we would have to pay for our tickets at the military rate which cost us about two dollars and fifty cents. We were very glad to do so, and we thanked the Captain warmly for his interest and trouble.

Before going to dinner we had got hold of a porter and arranged with him, by help of a tip, to hold our two seats in the first-class compartment. In going out to the train we had some difficulty in finding this man, but at last he came running, saying we were very early, and took us to our seats next to the window. Sentries with fixed bayonets guarded all cars and passed only those who could show a proper ticket. Again we were in a fine, clean car, and still it seemed strange to us, and we felt hardly in the right place.

The compartment soon filled. I had a very handsome young Lieutenant of the Polish Legion, in the French service, next to me. His bright clean uniform with silver stripes on the sleeves and silver buttons, with silver eagle on his Polish cap, and clean brown boots and belt, made my worn old battle uniform look very shabby. The other three men in the compartment were French civilians, well-dressed and well-fed. The car soon filled; people even sat in the corridor on luggage, and I did not envy these unfortunate folks the long night ride.

We pulled out at 8:30 p.m. and were soon running at a good rate of speed through the night, but our stops were more frequent than I expected on a through train. At every station there was a crowd that rushed the train, most of them in French uniform. Men would jump up and look in our window to see if there was an empty seat. The corridor soon got jammed full of people who stood and sat packed together all night. It must have been most uncomfortable. Several people tried to invade our compartment but were kept out by the French civilians, who protested violently with much gesturing of the hands. About eleven o'clock we closed the green cloth shade over the gas light and settled ourselves for what sleep we could get, sitting up or crouching down or anyway to get comfortable, which we did not succeed in doing and slept very little. At every stop the struggling crowd awoke us.

In the morning it was a tired and washed-out-looking group that sat in our compartment. None had had much sleep. One of the civilians produced a large bag of good white rolls which he passed around and he also contributed a bottle of wine. I had a small and very good cream cheese, given me by Herr Uhl and had carried it in my overcoat pocket ever since. On these things we made our breakfast and enjoyed it. We kept passing ruined towns until we got within an hour of Paris, which shows how close the Germans got to the city. At 10:30 a.m. we reached the station in Paris, having been running through the suburbs and the city itself for more than half an hour. It seemed an immense place after all the small cities we had been in.

There was the usual scramble for luggage, hats, and coats, and Walker had trouble in finding his overseas cap, but finally did find it under the seat cushion. Walking out of the crowded station, we were stopped by the military police and directed to stand in line in order to be registered and have our orders examined. Seeing us limping, an officer placed us at the head of the long line, and no one objected to this preference. We were given our passes and outside the station we got a taxi, after some waiting, but we had to climb into it through one door as its passengers left by the other.

When we reached the hospital at No. 3 Rue Chevreuse, the officer in charge made some trouble over red tape and said we had no orders from proper authorities to be admitted there. It seemed ridiculous, of course. I told the Colonel in charge about our situation and where we had come from and that it was not possible for us to have such orders. It came down to a case of taking us in or turning us out on the street, so they cut the red tape and made us welcome. Our adventures were over. We were back again in the great American Army and right glad to be there.

Epilogue: The Greatest War Story I Ever Heard

The title of this story, as given above, is a true one. For courage and devotion this tale is beyond all comparison the greatest I have ever heard,
and I know it is all true, for I had a very small part in it, but only as an
onlooker.

In December 1918 I was in the officers' convalescent hospital at
No. 12 Rue Boileau, Paris, France. It was, of course, an American Red
Cross hospital. All of the officers there were in condition to travel, and
were waiting for transportation home. One evening a stranger, a lieutenant colonel of the Army Medical Corps by the name of Harris, came
into my room and introduced himself. He asked me if it was true that
I had but recently come from a German military hospital. I told him it
was and that I had been in Trier, Germany, for the better part of the
month of November.

"Major, did you ever come across or hear of an American captain
by the name of William Harris of the 6th U.S. Engineers?" he asked
anxiously.

I thought over the names of the American officers I had met or
heard of in Germany and had to tell him that I had not. He was visibly
disappointed.

"I had so much hoped to get some information of him from you," he
said sadly.

I was naturally greatly interested in this fellow-prisoner and expressed not only my regret at not being able to give him information,
but also my interest. The Colonel told me that he himself was a brother
of General Peter B. Harris, Adjutant General of the Army at Washington, D.C., and that Captain Harris was the only son of General Harris,
and his own nephew.

"Last July," said the Colonel, "Captain Harris went into Belleau
Woods with his regiment in support of the attacking infantry, and from
that day to this, five months, in spite of every possible effort and the use
of every agency of the War Department and the Army, General Harris

has not been able to find out anything at all about his missing son. Not one word, not a single item of information in all these months about his only son."

I was deeply moved and felt a great sympathy for the General, obliged to carry on his important work in Washington, his heart breaking under the terrible strain. I told Colonel Harris how wonderfully well and how kindly the Germans had treated me and my prisoner comrades, how efficient their surgeons were, and how clean and well managed their hospitals were. How the food, although extremely plain, was plenty for our needs. I assured him that if Capt. Harris was a prisoner in a German hospital he would have the best of kindly care. I did not understand why he had not before this been returned to the American lines as all the prisoners had been. This phase of the matter was ominous, but I did not speak my thoughts to the Colonel, who, no doubt, had the same thoughts.

My description of the German doctors and hospitals and of the friendly care given the American wounded encouraged the Colonel a little, and he said he would at once send off a cablegram to General Harris telling him what I had said, in the hope of cheering him some. The Colonel thanked me for my encouragement. Promising to let me hear any news he got of Captain Harris, he went away to continue his search.

Some ten days later the Colonel came into my room and after greeting me said, "Well Major I can now tell you the rest of the story about my nephew, Capt. Harris, and it is a story of heroism and devotion such as I never heard before."

He went on, "A few days after I talked with you I chanced to hear that some returned prisoners of war who were members of the 6th U.S. Engineers, my nephew's regiment, were at Tours. I got into a staff car and hastened to that town and soon found these soldiers. Fortune at last favored me for two of these men, stretcher bearers and heroes, knew about my nephew, not all at that time, but enough to enable me with their help to learn the whole story of my nephew's fate.

"On the day of the Battle of Belleau Woods, these two stretcher bearers were following the 6th Engineers, which regiment had gone into the fight in support of the infantry, which was having a very hard time of it. As they advanced, the stretcher bearers came upon Capt.

Harris and realized that he was gravely wounded, being shot through the chest. They knew enough to realize that unless he had immediate medical attention he would die very soon.

"The advancing American lines had made such progress that the American first aid stations were now quite a distance in the rear. But there ahead of them, not far beyond the battle lines joined in stubborn contest, they could see the Red Cross flag of the German first aid station. Just how far away it was I cannot be sure, but it was very much nearer than the American first aid station. The Captain must have attention at once and to get it for him these two heroes, for that they most assuredly are, made the astonishing and heroic decision to carry him up to the American firing line, through it, across the interval to the German firing line, both lines firing all the time, and through the German line to that first aid station. Major, did you ever hear of greater devotion and courage?"

I never had. I was astonished and greatly impressed.

"Well they did it, and marvelous to say all three got through without a wound. Both of the firing lines must have been astounded at the sight. They got the Captain safely to the German first aid station, where the German surgeon took charge of him at once."

Here the stretcher bearers were separated from Captain Harris, and they could tell the Colonel no more about him.

"Could you find that first aid station if I took you to Belleau Woods in my car?" the Colonel asked them anxiously.

They were sure they could, so away all three went in the car. Arrived on the battlefield, they led the Colonel to the spot where the first aid station had been, and there nearby was a small graveyard, and on one of the crosses was the name "Captain William Harris, Sixth U.S. Engineers."

The Colonel's voice failed him. We sat there in that quiet room, our eyes full of tears, and when he got up to go we gripped hands hard.

"I wired the whole story to his poor father. At last he knows, and that is some relief," said the Colonel at parting.

The stretcher bearers received the Distinguished Service Cross. The General would not ask for the Congressional Medal of Honor for them, because he was Adjutant General of the Army, and the heroic act was performed for his son.

And here this wonderful tale of unequalled devotion and heroism should end, but it does not, for there is still another chapter of it. Some years afterwards I was up in the mountains of California at Randsburg, looking into a chemical proposition with some friends. In the evening we sat before the fire telling stories with the miners and prospectors. One of the miners, seeing my Silver Star wound button, said, "Here is a man who could tell us a war story."

And so I told them this wonderful tale. They were greatly interested and impressed. But my most intent and interested listener was a young woman who leaned over the small desk of the hotel office. When we broke up to go to bed she approached me and said, "It was wonderful to hear your story of Captain Harris. I was so deeply touched. Do you know I was General Harris' personal secretary during the War and I had charge of all the efforts that were constantly made to find out something about his son?"

I was astonished to learn who she was. Strange that we two should meet in this little mining town, and she should stand there and hear this tale in which she had had such a part herself. Perhaps some day I shall meet General Harris himself and tell him what little part I had in the search for his long-missing son.[1]

---

1. There are a few features of this story that are incorrect. The soldier's name was not William Harris but Charles Dashiell Harris. He was indeed the son of Major General Peter Harris. He graduated from West Point in 1917 and was a captain in the 6th Engineers. He was shot in the chest at Claires-Chenes Woods (not Belleau Wood) on October 20, 1918, while leading his men. He died in German captivity, as the story indicates.

Appendix A

Major Harry Dravo Parkin was awarded the Distinguished Service Cross "for extraordinary heroism in connection with military operations against an armed enemy at Hill 378, the Borne-du-Cornouiller, France, November 4, 1918."

In addition, Major Parkin was also awarded the Silver Star.

Notification of the Distinguished Service Cross award was made by Adjutant General Robert C. Davis on April 5, 1923, and its presentation and investiture was made by the Honorable John W. Weeks, Secretary of War, on May 25, 1923, at the Presidio, San Francisco, California.

The citation reads:

"He commanded one of the assaulting battalions and leading the attack received four wounds from enemy machine gun fire but declined to be evacuated remaining with his command on the position he had captured, temporarily assigning active command of the Battalion to his senior captain. Later, learning that this officer had been killed, Major Parkin, despite intense suffering from his wound, again assumed active command and under a terrific enemy concentration of artillery and machine gun fire, he defended the position with great bravery and gallantry against counter attacks by vastly superior numbers of enemy forces. His undaunted courage greatly inspired the men of his command, raising their morale to a high pitch."

Appendix B

Description of the attack on Hill 378, The Borne de Cornouiller, France, on November 4th, 1918, by Companies B and C, First Battalion, 316th Inf., 79th Division, AEF, under the command of Major H. D. Parkin.

Early on the morning of November 4th, 1918, complying with orders received the night before from Col. George Williams commanding the 316th Infantry, I left my line of defense with Company C 316th Infantry under command of 1st Lieut. William E. Drehr, and descended into the valley between the American and German lines. We came under German shell fire in the valley and started to suffer loss at once. On the lower slopes of Hill 378 we found Company B under Capt. Louis C. Knack. He had been sent out the previous afternoon to support Capt. Paul Strong, who had a reconnaissance in strength out against Hill 378. I had received orders to use only two companies in attacking Hill 378, and it was my intention to use Companies C and B.

Forming for attack, with Company C in the lead and Company B in support, we moved up the Hill, under heavy shell fire, until we neared the top, when it ceased. We passed through German trenches in which were German dead and broken machine guns, and through lines of wire, which were cut up and scattered. All evidence of good work on the part of our artillery, whose barrage had preceded us. Meeting the Captain of the Machine Gun Company assigned to the attack, I directed him to send two machine guns after me at one. This officer was wounded very soon afterwards, and the machine guns never reached me, or the result might have been different. I wanted them for defense against German counter attack, and needed them terribly later, when their assistance would, in my opinion, have broken up the German attack and they would never have regained a footing upon the Hill.

In this attack we were in touch with the companies of the Third Battalion of our regiment on our right, but we were entirely unable to gain touch with the French regiment supposed to be attacking on our left, although I sent a patrol out on that side, under Lt. Hurly of Company B for that purpose. We saw nothing at all of the French on our left during the time I was in the battle, and it is my opinion that they allowed their attack to be stopped by fire which my troops endured without being stopped. I can see no other reason for their absence, for Capt. Knack assured me that the French started the attack on our left. This left my left flank "in the air," and had fatal results later, for the German counter-attacks came up on our left flank. The presence of the French there would doubtless have prevented these attacks.

As we approached the summit of Hill 378 we came into fog, which enshrouded the top, and gave us protection from German rifle and machine gun fire, but made it difficult to locate the German positions. After considerable rifle fire by my front lines, we completely invaded the German positions and captured them without much trouble, taking a considerable number of prisoners, who were sent back to our lines under guard. I sent a written message back to Col. Williams telling him of our success, and giving him our position, on the crest of Hill 378.

Realizing that we had captured an important position from the Germans, I felt that they would endeavor to regain it by counter-attack, and so made preparations for defense. There were two lines of trenches, and in the one nearest the German lines, Company C, which had led the attack, had taken position. The line being long, this Company was necessarily considerably scattered along the trench, in order to cover the whole front. As I could not rely upon their line for much defense, I directed Capt. Knack to place Company B in the second trench, in two groups, one toward each end of the position, as counterattack units to meet the German attack. There were some sixty men in each group.

The need of machine guns for defense was impressed upon me now, and I sent another order for them by runner. These guns eventually reached the right of my position, and Lt. Drehr used them, with great effect, to stop the German rush from the left of my position, after it was recaptured, but they did not reach me on the left, where I happened to be when the German attack struck our line. Since Lt. Drehr stopped the Germans with these guns, I am convinced I could have done likewise on the left.

I also sent a message back to telephone head, which was in my dugout, asking our artillery to put down a barrage in the valley beyond

Hill 378 , to prevent the Germans from making attacks on our position. For some reason this artillery fire was long delayed, and was put down after the Germans had made their attacks, and in time to harass the American prisoners on their way to the German rear.

All this time the face of the Hill 378 towards the German lines, had been heavily swept by a barrage from German machine guns, firing up the slope from the foot of the Hill. We had suffered loss from this fire, and the men were cautioned to keep down, or back from the face of the Hill. Having made all possible preparations for defense, I was now anxious to make some observation of the German lines, and so crawled up to my front trench. I found that the heavy machine gun fire had resulted in our having no observation whatever of the enemy, as all the men were keeping well down in the trench. As this would result in our being surprised, it was necessary that some of the men be put on watch. In some angles of the trench men could observe the enemy and still have some protection from the fire. By crawling along the front, I placed a number of men so, and ordered them to open fire upon any visible enemy. To encourage these men in their dangerous work, I remained with them some time, and, taking a rifle from the ground, opened fire upon two individuals walking up and down behind the German position. They dropped abruptly.

Some time later I was in the second trench when I heard cries and rifle firing from our front trench. I saw a long line of German war helmets topping the rise. Calling to Capt. Knack to get the men in the left counterattack unit out of the trench and ready to attack, I stood on the top of the trench, and signaled Lt. Hurly, who was on our extreme left, on the crest of Hill 378 with his patrol, to close in on the Germans on that side, which he promptly did. Capt. Knack brought his men forward in good order. They attacked with great energy. I went forward with Capt. Knack. We discharged our pistols at the Germans, and an automatic rifleman also opened on them. The men did not fire, but followed with the bayonet. It looked like a bloody bayonet fight. Seeing us coming, the Germans halted, and stood in line with their rifles at the ready. We charged to within about twenty feet of them when the Germans broke, and turning their backs, ran back down the Hill. The men were now greatly excited, and wanted to follow them. The officers had great difficulty in stopping them, and did not succeed until we were all well out on the face of the Hill. As soon as the German Infantry had descended far enough, the German machine guns opened on us, and caused us heavy loss. It was at this time that I received four machine gun bullets in my legs and was no longer able to keep on my feet.

I passed the command to Capt. Knack, who was near, and was helped back into the rear trench. We had great difficulty in stopping the flow of blood from my wounds, and were finally able to do so by using the rawhide thong on my helmet. This loss of blood weakened me greatly, and I was unable to see distinctly for some time. Lt. Hurley came to me with the distressing news that Capt. Knack had just been killed. I had the greatest confidence in this officer, and felt easy with him in command. I had now only three young lieutenants left. I had not the slightest doubt of their personal courage, but did not feel that any of them had sufficient experience to assume the command in such a difficult situation. I therefore resumed the command myself, and directed Lt. Drehr to take command of the right of our position, and Lt. Hurley the left. I impressed upon them as forcibly as possible my absolute conviction that the Germans would attack us again very soon, and urged them to get their men ready to meet the attack. Lt. Hurley asked my permission to send a message to our lines for help. I thought this useless, knowing how far our lines were from us, and feeling sure that we would be attacked before we could receive any help, but I permitted him to send the message. Lying there in the trench, helpless, with no senior officers left to depend upon, and dreading the coming attack, I suffered great mental distress, fearing that we would not meet it successfully.

Shortly after the death of Capt. Knack, a German plane flew over us, very low, and dropped a yellow smoke signal. It had barely cleared off when the German shells began to burst on the Hill in great numbers. In the ensuing hour we endured the heaviest concentrated shell fire we had ever experienced. The continuous crashing and bursting of shells deafened and confused us. It seemed that everyone on the Hill must be killed or wounded, and most of us were. Sergeant-Major Robert S. MacCormack and I were alone in our section of the trench. We expected a shell in the trench every moment and were covered with dust from nearby explosions, which shook the ground. Our losses were very heavy and the survivors were demoralized. Suddenly the shell fire ceased, and almost immediately a large force of Germans poured over the position. The few dazed survivors were quickly surrounded and captured. The Sergeant-Major defended me with my pistol until I ordered him to stop and surrender, which he did unwillingly. Several grenades were thrown at us. We could not help the cause further. The Germans, seeing the Sergeant-Major disarmed, and noting my condition, did not molest us after an officer had spoken sharply to them.

By direction of the German Lieutenant in command of the attacking force, I was helped out of the trench, and two American soldiers, Sergeant-Major MacCormack, and a private, whose name I do not know, were ordered to help me to the German rear. I saw the Germans gathering the prisoners and there were not more than twenty-five of them, unwounded, standing in a group. These were all the survivors I could see out of considerably more than a hundred men we had on that part of our position (center of the crest). Such a small number of defenders, even if undemoralized by terrible artillery fire, could not have held the Hill against the large force of Germans which attacked it, unless they had been strongly supported by machine guns and artillery, both of which supports were entirely lacking.

The American prisoners were obliged to go to the German rear, through the intervening valley, under heavy American shell fire. Doubtless the barrage I had sent a message for, shortly after capturing the Hill, to prevent the German attack.

The co-operation between the German Infantry and Artillery in this attack was perfect. Hardly had the dust of the last exploding shell settled when the Infantry poured over our trenches. Our few survivors were covered by German rifles before they realized that the shell fire had ceased. However, machine guns in the second trench, had they survived the shell fire, could have slaughtered the German Infantry at point-blank range. A few determined machine gunners might have saved the situation.

On my way to the German rear I suffered greatly from being obliged to walk with my wounded legs, assisted by the two soldiers—not to speak of the heavy American shell fire, which harassed us all the way. My mental sufferings were equally great, and I was consumed with the bitterest thoughts of failure to hold the Hill. But upon reflection, I lost these bitter feelings, and became convinced that I had done all that was possible to save the situation, and that has ever since been my feeling. All the luck of war was against me. In fact, all help that I should have had failed me; —the machine guns, the artillery support, or the presence of the French on my left; any one of these might have saved the day.

[signature]
H. D. Parkin
Ex-Major 316th Inf. 79th Div.

Above is an extract from the War Memoirs of H. D. Parkin

Index

Page numbers in italics refer to photographs. Page numbers followed by *n* refer to notes, followed by the note number.

Eby, Mechanic, 277
Eckley, Paul, 208, 210
Eisenhower, Dwight D., 8
Enduring the Great War (Watson),
    263n2
Esnes, France, 134
Euwart, Corporal, 182, 188, 201,
    207–208, 217, 225–226, 235, 251,
    253, 255, 284, 310
Evans, Lieutenant, 67

Fatzinger, Robert L., 72, 115, 125, 142,
    153–154, 181, 184, 186, 196, 221
Faulkner, Richard, ix, 17n15
Fax, Gene, 183n2, 215n6
Ferrell, Robert, 19n17
Feuardent, Captain, 130, 189,
    202, 314
Filipinos, 55
Fitzharris, Joseph Christopher, death
    of, 202, 204
Fitzpatrick, Captain., 202
Fix Bayonets! (Thomason), 1
Flanders, Belgium, 152
Foch, Ferdinand, 14, 19, 269n6
Ford, Nancy Gentile, 87n8
Fort Niagara Training Camp, 40n7,
    107, 107n1, 110, 132
Fouraker, LeRoy, 145, 182, 186, 195,
    226, 239, 252–253, 264, 275, 277,
    279, 290, 305, 310, 316
Fourer-Selter, Lieutenant, 339–340
Fox, Lieutenant, 140, 151
France
    absence of male civilians, 108
    battlefield debris, 366–367
    beauty of, 64, 68, 70
    manure piles in, 64, 73, 76
    medieval history, 12, 83–85, 96
    military cemeteries, 122–123,
        267–268, 285
    train cars in, 66–67
    village life, 75

weather, 114
wine, 69, 90, 104
Franco-Prussian War, 354n3
French Army
    artillery, 122, 131
    colonial troops, 120, 305, 313,
        338–339, 338n, 366
    filthiness, 125
    instructors with AEF, 98, 99
    interactions with Americans, 234,
        240, 297, 314–315, 353–358
    reliability, 379–380
    use of tanks, 220n2, 229–231,
        230n6
French Colonies, 313, 338n1
French Foreign Legion, 2, 365
French Red Cross, 339
French 75mm, 122, 122n7
French Tank Squadron, 229

Gabriel, Lieutenant, 262
Gallagher, James A., *168*
General Staff, 97, 356
Genicourt, France, 237, 279, 288–290
German Army
    artillery, 219, 263–264, 334
    attitudes of POWs, *176*, 262–263,
        311
    defensive tactics, 16
    insubordination, 23–24, 342,
        343–344
    machine gunners, 145, 148, 185
    monuments, 285–286
    quarters, 206, 271
    retreat across Rhine, 24,
        344–345, 346
    snipers, 145–146, 158
    treatment of wounded, 324–326,
        327–328, 331, 337–344
German Red Cross, 324
German Republic, 346
Gettysburg College, ix, 1–2, 1n1, 4,
    29, *30*

Troyon sector, 4, 247, 253, 270, 282, 287, 299
Truman, Harry S., 7n7, 8, 9
Truman (McCullough), 9

Uhl, Albert, 358–362, 363, 371
Undertones of War (Blunden), 1
The Unsubstantial Air (Hynes), 40n8
US Navy, 2

Van Dyke, Captain, 90, 322, 343
Vaux-sous-Aubigny, France, 68, 71
Verdun, Battle of, 4, 273, 290–292, 295n1, 300, 302–303, 307, 320
Verdun, France, 14, 155, 187, 247, 253, 279, 292–296, 311
Vietnam War, 13
Violence Against Prisoners of War in the First World War (Jones), 341n3
V-J Day, 27

Wadonville, France, 247
Watson, Alexander, 263n2
Walker, Lieutenant, 338, 345–348, 353, 355–361, 363–364, 365–366, 369, 371
Walker, William, ix, 2, 2n2, 6n4, 6n5, 7n6, 16n14, 17, 17n16, 25n24, 26n25, 26n26, 46n12, 155n6, 196n6, 215n6

War in the Garden of Eden (Roosevelt), 2
Washington, DC, 1
Wawro, Geoffrey, 14n11, 15, 15n12
Weeks, John W., 377
West Point, 6, 110n3, 155, 155n6, 376n1
Whittlesey, Charles, 208n3
Wilhelm II (Kaiser), 14, 19, 22–24, 52, 52n15, 323, 327, 327n5, 330, 333, 344, 353
Williams, George, *164*, 280, 290–291, 295, 298, 308–309, 312–313, 379–380
Wilson, Woodrow, 7, 270n6
Winning and Losing on the Western Front (Boff), 263n2
Without Censor (Johnson), 1
Wood, Leonard, 7, 358, 358n4
Woods No. 268, 187, 202, 212
Woods No. 250. *See* Bois de Cunel
World War II, 4, 13, 35n5, 155n6
Wunderlich, Albert C., 184

X-Ray, 342

YMCA, 5, 9, 10n9, 43n9, 70, 119, 227, 231
A Youth in the Meuse-Argonne (Triplet), 3